Travelling Salesman Problem

Edited by

Federico Greco

Travelling Salesman Problem
Edited by Federico Greco

Republished by InTech
Janeza Trdine 9, 51000 Rijeka, Croatia

Additional hard copies can be obtained from orders@intechopen.com

Travelling Salesman Problem, Edited by Federico Greco
p. cm.
ISBN 978-953-7619-10-7

For EU product safety concerns:
IN TECH d.o.o., Prolaz Marije Krucifikse Kozulić 3, 51000 Rijeka, Croatia,
info@intechopen.com or visit our website at intechopen.com.

Preface

In the middle 1930s computer science was yet a not well defined academic discipline. Actually, fundamental concepts, such as 'algorithm', or 'computational problem', has been formalized just some year before.

In these years the Austrian mathematician Karl Menger invited the research community to consider from a mathematical point of view the following problem taken from the every day life. A traveling salesman has to visit exactly once each one of a list of m cities and then return to the home city. He knows the cost of traveling from any city i to any other city j. Thus, which is the tour of least possible cost the salesman can take?

The Traveling Salesman Problem (for short, TSP) was born.

More formally, a TSP instance is given by a complete graph G on a node set $V=\{1,2,\ldots m\}$, for some integer m, and by a cost function assigning a cost c_{ij} to the arc (i,j) , for any i, j in V.

TSP is a representative of a large class of problems known as combinatorial optimization problems. Among them, TSP is one of the most important, since it is very easy to describe, but very difficult to solve.

Actually, TSP belongs to the NP-hard class. Hence, an efficient algorithm for TSP (that is, an algorithm computing, for any TSP instance with m nodes, the tour of least possible cost in polynomial time with respect to m) probably does not exist. More precisely, such an algorithm exists if and only if the two computational classes P and NP coincide, a very improbable hypothesis, according to the last years research developments.

From a practical point of view, it means that it is quite impossible finding an exact algorithm for any TSP instance with m nodes, for large m, that has a behaviour considerably better than the algorithm which computes any of the $(m-1)!$ possible distinct tours, and then returns the least costly one.

If we are looking for applications, a different approach can be used. Given a TSP instance with m nodes, any tour passing once through any city is a feasible solution, and its cost leads to an upper bound to the least possible cost. Algorithms that construct in polynomial time with respect to m feasible solutions, and thus upper bounds for the optimum value, are called heuristics. In general, these algorithms produce solutions but without any quality guarantee as to how far is their cost from the least possible one. If it can be shown that the cost of the returned solution is always less than k times the least possible cost, for some real number $k>1$, the heuristic is called a k-approximation algorithm.

Unfortunately, k-approximation algorithm for TSP are not known, for any $k>1$. Moreover, in a paper appeared in 2000, Papadimitriou, and Vempala have shown that a k-approximation algorithm for TSP for any $97/96>k>1$ exists if and only if P=NP. Hence, also finding a good heuristic for TSP seems very hard.

Better results are known for NP-Hard subproblem of TSP. For example, a 3/2-approximation algorithm is known for Metric TSP (in a metric TSP instance the cost function verifies the triangular inequality).

Anyway, the extreme intractability of TSP has invited many researchers to test new heuristic technique on this problem. The harder is the problem you test on, the more significant are the result you obtain.

A large part of this book is devoted to some bio-inspired heuristic techniques that have been developed in the last years. Such techniques take inspiration from the nature. Actually, the animals that usually form great groups behave by instinct trying to satisfy the group necessity in the best possible way. Similarly, the natural systems develop in order to (locally) minimize their potential by finding a stationary point.

In chapter 1 [Population-Based Optimization Algorithms for Solving the Travelling Salesman Problem] the following bio-inspired algorithmic techniques are considered: Genetic Algorithms, Ant Colon Optimization, Particle Swarm Optimization, Intelligent Water Drops, Artificial Immune Systems, Bee Colony Optimization, and Electromagnetism-like Mechanisms. Every section briefly introduces one of these techniques and an algorithm applying it for solving TSP. In the last section the obtained experimental results are compared.

Chapter 2 [Bio-inspired Algorithms for TSP and Generalized TSP] is divided into two parts. In the first part, a new algorithm using the Ant Colon Optimization technique is considered. The obtained experimental results are then compared with other two algorithms using the same technique. In the second part, the combinatorial optimization problem called Generalized TSP (GTSP) is introduced, and a Genetic Algorithm for solving is proposed. We recall that a GSTP instance provides a complete graph $G = (V,E)$, and a cost function (as in a TSP instance), together with a partition of the node set V into p subsets. A feasible solution for GTSP is a tour passing at least once from each one of the p subsets of V. Clearly, GTSP is a generalization of TSP.

In Chapter 3 [Approaches to the Travelling Salesman Problem Using Evolutionary Computing Algorithms] an algorithm for TSP using the Genetic Local Search is considered. It is a hybrid technique, as it combines a genetic algorithm approach by a local search technique: As in a genetic algorithm the fitness of a population is the target, but a local search optimization phase is applied whenever a new individual is created during the evolutionary process. At the end of the chapter some experimental results are discussed.

Chapter 4 [Particle Swarm Optimization Algorithm for the Traveling Salesman Problem] and Chapter 5 [A Modified Discrete Particle Swarm Optimization Algorithm for the Generalized Traveling Salesman Problem] deals with the Particle Swarm Optimization (PSO) technique. In a PSO algorithm the current solution is seen as a particle whose movement in the solution space is controlled by a certain velocity operator. As the solution space of a TSP instance is discrete, it is more correct referring to discrete PSO approach for TSP.

In Chapter 4 the authors propose some velocity operators for a discrete PSO algorithm for TSP, and compare by computational experiments the results of the proposed approach with other known PSO heuristics for TSP.

In Chapter 5 a discrete PSO approach is considered for Generalized TSP. Afterwards, the proposed algorithm is hybridized with a local search improvement heuristic. In the last section some the computational results compare the proposed algorithm, and its improvement with other known discrete PSO algorithm for GTSP.

In Chapter 6 [Solving TSP via Neural Networks] and in Chapter 7 [A Recurrent Neural Network to Traveling Salesman Problem] Neural Network techniques for solving TSP are considered.

In particular, Chapter 6 is devoted to the recent progress in the transiently chaotic neural network (TCNN), a discrete-time neural network model, are presented. An algorithm for TSP using such technique is then introduced, and the obtained results are compared with other neural networks algorithms.

In Chapter 7 a technique based on the Wang's Recurrent Neural Networks with the "Winner Takes All" principle is used to solve the Assignment Problem (AP). By lightly modifying such technique, an algorithm for TSP is derived. Finally, some TSP instances taken from the TSP library are chosen for comparing the proposed algorithm with some other algorithms using different techniques.

Chapter 8 [Solving the Probabilistic Travelling Salesman Problem Based on Genetic Algorithm with Queen Selection Scheme] treats an extension of TSP, the Probabilistic TSP (PTSP). A PTSP instance provides a complete graph $G=(V,E)$, and a cost function (as in a TSP instance), together with a real number $0 \leq P_i \leq 1$ for each node i in V. P_i represents the probability of the node i to be visited by a tour. Clearly, the goal of PTSP is to find a tour of minimal expected cost. In this chapter an optimization procedure based on a Genetic Algorithm framework is presented.

In Chapter 9 [Niche Pseudo-Parallel Genetic Algorithms for Path Optimization of Autonomous Mobile Robot - A Specific Application of TSP] an application of TSP to the Path Optimization of Autonomous Mobile Robot is considered. An autonomous mobile robot has to find a non-collision path from initial position to objective position in an obstacle space trying to minimize the path cost. This problem can be modelled as a TSP instance. The authors consider a genetic algorithm, called Niche Pseudo-Parallel Genetic Algorithm, for solving TSP.

The last Chapter [The Symmetric Circulant Traveling Salesman Problem] gives an example of a theoretical research on TSP. Actually, it is interesting to investigate if TSP becomes easier or remains hard (from a computational complexity point of view) when it is restricted to a particular class of graphs. In this chapter the case in which the graph in the instance is symmetric, and circulant is deeply analyzed, and an overview on the most recent results is given.

By summing up, in this book the problem of finding algorithmic technique leading to good/optimal solutions for TSP (or for some other strictly related problems) is considered. An important thing has to be outlined here. As already said, TSP is a very attractive problem for the research community. Anyway, it arises as a natural subproblem in many applications concerning the every day life. Indeed, each application, in which an optimal ordering of a number of items has to be chosen in a way that the total cost of a solution is determined by adding up the costs arising from two successively items, can be modelled as a TSP instance. Thus, studying TSP can be never considered as an abstract research with no real importance.

It is time to start with the book.

Enjoy the reading!

September 2008

Editor

Federico Greco
Universita degli studi di Perugia, Italy

Contents

1

Population-Based Optimization Algorithms for Solving the Travelling Salesman Problem

Mohammad Reza Bonyadi, Mostafa Rahimi Azghadi
and Hamed Shah-Hosseini
Department of Electrical and Computer Engineering,
Shahid Beheshti University,
Tehran, Iran

1. Introduction

The Travelling Salesman Problem or the TSP is a representative of a large class of problems known as combinatorial optimization problems. In the ordinary form of the TSP, a map of cities is given to the salesman and he has to visit all the cities only once to complete a tour such that the length of the tour is the shortest among all possible tours for this map. The data consist of weights assigned to the edges of a finite complete graph, and the objective is to find a Hamiltonian cycle, a cycle passing through all the vertices, of the graph while having the minimum total weight. In the TSP context, Hamiltonian cycles are commonly called tours. For example, given the map shown in figure 1, the lowest cost route would be the one written (A, B, C, E, D, A), with the cost 31.

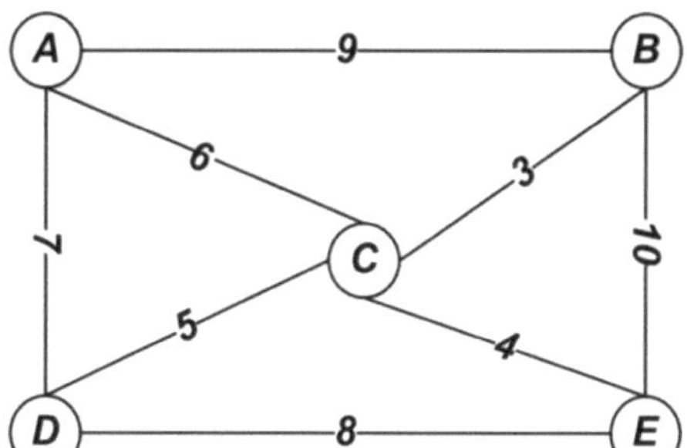

Fig. 1. The tour with A=>B =>C =>E =>D => A is the optimal tour.

In general, the TSP includes two different kinds, the Symmetric TSP and the Asymmetric TSP. In the symmetric form known as STSP there is only one way between two adjacent cities, i.e., the distance between cities A and B is equal to the distance between cities B and A (Fig. 1). But in the ATSP (Asymmetric TSP) there is not such symmetry and it is possible to have two different costs or distances between two cities. Hence, the number of tours in the ATSP and STSP on n vertices (cities) is $(n-1)!$ and $(n-1)!/2$, respectively. Please note that the graphs which represent these TSPs are complete graphs. In this chapter we mostly consider the STSP. It is known that the TSP is an NP-hard problem (Garey & Johnson, 1979) and is often used for testing the optimization algorithms. Finding Hamiltonian cycles or traveling salesman tours is possible using a simple dynamic program using time and space $O(2^n n^{O(1)})$, that finds Hamiltonian paths with specified endpoints for each induced subgraph of the input graph (Eppstein, 2007). The TSP has many applications in different engineering and optimization problems. The TSP is a useful problem in routing problems e.g. in a transportation system.

There are different approaches for solving the TSP. Solving the TSP was an interesting problem during recent decades. Almost every new approach for solving engineering and optimization problems has been tested on the TSP as a general test bench. First steps in solving the TSP were classical methods. These methods consist of heuristic and exact methods. Heuristic methods like cutting planes and branch and bound (Padherg & Rinaldi, 1987), can only optimally solve small problems whereas the heuristic methods, such as 2-opt (Lin & Kernighan, 1973), 3-opt, Markov chain (Martin et al., 1991), simulated annealing (Kirkpatrick et al., 1983) and tabu search are good for large problems. Besides, some algorithms based on greedy principles such as nearest neighbour, and spanning tree can be introduced as efficient solving methods. Nevertheless, classical methods for solving the TSP usually result in exponential computational complexities. Hence, new methods are required to overcome this shortcoming. These methods include different kinds of optimization techniques, nature based optimization algorithms, population based optimization algorithms and etc. In this chapter we discuss some of these techniques which are algorithms based on population.

Population based optimization algorithms are the techniques which are in the set of the nature based optimization algorithms. The creatures and natural systems which are working and developing in nature are one of the interesting and valuable sources of inspiration for designing and inventing new systems and algorithms in different fields of science and technology. Evolutionary Computation (Eiben & Smith, 2003), Neural Networks (Haykin, 99), Time Adaptive Self-Organizing Maps (Shah-Hosseini, 2006), Ant Systems (Dorigo & Stutzle, 2004), Particle Swarm Optimization (Eberhart & Kennedy, 1995), Simulated Annealing (Kirkpatrik, 1984), Bee Colony Optimization (Teodorovic et al., 2006) and DNA Computing (Adleman, 1994) are among the problem solving techniques inspired from observing nature.

In this chapter population based optimization algorithms have been introduced. Some of these algorithms were mentioned above. Other algorithms are Intelligent Water Drops (IWD) algorithm (Shah-Hosseini, 2007), Artificial Immune Systems (AIS) (Dasgupta, 1999) and Electromagnetism-like Mechanisms (EM) (Birbil & Fang, 2003). In this chapter, every section briefly introduces one of these population based optimization algorithms and applies them for solving the TSP. Also, we try to note the important points of each algorithm and every point we contribute to these algorithms has been stated. Section nine shows experimental results based on the algorithms introduced in previous sections which are implemented to solve different problems of the TSP using well-known datasets.

2. Evolutionary algorithms

2.1 Introduction

Evolutionary Algorithms (EAs) imitates the process of biological evolution in nature. These are search methods which take their inspiration from natural selection and survival of the fittest as exist in the biological world. EA conducts a search using a population of solutions. Each iteration of an EA involves a competitive selection among all solutions in the

population which results in survival of the fittest and deletion of the poor solutions from the population. By swapping parts of a solution with another one, recombination is performed and forms the new solution that it may be better than the previous ones. Also, a solution can be mutated by manipulating a part of it. Recombination and mutation are used to evolve the population towards regions of the space which good solutions may reside.
Four major evolutionary algorithm paradigms have been introduced during the last 50 years: genetic algorithm is a computational method, mainly proposed by Holland (Holland, 1975). Evolutionary strategies developed by Rechenberg (Rechenberg, 1965) and Schwefel (Schwefel, 1981). Evolutionary programming introduced by Fogel (Fogel et al., 1966), and finally we can mention genetic programming which proposed by Koza (Koza, 1992). Here we introduce the GA (Genetic Algorithm) for solving the TSP. At the first, we prepare a brief background on the GA.

2.2 Genetic algorithms

Genetic Algorithms focus on optimizing general combinatorial problems. GAs have long been studied as problem solving tools for many search and optimization problems, specifically those that are inherent in NP-Complete problems. Various candidate solutions are considered during the search procedure in the system, and the population evolves until a candidate solution satisfies the predefined criteria. In most GAs, a candidate solution, called an individual, is represented by a binary string (Goldberg, 1989) i.e. a string of 0 or 1 elements. Each solution (individual) is represented as a sequence (chromosome) of elements (genes) and is assigned a fitness value based on the value given by an evaluation function. The fitness value measures how close the individual is to the optimum solution. A set of individuals constitutes a population that evolves from one generation to the next through the creation of new individuals and deletion of some old ones. The process starts with an initial population created in some way, e.g. through a random process. Evolution can take two forms:

Crossover:

Two selected chromosomes can be combined by a crossover operator, the result of which will replace the lowest fitness chromosome in the population. Selection of each chromosome is performed by an algorithm to ensure that the selection probability is proportional to the fitness of the chromosome. A new chromosome has the chance to be better than the replaced one. The process is oriented towards the sub-regions of the search space, where an optimal solution is supposed to exist (Goldberg, 1989).

Mutation:

In mutation process, a gene from a selected chromosome is randomly changed. This provides additional chances of entering unexplored sub-regions. Finally, the evolution is stopped when either the goal is reached or a maximum CPU time has been spent (Goldberg, 1989).

In the following the GA operation pseudo code has been written:

1. Start
2. Population initialization
3. Repeat until (satisfying termination criteria)
    - Selection
    - Cross over
    - Mutation

- Making new population with the fittest solutions
- Evaluation
- Checking the termination criterion

4. Take the best solution as output
5. End

2.3 Solving the TSP using GA

As mentioned earlier, the TSP is known as a classical NP-complete problem, which has extremely large search spaces and is very difficult to solve (Louis & Gong, 2000). Hence, classical methods for solving TSP usually result in exponential computational complexities. These methods consist of heuristic and exact methods. Heuristic methods like cutting planes and branch and bound (Padherg & Rinaldi, 1987), can only optimally solve small problems while the heuristic methods, such as 2-opt (Lin & Kernighan, 1973), 3-opt, Markov chain (Martin et al., 1991), simulated annealing (Kirkpatrick et al., 1983) and tabu search are good for large problems. Besides, some algorithms based on greedy principles such as nearest neighbour, and spanning tree can be used as efficient solving methods. Nevertheless, because of the tremendous number of possible solutions and large search spaces, GAs seem to be wise approaches for solving the TSP especially when they are accompanied with carefully designed genetic operators (Jiao & Wang, 2000). GAs search the large space of solutions toward best answer and the operators can help the search process become faster and also they prepare the ability to avoid being trapped in local optima.

In recent years, solving the TSP using evolutionary algorithms and specially GAs has attracted a lot of attention. Many studies have been performed and researchers try to contribute to different parts of solving process. Some of researchers pose different forms of GA operators (Yan et al., 2005) in comparison to the former ones and others attempt to combine GA with other possible approaches like ACO (Lee, 2004), PSO and etc. In addition, some authors implement a new evolutionary idea or combine some previous algorithms and idea to create a new method (Bonyadi et al., 2007). Here we investigate some of these works and compare their results. Due to the spread of related works we can not mention all of them here. But The reader is referred to the prepared references for further information.

In all of the performed works, two instances are mentionable. First: all of the proposed algorithms work toward finding the nearest answer to the best solution. Second: solving the TSP in a more little time is a key point in this problem because of its special application which require, finding the best feasible answer fast.

In (Bonyadi et al., 2007), the authors made some changes to two previous local search algorithms i.e. the Shuffled Frog Leaping (SFL) and the Civilization and Society (CS) and combined these two algorithms with the GA idea. In this study, as it is common in a conventional GA, at first the elements of the population perform mutation or crossover in random order. Then for every element of this population, a local search algorithm, which is a mix of both SFL and CS, is performed. The results demonstrate significant improvements in terms of time complexity and reaching better solutions in comparison to the GAs which apply only SFL or CS in their usual forms. Hence, the main contribution in this work is combining two previous search methods and using them with the GA, simultaneously. The evaluation results of the proposed algorithm have been prepared in section nine.

In another work (Yan et al., 2005) a new algorithm based on Inver-over operator, for combinatorial optimization problems has been proposed. Inver-over is based on simple inversion; however, knowledge taken from other individuals in the population influences its action. In this algorithm some new strategies including selection operator, replace operator and some new control strategy have been applied. The results prove that these changes are very efficient to accelerate the convergence. A consequence, it is inferred that, one of the points for contribution is operators. Suitable changes in the conventional form of operators might lead to major differences in the search and optimization procedure.

Through the experiments, GAs are global search algorithms appropriate for problems with huge search spaces. In addition, heuristic methods can be applied for search in local areas. Hence, combination of these two search algorithms can result in producing high quality solutions. Cooperation between Speediness of local search methods in regional search and robustness of evolutionary methods in global search can be very useful to obtain the global optimum. Recently, (Nguyen et al., 2007) proposed a hybrid GA to find high-quality solutions for the TSP. The main contribution of this study is to show the suitable combination of a GA as a global search with a heuristic local search which are very promising for the TSP. In addition, the considerable improvements in the achieved results prove that the effectiveness and efficiency of the local search in the performance of hybrid GAs. Through these results, one of other points where it can be kept in mind is the design of the GA in a case that it balances between local and global search. Moreover, many other studies have been performed that all of them combine the local and global search mechanisms for solving the TSP.

As mentioned earlier, one of the points that solving the TSP can contribute is recombination operators i.e. mutation and crossover. Based on (Takahashi, 2005) there are two kinds of crossover operators for solving the TSP. Conventional encoding of the TSP which is an array representation of chromosomes where every element of this array is a gene that in the TSP shows a city. The first kind of crossover operator corresponds to this chromosome structure. In this operator two parents are selected and with exchanging of some parts in parents the children are reproduced. The second type performs crossover operation with mentioning epistasis. In this method it is tried to retain useful information about links of parent's edges which leads to convergence. Also, in (Tsai et al., 2004) another work on genetic operators has been performed which resulted in good achievements.

3. Ant colony optimization (ACO)

3.1 Introduction

The ACO (Ant Colony Optimization) heuristic is inspired by the real ant behaviour (figure 2) in finding the shortest path between the nest and the food (Beckers et al., 1992). This is achieved by a substance called pheromone that shows the trace of an ant. In its searching the ant uses heuristic information which is its own knowledge of where the smell of the food comes from and the other ants' decision of the path toward the food by pheromone information (Holldobler & Wilson, 1990).

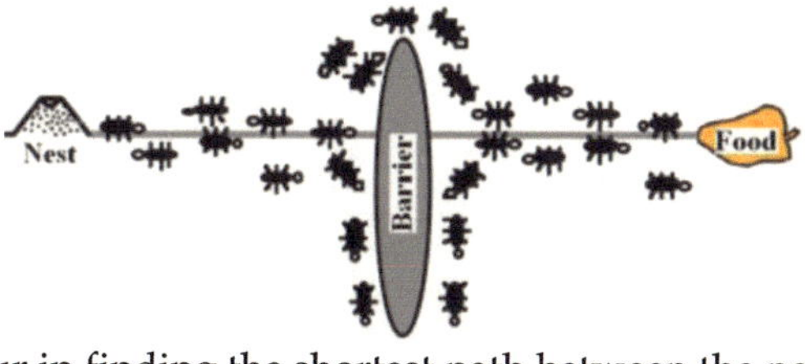

Fig. 2. Real ant behaviour in finding the shortest path between the nest and the food

In fact the algorithm uses a set of artificial ants (individuals) which cooperate to the solution of a problem by exchanging information via pheromone deposited on graph edges. The ACO algorithm is employed to imitate the behaviour of real ants and is as follows:

```
Initialize
Loop
          Each ant is positioned on a starting node
          Loop
                    Each ant applies a state transition rule to
                    incrementally build a solution and a local
                    pheromone updating rule
          Until all ants have built a complete solution
          A global pheromone updating rule is applied
Until end condition
```

3.2 State transition

Consider n is the city amount; m is the quantity of the ants in an ACO problem; dij is the length of the path between adjacent cities i and j; $\tau_{ij}(t)$ is the intensity of trail on edge (i, j) at time t . At the beginning of the algorithm, an initialization algorithm determines the ants positions on different cities and initial value $\tau_{ij}(0)$, a small positive constant c for trail intensity are set on edges. The first element of each ant's tabu list is set to its starting city.
The state transition is given by equation 1, which ant k in city i chooses to move to city j :

$$p_{ij}^{k}(t) = \begin{cases} \dfrac{(\tau_{ij}(t))^{\alpha}(\eta_{ij}(t))^{\beta}}{\sum\limits_{k \notin allowed_k} (\tau_{ik}(t))^{\alpha}(\eta_{ik}(t))^{\beta}}, & \text{if } j \notin allowed_k \\ 0, & \text{otherwise} \end{cases} \tag{1}$$

where $allowed_k$ = $\{N\text{-}tabu_k\}$, which is the set of cities that remain to be visited by ant k positioned on city i (to make the solution feasible) α and β are parameters that determine the relative importance of trail versus visibility, and $\eta = 1/d$ is the visibility of edge (i, j) .

3.3 Trial updating

In order to improve future solutions, the pheromone trails of the ants must be updated to reflect the ant's performance and the quality of the solutions found. The global updating rule is implemented as follows. Once all ants have built their tours, pheromone is updated on all edges according to the following formula (equations 2 to 4):

$$\tau_{ij}(t+1) = \rho\tau_{ij}(t) + \sum_{k=1}^{m} \Delta\tau_{ij}^{k} \tag{2}$$

where

$$\Delta\tau_{ij}^{k} = \begin{cases} \dfrac{Q}{L_k}, & \text{if edge } (i, j) \text{ is visited by the kth ant at current cycle} \\ 0, & \text{otherwise} \end{cases} \tag{3}$$

$$\Delta\tau_{ij} = \sum_{k=1}^{m} \Delta\tau_{ij}^{k} \qquad (4)$$

ρ ($0 < \rho < 1$) is trail persistence, L_k is the length of the tour found by kth ant , Q is a constant related to the quantity of trail laid by ants. In fact, pheromone placed on the edges plays the role of a distributed long-term memory (Dorigo & Gambardella, 1997). The algorithm iterates in a predefined number of iterations and the best solutions are saved as the results.

3.4 Solving the TSP using ACO

As it is mentioned, the ACO algorithm has good potential for problem solving and recently has attracted a lot of attentions specifically for solving NP-Hard set of problems. One of the earliest best works for solving the TSP uses the ACS (Ant Colony System) is presented in (Dorigo & Gambardella, 1997). They use the ACS algorithm for solving the TSP and they claim that the ACS outperforms other nature-inspired algorithms such as simulated annealing and evolutionary computation. In addition, they compared ACS-3-opt, a version of the ACS improved with a local search procedure, to some of the best performing algorithms for symmetric and asymmetric TSPs.

One of the other recent approaches for solving the TSP is proposed in (Song et al., 2006). In particular, the option that an ant hunts for the next step, the use of a combination of two kinds of pheromone evaluation models, the change of size of population in the ant colony during the run of the algorithm, and the mutation of pheromone have been studied. One of the most powerful attitudes in their paper was choosing the appropriate ACO model that proposed by M. Dorigo which were called ant-cycle, ant-quantity and ant-density models. These three models differ in the way the pheromone trail is updated. In ant-cycle algorithm, the trail is updated after all the ants finish their tours. In contrast, in the last two models, each ant lays its pheromone at each step without waiting for the end of the tour (Song et al., 2006). Furthermore they claim that in early stage of iterations, the convergence speed is faster using ant-density model in comparison with the other two models. Thus, at the beginning, the ant-density model is applied. Because the Ant-cycle system has the advantage of utilizing the global information, it is used at the other times. A mutation mechanism same as in genetic algorithm has been added to the improved ACO algorithm to assist the algorithm to jumping out from local optima's. In their proposed improved ACO, a population sizing method is used which changes the number of individuals (ants).

4. Particle swarm optimization (PSO)

4.1 Introduction

Particle Swarm Optimization (PSO) uses swarming behaviours observed in flocks of birds, schools of fish, or swarms of bees (figure 3), and even human social behaviour, from which intelligence emerges (Kennedy & Eberhart, 2001).

The standard PSO model consists of a swarm of particles. They move iteratively through the *feasible* problem space to find the new solutions. Each particle has a position represented by a position-vector $\vec{x}_i$ (*i* is the index of the particle), and a velocity represented by a velocity-vector $\vec{v}_i$. Each particle remembers its own best position so far in a vector $\vec{x}_i^{\#}$ and its *j*-th dimensional value is $x_{ij}^{\#}$. The best position-vector among the swarm heretofore is then stored in a vector x^* and its *j*-th dimension value is x^*_j.The PSO procedure is as follows:

Fig. 3. Birds or fish exhibit such a coordinated collective behaviour

Algorithm 1 Particle Swarm Algorithm
01. Begin
02. Parameter settings and swarm initialization
03. Evaluation
04. $g = 1$
05. While (the stopping criterion is not met) do
06. For each particle
07. Update velocity
08. Update position and local best position
09. Evaluation
10. EndFor
11. Update leader (global best particle)
12. $g + +$
15. End While
14. End

The PSO algorithm has several phases consist of Initialization, Evaluation, Update Velocity and Update Position. These phases are described in more details (See figure 5).

4.2 Initialization

The initialization phase is used to determine the position of the *m* particles in the first iteration. The random initialization is one of the most popular methods for this job. There is no guarantee that a randomly generated particle be a good answer and this will make the initialization more attractive. A good initialization algorithm make the optimization algorithm more efficient and reliable. For initialization, some known prior knowledge of the problem can help the algorithm to converge in less iterations. As an example, in 0-1 knapsack problem, there is a greedy algorithm which can generate good candidate answers but not optimal one. This greedy algorithm can be used for initializing the population and the optimization algorithm will continue the optimization from this good point.

4.3 Update velocity and position

In each iteration, each particle updates its velocity and position according to its heretofore best position, its current velocity and some information of its neighbours. Equation 5 is used for updating the velocity:

$$\overrightarrow{v_i(t)} = \underbrace{w\overrightarrow{v_i(t-1)}}_{inertia} + \underbrace{c_1 r_1 \left(\overrightarrow{x_i^{\#}(t-1)} - \overrightarrow{x_i(t-1)}\right)}_{Personal influence} + \underbrace{c_2 r_2 \left(\overrightarrow{x^{*}(t-1)} - \overrightarrow{x_i(t-1)}\right)}_{Social influence} \quad (5)$$

Where $\overrightarrow{x_i(t)}$ is the position-vector in iteration t (i is the index of the particle), $\overrightarrow{v_i(t)}$ is the velocity-vector in iteration t. $x_1^{\#}(t)$ is the best position so far of particle i in iteration t and its j-th dimensional value is $x^{\#}_{ij}(t)$. The best position-vector among the swarm heretofore is then stored in a vector $x^*(t)$ and its j-th dimension value is $x^*_j(t)$. $r1$ and $r2$ are the random numbers in the interval [0,1]. $c1$ is a positive constant, called as coefficient of the self-recognition component, $c2$ is a positive constant, called as coefficient of the social component. The variable **w** is called as the inertia factor, which value is typically setup to vary linearly from 1 to near 0 during the iterated processing. In fact, a large inertia weight facilitates global exploration (searching new areas), while a small one tends to facilitate local exploration. Consequently a reduction on the number of iterations required to locate the optimum solution (Yuhui & Eberhart, 1998). Figure 4 illustrates this reduction. The algorithm invokes the equation 6 for updating the positions:

$$\overrightarrow{x_i(t)} = \overrightarrow{x_i(t-1)} + \overrightarrow{v_i(t)} \quad (6)$$

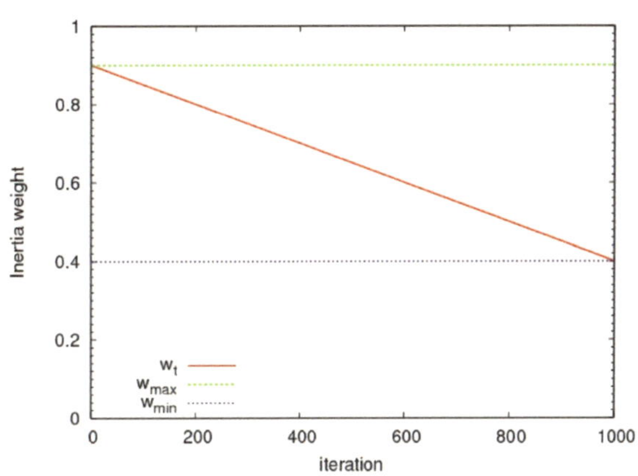

Fig. 4. The value of the inertia weight is decreased during a run

4.4 Solving the TSP using PSO

As it is described before, Particle Swarm Optimization (PSO) has a good potential for problem solving. The susceptibilities and charms of this nature based algorithm convinced researchers to use the PSO to solve NP-Hard problems such as TSP and Job-Scheduling. Here, we investigate some of these proposed approaches for solving the TSP.

One of the attractive works for solving the TSP was cited in (Yuan et al.., 2007). They propose a novel hybrid algorithm which invokes the sufficiency of both PSO and COA (Chaotic Optimization Algorithm) (Zhang et al., 2001). In fact, they exert the COA to restrain the particles from getting stock on local optima's in rudimentary iterations. In other word, they claim that the COA could considerably useful to keep particle's global searching ability.

One of the other exciting algorithms based on PSO for solving TSP is introduced in (Pang et al., 2004). In this paper they propose an algorithm based on PSO which uses the fuzzy matrices for velocity and position vectors. In addition, they use the fuzzy multiplication and addition operators for velocity and position updating formulas (equations (5) and (6)). The mentioned PSO algorithm in previous sections modified to an algorithm which works based on fuzzy means such as fuzzification and defuzzification. In each iteration, the position of each generated solution has been defuzzified to determine the cost of the individual. This cost will be used for updating the local best position.

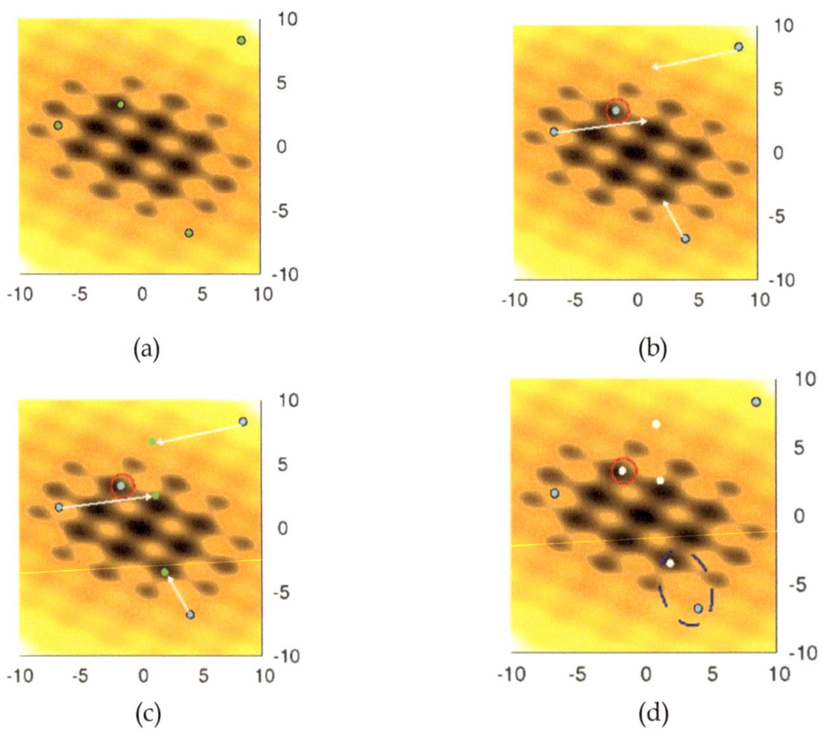

Fig. 5. (a) Create a 'population' of agents (called particles) uniformly distributed over X (feasible region) and Evaluate each particle's position according to the objective function, (b) Update particles' velocities according to equation (5), (c) Move particles to their new positions according to equation (6), (d) If a particle's current position is better than its previous best position, update it.

5. Intelligent water drops

5.1 Introduction

The last work on the population based optimization algorithms inspired by nature is a novel problem solving method proposed by Hamed Shah-hosseini (Shah-hosseini, 2007). This method is called "Intelligent Water Drops" or IWD algorithm which is based on the processes that happen in the natural river systems and the actions and reactions that take place between water drops in the river and the changes that happen in the environment that river is flowing. Here we prepare a complete description on this new and interesting method. To start with, the inspiration of IWD, natural water drops, will be stated. After that the IWD system has been introduced. And finally these ideas are embedded into the proposed algorithm for solving the Traveling Salesman Problem or the TSP.

5.2 Natural water drops

In nature, we often see water drops moving in rivers, lakes, and seas. As water drops move, they change their environment in which they are flowing. Moreover, the environment itself has substantial effects on the paths that the water drops follow. Consider a hypothetical river in which water is flowing and moving from high terrain to lower terrain and finally joins a lake or sea. The paths that the river follows, based on our observation in nature, are often full of twists and turns. We also know that the water drops have no visible eyes to be able to find the destination (lake or river). If we put ourselves in place of a water drop of the river, we feel that some force pulls us toward itself (gravity). This gravitational force as we know from physics is straight toward the center of the earth. Therefore with no obstacles and barriers, the water drops would follow a straight path toward the destination, which is the shortest path from the source to the destination. However, due to different kinds of obstacles in the way of this ideal path, the real path will have to be different from the ideal path and we often see lots of twists and turns in a river path. In contrast, the water drops always try to change the real path to make it a better path in order to approach the ideal path. This continuous effort changes the path of the river as time passes by. One feature of a water drop is the velocity that it flows which enables the water drop to transfer an amount of soil from one place to another place in the front. This soil is usually transferred from fast parts of the path to the slow parts. As the fast parts get deeper by being removed from soil, they can hold more volume of water and thus may attract more water. The removed soils which are carried in the water drops are unloaded in slower beds of the river. There are other mechanisms which are involved in the river system which we don't intend to consider them all here.

In summary, a water drop in a river has a non-zero velocity. It often carries an amount of soil. It can load some soil from an area of the river bed, often from fast flowing areas and unload them in slower areas of the river bed. Obviously, a water drop prefers an easier path to a harder path when it has to choose between several branches that exist in the path from the source to the destination. Now we can introduce the intelligent water drops.

5.3 Intelligent water drops

Based on the observation on the behavior of water drops, we develop an artificial water drop which possesses some of the remarkable properties of the natural water drop. This Intelligent Water Drop, IWD for short, has two important properties:

1. The amount of the soil it carries now, Soil (IWD).
2. The velocity that it is moving now, Velocity (IWD).

flows in its environment. This environment depends on the problem at hand. In an environment, there are usually lots of paths from a given source to a desired destination, which the position of the destination may be known or unknown. If we know the position of the destination, the goal is to find the best (often the shortest) path from the source to the destination. In some cases, in which the destination is unknown, the goal is to find the optimum destination in terms of cost or any suitable measure for the problem.

We consider an IWD moving in discrete finite-length steps. From its current location to its next location, the IWD velocity is increased by the amount nonlinearly proportional to the inverse of the soil between the two locations. Moreover, the IWD's soil is increased by removing some soil of the path joining the two locations. The amount of soil added to the IWD is inversely (and nonlinearly) proportional to the time needed for the IWD to pass from its current location to the next location. This duration of time is calculated by the simple laws of physics for linear motion. Thus, the time taken is proportional to the velocity of the IWD and inversely proportional to the distance between the two locations.

Another mechanism that exists in the behavior of an IWD is that it prefers the paths with low soils on its beds to the paths with higher soils on its beds. To implement this behavior of path choosing, we use a uniform random distribution among the soils of the available paths such that the probability of the next path to choose is inversely proportional to the soils of the available paths. The lower the soil of the path, the more chance it has for being selected by the IWD.

In this part, we specifically express the steps for solving the TSP. The first step is how to represent the TSP in a suitable way for the IWD. For the TSP, the cities are often modeled by nodes of a graph, and the links in the graph represent the paths joining each two cities. Each link or path has an amount of soil. An IWD can travel between cities through these links and can change the amount of their soils. Therefore, each city in the TSP is denoted by a node in the graph which holds the physical position of each city in terms of its two dimensional coordinates while the links of the graph denote the paths between cities. To implement the constraint that each IWD never visits a city twice, we consider a visited city list for the IWD which this list includes the cities visited so far by the IWD. So, the possible cities for an IWD to choose in its next step must not be from the cities in the visited list.

5.4 Solving the TSP using IWD

In the following, we present the proposed Intelligent Water Drop (IWD) algorithm for the TSP:

1. Initialization of static parameters: set the number of water drops N_{IWD}, the number of cities N_C, and the Cartesian coordinates of each city i such that $\mathbf{c}(i) = [x_i, y_i]^T$ to their chosen constant values. The number of cities and their coordinates depend on the problem at hand while the N_{IWD} is set by the user. Here, we choose N_{IWD} to be equal to the number of cities. For velocity updating, we use parameters $a_v = 1000$, $b_v = .01$ and $c_v = 1$. For soil updating, we use parameters $a_s = 1000$, $b_s = .01$ and $c_s = 1$. Moreover, the initial soil on each link is denoted by the constant $InitSoil$ such that the soil of the link between every two cities i and j is set by $soil(i, j) = InitSoil$. The initial velocity of IWDs is denoted by the constant $InitVel$. Both parameters $InitSoil$ and $InitVel$ are also user selected. In this paper, we choose $InitSoil = 1000$ and $InitVel = 100$. The best tour is denoted by T_B which is still unknown and its length is initially set to infinity: $Len(T_B) = \infty$. Moreover, we should specify the maximum number of iterations that the algorithm should be repeated or some other terminating condition suitable for the problem.

2. Initialization of dynamic parameters: For every IWD, we create a visited city list $V_c(IWD) = \{\ \}$ set to the empty list. The velocity of each IWD is set to *InitVel* whereas the initial soil of each IWD is set to zero.
3. For every IWD, randomly select a city and place that IWD on the city.
4. Update the visited city lists of all IWDs to include the cities just visited.
5. For each IWD, choose the next city j to be visited by the IWD when it is in city i with the following probability (equation 7):

$$p_i^{IWD}(j) = \frac{f\left(soil(i,j)\right)}{\sum_{k \notin vc(IWD)} f\left(soil(i,k)\right)} \tag{7}$$

such that $f(soil(i,j)) = \dfrac{1}{\varepsilon_s + g(soil(i,j))}$ and

$$g(soil(i,j)) = \begin{cases} soil(i,j) & if \ \min_{l \notin vc(IWD)} (soil(i,l)) \geq 0 \\ soil(i,j) - \min_{l \notin vc(IWD)} (soil(i,l)) & else \end{cases}$$

. Here ε_s is a small positive number to prevent a possible division by zero in the function $f(.)$. Here, we use $\varepsilon_s = 0.01$. The function $\min(.)$ returns the minimum value among all available values for its argument. Moreover, $vc(IWD)$ is the visited city list of the IWD.

6. For each IWD moving from city i to city j, update its velocity based on equation 8.

$$vel^{IWD}(t+1) = vel^{IWD}(t) + \frac{a_v}{b_v + c_v \, . soil(i,j)} \tag{8}$$

such that $vel^{IWD}(t+1)$ is the updated velocity of the IWD. $soil(i,j)$ is the soil on the path (link) joining the current city i and the new city j. With formula (8), the velocity of the IWD increases less if the amount of the soil is high and the velocity would increase more if the soil is low on the path.

7. For each IWD, compute the amount of the soil, $\Delta soil(i,j)$, that the current water drop IWD loads from its the current path between two cities i and j using equation 9.

$$\Delta soil(i,j) = \frac{a_s}{b_s + c_s . time\left(i,j; vel^{IWD}\right)} \tag{9}$$

such that $time\left(i,j; vel^{IWD}\right) = \dfrac{\left\| \mathbf{c}(i) - \mathbf{c}(j) \right\|}{\max\left(\varepsilon_v, vel^{IWD}\right)}$ which computes the time taken to travel from city i to city j with the velocity vel^{IWD}. Here, the function $\mathbf{c}(.)$ represents the two dimensional positional vector for the city. The function max(.,.) returns the maximum value among its arguments, which is used here to threshold the negative velocities to a very small positive number $\varepsilon_v = 0.0001$.

8. For each IWD, update the soil of the path traversed by that IWD using equation 10.

$$\begin{aligned} soil(i,j) &= (1-\rho).soil(i,j) - \rho.\Delta soil(i,j) \\ soil^{IWD} &= soil^{IWD} + \Delta soil(i,j) \end{aligned} \tag{10}$$

where $soil^{IWD}$ represents the soil that the IWD carries. The IWD goes from city i to city j. The parameter ρ is a small positive number less than one. Here we use $\rho = 0.9$.

9. For each IWD, complete its tour by using steps 4 to 8 repeatedly. Then, calculate the length of the tour traversed by the IWD, and find the tour with the minimum length among all IWD tours in this iteration. We denote this minimum tour by T_M.
10. Update the soils of paths included in the current minimum tour of the IWD, denoted by T_M which is computed based on equation 11.

$$soil(i,j) = (1-\rho).soil(i,j) - \rho.\frac{2.soil^{IWD}}{N_c\left(N_c - 1\right)} \quad \forall (i,j) \in T_M \tag{11}$$

11. 11. If the minimum tour T_M is shorter than the best tour found so far denoted by T_B, then we update the best tour by applying equation 12.

$$T_B = T_M \quad and \quad Len(T_B) = Len(T_M) \tag{12}$$

12. Go to step 2 unless the maximum number of iterations is reached or the defined termination condition is satisfied.
13. The algorithm stops here such that the best tour is kept in T_B and its length is $Len(T_B)$.

It is reminded that it is also possible to use only T_M and remove step 11 of the IWD algorithm. However, it is safer to keep the best tour T_B of all iterations than to count on only the minimum tour T_M of the last iteration. The IWD algorithm is experimented by artificial and some benchmark TSP environments. The proposed algorithm converges fast to optimum solutions and finds good and promising results. This research (Shah-Hosseini, 2007) is the beginning of using water drops ideas to solve engineering problems. So, there is much space to improve and develop the IWD algorithm.

6. Artificial immune systems

6.1 Introduction

Recently, there was an increasing interest in the area of Artificial Immune System (AIS) and its application for solving various problems specifically for the TSP (Zeng & Gu, 2007), (Lu et al., 2007). AIS is inspired by natural immune mechanism and uses immunology idea in order to develop systems capable of performing different tasks in various areas of research such as pattern recognition, fault detection, diagnosis and a number of other fields including optimization. Here we want to know the AIS completely. To start with, it might be useful to become more familiar with natural immune system.

Natural immune systems consist of the structures and processes in the living body that provide a defence system against invaders and also altered internal cells which lead to disease. In a glance, immune system's main tasks can be divided into three parts; recognition, categorization and defence. As recognition part, the immune system firstly has to recognize the invader and foreign antigens e.g. bacteria, viruses and etc. After recognition, classification must be performed by immune systems, this is the second part. And appropriate form of defence must to be applied for every category of foreign aggressive phenomenon as the third part. The most significant aspect of the immune systems in mammals is learning capability. Namely, the immune systems can grow during the life time and is capable of using learning, memory and associative retrieval in order to solve mentioned recognition and classification tasks. In addition, the studies show that the natural immune systems are useful phenomena in information processing and can be helpful in inspiration for problem solving and various optimization problems (Keko et al., 2003).

6.2 Artificial immune system

Like the natural immune systems the AIS is a set of techniques, which try to algorithmically mimic natural immune systems' behaviour (Dasgupta, 99). As mentioned earlier, the immune system is susceptible to all of the invaders, also the outer influences, like vaccines which are artificial ways of raising individual's immunity. Vaccines are other factors that can stimulate the immune system's susceptibility. This feature is the key point of the AIS structure. The vaccines in the AIS are abstracted forms of the preceding information. Vaccination modifies genes based on the useful knowledge of the problem to achieve higher fitness in comparison to the fitness that obtained from a random process when for example a classical GA is applied. Once again it is necessary to point out that, vaccines contain some important information about the problem and in consequence the vaccination process employed in a right manner can be very useful in the performance of the algorithm. Like classical GA and based on its structure the AIS can work. The GA operators (crossover and mutation) search the problem space randomly and hence they don't have enough capability of meeting the actual problem at the local level. GAs are known as incapable of search fine local tuning because they are global search algorithms. Immune method through vaccination tries to overcome such blindness of crossover and mutation (Keko et al., 2003). After vaccination, the immune method might leads to deterioration. This case happens when vaccination leads to smaller fitness values than previous ones. Hence, another important part of immune algorithm is prevention of deterioration when inserting vaccine. In short, immune operators perform in four steps: firstly, an individual is selected, randomly. Now as the second step, the vaccine is inserted at the individual's randomly chosen place. Vaccine insertion might leads to deterioration, the third step is checking for deterioration. And finally the forth step is discarding every individual that shows degeneration right after vaccine. This way of checking could be dangerous for diversity and could result in algorithm's inability to avoid local optima, especially when combined with small populations. The studies show that the use of immune systems resulted in faster convergence when population is large enough and diversity is secured. The combination of immune algorithm and GA, form the immune genetic algorithm (IGA). Many of previous works that are performed on the TSP used IGA. Now, we first investigate the IGA and its structure in detail and after that we have a look at some previous works around the TSP.

In summery, the IGA consists of these steps:

1. Creation of initial population in some way, e.g. through a random process
2. Abstract vaccines according to the former information
3. Checking the termination criterion (if it is satisfied go to step 10 and else go to next step)
4. Crossover on the randomly selected individuals
5. Mutation on the produced children
6. Vaccination on the former step outcome
7. Deterioration checking
8. Discarding every individual that shows degeneration right after vaccine
9. Go to step 3
10. End

As it is obvious from the ten steps which have been mentioned above, the IGA is very similar to the conventional GA, but they are different in operators. The IGA has vaccine operator to overcome the universality problem of the conventional GA. For more information on IGA you can refer to many cited papers which are prepared at the end of this chapter.

6.3 Solving the TSP using AIS and IGA

The first work in investigating potential application of the immune system in solving numerical optimization problems was the study by Bersini and Varela (Bersini & Varela, 90), who proposed immune employment mechanism. After that, many studies have been performed that focus on the AIS and IGA. Also, the IGA and AIS have been applied for solving the TSP in many cases. In (Jiao & Wang, 2000) the IGA and its parts have been introduced in detail and the IGA has been shown as an algorithm that accomplished in two steps: 1) a vaccination and 2) an immune selection. These phases are completely similar to that we mentioned about IGA and AIS in this section. In the mentioned paper, it is proved that the IGA theoretically converges with probability one. Besides, strategies and methods of selecting vaccines and constructing an immune operator are also given. Also, the IGA has been applied to the TSP and the results which are presented in this study illustrate that IGA is able to restrain the degenerate phenomenon effectively during the evolutionary process and can improve the searching ability, adaptability and greatly increase the converging speed. Recently, some works have been performed on the TSP which employ IGA. In (Zeng & Gu, 2007), a novel genetic algorithm based on immunity and growth for the TSP is presented. In this paper at first, a reversal exchange crossover and mutation operator is proposed which lead to preservation of the good sub-tours and making individuals various. At the next part, a new immune operator is proposed to restrain individuals' degeneracy. In addition, a novel growth operator is proposed to obtain the optimal solution with more chances. Results and investigations that performed in this study show that the algorithm is feasible and effective as it is claimed. In addition, in another study (Lu et al., 2007), a modified immune genetic algorithm is applied to solve the Travelling Salesman Problem. This method called an improved IGA by its authors. In this paper, at first, a new selection strategy is incorporated into the conventional genetic algorithm to improve the performance of genetic algorithm. Besides the authors changed the selection strategy and in a new form it includes three computational procedures: evaluating the diversity of genes, calculating the percentage of genes, and computing the selection probability of genes. Based on the prepared results it is inferred that, by incorporating inoculating genes into conventional procedures of genetic algorithm, the number of evolutional iterations to reach an optimal solution can be significantly reduced and in consequence it results in faster answer in comparison to conventional IGA.

In addition to the mentioned works, the biological immune idea can be combined with other population based optimization algorithms which all of them are prepared in this chapter. As an instance, the paper (Qin et al., 2006) proposes a new diversity guaranteed ant colony algorithm by adopting the method of immune strategy to ant colony algorithm and simulating the behaviour of biological immune system. This method has been applied to the TSP benchmarks and results show that the presented algorithm has strong capability of optimization; it has diversified solutions, high convergence speed and succeeds in avoiding the stagnation and premature phenomena.

Based on the performed studies some points can be inferred as mentioned in the following (Keko et al., 2003):

The simulation results show that the variation in population size has the same effect on the GA and IGA. In both of the mentioned techniques, large population sizes require more generation to achieve higher fitness, resulting in relatively slow rate of convergence. Hence new ideas are required for faster convergence. Some of these new ideas had been presented in some works as you see in some investigated papers.

Also, based on the simulation results, the running time of the IGA and the regular GA do not have large differences, since in the IGA all the vaccines are determined before the algorithm starts and when they are required they can be loaded from a look up table.

Combining immune operator with another local improving operator can be an additional idea for getting better answers from the IGA.

One of the advantages of the IGA over the plain GA is that it is less susceptible to changing control parameters such as crossover or mutation probability. The simulation results demonstrate that changing these parameters has slight influence to the overall performance.

It is worth mentioning that more studies and attentions in the AIS and IGA are employing other AIS features like adaptive vaccine selection.

7. Bee colony optimization

7.1 Introduction

Similar to other natural inspired and collective intelligence based algorithms such as PSO which is taken from the bird's life and ACO based on the ant colony social life, another kind of artificial intelligence systems that can be useful in solving many engineering, management, control and computational problems, is an algorithm inspired from Bee colonies in nature. The Bee Colony Optimization (BCO) algorithms are interesting metaheuristic algorithms that represent another direction in the field of swarm intelligence. Here, firstly we introduce the bee system and bee colony optimization briefly and then some recent works on the TSP which have used bee systems are investigated.

7.2 Bee colony optimization

The bee colony's function according to nature is as follows. At first, each bee belonging to a colony looks for the feed individually. When a bee finds the feed, it informs other bees by dancing. Other bees collect and carry the feed to the hive. After relinquishing the feed to the hive, the bee can take three different actions.

1. Abandon the previous food source and become again uncommitted follower.
2. Continue to forage at the food source without recruiting the nestmates.
3. Dance and thus recruit the nestmates before the return to the food source.

With a certain probability that is dependent on the obtained feed quality, its distance from the hive and the number of the bees which are now engaged with this feed resource, a bee selects one of the stated actions and follows its work in a similar repetitive form (Teodorovic & Dell'Orco, 2005). This behaviour can be applied to many complicated engineering problems including computational, control, optimization, transportation, etc. In the following we study such a method that focuses on the TSP solving.

7.3 BCO application

The BCO algorithm can be a significant method in local search applications. One of the most primary works on the bees and their life is (Sato & Hagiwara, 97). In this study, the authors applied bee system along with GA and introduced a modified and improved form of the conventional GA. Based on this fact that the regular GA lacks the global search ability; the improvement is regarding to overcome this shortcoming. Hence, a new GA inspired by the bee colony's function has been presented, the authors called it, bee system. The main purpose of this modified GA (bee system) is to improve the local search ability of GAs without degrading the global search ability. In the proposed bee system, firstly global search is performed using the simple GA structure. Through this global search step, some chromosomes with reasonable high fitness produced which are called superior chromosome. These superior chromosomes are kept for the local search procedure and each of them corresponds to a local population. At the beginning of the local search all of the chromosomes in each local population make couple (cross over) with its population superior chromosome. This crossover is named concentrated crossover which tries to search concentratedly around the related superior chromosome. Another difference between the bee system and ordinary GA is migration among the population. In this method, the bee system selects one individual per predetermined generation, and transfers it to the neighbouring population which is called migration. Using this migration technique, each population tries to search independently and cooperatively. Moreover, for a more effective search, a simplified Simplex Method named Pseudo-Simplex Method is introduced and employed in the proposed bee system. All of the mentioned operators are in the local search part. After passing the predetermined generations, the local search stops. If the best solution found so far does not suffice the ending condition, the global search starts again and the algorithm is repeated (Sato & Hagiwara, 97). It was a kind of application based on the bee colony's function which is used to solve the TSP. Simulation results depict that the introduced method has a good potential to solve the TSP and other complicated problems.

7.4 Solving the TSP using BCO

Another study around bee colony and its applications is a work performed for transportation modelling with focus on artificial life (ALife) approach (Lucic & Teodorovic, 2002). This paper shows that the ALife models that have been developed for solving complex transportation problems are inspired by social insect's behavior. Interaction between individual insects in a colony of social insects has been well documented. The examples of such interactive behavior are bee dancing during the food procurement, ants' pheromone secretion, and performance of specific acts which signal the other insects to start performing the same actions. Based on these studies we can construct the artificial systems such as bee systems. In the mentioned study, the artificial bee system has been applied to solve the TSP. Assume that, the graph in which the traveling salesman route should be discovered is shown by G = (N, A) that N= nodes (cities) and A= links connecting these nodes. This graph can correspond to the network that the artificial bees are collecting nectar. The hive can also be placed randomly in one of the network's nodes. For solving the TSP using the bee system it is necessary that two parameters correspond to each others, tour length and nectar quantity. Here, it is assumed that the nectar quantity that is possible to collect flying along a certain link is inversely proportional to the link length. In other words, the shorter the link, the higher the nectar quantity along that link. The artificial bees collect the nectar during the predetermined time interval. After that, the hive position is changed randomly and artificial bees start to collect the nectar from the new hive location. Each iteration is composed of a certain number of stages. The stage is an elementary time unit in the bees' environment. During one stage the artificial bee will visit nodes, create partial traveling salesman tour, and after that return to the hive (the number of nodes to be visited within one stage is prescribed by the analyst at the beginning of the search process). In the hive the bee will participate in a decision making process. The artificial bee will decide whether to abandon the food source and become again an uncommitted follower, continue to forage at the food source without recruiting nestmates, or dance and thus recruit nestmates before returning to the food source (Lucic & Teodorovic, 2002). During any stage, bees are choosing nodes to be visited in a random manner. The randomness in not useful here and the mentioned paper's authors assumed that the probability of choosing node j by the k-th bee, located in node i (during stage u +1 and iteration z) equals to equation 13:

$$P_{ij}^{k}(u+1,z)=\begin{cases}\dfrac{e^{-ad_{ij}\frac{z}{\sum_{r=\max(z-b,1)}^{z-1} n_{ij}(r)}}}{\sum_{l\in N_k(u,z)} e^{-ad_{il}\frac{z}{\sum_{r=\max(z-b,1)}^{z-1} n_{il}(r)}}}, & i=g_k(u,z),\ j\in N_k(u,z),\ \forall k,u,z\\ 0, & otherwise\end{cases} \tag{13}$$

Where:
i, j - Node indexes (i, j = 1, 2, …, N),
$d_{i,j}$ - Length of link (i, j),
k - Bee index (k = 1, 2, …, B),
B - The total number of bees in the hive,
z - Iteration index (z = 1, 2, …, M),
M - Maximum number of iteration,
u - Stage index $\left(u=1,2,\ldots,\left|\left(|N|-1\right)/s\right|\right)$,
s - Number of nodes visited by every artificial bee during one stage,

$n_{il}(r)$ - total number of bees that visited link (i, l) in r-th iteration,
b - Memory length,
$g_k(u, z)$ - Last node that bee k visits at the end of stage u in iteration z,
$N_k(u, z)$ - Set of unvisited nodes for bee k at stage u in iteration z (in one stage bee will visits s nodes; we have $|Nk(u, z)| = |N| - us$),
a - Input parameter given by analyst.
This equation is based on some simple rules in solving the TSP using the bee system. These rules have been prepared as follows:
The greater distance between nodes i and j leads to the lower probability that the k-th bee located in the node i will choose node j during stage u and iteration z.
The greater number of iterations (z) makes the higher influence of the distance. In other words, at the beginning of the search process, artificial bees have "more freedom of flight". It means that, the bees have more chance to search the entire solution space. But when more iterations have been performed the bees have less freedom to explore the solution space such as the search at first, because, near the end of the search process, with a high probability the solution is in our neighbourhood.
Probability of selecting a new link by a bee is related to the total number of the last bees which had been visited this link, before this. The greater total number of bees results in a higher probability of choosing that link in the future.
All of the above mentioned points have been employed in the equation 13. Another important point in this problem is the bee decision about the following of the search process. After relinquishing the food, the bee is making a decision about abandoning the food source or continuing the foraging at the food source. It is assumed that every bee can obtain the information about nectar quantity collected by every other bee. The probability that, at the beginning of stage u + 1, bee k will use the same partial tour that is defined in stage u in iteration z is equal to the following (equation 14):

$$p_k\left(u+1, z\right) = e^{-\frac{L_k(u,z) - \min\limits_{r \in w(u,z)}(L_r(u,z))}{uz}} \tag{14}$$

Where $L_k(u, z)$ is the length of partial route that is discovered by bee k in stage u in iteration z. Based on equation 14 if a bee has discovered the shortest partial travelling salesman tour in stage u in iteration z, the bee will fly along the same partial tour with the probability equal to one. Besides, the longer tour has the smaller chance to choose based on this equation. For having a global search it is better that the individual bees have interaction with each others. To follow this purpose the probability of that the artificial bee continues foraging at the food source without recruiting nestmates is tuned to a very low value and hence the probability of that the bee flies to the dance floor and dance with other bees becomes low. In other words, when at the beginning of a new stage, the bee does not follow the previous partial travelling salesman tour, it will follow other bees and interacts to their dancing. But the bee must select one of the advertised dancing arenas (partial travelling salesman tour) in the dancing area, and hence another selection must be performed. This selection can be carried out in terms of two conditions: 1) the length of that partial tour and 2) the number of bees which are engaged in that partial tour. It is clear that the selection can be done based on the smaller tour length and also the greater number of bees. Based on these conditions the authors prepare a relation as it is shown in equation 15, where:

ρ, θ - Parameters given by the analyst,

$\alpha_{\xi}(u,z)$ - The normalized value of the partial route length

$\beta_{\xi}(u,z)$ - The normalized value of the number of bees advertising the partial tour,

Y(u, z) - The set of partial tours that were visited by at least one bee.

$$p_{\xi}(u,z) = \frac{e^{\rho\beta_{\xi}(u,z)-\theta\alpha_{\xi}(u,z)}}{\sum_{\tau \in Y(u,z)} e^{\rho\beta\tau(u,z)-\theta\alpha\tau(u,z)}} \qquad \xi \in Y(u,z), \forall u, z \qquad (15)$$

As it is shown in the mentioned work (Lucic & Teodorovic, 2002), this bee system has been tested on a large number of well known test benches such as Eil51.tsp, Berlin52.tsp, St70.tsp, Pr76.tsp, Kroa100.tsp, Eil101.tsp, Tsp225.tsp and A280.tsp. Also, for improving the results in each step, the 2-opt or 3-opt algorithms have been applied. The results reveal that the mentioned method is very efficient. In all instances with less than 100 nodes, the bee system achieves the optimal solution and in the large cases it has a significant improvement in comparison to the other prevalent methods. The simulation results have been organized in section nine.

One of the recent work for solving the TSP using bee's behaviour and BCO algorithm is (Teodorovic et al., 2006). In this paper the authors propose the Bee Colony Optimization Metaheuristic (BCO). Moreover, this study, describes two BCO algorithms that the authors call them, the Bee System (BS) and the Fuzzy Bee System (FBS). In the case of FBS the agents (artificial bees) use approximate reasoning and rules of fuzzy logic in their communication and acting. In this way, the FBS is capable to solve deterministic combinatorial problems, as well as combinatorial problems characterized by uncertainty. In this paper, The BCO as a new computational paradigm is described in detail at first. After that the TSP as a case study has been solved using the proposed bee system. The proposed bee system is similar to that had been seen in the previous investigated study but in this paper the BCO algorithm has been described completely. For further information about the BCO algorithm please refer to the related resources prepared at the end of the chapter.

8. Electromagnetism

8.1 Introduction

The Electromagnetism-like mechanism is a heuristic that was introduced by (Birbil & Fang, 2003). The method utilizes an attraction-repulsion mechanism to move the sample points towards the optimality. In other words, EM simulates the attraction-repulsion mechanism of electromagnetism theory which is based on Coulomb's law. The main concentration of the first introduction of this heuristic was on the problems with bounded variables on the form equal to equation 16.

$$\mathbf{Min}(\mathbf{f}(x)) \text{ s.t. } x \in [\mathbf{l},\mathbf{u}] \qquad (16)$$

where l and u are defined as the following form (equation 17):

$$[l,u] = x \in \{x_n \mid l_k < x_k < u_k, k = 1,...n\} \tag{17}$$

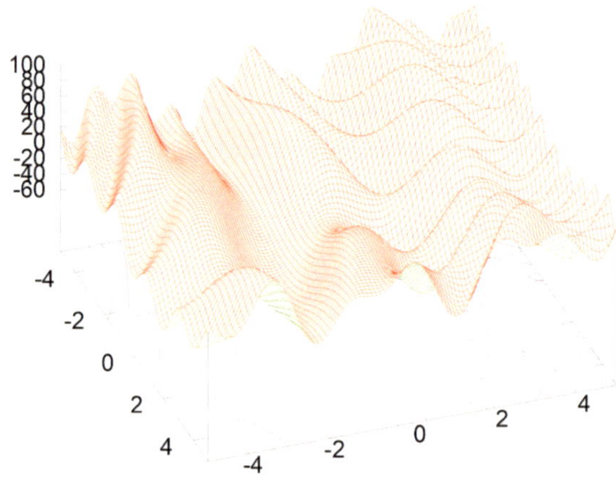

Fig. 6. A continuous optimization problem space

As an example, figure 6 illustrates continues problem space with l1=-60, l2=-4, l3=-4, u1=+100, u2=+4 and u3=+4. The aim is to find the minimum value of the shown surface.

In stochastic global optimization, population based algorithms start with sample points from feasible regions which are randomly selected. The regions of attraction are determined according to objective function values and then a mechanism is invoked for exploration of these candidate regions. The Genetic Algorithm is an example of this mechanism that corresponds to the crossover, reproduction and mutation operators (Michalewicz, 1994).

Similarly, Birbil et al. construct a mechanism that encourages the points to converge to the highly attractive valleys, and contrarily, discourages the points to move further away from steeper hills. This is similar to the charge of particles in elementary electromagnetism. In this approach, the *charge* of each point relates to the objective function value, which we are trying to optimize and also determines the magnitude of attraction or repulsion of the point over the sample population.

In addition, the combination force is exerted on the point via other points for finding a direction for each point to move in subsequence iterations. Like the electromagnetic forces, this force is calculated by adding vectorially the forces from each of the other points calculated separately.

Finally, similar to the hybrid population-based algorithms (Glover & Laguna, 1995), we may apply a local search procedure to improve some of the objective function values observed in the population.

Consider a problem in the form of (16) and the following parameters are given:

n dimension of the problem.

u_k upper bound in the kth dimension.

l_k lower bound in the kth dimension.

$f(x)$ pointer to the function that is minimized.

For solving such problem using Electromagnetism-Like method, the following algorithm is introduced by Birbil et al.

ALGORITHM 1. EM (*m, MAXITER, LSIT ER*, δ)
m: number of sample points
MAXITER: maximum number of iterations
LSIT ER: maximum number of local search iterations
δ: local search parameter, $\delta \in [0, 1]$
1: Initialize ()
2: iteration ←1
3: **while** iteration <*MAXITER* **do**
4: Local (*LSIT ER*, δ)
5: **F** ←CalcF ()
6: Move (**F**)
7: iteration ←iteration + 1
8: end while

The algorithm consists of four phases. The first phase is the initialization which determines the initial position of the particles, second is the local search which gathers the local information of each particle to improve it to its best local position, third is about calculating the force of each particle and finally moves the particles. These phases are described in more details as follows.

8.2 Initialization

The initialization procedure is used to determine the place of the *m* particles (size of population) at first iteration in an *n* dimensional feasible space. The distribution of the particles is uniform between the lower bound and upper bound of the corresponding variable. $f(x)$ is the objective function and x^{best} is the particle which has the best value of $f(x)$. The initialization algorithm is as follow:

ALGORITHM 2. Initialize ()
1: **for** $i = 1$ to m **do**
2: **for** $k = 1$ to n **do**
3: $\lambda \leftarrow U(0,1)$
4: $x_k^i \leftarrow l_k + \lambda(u_k - l_k)$
5: **end for**
6: Calculate $f(x^i)$
7: **end for**
8: $x_{best} \leftarrow \arg\min\{f(x^i), \forall i\}$

8.3 Local search

The local search procedure is used for gathering local information about x^i and replacing the particle with its best potential in its neighbour. The invoked local search by Birbil et al., works as follows: for each particle, in each dimension select a random step length and move the ith particle along the direction. If the attained point has the better objective value than the x^i, the x^i will be replaced by this point.

In this part of algorithm, any local search algorithm can be used but the following algorithm is introduced by Birbil et al.

This is a simple random line search algorithm applied coordinate by coordinate. This procedure does not require any gradient information to perform the local search. Instead of using other powerful local search methods (Solis & Wets, 1981), we have utilized this procedure because we wanted to show that even with this trivial method, the algorithm shows promising convergence properties.

ALGORITHM 3. Local($LSITER$, δ)

counter $\leftarrow 1$
Length $\leftarrow \delta(max_k\{u_k - l_k\})$
for $i = 1$ to m **do**
  for $k = 1$ to n **do**
    $\lambda_1 \leftarrow U(0, 1)$
    while counter $< LSITER$ **do**
      $y \leftarrow x^i$
      $\lambda_2 \leftarrow U(0, 1)$
      if $\lambda_1 > 0.5$ **then**
        $y_k \leftarrow y_k + \lambda_2$(Length)
      else
        $y_k \leftarrow y_k - \lambda_2$(Length)
      end if
      if $f(y) < f(x^i)$ **then**
        $x^i \leftarrow y$
        counter $\leftarrow LSITER - 1$
      end if
      counter $\leftarrow$ counter $+ 1$
    end while
  end for
end for
$x^{best} \leftarrow \text{argmin}\{f(x^i), \forall i\}$

8.4 Calculation of total force vector

The electrostatic force between two point charges is directly proportional to the magnitude of each charge and inversely proportional to the square of the distance between the charges. The fixed charge of particle i is shown as it is shown in equation 18 *(Cowan, 1968):*

$$q^i = \exp\left(-n\frac{f(x^i) - f(x^{best})}{\sum_{k=1}^{m}\left(f(x^k) - f(x^{best})\right)}\right), \forall i \tag{18}$$

where q^i is the charge of the ith particle and $f(x^i)$ is its objective value. $f(x^{best})$ is the objective value of the best individual and m is population size. In each iteration the charge of all particles will be computed according to their objective values. The charge of each particle determines the magnitude of an attraction and repulsion effect in the population. A better solution encourages other particles to converge to attractive valleys whereas a bad solution discourages particles to move toward this region. The force of particle i is calculate as follow (equation 19):

$$F^i = \sum_{j \neq i}^{m} \left\{ \begin{array}{ll} (x^j - x^i)\dfrac{q^i q^j}{\|x^j - x^i\|^2} & f(x^j) < f(x^i) \\ (x^i - x^j)\dfrac{q^i q^j}{\|x^j - x^i\|^2} & f(x^j) \geq f(x^i) \end{array} \right\} \forall i \tag{19}$$

Figure 7 represents an example. As it is clear from the figure, the particles 1, 2 and 3 have the objective values equal to 20, 15 and 10 respectively. The aim is calculating the force on particle 2 for example. The problem is minimization and particle 3 is the best particle. So particle 3 encourages the particle 2. Particle 1 is worse than the particle 2 and it represents a repulsion force on particle 2 and finally the force F is calculated.

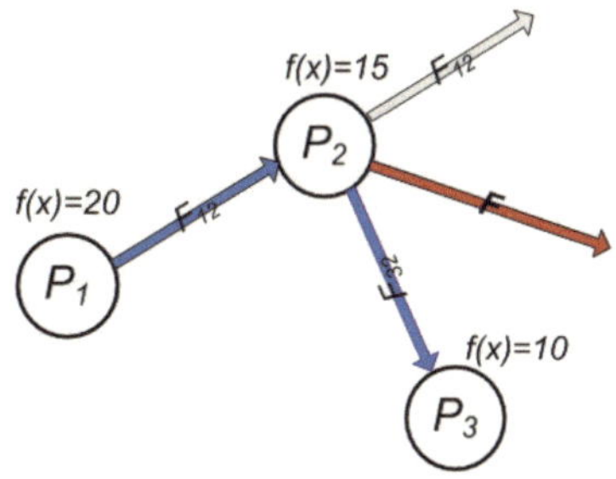

Fig. 7. F_{12} is the force from particle 1 to particle 2 (repulsion) and F_{32} is the force from particle 3 to particle 2 (attraction), F is the resultant force vector.

8.5 Movement according to the total force

After the total force vector for the ith particle is evaluated, the particle is moved in the direction of the force with the step length of λ which is selected randomly between 0 and 1. The following formula is used for the movement of particles:

$$x^i = x^i + \frac{F^i}{\|F^i\|}(RNG) \tag{20}$$

Where *RNG* is a vector whose components denote the allowed feasible movement toward the upper bound, u_k, or the lower bound, l_k, for the corresponding dimension (Algorithm 4, lines 6-10).

The following algorithm shows the movement procedure. Note that the best particle is not moved and is carried to the next generation.

ALGORITHM 4. Move(**F**)

1: **for** $i = 1$ to m **do**
2:     **if** $i \neq$ best **then**
3:         $\lambda \leftarrow U(0, 1)$
4:         $F^i \leftarrow \frac{F^i}{\|F^i\|}$
5:         **for** $k = 1$ to n **do**
6:             **if** $F_k^i > 0$ **then**
7:                 $x_k^i \leftarrow x_k^i + \lambda F_k^i (u_k - x_k^i)$
8:             **else**
9:                 $x_k^i \leftarrow x_k^i + \lambda F_k^i (x_k^i - l_k)$
10:            **end if**
11:        **end for**
12:    **end if**
13: **end for**

8.6 Termination criteria

There are 2 termination criteria introduced by Birbil et al. for electromagnetism as follow:

1. Maximum number of iterations. They claim that in general, 25 iterations per dimension (i.e., MAXITER=25n) is satisfactory for converging to the optimum point for moderate difficulty functions.
2. Successive number of iterations spent without changing the current best point. In other word, if the current best point is not improved for certain number of iterations, the algorithm may be stopped.

8.7 Solving the TSP using EM-like mechanism

One of the most attractive approaches for solving TSP using EM is cited in (Wu et al., 2006). In this study, a hybrid algorithm based on EM and K-OPT is introduced. They used a revised EM-like algorithm which proposed by (Birbil & Fang, 2005). In this version of EM, a parameter v belong to (0, 1) is introduced. The perturbed point x_p is selected as the farthest point from the current best point, x_{best}, in the current population. The calculation of the total force vector remains the same for all points except x_p. For x_p, the component forces are perturbed by a random number λ, where λ is uniformly distributed between 0 and 1. The directions of the component forces are perturbed; that is, if the random variable λ is less than the parameter v then the direction of the component force is reversed. Besides, they use a formulation for calculating the forces which proposed in (Maenhout & Vanhoucke, 2005) for solving the Nurse Scheduling problem. As we know, TSP is an integer value problem but the EM algorithm works in real valued problems (continues space). This problem makes the transformation very significant. In the proposed approach in (Wu et al., 2006), one of the well-known algorithms (Random Key (RK)) for transforming the continuous domain into the discrete domain has been used. The concept of RK technique is simple and can be applied easily. When we obtain a k-dimensional solution, we sort the value corresponding to each dimension. Any sorting algorithm can be used in the method. The indices of the sorted list will be the solution in discrete space. By applying the RK algorithm, any continuous algorithm like EM will be able to work in a discrete space.

9. Experimental results

In this section some results of discussed population based methods for solving the TSP have been prepared. At each subsection the mentioned algorithms and studies based on the some cited paper have been compared.

9.1 Evolutionary algorithms

The first study that has been cited in section 2 was (Bonyadi et al., 2007). In this work some changes to two previous local search algorithms i.e. Shuffled Frog Leaping (SFL) and Civilization and Society (CS) have been made and these algorithms are combined with the GA idea. The shown results illustrate that the mentioned hybrid algorithm has better results in comparison to the GA using the SFL method. The results have been shown in Table 1.

In another work (Yan et al., 2005) a new algorithm based on Inver-over operator, for combinatorial optimization problems has been proposed. The shown results prove that these changes are very efficient to accelerate the convergence speed. As a consequence, it is inferred that, one of the points for contribution is operators. Suitable changes in the conventional form of operators might lead to major differences in search and optimization procedure. The mentioned results have been prepared in Table 2.

Algorithm	*Average path value for 80 point input (million)*
GA	26
GA using SFL method	19
GA using Proposed approach	14
Exact solution	10

Table 1. (Bonyadi et al., 2007) simulation results

Instance	*Result in TSBLIB*	*Optimum in TSBLIB*	*Results by (Yan et al., 2005)*
Eil76	538	545.387	544.369
Pr136	96772	96772	96770.924

Table 2. (Yan et al., 2005) simulation results

As mentioned earlier, one of the points that solving the TSP can contribute is recombination operators i.e. mutation and crossover. Based on (Takahashi, 2005) there are two kinds of crossover operators for solving the TSP. Takahashi tries to retain useful information about links of parent's edges which leads to convergence. The Takahashi's experimental results suggest that changing crossover operators at arbitrary time according to city data structure is available to improve the performance of GAs.

9.2 ACO algorithms

The algorithm presented in (Dorigo & Gambardella, 1997) is listed in Table 3. As it is mentioned, the paper uses an algorithm based on ACS for solving the TSP.

Problem name	*ACS results (Dorigo & Gambardella 1997)*	*Optimum*
Eil50	427.96	425
Eil75	542.37	535

Table 3. (Dorigo & Gambardella, 1997) simulation results

9.3 PSO algorithms

Table 4 illustrates the results of the paper presented in (Yuan et al., 2007) which works based on ACO in combination with PSO.

Problem name	*Best*	*Worst*	*Average*
Oliver30	425.6542	457.2354	432.2231
Att48	33534	39679	34556

Table 4. (Yuan et al., 2007) simulation results

9.4 IWD algorithms

Based on the observation on the behavior of water drops, (Shah-Hosseini, 2007) develops an artificial water drop which possesses some of the remarkable properties of the natural water drop. The IWD algorithm is experimented by artificial and some benchmark TSP environments. The results show that the proposed algorithm converges fast to optimum solutions and finds good and promising results. Figures 8 and 9 depict the results of running this algorithm on some TSP benchmarks.

Fig. 8. The best tour found by the proposed algorithm after 300 iterations for the 76-city problem eil76. The algorithm gets a good local optimum with the tour length 559 which is quite close to the global optimum 538.

Fig. 9. The best tour found by the proposed algorithm after 1500 iterations for the 100-city problem kroA100. The algorithm gets a good local optimum with the tour length 23156 which is quite close to the global optimum 21282.

Figure 10 shows the average length of the best tours of the IWD algorithm in 10 independent runs for the TSP problems in which the cities are on a circle. The number of cities is increased from 10 to 100 by the value of five, and in each case the best average tour length over 10 runs is depicted.

Based on the simulation results, it is inferable that the IWD algorithm converges fast to optimum solutions and finds good and promising results.

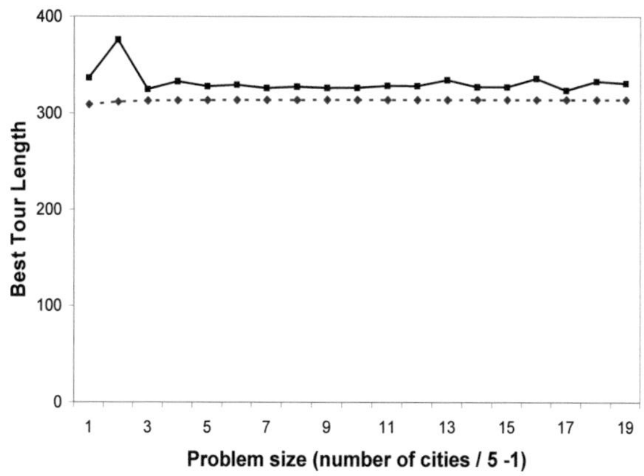

Fig. 10. The dotted lines show the global optimum tour length whereas the solid lines are the best tour lengths obtained by the IWD algorithm.

9.5 AIS algorithms

The IGA and AIS have been applied for solving the TSP in many cases. In (Jiao & Wang, 2000) it is proved that the IGA is theoretically convergent with probability one. Besides, strategies and methods of selecting vaccines and constructing an immune operator are also given. The simulation results illustrate that IGA is able to restrain the degenerate phenomenon effectively during the evolutionary process and can improve the searching ability and adaptability, while greatly increase the converging speed.

In another work, (Zeng & Gu, 2007), a novel genetic algorithm based on immunity and growth for the TSP is presented. The value obtained by the mentioned algorithm is prepared in Table 5. Results and investigations that performed in this study show that the algorithm is feasible and effective as it is claimed.

Problem	*Result in TSBLIB*	*Results by (Zeng & Gu, 2007)*
Eil51	429.983	428.872
Pr136	96772	96770.9

Table 5. (Zeng & Gu, 2007) simulation results

9.6 BCO algorithms

In section 7, one of the main work that had been studied was the study around bee colony and its applications for transportation modelling with focus on artificial life (ALife) approach (Lucic & Teodorovic, 2002). This paper shows that the ALife models that have been developed for solving complex transportation problems are inspired by social insect's behavior. The proposed algorithm in this work has been tested on a large number of well known TSP test benches such as Eil51.tsp, Berlin52.tsp, St70.tsp, Pr76.tsp, Kroa100.tsp, Eil101.tsp, Tsp225.tsp and A280.tsp. Also, for improving the results in each step, the 2-opt or 3-opt algorithms have been applied. Table 6 demonstrates the algorithm results. The results reveal that the mentioned method is very efficient. In all instances with less than 100 nodes, the bee system achieves the optimal solution and in the large cases it has a significant improvement in comparison to the other prevalent methods.

Problem	*Optimal value*	*Best value in (Lucic & Teodorovic, 2002)*	*Average value in (Lucic & Teodorovic, 2002)*
Eil51	428.87	428.87	428.87
Pr76	108159	108159	108159

Table 6. (Lucic & Teodorovic, 2002) simulation results obtained by the Bee System enriched with 3-opt heuristic.

Another work on the field of BCO and for solving the TSP is (Teodorovic et al., 2006). In this paper the authors propose the Bee Colony Optimization Metaheuristic (BCO). Moreover, this study, describes two BCO algorithms that the authors call them, the Bee System (BS) and the Fuzzy Bee System (FBS). In the case of FBS the agents (artificial bees) use approximate reasoning and rules of fuzzy logic in their communication and acting. The simulation results of the BS can be seen in Table 7.

Problem name	*Optimal value*	*Best value by (Teodorovic et al., 2006)*
Eil51	429.983	431.121
Pr76	108159	108790

Table 7. (Teodorovic et al., 2006) simulation results

9.7 Electromagnetism-like mechanisms

Table 8 illustrates the results for EM which introduced in (Wu et al., 2006).

9.8 Comparison of various algorithms

Figure 11 shows a comparison among various methods for two standard TSP problems named st70 and kroa100.

Problem name	*Best*	*Optimal*	*Average*
14 cities	30.879	30.879	31.80731
16 cities	3.2	3.2	3.30349

Table 8. (Wu et al., 2006) simulation results

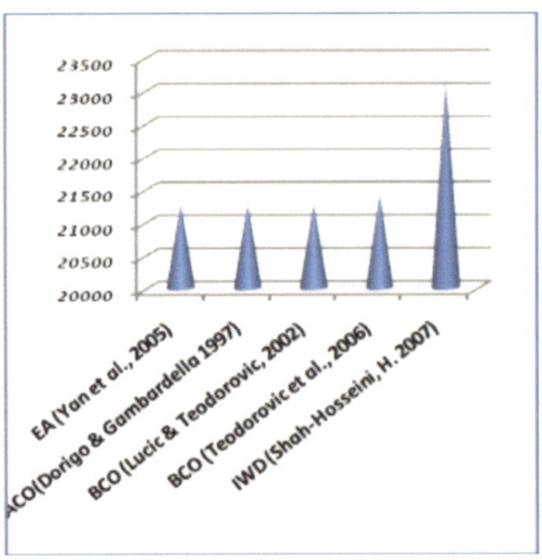

(a)

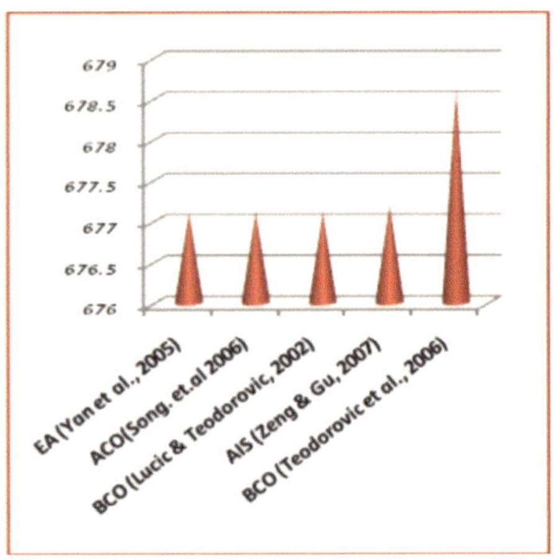

(b)

Fig. 11. (a) The results of various algorithm applied on Kroa100, (b) The results of various algorithm applied on st70 (The vertical axes show the best tour length obtained by each algorithm).

10. Conclusion

Maybe this chapter is the first versatile study on the population based optimization algorithms focused on solving the TSP. In this study, the state of the art of population based optimization algorithms such as Evolutionary Algorithms (EA), Ant Colony Optimization Algorithms (ACO), Particle Swarm Optimization Algorithms (PSO), Intelligent Water-Drops Algorithm (IWD), Artificial Immune Systems (AIS), Bee Colony Optimization Algorithms (BCO) and finally Electromagnetism-like Mechanisms (EM) has been introduced and investigated. The chapter includes nine parts before this; first one is introduction on the TSP and optimization algorithm, seven sections are about mentioned population based optimization algorithms and some related works which use these methods for solving the TSP, and finally the last part encompasses experimental results on the perused studies. All the sections try to introduce the related population based algorithm truly. Then the authors attempt to explore some useful studies that have been done by other researchers for solving the TSP. In addition some important points, where contribution or innovation in different parts of the related algorithm or in solving the TSP can be applied, have been pointed. The experimental results demonstrate a brief comparison among the various population based optimization methods. In this section you can find some tables, graphs and figures which compare the presented methods with their counterparts in terms of efficiency using some well known benchmarks on the TSP. The performed study shows that all of the stated methods have some weakness and some strength points which are noticed at the related section. As a consequence, the further research can focus on these points for amplification of strengths and eliminating or improving the weaknesses. In addition, an innovative population based method inspired by natural water drops behaviour is reviewed in this chapter.

11. References

Adleman, L. M. (1994). Molecular computation of solutions to combinatorial problem. *Science*, 1994, pp. 1021–1023.

Beckers, R. ; Deneubourg, J.L. ; Goss, S. (1992). Trails and U-turns in the selection of the shortest path by the ant Lasius Niger. *Journal of Theoretical Biology*, Vol. 159, pp. 397–415, 1992.

Bersini, H. & Varela, F. J., (1990). Workshop on Parallel Problem Solving from Nature. *LNCS*, Springer-Verlag 496 343, Proc. 1st.

Birbil, S. & Fang, Sh. (2003). An Electromagnetism-like Mechanism for Global Optimization. *Journal of Global Optimization*, , Kluwer Academic Publishers, Vol. 25, (2003), pp. 263-282, ISSN 263–282, 2003.

Birbil, S. & FANG, Sh. (2005). Convergence of a Population Based Global Optimization Algorithms. *Journal of Global Optimization*

Bonyadi, R. M.; Rahimi Azghadi S., M. & Shah-Hosseini, H. (2007). Solving Traveling Salesman Problem Using Combinational Evolutionary Algorithm. *In: IFIP International Federation for Information Processing, Volume 247, Artificial Intelligence and Innovations 2007: From Theory to Applications*, eds. Boukis, C, Pnevmatikakis, L., Polymenakos, L., pp. 37-44, (Boston: Springer).

Cowan, E. W. (1968), *Basic Electromagnetism*, Academic Press, New York.

Dasgupta D. (Ed.), (1999). *Artificial Immune Systems and Their Applications*. Springer-Verlag. Berlin.

Dorigo, M. & Stutzle, T. (2004). *Ant colony optimization*, Prentice hall,

Dorigo, M.; & Gambardella, L.M.; Ant Colony System: A Cooperative Learning Approach to the Traveling Salesman Problem, *IEEE TRANSACTIONS ON EVOLUTIONARY COMPUTATION*, VOL. 1, NO. 1, APRIL 1997, ISSN 1089-778X/97

Eberhart, C. & Kennedy, J. (1995). A new optimizer using particle swarm theory. *In Proc. Sixth Intl. Symposium on Micro Machine and Human Science*, Nagoya, Japan, 1995, pp. 39–43.

Eiben A. E. & Smith, J. E. (2003). *Introduction to Evolutionary Computing*. Springer-Verlag.

Eppstein, D. (2007). TSP for Cubic Graphs. *Journal of Graph Algorithms and Applications (JGAA)*, Vol. 11, No. 1, pp. 61–81.

Fogel, L. J.; Owens, A. J. & Walsh, M. J., (1966). *Artificial Intelligence through Simulated Evolution*. New York: John Wiley.

Garey, M. R. & Johnson, D. S. (1979). *Computers and Intractability: A Guide to the Theory of NP-Completeness*. W. H. Freeman.

Glover, J. K. F. & Laguna, M. (1995), Genetic algorithms and tabu search: Hybrids for optimization. *Computers and Operations Research*, 22: 111–134.

Goldberg, D. E., (1989). *Genetic Algorithm in Search, Optimization and Learning, Reading*, MA: Addison-Wesley.

Haykin, S. (1999). *Neural Networks*, Prentice-Hall, second edition.

Holland, J. (1975). *Adaptation in Natural and Artificial Systems*, University of Michigan Press, Ann Arbor.

Holldobler, B. & Wilson, E. O. (1990). *The Ants*. Berlin: Springer-Verlag.

Jiao L. & Wang L. (2000). Novel genetic algorithm based on immunity. *IEEE Transactions on Systems, Man and Cybernetics*, Part A, vol. 30, no. 5, pp. 552 -561.

Keko, H.; Skok, M. & Skrlec, D. (2003). Artificial Immune Systems in Solving Routing Problems. *EUROCON* 2003, pp. 62-66.

Kennedy, j. & Eberhart, R. (2001). *Swarm Intelligence*. Morgan Kaufmann.

Kirkpatrick, S.; Gelatt, C. D. & Vechi, M. P. (1983). Optimization by simulated annealing. *Science*, vol. 220, no.4598, pp. 671-680.

Kirkpatrik, S. (1984). Optimization by simulated annealing: quantitative studies. *Journal of Statistical Physics*, vol. 34, 1984, pp. 975-986.

Koza, J.R., (1992). *Genetic Programming: On the Programming of Computers by Means of Natural Selection*, MIT Press. ISBN 0-262-11170-5.

Lee Z. J. (2004). A Hybrid Algorithm Applied to Traveling Salesman Problem. *Proceedings of the 2004 IEEE International Conference on Networking, Sensing & Control*, pp. 237-242.

Lin, S. & Kernighan B., (1973). An effective heuristic algorithm for the traveling-salesman problem. *Operations Research*, vol. 21, no. 2, pp. 498-516.

Louis S. J. & Gong L., (2000). Case injected genetic algorithms for traveling salesman problems, *Information Sciences*, vol. 122, pp. 201-225.

Lu, J.; Fang, N.; Shao1, D. & Liu, C. (2007). An Improved Immune-Genetic Algorithm for the Traveling Salesman Problem. *Third International Conference on Natural Computation (ICNC 2007)*.

Lucic, P. & Teodorovic, D. (2002). Transportation Modeling: An Artificial Life Approach. *Proceedings of the 14th IEEE International Conference on Tools with Artificial Intelligence (ICTAI'02).*

Maenhout, B. & Vanhoucke, M. (2005). An Electromagnetic Meta-heuristic for the Nurse Scheduling Problem, *The 2nd Multidisciplinary International Conference on Scheduling: Theory and Applications*, New York, July (2005).

Martin, O.; Otto, S. & Felten E., (1991). Large-step markov chains for the traveling salesman problem. *Complex Systems*, vol. 5, no. 3, pp. 299-326.

Michalewicz, Z. (1994), *Genetic Algorithms + Data Structures = Evolution Programs*, Springer, Berlin.

Nguyen, H. D.; Yoshihara, I.; Yamamori, K. & Yasunaga, M. (2007). Implementation of an Effective Hybrid GA for Large-Scale Traveling Salesman Problems. *IEEE Transactions on Systems, Man, and Cybernetics-Part B: Cybernetics*, Vol. 37, No. 1, pp. 92-99.

Padherg M. & Rinaldi R., (1987). Optimization of a 532-city symmetric travelling salesman problem by branch and cut. *Operations Research Letters*, vol. 6, no.1, pp. 1-7.

Pang, W.; Wang, K.; Zhou, C.; Dong, L. (2004), Fuzzy Discrete Particle Swarm Optimization for Solving Traveling Salesman Problem, *Proceedings of the Fourth International Conference on Computer and Information Technology (CIT'04).*

Qin, L.; Chen, Y.; Luo, J.; Chen, L. & Guo, J. (2006). A Diversity Guaranteed Ant Colony Algorithm Based on Immune Strategy. *Proceedings of the First International Multi-Symposiums on Computer and Computational Sciences (IMSCCS'06).*

Rechenberg, I.; (1965). *Cybernetic Solution Path of an Experimental Problem*, Royal Aircraft Establishment, Library Translation, No. 1122.

Sato, T. & Hagiwara, M. (1997). Bee System: Finding Solution by a Concentrated Search. *Computational Cybernetics and Simulation apos; 1997 IEEE International Conference* on. Vol. 4, pp.3954 - 3959.

Schwefel, H. P., (1981). *Numerical optimization of computer models*, Chichester: Wiley & Sons.

Shah-Hosseini, H. (2006). The time adaptive self-organizing map is a neural network based on Artificial Immune System. *In Proc. IEEE World Congress on Computational Intelligence, Vancouver, Canada, July 2006*, pp. 1007-1014.

Shah-Hosseini, H. (2007). Problem Solving by Intelligent Water Drops. *2007 IEEE Congress on Evolutionary Computation (CEC 2007)*, pp. 3226-3231.

Solis, F. J. and Wets, R. J-B. (1981), Minimization by random search techniques, *Mathematics of Operations Research*, 6: 19–30.

Song, X; Li, B.; Yang H. (2006); IMPROVED ANT COLONY ALGORITHM and ITS APPLICATIONS in TSP, *Proceedings of the Sixth International Conference on Intelligent Systems Design and Applications (ISDA'06)*, 0-7695-2528-8/06

Takahashi, R. (2005). Solving the Traveling Salesman Problem through Genetic Algorithms with Changing Crossover Operators. *Proceedings of the Fourth International Conference on Machine Learning and Applications (ICMLA'05).*

Teodorovic, D. & Dell'Orco, M. (2005). Bee colony optimization: A cooperative learning approach to complex transportation problems. *Advanced OR and AI Methods in Transportation*, pp. 51-60.

Teodorovic, D.; Lucic, P.; Markovic, G. & Dell'Orco, M. (2006). Bee Colony Optimization: Principles and Applications. *8th Seminar on Neural Network Applications in Electrical Engineering, NEUREL-2006.*

Teodorovic, D.; Lucic, P.; Markovic, G. & Dell'Orco, M. (2006). Bee Colony Optimization: Principles and Applications. *8th Seminar on Neural Network Applications in Electrical Engineering, NEUREL-2006.*

Tsai, H. K.; Yang, J. M.; Tsai, Y. F. & Kao, C. Y. (2004). An Evolutionary Algorithm for Large Travelling Salesman Problems. IEEE Transactions on Systems, *Man, and Cybernetics-Part B: Cybernetics*, Vol. 34, No. 4, pp. 1718-1729.

Wu, P.; Yang, K.; Fang, H. (2006). A Revised EM-like Algorithm + K-OPT Method for Solving the Traveling Salesman Problem. *Proceedings of the First International Conference on Innovative Computing, Information and Control.* ISBN 0-7695-2616-0/06

Yan, X. S.; Li H.; CAI, Z. H. & Kang L. S. (2005). A fast evolutionary algorithm for combinatorial optimization problem. *Proceedings of the Fourth International Conference on Machine Learning and Cybernetics*, pp. 3288-3292.

Yuan, Z.; Yang, L.; Wu, Y.; Liao, L.; Li, G. (2007). Chaotic Particle Swarm Optimization Algorithm for Traveling Salesman Problem. *Proceedings of the IEEE International Conference on Automation and Logistics*, 1-4244-1531-4, Jinan, China.

Yuhui, S. & Eberhart, R. (1998). A modified particle swarm optimizer. *Proceedings of the IEEE International Conference on Evolutionary Computation*, pp 69–73, Piscataway, NJ, USA, 1998. IEEE Press.

Zeng, C. & Gu T. (2007). A Novel Immunity-Growth Genetic Algorithm for Traveling Salesman Problem. *Third International Conference on Natural Computation (ICNC 2007).*

Zhang, G.P.; Wang, Z.O.; Yuan, G.L. (2001),A Chaotic Search Method for a Class of Combinatorial Optimization Problems, *Systems Engineering-Theory & Practice* , pp.102-105

2

Bio-inspired Algorithms for TSP and Generalized TSP

Zhifeng Hao, Han Huang and Ruichu Cai
South China University of Technology
China

1. Introduction

The Traveling Salesman Problem (TSP) is to find a Hamiltonian tour of minimal length on a fully connected graph. The TSP is a NP-Complete, and there is no polynomial algorithm to find the optimal result. Many bio-inspired algorithms has been proposed to address this problem. Generally, generic algorithm (GA), ant colony optimization (ACO) and particle swarm optimization (PSO) are three typical bio-inspired algorithm for TSP. In this section we will give a brief introduction to the above three bio-inspired algorithms and their application to the TSP.

1.1 GAs for TSP

GAs were introduced by Holland in the 1970s [1]. These algorithms are adaptive search techniques based on the mechanisms of natural selection and the survival of the fittest concept of biological evolution. By simulating biological evolution, GAs can solve searching problem domains effectively and easily apply to many of the current engineering problems. GAs have been widely used in many applications of TSP and its extensions throughout the literature [2-4].

A particularly nice introduction to GAs is given in Goldberg's book [5]. The main idea behind GAs is to start with randomly generating initial solutions and implements the "survival of the fittest" strategy to increasing better solutions through generations. A traditional GA process includes initial population generation, fitness evaluation, chromosome selection, applying genetic operators for reproduction, and suspension condition.

In designing a GA, how to encode a search solution is a primary and key issue [6]. Many optimization operators for TSP were proposed by Goldberg [5]. A commonly used encoding strategy is transposition expression [7]. In the transposition expression strategy, each city of the TSP is encoded as a gene of the chromosome with the constraint that each city appears once and only once in the chromosome. Transposition expression is the most nature expression for TSP which based on the order of tour. While such method may leads to infeasible tour after traditional crossover operator [7]. This is a common occurrence for TSP. Although feasibility can be maintained in many ways named 'repair algorithms', such algorithms can consume a considerable amount of time and can inhibit convergence.

3	2	1	5	4	6	8	7

Figure 1. Transposition expression encoding method for TSP

Another typical encoding method is Random Keys encoding [8] which is introduced by Bean. In Random Keys encoding a random numbers encode the structure of the solution. Such representation ensures that feasible tours are maintained during the application of genetic operators.

In the GA, the crossover and mutation are two of most important method for the success of the algorithm. A crossover operator generates new individuals through recombining the current population hopefully to retain good features from the parents. Numbers of different crossovers have been proposed in the literatures to solve the TSP using a GA. The partially mapped crossover [5,11-12], linear order crossover [13] and order based crossover [5,8,11,12,14] are the commonly used crossover strategy in the TSP context. Expect the commonly used crossover strategy, many different crossover strategy are proposed for the TSP problem, for example: sub-tour crossover[15,16], edge recombination [17-20], distance preserving crossover [21-22], generic crossover [23], NGA [24], EAX [25-26], GSX [27-28], heuristic based crossover [29-35].

A mutation operator is used to enhance the diversity and provide a chance to escape from local optima. Many mutation operators were proposed such as inverse, insert, displace, swap, hybrid mutation [34], and heuristic mutation. The former five are realized by small alterations of genes. Heuristic mutation was proposed by Cheng and Gen [37-38], which adopts a neighborhood strategy to improve the solution.

At present, the genetic algorithm to solve the TSP has been to promote large-scale TSP, as well as a multiple TSP (MTSP) and generalized TSP. A lot of progress was made recently. Arthur E. Carter and Cliff T. Ragsdale propose a new GA chromosome and related operators for the MTSP [39]. H. D. Nguyen, et al described a hybrid GA based on a parallel implementation of a multi population steady-state GA involving local search heuristics [40]. Samanlioglu et.al proposes a methodology uses a "target-vector approach" in which the evaluation function is a weighted Tchebycheff metric with an ideal point for a symmetric multi-objective traveling salesman problem [41-43].

1.2 Ant colony optimization (ACO) for TSP

Ant Colony Optimization (ACO), first proposed by M. Dorigo et al. [44-46], is a population-based, general-purpose heuristic approach to combinational optimization problems. The earliest ACO algorithm [44-45], Ant System (AS), was applied to the TSP (mainly because the TSP is "a shortest path problem to which the ant colony metaphor is easily adapted and that it is a didactic problem" [4]. After that, most improved ACO algorithms also used the TSP as a test problem and the result is promising.

As the name suggests, ACO took inspiration from the foraging behavior of real ant colonies. Ants deposit pheromone on the ground they cover while working, forming a pheromone trail. Other ants tend to follow the pheromone trail. Consider an ant colony exploring the paths between their nest to a food source. At the beginning, the ants choose paths randomly in equal rate since there's no pheromone on the paths help them make the decision. Suppose that every ant walk in the same speed, shorter paths accumulate pheromone faster than longer paths because ants on those paths return earlier. A moment later, the difference in the amount of pheromone on the paths becomes sufficient large so that the ants' decision are influenced and more ants select the shorter paths. Experiments show that this behavior can lead the ant colony to the shortest path.

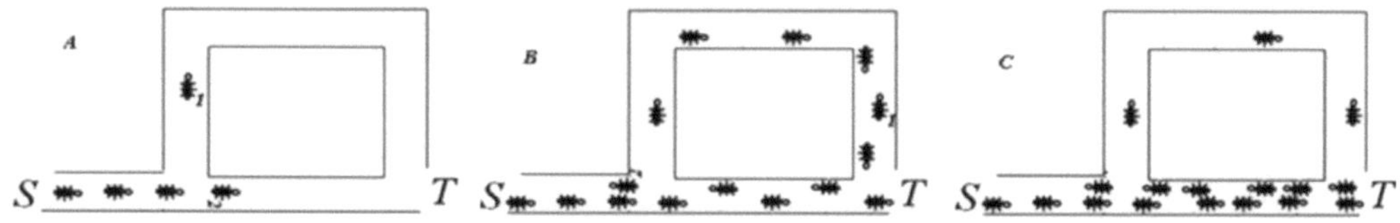

Figure 2. an ant colony exploits the paths between *S* and *T*. (A) The two paths are selected with the same probability at first. (B) Ant 2 choosing the lower path returns to *S* earlier. Thus pheromone on the lower path rises faster. (C) Most ants walk on the lower path after a minute.

Typical ant algorithms stimulate the above foraging behavior of ant colonies using a set of agents (artificial ants) and an indirect communication mechanism employing (artificial) pheromone. A simple framework may look like this:

```
Loop /* at this level each loop is called iteration */
    Each ant is positioned on a starting node.
    Loop /* at this level each loop is called a step */
        Each ant applies a stochastic state transition rule to incrementally build a solution
    Until all ants have built a complete solution
    A pheromone updating rule is applied
Until End condition
```

The stochastic state transition rule and the pheromone updating rule are two factor to the success of the ACO. And many strategies have been proposed for these two operators. The Ant Colony System (ACS) [48-50] and MAX-MIN Ant System (MMAS) [51] are among the most successful algorithms [52]. Recent researches focus most on extending the applications of ACO algorithms to more challenge problems. There're also some studies on the convergence theory of ACO algorithms too [47, 53-58].

1.3 PSO for TSP

The particle swarm optimization (PSO) was originally presented by Kennedy and Eberhart in 1995 [59]. It is an algorithm based stochastic optimization technique which inspired by social behavior among individuals. In the PSO system, individuals (we call them particles) move around a multidimensional search space. Each particle represents a potential solution of the problem, and can remember the best position (so1ution) it has reached. All the particles can share their information about the search space, so there is a global best solution.

In each iteration, every particle adjusts its velocity v_i and position x_i according to the following formulas:

$$\begin{aligned} v_i &= v_i + c_1 * r_1 * (x_{i,pbest} - x_i) + c_2 * r_2 * (x_{i,gbest} - x_i) \\ x_i &= x_i + v_i \end{aligned} \quad (1)$$

Where w is inertia weight, c_1 and c_2 are acceleration coefficients, r_1 and r_2 are two independent random values between 0 and 1. $x_{i,pbest}$ is the best solution this particle has reached; $x_{i,gbest}$ is the global best solution of all the particles until now.
Due to the continuous characters of the position of particles in PSO, the standard encoding scheme of PSO can not be directly adopted for TSP. Much work was published to avoid such problem. Clerc adopted discrete particle swarm optimization (DPSO)[60] to make PSO suitable for solving TSP. Bo Liu, et al. proposes a PSO-based MA [61](PSOMA) for TSP, which combined evolutionary searching mechanism of PSO and adaptive local search. Yong-Qin Tao, et al. proposed a GRPSAC algorithm [62] combined ACO with PSO organically and adds gene regulation operator at the same time, which make solution of TSP problem more efficiency. Other recently work such as heuristic information method based on improved fuzzy discrete PSO [63] and chaotic PSO algorithm [64] were proved to be effective for TSP.

2. Ant colony optimization (ACO) for TSP

2.1 The method of ant colony optimization solving TSP

Among the bio-inspired algorithms, the ant colony optimization (ACO) is a popular approach for TSP since it's proposed by M.Dorigo in early nineties [65-66]. Ant colony optimization (ACO) takes inspiration from the foraging behavior of some ant species. These ants deposit pheromone on the ground in order to mark some favorable path that should be followed by other ants of the colony. Ant colony optimization exploits a similar mechanism for solving optimization problems.
In TSP, a set of cities is given and the distance between each of them is known. The goal is to find a Hamiltonian tour of minimal length on a fully connected graph. This goal is very similar with the ants to find the shortest path between the nest and the food source. In ant colony optimization, the problem is tackled by simulating a number of artificial ants moving on a graph that encodes the problem itself. A variable called pheromone is associated with each edge and can be read and modified by ants. The artificial ants explore the pheromone to find the most favorable path which is the shortest Hamiltonian Tour in TSP.
Ant colony optimization is an iterative algorithm. In an iterative step, each ant of the colony builds a solution by walking from vertex to vertex on the graph with the constraint of not visiting any vertex that has been visited before. The solution construction and the pheromone updating are two main steps for the ACO. In the solution construction step, an ant selects the next vertex to be visited according to a stochastic mechanism that is biased by the pheromone. After the solution construction step, the pheromone is updated on the basis of the quality of the solutions.
Under the above framework, many different version of the algorithm are proposed. According to the M.Dorigo's work [46,67], the Ant System (AS), MAX−MIN Ant System (MMAS) and Ant Colony System (ACS) are three of most popular ant algorithms. Following, we will give a short brief of those three algorithms on TSP.

2.1.1 Ant System (AS)

Ant System is the first ACO algorithm proposed in the literature [44,65-66]. Its main characteristic is that, at each iteration, the pheromone values are updated by all the m ants that have built a solution in the iteration itself. The pheromone τ_{ij}, associated with the edge joining cities i and j, is updated as follows:

$$\tau_{ij} \leftarrow (1-\rho)\cdot\tau_{ij} + \sum_{k=1}^{m} \Delta\tau_{ij}^{k} \qquad (1)$$

where ρ is the evaporation rate, m is the number of ants, and $\Delta\tau_{ij}^{k}$ is the quantity of pheromone laid on edge (i, j) by ant k:

$$\Delta\tau_{ij}^{k} = \begin{cases} Q/L_k & \text{if ant } k \text{ used edge}(i,j) \text{ in its tour,} \\ 0 & \text{otherwise,} \end{cases} \qquad (2)$$

where Q is a constant, and L_k is the length of the tour constructed by ant k.
In the construction of a solution, ants select the following city to be visited through a stochastic mechanism. When ant k is in city i and has so far constructed the partial solution S^p, the probability of going to city j is given by:

$$P_{gs}^{k}(t) = \begin{cases} \dfrac{[\tau_{gs}(t)]^{\alpha}[\eta_{gs}]^{\beta}}{\sum_{r\in J_k(g)} [\tau_{gr}(t)]^{\alpha}[\eta_{gr}]^{\beta}} & \text{if } s \in J_k(g) \\ 0 & \text{otherwise} \end{cases} \qquad (3)$$

where $J_k(g)$ is the set of cities not visited yet by ant k when at city g. The parameters α and β control the relative importance of the pheromone versus the heuristic information η_{ij}, which is given by $\eta_{ij} = \dfrac{1}{d_{ij}}$, where d_{ij} is the distance between cities i and j.

2.1.2 MAX −MIN Ant System (MMAS)

The MAX −MIN Ant System [51] is an improvement over the original Ant System. In the MMAS, only the best ant updates the pheromone trails and the value of the pheromone is bound. The pheromone update is implemented as follows:

$$\tau_{ij} = \begin{cases} \tau_{\max} & \text{if } (1-\rho)\cdot\tau_{ij} + \Delta\tau_{ij}^{best} > \tau_{\max}, \\ \tau_{\min} & \text{if } (1-\rho)\cdot\tau_{ij} + \Delta\tau_{ij}^{best} < \tau_{\min}, \\ (1-\rho)\cdot\tau_{ij} + \Delta\tau_{ij}^{best} & \text{otherwise;} \end{cases} \qquad (4)$$

where $\tau_{\max}$ and $\tau_{\min}$ min are respectively the upper and lower bounds imposed on the pheromone and $\Delta\tau_{ij}^{best}$ is:

$$\Delta\tau_{ij}^{best} = \begin{cases} 1/L_{best} & \text{if } (i,j) \text{ belongs to the best tour} \\ 0 & \text{otherwise;} \end{cases} \qquad (5)$$

where L_{best} is the length of the tour of the best ant.

For the $\tau_{\max}$ and $\tau_{\min}$, they are typically obtained empirically and tuned on the specific problem considered [68]. And some guidelines have been provided for defining $\tau_{\min}$ and $\tau_{\max}$ on the basis of analytical considerations [51].

2.1.3 Ant Colony System (ACS)

The ACS was considered the most efficient algorithm on the TSP problem. The main contribution of ACS [48, 50, 69] is introducing a novel local pheromone update in addition to the global pheromone.

The local pheromone update is performed by all the ants after each construction step. Each ant applies it only to the last edge traversed:

$$\tau_{ij} = (1-\varphi)\cdot\tau_{ij} + \varphi\cdot\tau_0 \tag{6}$$

where $\varphi \in (0,1]$ is the pheromone decay coefficient, and τ_0 is the initial value of the pheromone.

Using the local update strategy, the pheromone concentration on the traversed edges is decreased. So, the subsequent ants are encouraged to choose other edges and to produce different solutions. This makes it less likely that several ants produce identical solutions during one iteration.

2.2 An adaptive strategy for weight parameter

Many strategies for ACO have been studied, but little theoretical work has been done on ACO's parameters α and β, which control the relative weight of pheromone trail and heuristic value. In this part, we will theoretical show the importance and functioning of α and β. The theoretical analysis show that a fixed β may not enable ACO to use both heuristic and pheromone information for solution when $\alpha = 1$. An adaptive β strategy and a new ACO called adaptive weight ant colony system (AWACS) with the adaptive β and $\alpha = 1$ is introduced. The numerical experiment results show that the AWACS is more effective and steady than traditional ACS.

2.2.1 Theoretical analysis of the weight parameter

Given $a, b \in J_k(g)$, if $P_{ga}{}^k(t) > P_{gb}{}^k(t)$, which means that city a may be chosen by the ant k as the next city to city g with higher probability than city b, then α and β satisfies the following formula: $P_{ga}{}^k(t) > P_{gb}{}^k(t) \Leftrightarrow [\tau_{ga}(t)]^\alpha[\eta_{ga}]^\beta > [\tau_{gb}(t)]^\alpha[\eta_{gb}]^\beta$.

When $\tau_{ga}(t)=\tau_{gb}(t)$ or $\eta_{ga}=\eta_{gb}$, for $\forall\alpha,\beta>0$, the formula above holds, so we have:

$$P_{ga}{}^k(t) > P_{gb}{}^k(t) \Leftrightarrow \begin{cases} \eta_{ga} > \eta_{gb} & \tau_{ga} = \tau_{gb} \\ \tau_{ga} > \tau_{gb} & \eta_{ga} = \eta_{gb} \end{cases} \tag{8}$$

However, when $\tau_{ga}(t) \neq \tau_{gb}(t), \tau_{ga}(t) > 0, \tau_{gb}(t) > 0$ and $\eta_{ga} \neq \eta_{gb}(\eta_{ga}(t) > 0, \eta_{gb}(t) > 0)$, one has: $P_{ga}^{\ k}(t) > P_{gb}^{\ k}(t) \Leftrightarrow [\tau_{ga}(t)]^{\alpha}[\eta_{ga}]^{\beta} > [\tau_{gb}(t)]^{\alpha}[\eta_{gb}]^{\beta} \Leftrightarrow \log\tau_{ga}(t) - \log\tau_{gb}(t) > \frac{\beta}{\alpha}(\log\eta_{gb} - \log\eta_{ga})$.

And we have:

$$\begin{cases} \dfrac{\beta}{\alpha} < \dfrac{\log\tau_{ga}(t) - \log\tau_{gb}(t)}{\log\eta_{gb} - \log\eta_{ga}} & \eta_{gb} > \eta_{ga} \\ \dfrac{\beta}{\alpha} > \dfrac{\log\tau_{ga}(t) - \log\tau_{gb}(t)}{\log\eta_{gb} - \log\eta_{ga}} & \eta_{gb} < \eta_{ga} \end{cases} \tag{7}$$

Particularly, when α=1, which exists in ACO algorithms like ACS, a conclusion can be drawn:

$$P_{ga}^{\ k}(t) > P_{gb}^{\ k}(t) \Leftrightarrow \begin{cases} \beta < \dfrac{\log\tau_{ga}(t) - \log\tau_{gb}(t)}{\log\eta_{gb} - \log\eta_{ga}} & \eta_{gb} > \eta_{ga} \\ \beta > \dfrac{\log\tau_{ga}(t) - \log\tau_{gb}(t)}{\log\eta_{gb} - \log\eta_{ga}} & \eta_{gb} < \eta_{ga} \end{cases} \tag{8}$$

For the sake of convenience, some symbols about the pheromone trail are defined as follows: $\tau_g^{\max}(t) = \max\limits_{r \in J_k(g)}\{\tau_{gr}(t)\}$ is the highest pheromone trail among all the cities feasible to be selected as next stop to city g. $\tau_g^{\min}(t) = \min\limits_{r \in J_k(g)}\{\tau_{gr}(t)\}$ is the lowest one, and $\tau_g^{ave}(t) = |J_k(g)|^{-1}\sum\limits_{r \in J_k(g)}\tau_{gr}(t)$ is the average pheromone trail, where $|J_k(g)|$ is the number of elements in the set $J_k(g)$. $\eta_g^{\max} = \max\limits_{r \in J_k(g)}\{d_{gr}^{\ -1}\}$ is the highest heuristic value of elements in the set $J_k(g)$. $\eta_g^{\min} = \min\limits_{r \in J_k(g)}\{d_{gr}^{\ -1}\}$ stands for the lowest heuristic value, and $\eta_g^{ave} = |J_k(g)|^{-1}\sum\limits_{r \in J_k(g)}\eta_{gr} = |J_k(g)|^{-1}\sum\limits_{r \in J_k(g)}d_{gr}^{\ -1}$ is the average heuristic value.

Let $\alpha = 1$, two cases are discussed in the following:

① $[\tau_g^{\max}(t)]^{\alpha}[\eta_g^{\min}]^{\beta} > [\tau_g^{ave}(t)]^{\alpha}[\eta_g^{\max}]^{\beta}$. It means that the ants will select the paths with the maximum pheromone trail with a very high probability ACS. According to Formula (3), one has $\beta < \dfrac{\log\tau_g^{\max}(t) - \log\tau_g^{ave}(t)}{\log\eta_g^{\max} - \log\eta_g^{\min}} = M_1(g,t)$, because it is obvious that $\eta_g^{\max} > \eta_g^{\min}$ holds in TSPLIB problems.

② $[\tau_g^{\min}(t)]^{\alpha}[\eta_g^{\max}]^{\beta} > [\tau_g^{\max}(t)]^{\alpha}[\eta_g^{ave}]^{\beta}$. It means that the ants will select the paths with the maximum heuristic value with a very high probability in ACS. It is obvious that $\beta > \frac{\log \tau_g^{\min}(t) - \log \tau_g^{\max}(t)}{\log \eta_g^{ave} - \log \eta_g^{\max}} = M_2(g,t)$ holds, when $\eta_g^{\max} > \eta_g^{ave}$ and $\tau_g^{\min}(t) > 0$.

According to the analysis of case ① and ②, ACO may work as a non-heuristic searching when $\beta < M_1(g,t)$, and as a greedy searching without using pheromone trail when $\beta > M_2(g,t)$. Therefore, a fixed β may not enable ACO to find optimal solution by using both heuristic and pheromone information. However, the process of ACO will not be in the extreme as non-heuristic or greedy searching when $M_1(g,t) \le \beta \le M_2(g,t)$. So a new adaptive parameter β is designed as follows:

$$\alpha = 1, \beta(g,t) = \frac{\log \tau_g^{ave}(t) - \log \tau_g^{\max}(t)}{\log \eta_g^{ave} - \log \eta_g^{\max}} \quad (\tau_g^{\min}(t) > 0) \tag{9}$$

where $M_1(g,t) \le \beta(g,t) \le M_2(g,t)$ can be proved.

Based on the adaptive parameter $\beta(g,t)$ strategy shown in Formula (4), a novel ACO algorithm, which is called adaptive weight ant colony system (AWACS) can be described as follows.

```
Initialize /* β is chosen in [0, 5] randomly, q0=0.6 */
Loop /* at this level each loop is called iteration */
    Each ant is positioned on a starting node.
    Loop /* at this level each loop is called a step */
        Each ant applies a stochastic state transition rule to incrementally build a solution
        and a local pheromone updating rule
    Until all ants have built a complete solution
    A global pheromone updating rule is applied
    β(g,t) is updated (g = 1,…,n) following Formula (11)
Until End condition
```

The proof of its convergence (g = 1,…,n) is the same as the one in Ref. [54]. According to the work of Ref. [54], it still holds that $\tau_g^{\min}(t) > 0$ and $\tau_g^{\max}(t) < +\infty$ (g = 1,…,n) when the adaptive parameter $\beta(g,t)$ strategy in Formula (4) is applied. Then, AWACS can be proved to find the optimal solution with probability one following the conclusion given by T. Stützle and M. Dorigo [54,69].

2.2.2 Numerical results and analyses

A comparison of the performance of ACS and AWACS is given in this section. In our experiments, the parameters are set as follows: m = 10, $\alpha = \rho = 0.1$, $\tau_0 = (nL_{nn})^{-1}$. q_0 is set q_0 =0.9 in ACS, and q_0 =0.6 in AWACS , respectively. The initial value of β in AWACS is a

random figure changing in the interval [1,5]. The initial feasible solutions of TSP are generated in the way from Ref [49]. What's more, no local search strategy is used in experiment.
The experiments are conducted on two set of TSP problems. In the first set of 10 TSP, the distances between cities are measured by integers and in the left 10 TSP, and the distances are measured by real values. The datasets can be found in TSPLIB: http://www.iwr.uni-heidelberg.de/ iwr/comopt/soft/TSPLIB95/TSPLIB.html. The detail of the experiment result is given at table 1, table 2 and table 3.

Instance	Optimal	Best (ACS)	Best (AWACS)	Average (ACS)	Average (AWACS)	T_{avg}(s) (ACS)	T_{avg} (s) (AWACS)	Best β (ACS)
st70	654	657	657	675.9	675.5	16.9	27.4	4
rat99	unknown	1188	1188	1211.7	1199.4	53.2	59.7	3
pr107	unknown	44539	44398	44906.3	44783.9	39.5	55.4	4
pr124	unknown	59205	59067	59819.9	59646.6	59.2	42.3	4
eil101	612	614	613	634.6	631.4	22.4	76.3	5
rd100	7858	7909	7861	8100.4	8066.2	59.5	54.1	3
eil51	415	415	415	423.9	423.7	6.7	7.8	3
lin105	14345	14376	14354	14509.3	14465.6	73.7	50.8	4, 5
kroD100	21249	21486	21265	21893	21628.2	25.8	60	5
kroC100	20703	20703	20703	21165.3	20914.9	29.5	67.7	4

Table 1. Comparison I of the results obtained by ACS and AWACS

Instance	Optimal	Best (ACS)	Best (AWACS)	Average (ACS)	Average (AWACS)	T_{avg}(s) (ACS)	T_{avg} (s) (AWACS)	Best β (ACS)
kroA100	21282	21285.44	21285.44	21345.78	21286.33	51.3	51.8	2, 3
kroE100	22068	22078.66	22068.75	22206.62	22117.16	56.3	64.5	5
berlin52	7542	7544.36	7544.36	7544.36	7544.36	8.7	9.8	5
kroB150	26130	26127.35	26127.71	26332.75	26214.10	177.8	164.8	5
ch150	6528	6530.90	6530.90	6594.94	6559.66	373.6	118.1	2
kroB100	22141	22139.07	22139.07	22335.72	22177.47	55.5	68.6	4
kroA150	26524	26618.33	26524.86	26809.08	26685.73	204.5	242.9	5
u159	42080	42075.67	42075.67	42472.04	42168.54	356.7	80.2	1
pr76	108159	108159.4	108159.4	108610.6	108581.7	50.5	42.8	1
pr136	96772	96870.89	96785.86	97854.16	97236.61	344.3	158.9	14,5

Table 2. Comparison II of the results obtained by ACS and AWACS

Instance \Standard deviation	AWACS	ACS $\beta = 1$	ACS $\beta = 2$	ACS $\beta = 3$	ACS $\beta = 4$	ACS $\beta = 5$
kroA100	8.49	460.04	338.84	183.55	625.81	447.03
kroE100	123.82	327.01	467.75	529.73	330.12	366.49
berlin52	0.00	376.98	376.19	357.76	548.34	0.00
kroB150	221.98	447.98	652.57	821.48	664.54	486.91
ch150	54.50	114.76	153.71	109.36	171.66	54.81
kroB100	132.37	554.43	579.73	1091.25	558.86	233.01
kroA150	384.39	522.81	942.11	974.79	640.34	432.72
u159	623.16	726.99	3531.45	2458.43	1509.09	1661.63
pr76	1158.43	1180.56	5058.92	2088.68	1677.73	1411.15
pr136	1300.78	2386.53	5303.40	4572.69	3304.40	2173.27

Table 3. Comparison of standard deviations of the tour lengths obtained by AWACS and ACS

As shown in the above tables, there might be something like precision and time cost in the result of our experiments different from those in the former research because of the different program tools, systems and computing machines. Another possible reason is that the distances between cities in the first 10 instances are measured by integer numbers. But ACS and AWACS are running in the same setting, so the result remains helpful to compare the performance of these two algorithms.

From Table 1-2, it could be seen that AWACS performs better than ACS with the fixed β. The shortest lengths and the average lengths obtained by AWACS are shorter than those found by ACS in all of the TSP instances. As Table 3 shows, it can be concluded that the standard deviations of the tour lengths obtained by AWACS are smaller than those of ACS with the fixed β. Therefore, we can conclude that AWACS is proved to be more effective and steady than ACS.

ACS has to change the best integer value of parameter β with respect to different instances in the experiments. AWACS can avoid the difficulty about how to choose the experimental value of β, because its adaptive strategy can be considered as a function trying to find the best setting for each path search via meeting the request of Formula 4. Though, the time cost t_{avg} of AWACS is more than ACS in some case, it is less than the sum of time ACS costs with $\beta = 1,2,3,4,5$ in all of the instances. As a result, the adaptive setting can save much time in choosing the experimental β. Item t_{avg} of AWACS is not less than ACS in all of the instances because it needs to compute the value of β n (number of cities) times in each iteration. However, the adaptive function of AWACS is feasible to use because of its acceptable time cost.

2.3 Bi-directional searching ant colony system

In 2.2, an adaptive strategy for the weight parameter is proposed by exploring the function of the parameter in the stochastic mechanism. In this section, we will further explore the stochastic mechanism and a bi-directional searching ant colony system is proposed.

2.3.1 Bi-directional searching strategy using adaptive weight parameter

In the proposed ACO algorithms, the state transition rule of the artificial ants is given as follows:

$$P_{gs}^{\;k}(t)=\begin{cases}\dfrac{[\tau_{gs}(t)]^{\alpha}[\eta_{gs}]^{\beta(g,t)}}{\sum\limits_{r\in J_k(g)}[\tau_{gr}(t)]^{\alpha}[\eta_{gr}]^{\beta(g,t)}} & if \quad s\in J_k(g)\\ 0 & otherwise\end{cases} \tag{10}$$

The only difference between the (10) and (3) is the setting of the parameter $\beta(g,t)$. In the Bi-directional case, the parameter is set with one of the following two methods by probability 0.5

1). $\beta(g,t)=\dfrac{\log\tau_g^{\max}(t)-\log\tau_g^{ave}(t)}{\log\eta_g^{\max}-\log\eta_g^{\min}}-\varepsilon_0$ 2). $\beta(g,t)=\dfrac{\log\tau_g^{\min}(t)-\log\tau_g^{\max}(t)}{\log\eta_g^{ave}-\log\eta_g^{\max}}+\varepsilon_0$.

where $\tau_g^{\max}(t)=\max\limits_{i\in J_k(g)}\{\tau_{gi}(t)\}$ is the highest pheromone trail among all the cities feasible to be selected as next stop to city g. $\tau_g^{\min}(t)=\min\limits_{i\in J_k(g)}\{\tau_{gi}(t)\}$ is the lowest one, and $\tau_g^{ave}(t)=|J_k(g)|^{-1}\sum\limits_{i\in J_k(g)}\tau_{gi}(t)$ is the average pheromone trail, where $|J_k(g)|$ is the number of elements in the set $J_k(g)$. $\eta_g^{\max}=\max\limits_{i\in J_k(g)}\{d_{gi}^{\;-1}\}$ is the highest heuristic value of elements in the set $J_k(g)$. $\eta_g^{\min}=\min\limits_{i\in J_k(g)}\{d_{gi}^{\;-1}\}$ stands for the lowest heuristic value, $\eta_g^{ave}=|J_k(g)|^{-1}\sum\limits_{i\in J_k(g)}\eta_{gi}=|J_k(g)|^{-1}\sum\limits_{i\in J_k(g)}d_{gi}^{\;-1}$ is the average heuristic value, and $\varepsilon_0>0$..

For the first method,

$$\beta(g,t)<\frac{\log\tau_g^{\max}(t)-\log\tau_g^{ave}(t)}{\log\eta_g^{\max}-\log\eta_g^{\min}}\Leftrightarrow\frac{[\tau_g^{\max}(t)]^{\alpha}[\eta_g^{\min}]^{\beta(g,t)}}{\sum\limits_{r\in J_k(g)}[\tau_{gr}(t)]^{\alpha}[\eta_{gr}]^{\beta(g,t)}}>\frac{[\tau_g^{ave}(t)]^{\alpha}[\eta_g^{\max}]^{\beta(g,t)}}{\sum\limits_{r\in J_k(g)}[\tau_{gr}(t)]^{\alpha}[\eta_{gr}]^{\beta(g,t)}}.$$

It means that the ants will select the paths with the maximum pheromone trail by the higher probability than most of the other feasible paths, even if they are paths with the highest heuristic value.

For the second one,

$$\beta(g,t)>\frac{\log\tau_g^{\min}(t)-\log\tau_g^{\max}(t)}{\log\eta_g^{ave}-\log\eta_g^{\max}}\Leftrightarrow\frac{[\tau_g^{\min}(t)]^{\alpha}[\eta_g^{\max}]^{\beta(g,t)}}{\sum\limits_{r\in J_k(g)}[\tau_{gr}(t)]^{\alpha}[\eta_{gr}]^{\beta(g,t)}}>\frac{[\tau_g^{\max}(t)]^{\alpha}[\eta_g^{ave}]^{\beta(g,t)}}{\sum\limits_{r\in J_k(g)}[\tau_{gr}(t)]^{\alpha}[\eta_{gr}]^{\beta(g,t)}}$$

It means that the ants will select the paths with the maximum heuristic value by the higher probability than most of the other feasible paths, even if they are paths with the highest pheromone trail.

Combing the above two methods of the parameter setting, the new ACO algorithm BSACS is designed as:

```
Initialize
/*β is chosen between 0 and 5 randomly, q0=0.6 */
Loop /* at this level each loop is called iteration */
        Each ant is positioned on a starting node
        Loop /* at this level each loop is called a step */
            Each ant applies a state transition rule to incrementally build a solution and
            a local pheromone updating rule is applied
        Until all ants have built a complete solution
        A global pheromone updating rule is applied
β(g,t)is updated by either of the two methods by probability 0.5 (g=1,…,n)
Until End_condition
```

2.3.2 Numerical results and analyses

In this section, several large TSP instances of TSPIB [70] are tested by BSACS and ACS to show the efficiency of the BSACS. The parameters are set as follows: $m = 10$, $a = \rho = 0.1$, $\tau_0 = (nL_{nn})^{-1}$, and $\alpha=1$. $q_0=0.9$ in ACS, $\varepsilon_0=0.001$ and $q_0=0.6$ in BSACS , respectively. All the instances are computed by BSACS 10 times, and so does ACS with each $\beta(\beta =1,2,3,4,5)$. As shown in Table 4 and Table 5, Item (1) is the length of the best tour obtained by ACS and BSACS. Item (6) is the length of optimal solution published in the TSPLIB: http://www.iwr.uniheidelberg.de/iwr/comopt/soft/TSPLIB95/TSPLIB.html. Item (2) is the relative error which can be computed by $(2) = ((1)-(3))\times(3)^{-1}\times 100\%$. Item (1) and (2) show that BSACS can obtain better solution than ACS in all of the instances. Item (4) is the average length of the solutions found by both ACS and BSACS. Item (5) is the best value of β which can make ACS perform the best according to Item (1) or Item (4).

The experiment result shows that BSACS can perform better than ACS in every computation. What's more, ACS has to change the selection of β in different instances and cannot solve different large size TSP problems steadily with a fixed value of β. The reason is that ACS is not able to effectively use the pheromone trail and heuristic value in searching when β of the transition rule is fixed and unchanged in iterations. This disadvantage could be avoided by using BSACS because the new rule of BSACS (Formula 1) functions based on both pheromone trail and heuristic value adaptively. For the computational complexity, the BSACS need more time than ACS, because $\beta(g,t)$(g=1,…, n) has to be updated at each iteration. However, it doesn't mean that the cost of BSACS is more than ACS in the application, because the cost of ACS for the best parameter selection (Item (5) in Table 2) has not been calculated here. Therefore, BSACS can save the time in choosing the experimental value of the parameter. Generally, the BSACS improves the performance of ACS in solving large size TSP problems.

Instance	Algorithm	(1)Best	(2)%Error	(3)Optimal
bier127	ACS	118773	0.423	118282
	BSACS	118372	0.076	
d198	ACS	15888	0.68	15780
	BSACS	15780	0.00	
ts225	ACS	128829	1.734	126643
	BSACS	126905	0.206	
pcb442	ACS	51286	0.96	50799
	BSACS	51271	0.93	
att532	ACS	28147	1.67	27686
	BSACS	27939	0.91	
u574	ACS	38318	3.829	36905
	BSACS	37662	2.052	
rat783	ACS	9015	2.37	8806
	BSACS	8819	0.14	
fl1577	ACS	22977	3.27	222490.
	BSACS	22611	1.63	

Table 4. Comparison of the best solution obtained by ACS and BSACS

Instance	Algorithm	(4) Average	(5)Best β of ACS	(6) t_{avg} (second)
bier127	ACS	119185.3	2, 3	45.6
	BSACS	118826.8	-	91.0
d198	ACS	16054.8	2	97.8
	BSACS	15842.1	-	124.5
ts225	ACS	129102.5	4, 5	32.0
	BSACS	127262.8	-	67.0
pcb442	ACS	51690.2	2	281.6
	BSACS	51642.8	-	461.2
att532	ACS	28532.0	2	401.5
	BSACS	28163.7	-	539.7
u574	ACS	38657.8	1, 5	305.3
	BSACS	38291.9	-	504.3
rat783	ACS	9066.0	2	1185.4
	BSACS	8985.8	-	1559.8
fl1577	ACS	23163.5	2	3884.0
	BSACS	22680.3	-	6290.2

Table 5. Comparison of the average solution obtained by ACS and BSAC

2.4 An adaptive volatility rate of pheromone trail

The following presents a trial work of setting the parameters of ACO adaptively. First, a tuning rule for ρ is designed based on the quality of the solution constructed by artificial ants. Then, we introduce the adaptive ρ to form a new ACO algorithm, which is tested to compute several benchmark instances of traveling sales-man problem and film-copy deliverer problem.

2.4.1 An adaptive volatility rate setting strategy

After constructing its tour, an artificial ant also modifies the amount of pheromone on the visited edges by applying the pheromone updating rule. The rule is designed so that it tends to give more pheromone to the edges which should be visited by ants. The classical pheromone updating rule is as (1). And the optimal ρ was set ρ =0.1 experimentally [46, 49, 55], which means that 90 per cent of the original pheromone trail remains and its 10 per cent is replaced by the increment.

In order to update the pheromone according to the quality of solutions found by ants, an adaptive rule for volatility of the pheromone trail is designed as follows:

$$\rho_m = L_m^{-1} / (L_m^{-1} + L_P^{-1}) \tag{11}$$

where L_m is the length of the solution S_m found by ant m, and L_p is the length of the solution S_p built based on the pheromone matrix, shown as $s = \arg\max_{u \in J_m(r)} \{[\tau(r,u)\}$ where s is the city selected as the next one to city r for any $(r,s) \in S_p$.

The motivation of the proposed rule is: better solutions should contribute more pheromone, and the worse ones contribute less. And a new ACO algorithm with the adaptive rule (shown as Equation 3) is introduced as follows:

```
Initialize
/*β is chosen between 0 and 5 randomly, q0=0.6 */
Loop /* at this level each loop is called iteration */
        Each ant is positioned on a starting node
        Loop /* at this level each loop is called a step */
            Each ant applies a state transition rule to incrementally build a solution and
            a local pheromone updating rule is applied
            Each ant the calculate the ρi is based on its solution's length
        Until all ants have built a complete solution
        ρbest is calculated based on the best solution Sbest.
        Carry out the pheromone updating rule with ρi (i=1,...,k) and ρbest.
Until End_condition
```

2.4.2 Numerical results

This section indicates the numerical results in the experiment that the proposed ACO algorithm is used to solve TSP problems [69]. Several TSP instances are computed by ACS [49], ACO [71] and the proposed ACO on a PC with an Intel Pentium 550MBHz Processor and 256MB SDR Memory, and the results are shown in Table 1.

It should be noted that every instance is computed 20 times. The algorithms are both programmed in Visual C++6.0 for Windows System. They would not stop until a better solution could be found in 500 iterations, which is considered as a virtual convergence of the algorithms. Table 6 shows that the proposed ACO algorithm (PACO) performs better than ACS [49] and ACO [71]. The shortest lengths and the average lengths obtained by PACO are shorter than those found by ACS and ACO in all of the TSP instances. Furthermore, it can be concluded that the standard deviations of the tour lengths obtained by PACO are smaller than those of another algorithms. Therefore, we can conclude that PACO is proved to be more effective and steady than ACS [49] and ACO [71]. Computation time cost of PACO is not less than ACS and ACO in all of the instances because it needs to compute the value of volatility rate $k+1$ times per iteration. Although all optimal tours of TSP problems cannot be found by the tested algorithms, all of the errors for PACO are much less than that for another two ACO approaches. The algorithms may make improvement in solving TSP when reinforcing heuristic strategies like local search like ACS-3opt [49] and MMAS+rs [51] are used.

Problem	Algorithm	best	ave	time(s)	standard deviation
kroA100	ACS	21958	22088.8	65	1142.77
	ACO	21863	22082.5	94.6	1265.30
	PACO	21682	22076.2	117.2	549.85
ts225	ACS	130577	133195	430.6	7038.30
	ACO	130568	132984	439.3	7652.80
	PACO	130507	131560	419.4	1434.98
pr226	ACS	84534	86913.8	378.4	4065.25
	ACO	83659	87215.6	523.8	5206.70
	PACO	81967	83462.2	762.2	3103.41
lin105	ACS	14883	15125.4	88.8	475.37
	ACO	14795	15038.4	106.6	526.43
	PACO	14736	14888	112.2	211.34
kroB100	ACS	23014	23353.8	56.2	685.79
	ACO	22691	23468.1	102.9	702.46
	PACO	22289	22728	169.6	668.26
kroC100	ACS	21594	21942.6	54.8	509.77
	ACO	21236	21909.8	78.1	814.53
	PACO	20775	21598.4	114.8	414.62
lin318	ACS	48554	49224.4	849.2	1785.21
	ACO	48282	49196.7	902.7	2459.16
	PACO	47885	49172.8	866.8	1108.34

Table 6. Comparison of the ACS [49], ACO [51] and the proposed ACO (PACO) in TSP instances

3. Genetic algorithm for generalized TSP

3.1 Generalized TSP (GTSP)

The generalized traveling salesman problem (GTSP) is a kind of combinatorial optimization problem, which has been introduced by Henry-Labordere [72] and Saksena [73] in the context of computer record balancing and of visit sequencing through welfare agencies since 1960s. The GTSP can be described as the problem of seeking a special Hamiltonian cycle with lowest cost in a complete weighted graph.

Let G=(V, E, M) be a complete weighted graph where $V=\{v_1,v_2,\cdots,v_n\}$ $(n>3)$, $E=\{e_{ij} \mid v_i,v_j \in V\}$ and $W=\{w_{ij} \mid w_{ij} \geq 0\, and\, w_{ii}=0, \forall i,j \in N(n)\}$ are vertex set, edge set, and cost set, respectively. The vertex set V is partitioned into m possibly intersecting groups $V_1,V_2,\cdots V_m$ with $|V_j| \geq 1$ and $V=\bigcup_{j=1}^{m} V_j$. The GTSP is required to pass through all of the groups, but not all of the vertices differing from that of TSP. For convenience, we also call **W** as the cost matrix and take it as $\mathbf{W}=(w_{ij})_{n\times n}$. There are two different kinds of GTSP under the abovementioned framework of the special Hamiltonian cycle [75-76]: (1) the cycle passes exactly one vertex in each group (refer to Fig. 1) and (2) the cycle passes at least one vertex in each group (refer to Fig. 2). The first kind of GTSP is also known as E-GTSP, where E stands for equality [76]. In this paper we only discuss the GTSP for the first case and will still call it as GTSP for convenience.

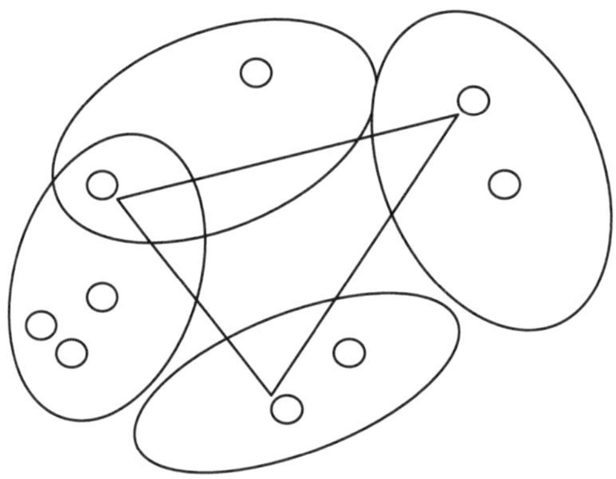

Figure 3. Exactly one vertex is visited in a GTSP cycle.

GTSP has extensive application fields. Laport et al. [75], Lien et al. [77], and Castelino et al. [78] reported the applications of GTSP. Just as mentioned in Ref. [77], "for many real-world problems that are inherently hierarchical, the GTSP offers a more accurate model than the TSP." Generally, GTSP provides a more ideal modeling tool for many real problems. Furthermore, GTSP can include the grouped and isolated vertices at the same time according to our present extension. Therefore, GTSP includes TSP theoretically (see Fig. 3) and application fields of GTSP are wider than those of TSP.

Although since late 1960s GTSP has been proposed [72-74], the related reported works are very limited compared with those on TSP [79–82] and the existing algorithms for GTSP are mainly based on dynamic programming techniques [72-74,76,83-84]. However, because of its NP-hard quality, only a few solutions of modest-size problems are supported by the current hardware technology and most of them fail to obtain the results due to the huge memory required in dynamic programming algorithms and the problem of lengthy computational time.

The main methodology of the dynamic programming algorithms is to transform the GTSP into TSP and then to solve the TSP using existing algorithms [76, 84–86]. The shortcomings of these methods are that the transformation increases the problem dimension dramatically and in some cases the dimension would expand up to more than three times of the original [77, 87-89]. Therefore, although theoretically the GTSP could be solved using the corresponding transformed TSP, the technological limitation ruins its practical feasibility. Some studies have been performed to discuss and solve the problem [90–92]. This study, we will show some bio-inspired method on the GTSP problem.

3.2 Genetic algorithm for generalized TSP

Genetic algorithm (GA) is one of the powerful tools to deal with NP-hard combinatorial optimization problems and has been widely applied for finding the solution of TSP due to its high efficiency and strong searching ability. However, theoretical and application studies related to using GA methods to solve GTSP are very few. The [90] and [93] are two of most interesting work on this problem. In [90], a hybrid GTSP solving algorithm is proposed based on random-key GA and local search method, the main difficult of the method it is hard to handle large scale problems. In [93], a generalized chromosome is used and a generalized chromosome- based GA (GCGA) is proposed accordingly. The advantages of the GCGA are that it does not require the transformation from GTSP to TSP and remove the limitation of triangle inequality of the cost matrix, which enables the GCGA to be able to run with high efficiency.

3.2.1 Generalized chromosome

The solution of GTSP is a special Hamiltonian cycle, which passes through all of the groups. The encoding for solution of GTSP is designed similarly to the one proposed by Huang et al. [94]. A hybrid encoding, which includes a head encoded with binary number and a body encoded with integer number, is given for the solution as figure 1 shows.

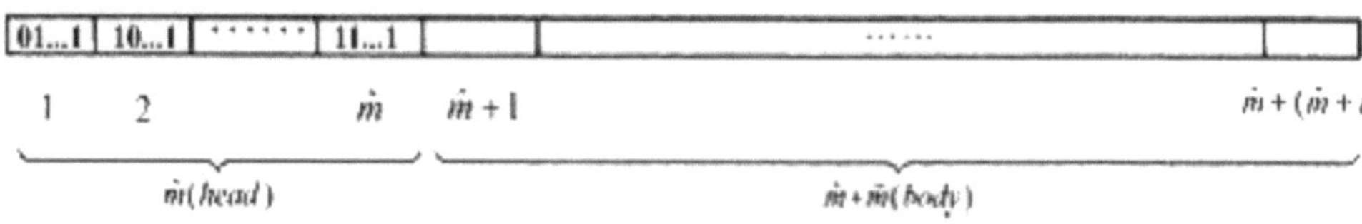

Figure 4. Hybrid Encoding for Solution of GTSP

In the body, there are m integer elements representing m groups ($m = \hat{m} + \tilde{m}$, $\hat{m}$ supper vertexes and $\tilde{m}$ scattering vertexes[93]. In the head, there are $\hat{m}$ binary elements representing vertexes in groups.

Let $[e_1,...,e_i,...,e_{\hat{m}}, g_1,..., g_j,..., g_m]$ be a GTSP solution, where e_i (encoded in binary number) is the sequence number of the vertex in Group i, and g_j (encoded in integer number) is the sequence number of the jth group in the cycle. The set of hybrid encoding can be denoted by $D = \{x | x = h \oplus b, h \in H, b \in B\}$, and each solution for GTSP can be encoded as $x \in D$, where $H = \{h \mid h = e_1,...,e_{\hat{m}}; e_i \le |V_i|, i \le \hat{m}\}$ represents the head and $B = \{b \mid b = g_1,..., g_m\}$) represents the body.

3.2.2 The framework of the GCGA

The special designed operators are needed to conduct random search on the generalized chromosome. The GCGA contains the following four operators: Initializing operator **P**, Generalized crossover operator **C**, Generalized crossover operator **C** and Generalized reversion operator **R**. We give a brief introduction to these five steps in this section. More information about the GCGA can refer to [93].

1. Initializing operator P

Initializing operator **P** is used to generate an initial population. It is a two-element random operator. Its two variables are H and B, and its result is a subset of D. Denoting P as a population, then the initialization of P can be represented as $P_N=(H,B)$, where PN is an operator to randomly generate an initial population with size *N*.

2. Generalized crossover operator C

To implement the crossover operation and generate new chromosomes, a generalized crossover operator is defined as $C{:}D\times D\rightarrow D\times D$. It is a two-element random operator. Its variables are the elements of D. The behavior of the operator is somewhat similar to the two-point crossover in the standard GA. Let the two crossover points selected randomly be i_1 and i_2 (assume $i_1 < i_2$), where $i_1 = random(2\hat{m}+\tilde{m})$, and $i_2 = random(2\hat{m}+\tilde{m})$. If $i_1 > \hat{m}$ then the crossover takes place in the body parts. In this case, the effect of crossover operator is equal to the conventional crossover in some extent, because the body parts of GC are equivalent to two normal chromosomes. If $i_2 \le \hat{m}$, then the crossover takes place in the head parts. In this case, it is only needed to exchange the genes within the crossover segments. If $i_1 \le \hat{m} < i_2$, then the generalized crossover can be treated as the combination of the above cases.

3. Generalized mutation operator M

To increase the diversity of the gene segments, the generalized mutation operator M is designed based on the insertion mutation used in standard GA. Preliminary gene $i_2 = random(2\hat{m}+\tilde{m})$ is randomly selected, which is taken as the gene to be mutated. The difference between GCGA and standard GA is that if $i < \hat{m}$ then the preliminary gene lies in the head part and its corresponding body part also need to be generated.

4. Generalized reversion operator R

To enhance the convergent speed of the GCGA, the generalized reversion operator is designed which is similar to the conventional reversion operation. Operator **R** can be used to select two reversion points i_1 and i_2 according to $i_1 = random(\hat{m}+\tilde{m})$, and $i_2 = random(\hat{m}+\tilde{m})$. If the solution generated after the reversion operator, then the operator R is taken, otherwise the operator won't taken.

3.3 Improved Evolutionary Algorithm (EA) for GTSP

3.3.1 The framework of EA for GTSP

In this section, an improved EA for the GTSP (EA-GTSP) has been proposed. In the EA-GTSP, the generalized chromosome described in 3.2 is used to encode the problem. And the following three operators are specially designed to improve the efficiency of the algorithm on the GTSP: crossover operator, mutation operator and local optimization strategy.

a. Crossover

At Step 3, pairs of solutions may be selected to carry out the crossover operator by the crossover probability P_c. Given two solutions $S_x = h_x \oplus b_x$ and $S_y = h_y \oplus b_y$ selected at Step 3 ($h_x, h_y \in H. b_x, b_y \in B$), the process of crossover can be shown as follows:

Two integer numbers i_1, i_2 $(i_1, i_2 \le \hat{m} + (\hat{m} + \tilde{m}),\ i_1 < i_2)$ are generated randomly to set the crossing position. If $i_1 > \hat{m}$, then, $b_x \otimes b_y \to (b'_x, b'_y)$, which is the same operator as the GCGA, $x' = h_x \oplus b'_x$, $y' = h_y \oplus b'_y$. If $i_2 \le \hat{m}$, $h_x \otimes h_y \to (h'_x, h'_y)$, $x' = h'_x \oplus b_x$, $y' = h'_y \oplus b_y$. If $i_1 < \hat{m}$ and $i_2 \ge \hat{m}$, $h_x \otimes h_y \to (h'_x, h'_y)$ and $b_x \otimes b_y \to (b'_x, b'_y)$, $x' = h'_x \oplus b'_x$ and $y' = h'_y \oplus b'_y$.

If the GTSP solution S_x costs less than S_y $(i_2 \le \hat{m})$,

$$h'_x = \{e_{x1}, \ldots, e_{xi_1 - 1}, e_{xi_1}.\mathrm{AND}.e_{yi_1}, \ldots, e_{xi_2}.\mathrm{AND}.e_{yi_2}, e_{xi_2+1}, \ldots, e_{x\hat{m}}\}$$

$$h'_y = \{e_{x1}, \ldots, e_{xi_1 - 1}, e_{xi_1}.\mathrm{OR}.e_{yi_1}, \ldots, e_{xi_2}.\mathrm{OR}.e_{yi_2}, e_{xi_2+1}, \ldots, e_{x\hat{m}}\};$$

otherwise,

$$h'_x = \{e_{y1}, \ldots, e_{yi_1 - 1}, e_{xi_1}.\mathrm{AND}.e_{yi_1}, \ldots, e_{xi_2}.\mathrm{AND}.e_{yi_2}, e_{yi_2+1}, \ldots, e_{y\hat{m}}\}$$

$$h'_y = \{e_{y1}, \ldots, e_{yi_1 - 1}, e_{xi_1}.\mathrm{OR}.e_{yi_1}, \ldots, e_{xi_2}.\mathrm{OR}.e_{yi_2}, e_{yi_2+1}, \ldots, e_{y\hat{m}}\}.$$

If the GTSP solution S_x costs less than S_y $(i_1 < \hat{m}$ and $i_2 \ge \hat{m})$,

$$h'_x = \{e_{x1}, \ldots, e_{xi_1 - 1}, e_{xi_1}.\mathrm{AND}.e_{yi_1}, \ldots, e_{x\hat{m}}.\mathrm{AND}.e_{y\hat{m}}\}$$

$$h'_y = \{e_{x1}, \ldots, e_{xi_1 - 1}, e_{xi_1}.\mathrm{OR}.e_{yi_1}, \ldots, e_{x\hat{m}}.\mathrm{OR}.e_{y\hat{m}}\};$$

otherwise,

$$h'_x = \{e_{y1}, \ldots, e_{yi_1 - 1}, e_{xi_1}.\mathrm{AND}.e_{yi_1}, \ldots, e_{x\hat{m}}.\mathrm{AND}.e_{y\hat{m}}\}$$

$$h'_y = \{e_{y1}, \ldots, e_{yi_1 - 1}, e_{xi_1}.\mathrm{OR}.e_{yi_1}, \ldots, e_{x\hat{m}}.\mathrm{OR}.e_{y\hat{m}}\}.$$

b. Mutation

The mutation operator is added to help EA-GTSP converge to the global optimal solution. Each solution is affected by the mutation operator by probability P_m. There are two procedures called head mutation and body mutation in the operator.

In the head mutation, given a head of a solution, the procedure of head mutation is:

Head mutation: $h_z \to h'_z$, $h'_z = \{e_{z1}, \ldots, e_{zi_3 - 1}, rebuild(e_{zi_3}), e_{zi_3+1}, \ldots, e_{z\hat{m}}\}$

where $h_z = \{e_{z1}, ..., e_{zi_3-1}, e_{zi_3}, e_{zi_3+1}, ..., e_{z\hat{m}}\}$. $rebuild(e_{zi_3})$ will generate a segment of binary bits randomly. Every binary element of solution S_Z may be affected by $rebuild(e_{zi_3})$ when $r_{mh} < P_{mh}$ (r_{mh} is generated randomly in [0,1] for each binary element of the solution obtained at Steps 3 and 4).

In the body mutation, the procedure is described as follows:

Body mutation: $b_z \rightarrow b'_z, b'_z = \{g'_{z1}, ..., g'_{zi-1}, g'_{zi}, g'_{zi+1}, ..., g'_{z\hat{m}}\}$

where $b_z = \{g_{z1}, ..., g_{zi}, ..., g_{z\hat{m}}\}$ and $r_{mb} < P_{mb}$ (r_{mb} is generated randomly in [0,1] for each solution obtained at Steps 3 and 4).

So the mutation operator of the EA-GTSP is defined as follows:

Mutation of EA-GTSP: $S_z = h_z \oplus b_z \xrightarrow{mutation} S_z' = h'_z \oplus b'_z$.

c. Local Optimal Strategy

The local optimal strategy is helpful to find the best solution in a local searching space. Each solutions of the population are optimized according to a heuristic algorithm as follows:

```
Input: GTSP solution S_q
For i=1 to m̂ do      //optimization for head
   Choose a vertex in Group i to make S_q cost the lest
End for
For j=1 to m̂ + m̃ -1 do //optimization for body
   Choose an order for g_qj and g_qj+1 to make S_q cost the least.
End for
Output: a new solution S'_q (S_q is changed into S'_q.)
```

d. Decoding for solution of GTSP

Because the head encoding is designed as binary number, it needs to be decoded in the following function.

$$h = [e_1, \ldots, e_{\hat{m}}] \xrightarrow{decoding} [e_1 . \text{MOD} . |V_1|, \ldots, e_i . \text{MOD} . |V_i|, \ldots, e_{\hat{m}} . \text{MOD} . |V_{\hat{m}}|]$$

where $|V_i|$ is the number of vertexes in Group i (V_i).

Until now, we can summarize the algorithm of the improved EA for the GTSP as follows.

```
Initialize parameters.
Encode and initialize a population of solutions.
/*β is chosen between 0 and 5 randomly, q0=0.6 */
Loop /* at this level each loop is called iteration */
    Crossover Operator: select pairs of solutions and change them into pairs of new Local
    solutions with the crossover operator by the crossover probability.
    Optimal Strategy: optimize all of the solutions with a heuristic algorithm locally.
    Mutation Operator: select several solutions by the mutation probability and change
End_condition
Decoding for solution of GTSP
```

3.3.2 Numerical result

In this section, the efficiency of the EA-GTSP and other algorithms are compared on some benchmark problems [93].

Problem \five runs	EA-GTSP Best	EA-GTSP Average	GCGA Best	GCGA Average	HCGA Best	HCGA Average
30KROA150	11018	11018	11018	11022	11018	11018
30KROB150	12195	12195	12196	12314	12195	12195
31PR152	51573	51573	51586	53376	51573	51573
32U159	22664	22664	22664	22685	22664	22664
40KROA200	13408	13408	13408	13617	13408	13408
40KROB200	13113	13114	13120	13352	13113	13119
45TS225	68340	68403	68340	68789	68340	68432
46PR226	64007	64007	64007	64574	64007	64007
53GIL262	1011	1011	1011	1057	1011	1011
53PR264	29546	29546	29549	29791	29546	29546
60PR299	22617	22631	22638	22996	22631	22638
64LIN318	20769	20799	20977	22115	20788	20914
80RD400	6446	6480	6465	6604	6456	6498
84FL417	9663	9663	9663	9725	9663	9663
88PR439	60099	60249	61273	62674	60184	60558
89PCB442	21695	21735	21978	22634	21768	21860

Table 7. Comparison of solution among EA-GTSP, GCGA and HCGA

The instances can be obtained from TSPLIB library which were originally generated for testing standard TSP algorithms. To test GTSP algorithms, Fischetti et al. [95] provided a partition algorithm to convert the TSP instances to GTSP instances.

In our experiments, we set the population size as 100 (*pop_size*=100), crossover probability as 0.5 ($P_c = 0.5$), and mutation probability as 0.09 (P_m=0.09, P_{mh}=0.001, P_{mb}=0.005). The algorithms would stop when no better solution could be found in 500 iterations. All of the instances are computed by EA-GTSP, HCGA [94] and GCGA [93] twenty times on a PC with 2.0 GHz processor and 256 MB SDR memory, and the results are shown in Table 1.

In Table 7, not only the best solution obtained by EA-GTSP is shorter than the one obtained by HCGA and GCGA does, but also the one on average, in all of the examples. It can show global optimal function of EA-GTSP. In order to show the performance of EA-GTSP, there is a comparison between it and several heuristic algorithms [96] by computing the same GTSP instances. As Table 2 shows, EA-GTSP is more efficient and steady than all of the test algorithms because it can get the best solution in most of the instances.

Problem\five runs	EA-GTSP	NN (G-opt)	NN (G2-opt)	CI (G-opt)	CI (G2-opt)	MO (G-opt)	MO (G2-opt)	CI^2	GI^3
30KROA150	11018	11018	11018	11018	11018	11018	11018	11018	11018
30KROB150	12195	12196	12196	12196	12196	12196	12196	12196	12196
31PR152	51573	52506	52506	51915	51915	51820	51820	51820	51820
32U159	22664	23296	23296	22664	22664	22923	22923	23254	23254
40KROA200	13408	14110	14110	14059	14059	13887	13887	13406	13406
40KROB200	13113	13932	13111	13117	13117	13117	13117	13111	13111
45TS225	68340	68340	68340	69279	69279	68756	68756	68756	68756
46PR226	64007	65811	65395	65395	65395	64007	64007	64007	64007
53GIL262	1011	1077	1032	1036	1036	1021	1021	1064	1064
53PR264	29546	31241	31241	31056	31056	30779	30779	29655	29655
60PR299	22617	24163	23069	23119	23119	23129	23129	23119	23119
64LIN318	20769	22233	21787	21858	21858	22403	22403	21719	21719
80RD400	6446	7083	6614	6550	6550	6546	6546	6439	6439
84FL417	9663	9754	9754	9662	9662	9697	9697	9932	9697
88PR439	60099	63736	62514	61126	61126	62091	62091	62215	62215
89PCB442	21695	23364	21704	23307	23307	22697	22697	22936	22936

Table 8. Comparison of solution among EA-GTSP, GCGA and HCG

4. Conclusion and discussions

The chapter introduces two examples of bio-inspired algorithm for traveling sales-man problems and its extended version. The first algorithm, named ant colony optimization (ACO) which is designed inspired by the natural ants' behavior, is a novel method to deal with TSPs. The experimental results prove the performance of ACO approach, which is feasible to solve TSP instances as well as the traditional method. The research results about the self-adaptive parameters of ACO are presented in the chapter, which indicates how to set an optimal ACO algorithm for different TSPs. Another algorithm is genetic algorithm, which is used to solve generalized traveling sales-man problem (GTSP) that is one extended style of TSPs. The best-so-far genetic algorithm for GTSP is introduced in the final sub-section. Bio-inspired algorithms are the feasible methods for TSPs, and can attain better performance with the modified setting like self-adaptive parameters and hybrid coding, which are described in the chapter.

5. References

J.H. Holland, Adaptation in Natural and Artificial Systems. MIT Press, Cambridge, MA. 1975

R. Cheng, & M. Gen, Crossover on intensive search and traveling salesman problem. Computers & Industrial Engineering, 27(1-4), pp. 485-488, 1994.

R. Cheng, M. Gen, & M. Sasaki, Film-copy deliverer problem using genetic algorithms. Computers & Industrial Engineering, 29(1-4):pp. 549-553, 1995.

N. Kubota, T. Fukuda, & K. Shimojima, Virus-evolutionary genetic algorithm for a self-organizing manufacturing system. Computers and Engineering, 30(4), 1015-1026, 1996.

D. E. Goldberg, Genetic Algorithms in Search, Optimization and Machine Learning, Addison-Wesley, Reading, MA.1989.

R. Cheng, M. Gen and Y. Tsujimura, "A tutorial survey of jobshop scheduling problems using genetic algorithms - I. Representation", Computers and Industrial Engineering, pp. 983-997, 1996.

C. R. Reeves, "A genetic algorithm for flowshop sequencing", Computers and Operations Research, 22(1), pp. 5-13, 1995

J. C. Bean, Genetic algorithms and random keys for sequencing and optimization. ORSA Journal on Computing, 6(2), pp.154-160,1994.

L. Davis, Job shop scheduling with genetic algorithms. In: Proceedings of the International Conference on Genetic Algorithms, London, pp. 136-140, 1985.

D.E. Goldberg, R.J. Lingle, Alleles, loci and the traveling salesman problem. In: Proceedings of the International Conference on Genetic Algorithms, London, pp.154-159, 1985.

I. Oliver, D. Smith, J. Holland, A study of permutation crossover operators on the traveling salesman problem. In: Proceedings of the Second International Conference on Genetic Algorithms, London, pp. 224-230, 1987.

T. Starkweather, et al., A comparison of genetic sequencing operators. In: Proceedings of the Fourth International Conference on Genetic Algorithms, Los Altos, CA, pp. 69-76, 1991.

F. D. Croce, R. Tadei and G. Volta, "A genetic algorithm for the job shop problem", Computers and Operations Research, 22(1), pp. 15-24, 1995.

G. Syswerda, Uniform crossover in genetic algorithms.In: Proceedings of the Third International Conference on Genetic Algorithms, Los Altos, pp. 502-508, 1989.

M. Yamamura, , T Ono, and S. Kobayashi, Character-preserving genetic algorithms for traveling salesman problem, Journal of Japan Society for Artificial Intelligence, vol. 6.pp. 1049-1059, 1992.

M. Yamamura, T Ono, and S. Kobayashi, Emergent search on double circle TSPs using subtour exchange crossover, in: Proceedings of the Third IEEE Conference on Evolutionary Computation, IEEE Press, Nagoya, Japan, pp. 535-540, 1996.

J. Dzubera and D. Whitley, "Advanced correlation analysis of operators for the traveling salesman problem," in Parallel Problem Solving From Nature—PPSN III, Y. Davidor, H.-P. Schwefel, and R. Männer, Eds. New York: Springer-Verlag, pp. 68-77, 1994.

K. Mathias and D. Whitley, "Genetic operators, the fitness landscape, and the traveling salesman problem," in Parallel Problem Solving From Nature. Amsterdam, The Netherlands: Elsevier, pp. 219–228, 1992.

H. D. Nguyen, I. Yoshihara, and M. Yasunaga, "Modified edge recombination operators of genetic algorithms for the traveling salesman problem," in Proc. 3rd Asia-Pacific Conf. Simul. Evol. and Learn., Nagoya, Japan, pp. 2815–2820, 2000.

T. Starkweather, S. McDaniel, K. Mathias, C. Whitley, and D. Whitley, "A comparison of genetic sequencing operators," in Proc. 4th Int. Conf. Genetic Algorithms, pp. 69–76, 1991.

B. Freisleben and P. Merz, "A genetic local search algorithm for solving symmetric and asymmetric traveling salesman problems," in Proc. IEEE Int. Conf. Evol. Comput., pp. 616-621, 1996.

P. Merz and B. Freisleben, "Genetic local search for the TSP: New results,"in Proc. IEEE Int. Conf. Evol. Comput., pp. 159–164, 1997.

— —, "Memetic algorithms for the traveling salesman problem," Complex Syst., 13(4), pp. 297–345, 2001.

S. Jung and B. Moon, "The natural crossover for the 2D Euclidean TSP," in Proc. Genetic and Evol. Comput. Conf, pp. 1003–1010, 2001.

Y. Nagata and S. Kobayashi, "Edge assembly crossover: A high-power genetic algorithm for the traveling salesman problem," in Proc. 7th Int. Conf. Genetic Algorithms, pp. 450–457, 1997.

Y. Nagata, "The EAX algorithm considering diversity loss," in Parallel Problem Solving From Nature—PPSN VIII. New York: Springer-Verlag, pp. 332–341, 2004.

H. D. Nguyen, I. Yoshihara, K. Yamamori, and M. Yasunaga, "Greedy genetic algorithms for symmetric and asymmetric TSPs," IPSJ Trans. Math. Modeling and Appl., 43, SIG10 (TOM7), pp. 165–175, 2002.

H. Sengoku and I. Yoshihara, "A fast TSP solver using GA on JAVA," in Proc. 3rd Int. Symp. Artif. Life and Robot , pp. 283–288, 1998.

J. Grefenstette, et al. Genetic algorithms for the traveling salesman problem, in: Proceedings of the First International Conference on Genetic Algorithms, Lawrence Erlbaum Associates, Hillsdale, pp. 160-168,1985.

G. Liepins, et al. Greedy genetics, in: Proceedings of the First International Conference on Genetic Algorithms, Lawrence Erlbaum Associates, Hillsdale, pp.90-99, 1985.

P.W. Poon, J.N. Carter. Genetic algorithm crossover operators for ordering applications. Computers and Operations Research 22 (1), pp. 135–147,1995.

L. Qu, R. Sun, A synergetic approach to genetic algorithms for solving traveling salesman problem. Information Sciences 117 (3–4), pp. 267–283, 1999.

C. Liaw. A hybrid genetic algorithm for the open shop scheduling problem. European Journal of Operational Research 124 (1), pp. 28–42, 2000.

K. Katayama, H. Sakamoto, H. Narihisa. The efficiency of hybrid mutation genetic algorithm for the traveling salesman problem. Mathematical and Computer Modeling 31 (10–12), pp.197–203, 2000.

R. Knosala, T. Wal. A production scheduling problem using genetic algorithm. Journal of Materials Processing Technology 109 (1–2), 90–95, 2001.

C. Moon, et al., An efficient genetic algorithm for the traveling salesman problem with precedence constraints. European Journal of Operational Research 140 (3), pp. 606–617, 2002.

R. Cheng, M. Gen, Resource constrained project scheduling problem using genetic algorithms. International Journal of Intelligent Automation and Soft Computing, 1996.

K. Katayama and H. Sakamoto. The Efficiency of Hybrid Mutation Genetic Algorithm for the Travelling Salesman Problem. Mathematical and Computer Modelling 31,pp. 197-203,1990.

Arthur E. Carter, Cliff T. Ragsdale. A new approach to solving the multiple traveling salesperson problem using genetic algorithms. European Journal of Operational Research 175, pp. 246–257 , 2006.

H. D. Nguyen, et al. Implementation of an Effective Hybrid GA for Large-Scale Traveling Salesman Problems: IEEE Transactions on Systems, Man and Cybernetics-Part B: Cybernetics, 37(1):92-99,2007

F. Samanlioglu, M.E. Kurz, , & W.G. Ferrell Jr.. A genetic algorithm with random-keys representation for a symmetric multiobjective traveling salesman problem. In: Proceedings of the Institute of Industrial Engineers Annual Conference. Orlando: Florida, 2006.

F. Samanlioglu, M. E. Kurz, W. G. Ferrell Jr., & Tangudu, S. A hybrid random-key genetic algorithm for a symmetric traveling salesman problem. International Journal of Operations Research, 2(1), 47–63, 2007.

F.Samanlioglu et al. A memetic random-key genetic algorithm for a symmetric multi-objective traveling salesman problem. Computers & Industrial Engineering. www.sciencedirect.com, 2008.

M. Dorigo, V. Maniezzo, and A. Colorni. Ant System: Optimization by a Colony of Cooperating Agents. IEEE Transactions on Systems, Man, and Cybernetics-Part B: CYBERNETIC, 26(1), FEBRUARY, 1996.

M. Dorigo. Optimization, Learning and Natural Algorithms (in Italian). PhD thesis, Dipartimento di Elettronica e Informazione, Politecnico di Milano, IT, 1992.

M. Dorigo, G.D. Caro, L.M. Gambardella. Ant algorithms for Discrete Optimization. Massachusetts Institute of Technology, Artificial Life 5, pp. 137-172, 1999.

W.J. Gutjahr. ACO algorithms with guaranteed convergence to the optimal solution. Information Processing Letters 82, pp.145-153, 2002.

M. Dorigo and L.M. Gambardella. Ant colonies for the traveling salesman problem. BioSystems, 43, pp. 73-81, 1997.

M. Dorigo and L.M. Gambardella. Ant Colony System: A cooperative learning approach to the traveling salesman problem. IEEE Transactions on Evolutionary Computation, 1(1), pp. 53-66, 1997.

L.M. Gambardella and M. Dorigo. Solving symmetric and asymmetric TSPs by ant colonies. Proceedings of IEEE International Conference on Evolutionary Computation. 1996.

T. Stutzle and H.H. Hoos. MAX-MIN Ant System. Future Generation Computer Systems,16(8), pp. 889-914, 2000.

M. Dorigo, M. Birattari, T. Stutzle. Ant colony optimization. Computational Intelligence Magazine, IEEE, Vol. 1, Nov., pp.28-39, 2006.

W.J. Gutjahr. A graph-based ant system and its convergence. Future Generation Computer Systems 16(9), pp. 873-888, 2000.

T. Stutzle, M. Dorigo. A Short Convergence Proof for a Class of Ant colony Optimization Algorithms. IEEE Transactions on Evolutionary Computation, 6(4), 2002.

M. Dorigo, C. Blum. Ant colony optimization theory: A survey. Theoretical Computer Science, 344, pp. 243-278, 2005.

A. Badr, A. Fahmy. A proof of convergence for Ant algorithms. Information Sciences 160, pp. 267-279, 2004.

S. Fidanova. ACO Algorithm with Additional Reinforcement. M. Dorigo et al. (Eds): ANTS 2002, LNCS 2463, pp. 292-293, 2002.

S. Fidanova. Convergence Proof for a Monte Carlo Method for Combinatorial Optimization Problems. M. Bubak et al. (Eds.): ICCS 2004, LNCS 3039, pp. 523-530, 2004

J. Kennedy and R.C. Eberhart. Particle Swarm Optimisation. In Proceedings of the International Conference on Neural Networks, pp.1942–1948, 1995.

Clerc, M.. Discrete Particle Swarm Optimization, Illustrated by Traveling Salesman Problem. In New Optimization Techniques in Engineering. Springer-Verlag, Berlin , 2004.

Bo Liu, Ling Wang, Yi-hui Jin, and De-xian Huang, An Effective PSO-Based Memetic Algorithm for TSP, In: D.-S. Huang, K. Li, and G.W. Irwin (Eds.): ICIC 2006, LNCIS 345, pp. 1151 - 1156, 2006.

Yong-Qin Tao, Du-Wu Cui, Xiang-Lin Miao, and Hao Chen, An Improved Swarm Intelligence Algorithm for Solving TSP Problem. In D.-S. Huang, L. Heutte, and M. Loog (Eds.): ICIC 2007, LNAI 4682, pp. 813–822, 2007.

Bin Shen, Min Yao, and Wensheng Yi., Heuristic Information Based Improved Fuzzy Discrete PSO Method for Solving TSP. In Computer Science, PRICAI 2006, LNAI 4099, pp. 859 - 863, 2006.

Yuan, Zhenglei, et al. Chaotic Particle Swarm Optimization Algorithm for Traveling Salesman Problem.Automation and Logistics, 2007 IEEE International Conference on 18-21. pp. 1121 - 1124, 2007.

M. Dorigo, V. Maniezzo, and A. Colorni, "Positive feedback as a search strategy," Dipartimento di Elettronica, Politecnico di Milano, Italy, Tech. Rep. 91-016, 1991.

M. Dorigo, "Optimization, learning and natural algorithms (in italian)," Ph.D. dissertation, Dipartimento di Elettronica, Politecnico di Milano, Italy, 1992.

M. Dorigo and G. Di Caro, "The Ant Colony Optimization meta-heuristic," in New Ideas in Optimization, D. Corne et al., Eds., McGraw Hill, London, UK, pp. 11–32, 1999.

Sun, J., Xiong, S. W., Guo, F. M.: A new pheromone updating strategy in ant colony optimization, Proceedings of 2004 International Conference on Machine Learning and Cybernetics, 1, pp. 620-625, 2004

Dorigo, M., Stützle, T.: Ant Colony Optimization. MIT Press, Cambridge, MA. 2004.

G. Reinelt, "TSPLIB. A traveling salesman problem library," ORSA Journal on Computing, 3(4), pp. 376-384, 1991.

K. Socha, J. Knowles, and M. Sampels, "A MAX-MIN ant system for the university timetabling problem," in Proc. ANTS 2002, ser. LNCS, M. Dorigo et al., Eds., vol. 2463, p. 1, Berlin, Germany: Springer Verlag, 2002.

A. L. Henry-Labordere, RIRO B 2, 43, 1969.

J. P. Saskena, CORS J. 8, 185, 1970.

S. S. Srivastava, S. Kumar, R. C. Garg, and P. Sen, CORS J. 7, 7 ,1969.

G. Laporte, A. Asef-vaziri, and C. Sriskandarajah, J. Oper.Res. Soc. 47, 1461, 1996.

M. Fischetti, J. J. Salazar, and P. Toth, Oper. Res. 45, 378, 1997.

Y. N. Lien, E. Ma, and B. W.-S. Wah, J. Chem. Inf. Comput. Sci. 74, 177, 1993.

K. Castelino, R. D'Souza, and P. K. Wright, http://kingkong.me.berkeley.edu/_kenneth/

N. E. Bowler, T. M. A. Fink, and R. C. Ball, Phys. Rev. E 68,036703, 2003.

M. Andrecut and M. K. Ali, Phys. Rev. E 63, 047103, 2001.

T. Munakata and Y. Nakamura, Phys. Rev. E 64, 046127, 2001.

J. Bentner, G. Bauer, G. M. Obermair, I. Morgenstern, and J.Schneider, Phys. Rev. E 64, 036701 2001.

G. Laporte and Y. Nobert, INFOR 21, 61, 1983.

C. E. Noon and J. C. Bean, Oper. Res. 39, 623, 1991.

D. Ben-Arieh, G. Gutin, M. Penn, A. Yeo, and A. Zverovitch,Int. J. Prod. Res. 41, 2581, 2003.

D. Ben-Arieh, G. Gutin, M. Penn, A. Yeo, and A. Zverovitch,Oper. Res. Lett. 31, 357, 2003.

V. Dimitrijevic and Z. Saric, J. Chem. Inf. Comput. Sci. 102,105, 1997.

G. Laporte and F. Semet, INFOR 37, 114, 1999.

C. E. Noon and J. C. Bean, INFOR 31, 39, 1993.

L. V. Snyder and M. S. Daskin, A Random-key genetic algorithm for the generalized traveling salesman problem (Northwestern University, see, l-snyder3@northweatern.edu, m-daskin@northwestern.edu)

O. Jellouli, in IEEE International Conference on Systems, Man, and Cybernetics, 4, pp. 2765-2768, 2001.

Y. Matsuyama, Trans. Inst. Electron., Inf. Commun. Eng. D-II J74D-II, 416, 1991.

C. G., Wu, Y. C., Liang, H. P., Lee, and C., Lu, Generalized chromosome genetic algorithm for generalized traveling salesman problems and its applications for machining, Physical Review E. 69, 1, 2004

Huang H, Yang XW, Hao ZF, Liang YC, Wu CG, Zhao X. Hybrid chromosome genetic algorithm for generalized traveling salesman problems, Lecture Notes in Computer Science 3612: 137-140 2005.

M. Fischetti, J. J. Salazar, and P. Toth, Branch-and-cut algorithm for the symmetric generalized traveling salesman problem, Operations Research. 45(3), pp.378-394, 1997.

J., Renaud, F. F., Boctor, An efficient composite heuristic for the symmetric generalized traveling salesman problem, European Journal of Operational Research 108, pp.571-584, 1998.

Huang H, Yang XW, Hao ZF, Cai RC. A novel ACO algorithm with adaptive parameter, Lecture Notes in Bioinformatics 4115: 12-21 2006.

Huang H, Hao ZF. ACO for continuous optimization based on discrete encoding. Lecture Notes in Computer Science 4150: 504-505 2006.

Huang H, Hao ZF. An ACO algorithm with bi-directional searching rule. Dynamics of Continuous Discrete and Impulsive Systems-Series B-Applications & Algorithms 13: 71-75, 2006.

Hao ZF, Huang H, Zhang XL, Tu K. A time complexity analysis of ACO for linear functions, Lecture Notes in Computer Science 4247: 513-520 2006.

Zhifeng Hao, Han Huang, Yong Qin, Ruichu Cai. An ACO Algorithm with Adaptive Volatility Rate of Pheromone Trail, Lecture Notes in Computer Science 4490: 1167–1170, 2007.

3

Approaches to the Travelling Salesman Problem Using Evolutionary Computing Algorithms

Jyh-Da Wei
Chang-Gung University
Taiwan

1. Introduction

Genetic algorithms (GAs) were developed as problem independent search algorithms (Goldberg, 1989; Holland, 1975; Man et al., 1999), which simulate the biological evolution to search for an optimal solution to a problem. Figure 1(a) shows the main processes of genetic algorithms. When developing a genetic algorithm, we analyze the properties of the problem and determine the "gene encoding" policy -- Several parameters are chosen as genes and the parameter set is regarded as a chromosome, which reflects an individual. Following the gene encoding policy, we scatter many individuals in a population, and then repeatedly evaluate the individuals' fitness values and select the fittest ones to reproduce the offspring by crossover and mutation operators. Genetic algorithms follow the criterion of "survival of the fittest" to develop increasingly fit individuals.

Hybrid with local search heuristics, Genetic Local Search (GLS) is an upgraded version that replaces each individual with its local optimal neighbour. As shown in Fig. 1(b), a local search process is launched in evaluation. GLS is thereby regarded as a method to mimic the cultural evolution instead of biological evolution, and also referred to as Mimetic Algorithm (MA) or Lamarckian Evolutionary Algorithm (Digalakis & Margaritis, 2004).

Using these "evolutionary computing algorithms" for combinatorial optimization problems has been a well-studied problem-solving approach. The benefit of evolutionary computing is not only its simplicity but also its ability to obtain global optima. Many research findings have indicated that a well-adapted genetic local search algorithm can acquire a near-optimal solution better than those found by simply local searching algorithms (Goldberg, 1989; Pham & Karaboga, 2000). Therefore, numerous results on evolutionary optimization have been published in recent years (Larranaga et al., 1999; Man et al., 1999; Mohammadian et al., 2002). Using genetic algorithms to solve the travelling salesman problem (TSP) is one of the popular approaches (Larranaga et al., 1999).

The TSP is a classical NP-hard combinatorial optimization problem which has been extensively studied. Given n cities and the distances (costs) between each pair of cities, we want to find a minimum-cost tour that visits each city exactly once. Assuming that $d_{i,j}$ is the cost traveling from city i to city j, the TSP is formulated as to find a permutation π of $\{1, 2, \ldots, n\}$ that minimizes

$$C(\pi) = \sum_{i=1}^{n-1} d_{\pi(i),\pi(i+1)} + d_{\pi(n),\pi(1)} \tag{1}$$

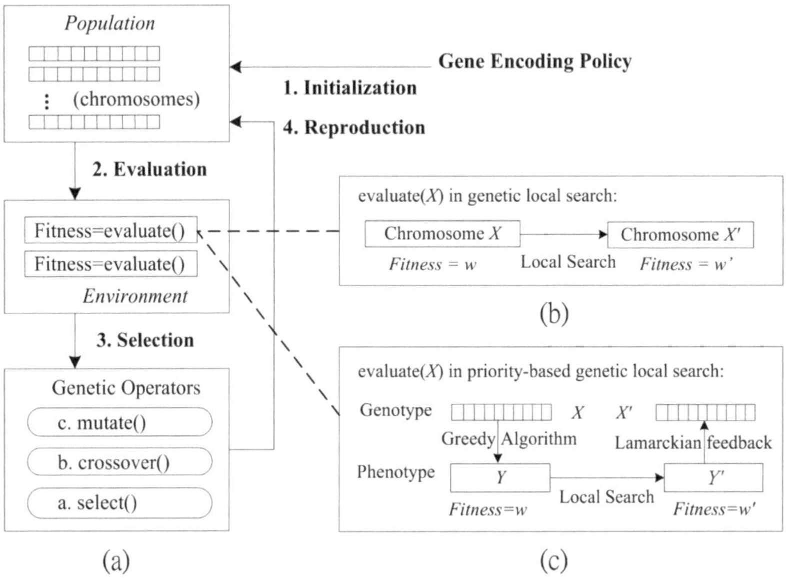

Figure 1. Genetic Algorithm (GA) and Genetic Local Search (GLS). (a) GA flowchart; (b) GLS is a combination of GA and local search heuristics; (c) Priority-Based GLS (PB-GLS) uses a greedy algorithm and a Lamarckian feedback process to alternate between genotype and phenotype.

In the symmetric TSP (STSP), $d_{i,j}$ is equal to $d_{j,i}$ for any two cities i and j, while in the asymmetric TSP (ATSP) this condition might not hold. The Euclidean TSP is a special case of STSP, where the cities are located in R^m space for some m, and the cost function satisfies the triangle inequality, i.e., $d_{i,k} + d_{k,j}$ is greater than or equal to $d_{i,j}$ for distinct i, j and k. The two-dimensional Euclidean TSP is the most popular version studied in the literature.

According to Rego and Glover's classification, the heuristic local search algorithms for the TSP are divided into two categories (Rego & Glover, 2002). Tour construction procedures build a tour by sequentially adding a new node into the current partial tour. Some instances of these procedures include nearest neighbour, nearest insertion, and shortest edge first algorithms (Johnson & McGeoch, 2002). On the other hand, tour improvement procedures start with an initial tour and iteratively seek a better one to replace the current tour. The *k-opt* and *LK* (Lin & Kernighan, 1973; Rego & Glover, 2002) algorithms are examples of these procedures. Subsequently developed algorithms for the TSP also include stochastic search methods, such as Tabu search (Fiechter, 1994; Zachariasen & Dam, 1995), simulated annealing (Kirkpartrick et al., 1983; Moscato & Norman, 1992), ant colony (Dorigo & Gambardella, 1997; Gambardella & Dorigo, 1995) and artificial neural networks (Miglino et al., 1994; Naphade & Tuzun, 1995).

As convenient and powerful searching tools, evolutionary computing algorithms have been applied to the TSP. Genetic algorithms and GLS algorithms are characterized by their population-based global searching, and often find a near-optimal solution better than most previously known methods. However, the TSP requires that each city be visited exactly once. This critical requirement puts a great constraint for us to encode the genes. Directly encoding cities into the chromosomes (the order representation to be given in more detail in

the next section) may not work altogether with traditional crossover methods. As Fig. 2 shows, the offspring becomes an illegal tour if we use traditional crossover operators.
To overcome this difficulty, new crossover operators built upon detection and repair procedures have been developed. Although these operators make evolutionary computing algorithms applicable to the TSP, they are ad hoc and lose generality in problem solving. In Section 2, we provide a relevant survey of developing particular crossover operators for the TSP. Then in Section 3, we present a priority-based encoding scheme instead. This alternative method not only maintains the general-purpose characteristics of evolutionary computing, but also acquires remarkable searching results. In Section 4, we discuss the experimental results, and we give conclusions in Section 5.

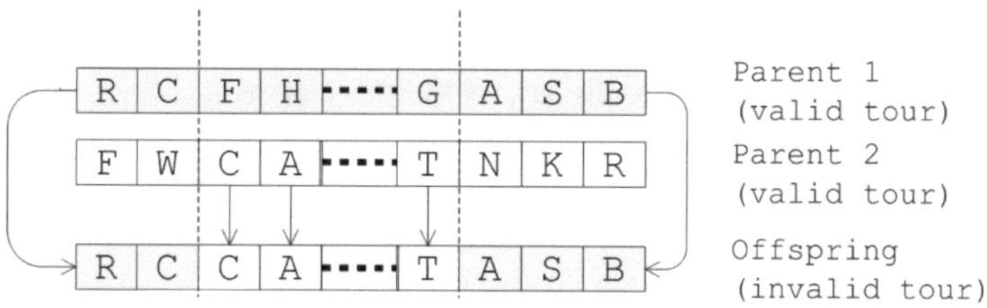

Figure 2. Directly encoding cities into the chromosomes does not work altogether with traditional crossover methods. The offspring may become an invalid TSP tour.

2. Specialized crossover operators for the TSP

Traditional genetic evolution appears to contradict the TSP definition. Therefore, we need additional operators to assist genetic algorithms. Many of these operators depend on the tour representation in the algorithms, such as the order, adjacency and locus representations.

Order representation: The order representation is the most natural to represent a tour since the TSP is a permutation problem. This tour representation encodes the cities in the chromosome as gene values. For example, the partially matched crossover (PMX) (Goldberg & Lingle, 1985; Goldberg, 1989) adopts two crossover points to enclose a crossover interval. The genes (cities) within the crossover intervals are exchanged to initiate the offspring chromosome, and then an automaton is established to transform the genes duplicated outside the intervals.

Adjacency list representation: The adjacency list can also represent a tour. In this representation, recording city j in position i reflects travelling from city i to city j. Because adjacency lists might yield illegal tours, detection and repair procedures are also necessary. For example, the greedy crossover (GX) (Boukreev, 2007; Julstrom, 1995) iteratively selects the shortest edge from the parents to extend the current subtour. If this edge causes a cycle that is not a complete tour, we need to choose another edge connecting to the current subtour.

Adjacency matrix representation: Instead of adjacency lists, the matrix crossover (MX) (Homaifar et al., 1992; Homaifar et al., 1992) uses adjacency matrix to represent the tour. In this binary matrix, the element $m_{i,j}$ is 1, if city j is visited after city i; otherwise the value is 0. Based on this encoding method, the MX exchanges columns of two parents to generate offspring matrix. If the offspring matrix is infeasible due to duplicate adjacency or disconnected cycles, repair procedures are also invoked.

Locus representation: The locus representation regards the graphic image itself of a tour as a chromosome. This representation retains geographical relationships among the cities, but does not embody a gene-encoding method. Therefore, geometrical computations might be necessary in the crossover operators. The natural crossover (NX) published in 2002 (Jung & Moon, 2002) used the locus representation. This crossover operator randomly generates curves to partition the chromosomal space. Cities in some regions inherit the paths from one parent, and those in other regions inherit the paths from the other parent. Finally, repair procedures are also needed to reconnect the subtours.

Other representation-independent approaches: There are genetic operators independent of tour representations. These operators directly analyze the parent tours to create the offspring. Edge-recombination crossover (ERX) (Whitley et al., 1989; Whitley et al., 1991) collects the adjacency information from the parent tours and generates a new tour from this information. Distance preserving crossover (DPX) (Freisleben & Merz, 1996) generates an offspring satisfying the condition that the numbers of differences between the two parents and the offspring are all the same. By doing so, this crossover operator allows "jumps" in the search space. Although these approaches are representation independent, they also act according to the principle that the offspring must inherit the characteristics of the two parents.

The renowned approaches listed above can improve genetic algorithms to solve the TSP. However, these approaches have some drawbacks. The order and adjacency list representations do not ensure a unique representation for a TSP tour. This situation usually retards the evolutionary process. The adjacency matrix representation is time-consuming and does not have a significant performance. The locus representation is not general enough even for an STSP case; and it can only perform on the Euclidean TSP. Most importantly, these crossover operators are specialized mainly for the TSP and involve repair procedures to generate a valid tour. In contrast with the original intention of genetic algorithms, these operators are short of general practical values. In the next section, we present a Genetic Local Search method with Priority-Based encoding, dubbed the "PB-GLS" model (Wei & Lee, 2004; Wei & Lee, 2006). This model retains generality in applications, supports schema analysis during searching process, and has been empirically proven to gain remarkable search results for the travelling salesman problem.

3. Priority-based genetic local search

For a combinatorial optimization problem for which a near-optimal solution can be obtained by using a greedy algorithm, certain entities, such as the nodes of the dMST and TSP problems (Freisleben & Merz, 1996; Zeng & Wang, 2003) and the jobs in the flowshop scheduling (Arroyo & Armentano, 2005) are selected step by step. Herein, the links between two consecutively selected entities are called "consecutive selections". The priority-based encoding policy assigns priorities to all the links between entities and it is expected to set high priority to the correct consecutive selections. The greedy algorithm employed remains the same, except that we select the next entity in consideration of the link priority prior to the original ranking key. By doing so, the greedy algorithm leads to a valid solution and the priority encoding makes it possible to follow traditional genetic evolutions. This approach does not lose generality in applications because we only need to provide a chromosome conformation that is simply a priority assignment.

3.1 Priority-based encoding with local search method

As Fig. 1(c) shows, the priority-based encoding is based on Mendelian inheritance that distinguishes genotype and phenotype in inheritance process. A greedy algorithm plays the role as the biochemical process that transfers the genotype encoding to the phenotype of each individual. The PB-GLS model further conducts a local search method to improve this phenotype. After that, we need a Lamarckian feedback process for encoding the local optimal solution and converting it back to its genotype. This process can be done if we enable all consecutive selections in the given solution by assigning them with higher priorities and disable potentially incorrect links by setting lower priorities. The range of priorities can be determined experimentally, although two priority levels are sufficient in any case.

3.2 Characteristics of the priority-based GLS

The priority-based genetic local search has three main features, i.e., broad applicability, problem transformation, and simulation of Mendelian inheritance theory.

Broad applicability: The priority-based encoding policy suits to any problem whose optimal solution can be approximated by a greedy algorithm, because the greedy algorithm is characterized by two features, i.e., (a) the candidate entities are selected one after another sequentially, and (b) the selected entities are not discarded thereafter.

Problem transformation: The PB-GLS transforms combination and permutation problems into priority assignment problems. This problem transformation suggests a new direction to tackle the given problems. Imagine that the perfect optimal solution contains some crucial consecutive selections of problem entities (e.g. crucial edges in the TSP). Assigning higher priorities to these links leads to a near-optimal solution. Naturally, priority-based encoding allows us to analyze searching schema during the search process.

Simulation of Mendelian inheritance theory: We use greedy algorithms to simulate chemical processes, and use the priority-based encoding policy to simulate the gene codes in inheritance procedure. These priorities control the biochemical processes to "enable" and "disable" some biological functions, and finally develop a phenotype that fits the definition of the genotype.

3.3 Using the priority-based GLS to solve the TSP

A greedy algorithm known as double-ended nearest neighbour (DENN) is used to demonstrate using the PB-GLS model to solve the TSP. Let E(A,B) denote the edge between city A and city B, and assume E(A,B) is identical to E(B,A) for any two distinct cities A and B. The DENN algorithm is described as follows:

Step 1 Sort the edges by their costs into a sequence *S*.

Step 2 Initialize a partial tour *T* = *{S[1]}*. Let *S[1]* = *E(A,B)* be the current subtour from *A* to *B*.

Step 3 Suppose the current subtour is from *X* to *Y* . We trace the sequence *S* to find the first edge *E(P,Q)* that could extend the subtour at either end city *X* or city *Y* without creating a cycle, i.e., a complete tour that does not visit all the cities.

Step 4 If the above edge *E(P,Q)* is found, add it into *T* to extend the current subtour and repeat step 3; otherwise, add *E(Y,X)* into *T* and return *T* as the searching result.

Note that the current state is extended by adding new nodes (cities) repeatedly. We now add priorities to the edges and change the sorting step by considering priorities of these edges first and then their costs in the first step. This change never affects the validity of tours, because the other steps of this greedy algorithm remain unchanged. The most concerned question is whether any tour can be represented by this encoding method. Considering that a greedy algorithm never discards an object once this object is selected, we can construct any given tour "*T*" by a greedy algorithm as the following formula describes:

$$\begin{aligned}&(\forall\ (r, s, t, k, |\{r,s,t,k\}| = 4)\ (\ \{E(r,s), E(s,t)\} \subseteq T\ \wedge \\ &C(k,s) \leq \min\{C(r,s),C(s,t)\}\ \Rightarrow\ P(k,s)\ > \max\{P(r,s), P(s,t)\}\ )\ ) \\ &\Rightarrow \text{The greedy algorithm constructs T,}\end{aligned} \tag{2}$$

where $C(a, b)$ and $P(a, b)$ are the cost and priority of edge $E(a, b)$ respectively, and a lower priority value $P(a, b)$ reflects a higher priority of edge $E(a, b)$ to be included in the tour.
The above description implies that the priority-based encoding can be used to search the global optimal solution. Two levels of priorities are sufficient to guarantee such an optimal solution. Formula (2) is also used in the Lamarckian feedback process of the *PB-GLS* model. We apply the *LK* heuristic (Lin & Kernighan, 1973) as the local search method in the following experiments.

3.4 Complexity analysis

It is well-known that an exhausted search for a TSP has an exponential time complexity. Suppose that n is the number of vertices. An exact solution takes $O(n!)$ time, which is prohibitively long. Therefore, polynomial-time heuristic search approaches are proposed. Heuristic or local search algorithms have complexities ranging from $O(n^2)$ (e.g., nearest neighbour, double ended nearest neighbour, and nearest insertion), $O(n^2 \log(n))$ (e.g., shortest edge first) to $O(n^{2.2})$ (e.g., LK) or higher order (e.g., k-opt).
The genetic algorithms with specialized crossover operators have time complexity $O(kmn^2)$, where k is the generation number and m is the population size. The n^2 factor is due to the fact that all the repair procedures need to scan all the possible pairs of the vertices which is $O(n^2)$. If we combine genetic algorithms with a local search algorithm, the latter affects the time complexity. For example, the genetic local search algorithm incorporating the DPX operator with the LK heuristic (Freisleben & Merz, 1996) has time complexity $O(kmn^{2.2})$. This model, referred to as DPX-LK model, is currently known as the most powerful model and will be compared with the PB-GLS model in the next section.
The time complexity of the PB-GLS model depends on the selected greedy algorithm, the Lamarckian feedback process, and the local search heuristic. When the DENN algorithm and LK heuristic are used, the PB-GLS needs $O(n^2)$ time to crossover the parent chromosomes and $O(n^2+n^{2.2}+n^2)$ time to construct the tour, search the local optimum, and feedback the upgraded gene information. Therefore, the total time complexity is also $O(kmn^{2.2})$.

4. Experimental results

In this section, we conduct three parts of experiments applying PB-GLS to solve the TSP. The first part used our own data to demonstrate how priority encoding is used and how it supports schema analysis. The second part used benchmark instances released by the TSPLIB *(http://www.iwr.uni-heidelberg.de/groups/comopt/software/tsplib9)* and proved that the PB-GLS model can find near-optimal solutions identical to the best known results, in cases where the number of cities was no more than *400*. In the last part, we generated sparsely connected maps from the TSPLIB data instance and compared the experimental results between the PB-GLS model and the currently most efficient DPX-LK hybrid searching model. The PB-GLS model in these experiments uses Holland's simple genetic algorithm model with the uniform crossover operator and conducts the LK heuristic for local searching every five generation. To reduce the searching space and simplify the result discussion, priority encoding in these experiments used only two-level priority, i.e., the high priority was 1 and the low priority was 2. The population size and mutation rate were set as *100* and *0.2* respectively.

city	coordinates		city	coordinates		city	coordinates		city	coordinates	
1	0.047	0.692	6	0.259	0.085	11	0.436	0.367	16	0.684	0.292
2	0.054	0.577	7	0.326	0.748	12	0.525	0.222	17	0.694	0.585
3	0.095	0.004	8	0.336	0.530	13	0.534	0.031	18	0.732	0.811
4	0.146	0.855	9	0.399	0.143	14	0.542	0.602	19	0.891	0.082
5	0.157	0.319	10	0.399	0.275	15	0.586	0.982	20	0.946	0.728

Table 1. Cities in the first part of experiments

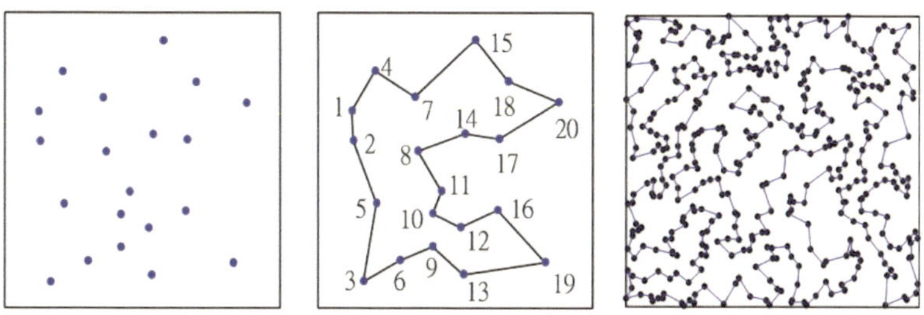

(a) (b) (c)

Figure 3. Experimental results of the TSP. (a) map of the cities of Table 1; (b) near-optimal solution of the above listed cities; (c) near-optimal solution of the rd400 data instance.

	cost	adjacency		p1	p2	p3	p4	T		cost	adjacency		p1	p2	p3	p4	T
1	0.100	10	11	1	1	1	1	Yes	41	0.295	16	19	1	2	1	1	Yes
2	0.115	1	2	1	1	1	1	Yes	42	0.299	5	9	2	2	2	1	-
3	0.132	9	10	2	2	2	2	-	43	0.299	6	12	2	2	1	2	-
4	0.137	10	12	1	1	1	1	Yes	44	0.301	13	16	1	2	1	1	-
5	0.149	9	12	2	2	2	2	-	45	0.320	3	5	1	1	1	1	Yes
6	0.151	6	9	1	1	1	1	Yes	46	0.321	2	7	2	2	2	1	-
7	0.152	14	17	1	1	1	1	Yes	47	0.322	9	16	1	2	2	1	-
8	0.170	11	12	2	2	2	2	-	48	0.331	1	8	2	2	2	2	-
9	0.174	12	16	1	1	1	1	Yes	49	0.333	6	11	2	2	1	2	-
10	0.176	9	13	1	1	1	1	Yes	50	0.334	3	9	1	1	1	2	-
11	0.183	3	6	1	1	1	2	Yes	51	0.337	11	17	1	2	1	1	-
12	0.190	8	11	1	1	1	1	Yes	52	0.340	14	16	1	2	2	1	-
13	0.191	1	4	1	1	1	1	Yes	53	0.350	7	15	1	1	1	1	Yes
14	0.191	12	13	2	1	1	2	-	54	0.351	11	13	1	1	1	2	-
15	0.209	4	7	1	1	1	1	Yes	55	0.357	10	14	2	1	1	2	-
16	0.218	8	14	1	1	1	1	Yes	56	0.361	8	12	2	1	1	1	-
17	0.218	7	8	2	1	1	2	-	57	0.361	13	19	1	1	1	1	Yes
18	0.225	15	18	1	1	1	1	Yes	58	0.361	8	17	2	1	2	2	-
19	0.228	9	11	1	1	2	2	-	59	0.376	4	8	2	1	2	1	-
20	0.230	17	18	2	2	2	2	-	60	0.380	12	14	2	2	2	1	-

Table 2. Searching results of the first part experiment (partially listed). The edges are sorted by their costs. Columns from *p1* to *p4* are the converged priorities on four distinct chromosomes.

Table 1 lists the locations of the cities in the first part of experiments. These cities were randomly generated in the *[0, 1] × [0, 1]* square. Figure 3(a) and (b) show the city map and the near-optimal solution respectively, found by both the DPX-LK hybrid model and the PB-GLS model within 100 generations. According to repeated experimental results, we believe that this tour with cost=*4.35* is very close to the optimal tour. Table 2 lists the searching results of gene values partially, and the edges by their costs in ascending order. Columns from *p1* to *p4* are four converged near-optimal chromosomes. All these chromosomes can develop the near-optimal TSP tour that is shown in Fig. 3(b). The final column denotes whether the edge under consideration is selected to be part of the tour.
Edges *E(3, 5), E(7, 15)* and *E(13, 19)* in the *45th, 53rd,* and *57th* rows are the longest three edges contained in the tour. We can observe that they all receive a high priority. They are likely the crucial edges in the optimal tour. Interestingly, the three edges excluded from the tour, i.e., *E(9, 10), E(9, 12)* and *E(11, 12),* are also remarkable because they are quite short and all receive a low priority. This result demonstrates that priority encoding allows schema explanation in searching optimal TSP tours. This schema is also likely to be useful when the number of cities increases or decreases.

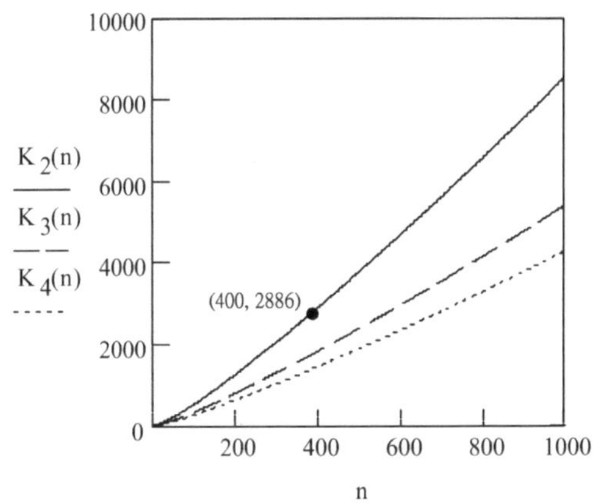

Fig 4. Assuming p priority levels are used for searching in a sparsely connected map with k edges and n cities, $K_p(n)=log_p(n!)$ represents the highest tolerable values of k to ensure the searching space of PB-GLS less than that of the DPX-LK model, i.e., $p^k < n!$.

	DPX-LK		Priority-based GLS	
#(Edges)	Generations	CPU time (sec)	Generations	CPU time (sec)
6000	268	11768	695	20949
5000	205	8933	389	11663
4000	144	6357	207	6195
3000	93	4102	74	2203
2000	35	1512	27	804

Table 3. Applying DPX-LK and PB-GLS models to find TSP tours in sparsely connected *rd400* maps

In the second part of experiments, we used the instances released on the TSPLIB website to test the PB-GLS method. Experimental results reveal that the PB-GLS can find near-optimal solutions in maps with no more than *400* cities, such as the *st70, ch150, a280* and *rd400* data instances. The solutions obtained are identical to the presently best known results. For example, Fig. 3(c) is the experimental result for the rd400 data instance with the tour cost equal to *15281*.

The time complexity of the PB-GLS model is described in the previous section as $O(kmn^{2.2})$, where k, m and n are respectively the generation number, population size and city size. The running time increases quickly as more cities are added. For the first part of experiments, the searching result converged within *100* generations and took less than *3* seconds running on Sun's Ultra SPARC III Workstation with 750-MHz clock rate. In case of *400* cities, it takes an average of *6216* generations and almost *3000*-minute CPU time before the evolution converges to the best known solution.

If we do not want to enlarge the population size and the generation number, it could be necessary that we prune the longest edges from the chromosomes to improve the performance for a large scale TSP. The pruning is reasonable because fully connected maps are eventually not usual in the real word. In the third part of experiments, we generated sparsely connected maps from *rd400* data instance. In addition to the *400* edges in the best-known optimal tour, another *1600, 2600, 3600, 4600,* and *5600* edges were randomly selected and added into the testing bed. We then conducted five experiments using these *2000, 3000, 4000, 5000* and *6000* edges as the test data respectively; these *400* nodes each had *10, 15, 20, 25* and *30* adjacent nodes in average. The PB-GLS model was compared with the DPX-LK hybrid model.

Assuming the p priority levels are used for testing a data instance with k edges and n nodes, the searching spaces of the PB-GLS model and the DPX-LK hybrid model are of sizes p^k and $n!$ respectively. The condition to let $p^k < n!$ can be derived as

$$p^k < n! \Leftrightarrow k < \log_p(n!) = \sum_{v=1}^{n}(\log_p v) \tag{3}$$

Figure 4 draws the right part of formula (3), denoted as function $K_p(n)$, with $n \in \{1,2,\ldots,1000\}$ and $p \in \{2,3,4\}$. Given p = *2* and n = *400*, k must be less than *2886* to ensure search space $p^k < n!$. However, the experimental results listed in Table 3 reveal that the PB-GLS model converged efficiently than the DPX-LK model even with k = *4000*. This result implies that using permutation based algorithms in search sparsely connected maps may suffer an overhead that does not occur when we use priority-based algorithms.

5. Conclusion

Genetic algorithms and genetic local search are population based general-purpose search algorithms that have been examined to search efficiently for the near-optimal solutions to certain combinatorial optimization problems, such as the constraint satisfaction problem (Marchiori & Steenbeek, 2000), flowshop scheduling problem (Arroyo & Armentano, 2005), constraint minimum spanning tree problem (dMST) (Zeng & Wang, 2003), and travelling salesman problem (TSP) (Freisleben & Merz, 1996). Notably, these optimization problems usually have critical requirements that have forced researchers to develop new genetic operators. For example, for the dMST we have an upper bound on the node degrees and for the TSP we require that each city be visited exactly once.

Previous results made use of specialized genetic operators to enhance the GA and GLS. Alternatively, we have presented another approach to the TSP using evolutionary computing algorithms, i.e., the priority-based encoding method in conjunction with greedy algorithms. This coding policy encodes link priorities as chromosomes, and then uses the underlying greedy algorithms to construct the corresponding solution as the phenotype. By doing so, traditional genetic algorithms can be exploited as usual.

Priority-based encoding supports not only broad applications but also schema analysis. In addition, the priority-based genetic local search is empirically tested to achieve remarkable searching results for the TSP by iteratively converging to crucial edges. According to experimental results, this model found near-optimal solutions to TSPLIB instances -- in cases where the number of cities is no more than 400, the results are identical to the best previously known results. Experimental results also reveal that the permutation-based algorithms using specialized GA operators have an overhead in searching sparsely connected maps. This overhead does not occur when we use priority-based algorithms, because it is not necessary to encode the disconnected links into the chromosome.

6. Acknowledgements

This work was supported in part by the Taiwan National Science Council under the Grants NSC95-2221-E-001-016-MY3 and NSC-95-2752-E-002-005-PAE.

7. References

Arroyo, J. & Armentano, V. (2005): *Genetic local search for multi-objective flowshop scheduling problems,* European Journal of Operational Research, Vol. 167, 717–738

Boukreev, K. (2007): *Genetic algorithms and the traveling salesman problem,* The Code Project Website, (http://www.codeproject.com/cpp/tspapp.asp)

Digalakis, J. & Margaritis, K. (2004): *Performance comparison of memetic algorithms,* Applied Mathematics and Computation, Vol. 158, 237–252

Dorigo, M. & Gambardella, L. M. (1997): *Ant colony system: A cooperative learning approach to the traveling salesman problem,* IEEE Transactions on Evolutionary Computation, Vol. 1, 53–66

Fiechter, C. N. (1994): *A parallel tabu search algorithm for large traveling salesman problems,* Discrete Applied Mathematics and Combinatorial Operations Research and Computer Science, Vol. 51, 243–267

Freisleben, B. & Merz, P. (1996a): A genetic local search algorithm for solving symmetric and asymmetric traveling salesman problems, *Proceedings of the 1996 IEEE International Conference on Evolutionary Computation,* pp. 616–621

Freisleben, B. & Merz, P. (1996b): New genetic local search operators for the traveling salesman problem, *Proceedings of the Fourth Conference on Parallel Problem Solving from Nature,*Vol. 1141, (1996) pp. 890–899, Springer, Berlin

Gambardella, L. M. & Dorigo, M.: Ant-Q (1995): A reinforcement learning approach to the traveling salesman problem, *Proceedings of International Conference on Machine Learning,* pp. 252–260

Goldberg, D. E. & Lingle, R. (1985): Alleles, loci, and the traveling salesman problem, *Proceedings of an International Conference on Genetic Algorithms and Their Applications,* pp. 154–159, Pittsburgh, PA

Goldberg, D. E. (1989): *Genetic Algorithms in Search, Optimization, and Machine Learning,* Addison-Wesley

Holland, J. H. (1975): *Adaptation in Nature and Artificial Systems,* The University of Michigan

Homaifar, A.; Guan, S. & Liepins, G. (1992): *Schema analysis of the traveling salesman problem using genetic algorithms,* Complex Systems, Vol. 6, 533-552

Homaifar, A. & Guan, S., Liepins, G. (1993): A new approach on the traveling salesman problem by the genetic algorithms, *Proceedings of the Fifth International Conference on Genetic Algorithms,* pp. 460-466, San Mateo, CA, Morgan Kaufman

Johnson, D. S. & McGeoch, L. A. (2002): Experimental analysis of heuristics for the STSP, In: Gutin, G. & Punnen, A. P. (Eds), *The Traveling Salesman Problem and Its Variations,* 369-443, Kluwer Academic Publishers, Dordrecht, Netherlands

Julstrom, B. A. (1995): Very greedy crossover in a genetic algorithm for the traveling salesman problem, *Proceedings of the 1995 ACM symposium on Applied computing,* pp. 324-328

Jung, S. & Moon, B.R. (2002): *Toward minimal restriction of genetic encoding and crossovers for the two-dimensional Euclidean TSP.* IEEE Transactions on Evolutionary Computation, Vol. 6, 557-565

Kirkpartrick, S.; Gelatt Jr., C. D.; Vecchi, M. P. (1983): *Optimization by simulated annealing,* Science, Vol. 220, 671-680

Larranaga, P.; Kuijpers, C. M. H.; Murga, R. H.; Inza, I. & Dizdarevic, S. (1999): *Genetic algorithms for the travelling salesman problems: A review of representations and operators,* Artificial Intelligence Review, Vol. 13, 129-170

Lin, S. & Kernighan, B. (1973): *An effective heuristic algorithm for the traveling salesman tours,* Operations Research, Vol. 21, 498-516

Man, K.; Tang, K. & Kwong, S. (1999): *Genetic Algorithms :Concepts and Designs,* Springer, London

Marchiori, E. & Steenbeek, A.(2000): *A genetic local search algorithm for random binary constraint satisfaction problems,* SAC Vol. 1, 458-462

Miglino, O.; Menczer, D. & Bovet, P. (1994): *A neuro-ethological approach for the TSP: Changing methaphors in connectionist models,* Journal of Biological Systems, Vol. 2, 357-366

Mohammadian, M.; Sarker, R. & Yao, X. (2002): *Evolutionary Optimization,* Kluwer Academic Publishers, Boston

Moscato, P. & Norman, M.G. (1992): A "memetic" approach for the traveling salesman problem implementation of a computational ecology for combinatorial optimization on message-passing systems, In: Valero, M.; Onate, E.; Jane, M.; Larriba, J. L.& Suarez, B. (Eds), *Parallel Computing and Transputer Applications,* 177-186, Amsterdam IOS Press

Naphade, K. S. & Tuzun, D. (1995): Initializing the Hopfield-tank network for the TSP using a convex hull: A computational study, *Proceedings of the Artificial Neural Networks in Engineering conference,* Vol. 5, pp. 399-404, St. Louis

Pham, D. T. & Karaboga, D. (2000): *Intelligent Optimization Techniques: Genetic Algorithms,Tabu Search, Simulated Annealing and Neural Networks,* Springer, London

Rego, C. & Glover, F. (2002): Local search and metaheuristics, In: Gutin, G. & Punnen, A. P. (Eds.), *The Traveling Salesman Problem and Its Variations,* 309-368, Kluwer Academic Publishers, Dordrecht, Netherlands

Wei, J. D. & Lee, D. T. (2004): A new approach to the traveling salesman problem using genetic algorithms with priority encoding, *Proceedings of the 2004 IEEE Congress on Evolutionary Computation,* pp. 1457-1464

Wei, J. D. & Lee, D. T. (2006): *Priority-based genetic local search and it's application to the traveling salesman problem,* Lecture Notes in Computer Science, No. 4274, 424–432

Whitley, D.; Starkweather, T. & Fuquay, D. (1989): Scheduling problems and traveling salesman: the genetic edge recombination, *Proceedings of the third international conference on Genetic algorithms,* pp. 133–140

Whitley, D.; Starkweather, T. & Shaner, D. (1991): The traveling salesman and sequence scheduling: Quality solutions using genetic edge recombination; In: Davis, L. (Ed.), *Handbook of Genetic Algorithms,* 350–372, Van Nstrand Reinhold, New York

Zachariasen, M. & Dam, M. (1995): Tabu search on the geometric traveling salesman problem, *Proceedings of Metaheuristics International Conference,* pp. 571–587, Colorado

Zeng, Y. & Wang, Y. P. (2003): A new genetic algorithm with local search method for degree-constrained minimum spanning tree problem, *Proceedings of the Fifth International Conference on Computational Intelligence and Multimedia Applications,* pp. 218–222

4

Particle Swarm Optimization Algorithm for the Traveling Salesman Problem

Elizabeth F. G. Goldbarg, Marco C. Goldbarg and Givanaldo R. de Souza
Universidade Federal do Rio Grande do Norte
Brazil

1. Introduction

Particle swarm optimization, PSO, is an evolutionary computation technique inspired in the behavior of bird flocks. PSO algorithms were first introduced by Kennedy & Eberhart (1995) for optimizing continuous nonlinear functions. The fundamentals of this metaheuristic approach rely on researches where the movements of social creatures were simulated by computers (Reeves, 1983; Reynolds, 1987; Heppner & Grenander, 1990). The research in PSO algorithms has significantly grown in the last few years and a number of successful applications concerning single and multi-objective optimization have been presented (Kennedy& Eberhart, 2001; Coello et al., 2004). This popularity is partially due to the fact that in the canonical PSO algorithm only a small number of parameters have to be tuned and also due to the easiness of implementation of the algorithms based on this technique. Motivated by the success of PSO algorithms with continuous problems, researchers that deal with discrete optimization problems have investigated ways to adapt the original proposal to the discrete case. In many of those researches, the new approaches are illustrated with the Traveling Salesman Problem, TSP, once it has been an important test ground for most algorithmic ideas.

Given a graph $G = (N,E)$, where $N = \{1,...,n\}$ and $E = \{1,...,m\}$, and costs, c_{ij}, associated with each edge linking vertices i and j, the TSP consists in finding the minimal total length Hamiltonian cycle of G. The length is calculated by the summation of the costs of the edges in the considered cycle. If for all pairs of nodes {i,j}, the costs c_{ij} and c_{ji} are equal then the problem is said to be symmetric, otherwise it is said to be asymmetric. The main importance of TSP regarding applicability is due to its variations, nevertheless some applications of the basic problem in real world problems are reported for different areas such as VLSI chip fabrication, X-ray crystallography, genome map and broadcast schedule, among others.

Although, a great research effort has been done to accomplish the task of adapting PSO to discrete problems, many approaches still obtain results very far from the best results known for the TSP. Some of those works are summarized in section 2.

An effective PSO approach for the TSP is presented by Goldbarg et al. (2006a), where distinct types of velocity operators are considered, each of them concerning one movement the particles are allowed to do. This proposal is presented and extended in this chapter, where search strategies for Combinatorial Optimization problems are associated with the velocity operators. Rather than a metaheuristic technique, the PSO approach in this context can be thought as a framework for heuristics hybridization. The extension of the approach proposed previously comprehends methods to combine the distinct velocity operators. Computational experiments with a large set of benchmark instances show that the proposed algorithms produce high quality solutions when compared with effective heuristics for the TSP.

The chapter begins with a brief review of Particle Swarm Optimization. Some proposals for applying this metaheuristic technique to discrete optimization problems and, in particular, to the Traveling Salesman Problem are presented in section 2. In section 3, our proposal for velocity operators in the discrete context is presented. Computational experiments compare the results of the proposed approach with other PSO heuristics presented previously for the TSP. In section 4, the combination of velocity operators is investigated. Conclusions and directions for future works are presented in sections 5 and 6, respectively.

2. Particle swarm optimization

Kennedy & Eberhart (1995) proposed the bio-inspired PSO approach, which can be seen as a population-based algorithm that performs a parallel search on a space of solutions. In the optimization context, several solutions of a given problem constitute a population (the swarm). Each solution is seen as a social organism, also called particle. The method attempts to imitate the behavior of real creatures making the particles "fly" over a solution space. These particles search the problem's solution space balancing the intensification and the diversification efforts. Each particle has a value associated with it. In general, particles are evaluated with the objective function of the considered optimization problem. A velocity is also assigned to each particle in order to direct the "flight" through the problem's solution space. The artificial creatures have a tendency to follow the best ones among them. At each iteration step, a new velocity value is calculated for each particle. This velocity value is used to update the particle's position. The process iterates until reaching a stopping condition.

In the classical PSO algorithm, each particle

- has a position and a velocity
- knows its own position and the value associated with it
- knows the best position it has ever achieved, and the value associated with it
- knows its neighbors, their best positions and their values

The best position a given particle has ever achieved is called *pbest*. In some versions of particle swarm algorithms the particles also track the best position achieved so far by any particle of the swarm. This position is called *gbest*. By changing their velocities with individualistic moves or toward *pbest* and *gbest*, the particles change their positions. The move of a particle is a composite of three possible choices (Onwubolu & Clerc, 2004):

- To follow its own way
- To go back to its best previous position
- To go towards its best neighbor's previous or present position

The neighborhood may be physical or social. Physical neighborhoods take distances into account, thus a distance metric has to be established. This approach tends to be time consuming, since each iteration distances must be computed. In general, social neighborhoods are based upon "relationships" defined at the very beginning of the algorithm.

A general framework of a particle swarm optimization algorithm is presented in figure 1. Initially, a population of particles is generated. After, all particles are evaluated and, if necessary, $pbest_p$ is replaced by x_p, p's position. The best position achieved so far by any of the p's neighbors is set to $gbest_p$. Finally, the velocities and positions of each particle are updated. The procedure *compute_velocity( )* receives three inputs. This is done to show that, in general, p's position, x_p, $pbest_p$ and $gbest_p$ are used to update p's velocity, v_p. The process is repeated until some stopping condition is satisfied.

```
procedure PSO
   Initialize a population of particles
   do
       for each particle p with position x_p do
           if (x_p is better than pbest_p) then
              pbest_p ← x_p
           end_if
       end_for
       Define gbest_p as the best position found so far by any of p's neighbors
       for each particle p do
          v_p ← Compute_velocity(x_p, pbest_p, gbest_p)
          x_p ← update_ position(x_p, v_p)
       end_for
   while (a stop criterion is not satisfied)
```

Fig. 1. Framework of a particle swarm optimization algorithm

Kennedy & Eberhart (1995) suggest equations (1) and (2) to update the particle's velocity and position, respectively. In these equations, $x_p(t)$ and $v_p(t)$ are the particle's position and velocity at instant t, $pbest_p(t)$ is the best position the particle achieved up to instant t, $gbest_p(t)$ is the best position that any of p's neighbors has achieved up to instant t, c_1 is a cognitive coefficient that quantifies how much the particle trusts its experience, c_2 is a social coefficient that quantifies how much the particle trusts its best neighbor, $rand_1$ and $rand_2$ are random numbers.

$$v_p(t) = v_p(t\text{-}1) + c_1.rand_1.(pbest_p(t\text{-}1) - x_p(t\text{-}1)) + c_2.rand_2.(gbest_p(t\text{-}1) - x_p(t\text{-}1)) \quad (1)$$

$$x_p(t) = x_p(t\text{-}1) + v_p(t) \quad (2)$$

An inertia factor is introduced in equation (1) by Shi & Eberhart (1998). Considering the inertia factor w, equation (3) replaces equation (1). The inertia factor multiplies the velocity of the previous iteration. It is decreased throughout the algorithm execution. The inertia factor creates a tendency for the particle to continue moving in the same direction it was going previously. The motivation for the use of the inertia factor was to be able to better control intensification and diversification. Shi & Eberhart (1998) observed that suitable values for the inertia factor yielded a good trade-off between exploration and exploitation.

$$v_p(t) = wv_p(t\text{-}1) + c_1.rand_1.(pbest_p(t\text{-}1) - x_p(t\text{-}1)) + c_2.rand_2.(gbest_p(t\text{-}1) - x_p(t\text{-}1)) \quad (3)$$

Constriction factors were introduced by Clerc (1999) who observed that the use of a constriction factor was necessary to insure the convergence of the PSO algorithm. A simple way to incorporate a constriction factor in PSO algorithms is to replace equation (1) by equations (4) and (5), where K is the constriction factor. In equation (5), c_1 and c_2 are usually set to 1.49445 (Eberhart & Shi, 2001).

$$v_p(t) = K[v_p(t\text{-}1) + c_1.rand_1.(pbest_p(t\text{-}1) - x_p(t\text{-}1)) + c_2.rand_2.(gbest_p(t\text{-}1) - x_p(t\text{-}1))] \quad (4)$$

$$K = \frac{2}{2-\alpha-\sqrt{\alpha^2-4\alpha}}, \quad \alpha = c_1 + c_2, \quad \alpha > 4 \quad (5)$$

The canonical PSO algorithm, however, needs an adaptation in order to be applied to discrete optimization problems. Kennedy & Eberhart (1997) propose a discrete binary PSO version, defining particles' trajectories and velocities in terms of changes of probabilities that a bit is set to 0 or 1 (Shi et al., 2007). The particles move in a state space restricted to 0 and 1 with a certain probability that is a function of individual and social factors. The probability of $x_p(t) = 1$, $Pr(x_p = 1)$, is a function of $x_p(t\text{-}1)$, $v_p(t\text{-}1)$, $pbest_p(t\text{-}1)$ and $gbest_p(t\text{-}1)$. The probability of $x_p(t) = 0$ equals 1 - $Pr(x_p = 1)$. Thus equation (2) is replaced by equation (6), where $rand_3$ is a random number, $\psi(v_p(t))$ is a logistic transformation which can constrain $v_p(t)$ to the interval [0,1] and can be considered as a probability.

$$x_p(t) = \begin{cases} 1, \ if \ rand_3 < \psi(v_p(t)) \\ 0, \ otherwise \end{cases} \quad (6)$$

PSO for permutation problems is investigated by several researchers. In several of these research works the TSP is the target problem.

Hu et al. (2003) define velocity as a vector of probabilities in which each element corresponds to the probability of exchanging two elements of the permutation vector that represents a given particle position. Pairwise exchanging operations, also called 2-swap or 2-exchange, are very popular neighborhoods in local search algorithms for permutation problems. Let V be the velocity of a particle whose position is given by the permutation vector P. Given integers i and j, $V[i]$ is the probability of elements $P[i]$ and $P[j]$ be exchanged. The element $P[j]$ corresponds to $P_{nbest}[i]$, where P_{nbest} is the vector that represents the permutation associated with the position of the best neighbor of the considered particle. The authors introduce a *mutation* operator in order to avoid premature convergence of their algorithm. The mutation operator does a 2-swap move with two elements chosen at random in the considered permutation vector.

Another approach is proposed by Clerc (2004) that utilizes the Traveling Salesman Problem to illustrate the PSO concepts for discrete optimization problems. In the following we list the basic ingredients Clerc (2004) states that are necessary to construct a PSO algorithm for discrete optimization problems:

- a search space, $S = \{s_i\}$
- an objective function f on S, such that $f(s_i) = c_i$
- a semi-order on $C = \{c_i\}$, such that for every $c_i, c_j \in C$, we can establish whether $c_i \geq c_j$ or $c_j \geq c_i$
- a distance d in the search space, in case we want to consider physical neighborhoods.

S may be a finite set of states and f a discrete function, and, if it is possible to define particles' positions, velocity and ways to move a particle from one position to another, it is possible to use PSO. Clerc (2004) presents also some operations with position and velocity such as: the opposite of a velocity, the addition of position and velocity (move), the subtraction of two positions, the addition and subtraction of two velocities and the multiplication of velocity by a constant. A distance is also defined to be utilized with physical neighborhoods. To illustrate his ideas about tackling discrete optimization problems with PSO, Clerc (2004) develops several algorithm variants with those operations and methods and applies them to the asymmetric TSP instance br17.atsp. In his algorithm the positions are defined as TSP tours represented in vectors of permutations of the $|N|$ vertices of the graph correspondent to the considered instance. These vertices are also referred as cities, and the position of a particle is represented by a sequence (n_1, ..., $n_{|N|}$, $n_{|N|+1}$), $n_1 = n_{|N|+1}$. The value assigned to each particle is calculated with the TSP objective function, thus corresponding to the tour length. The velocity is defined as a list of pairs (i,j), where i and j are the indices of the elements of the permutation vector that will be exchanged. This approach was applied to tackle the real problem of finding out the best path for drilling operations (Onwubolu & Clerc, 2004) .

Wang et al. (2003) present a PSO algorithm for the TSP utilizing, basically, the same structure proposed by Clerc (2004) and apply their algorithm to the benchmark instance burma14.

Hendtlass (2003) proposes the inclusion of a memory for the particles in order to improve diversity. The memory of each particle is a list of solutions (target points) that can be used as an alternative for the current local optimal point. There is a probability of choosing one of the points of the particle's memory instead of the current $gbest_p$. The size of the memory list and the probability are new parameters added to the standard PSO algorithm. The algorithm is applied to the benchmark TSP instance burma14. The results obtained with algorithmic versions with several parameter settings are compared with the results of an Ant Colony Optimization algorithm. The author shows that his algorithm outperformed the PSO version without the use of memory and presented quality of solution comparable to the results produced by the ACO algorithm, for instance burma14.

Pang et al. (2004a) extend the work of Wang et al. (2003). Their algorithm alternates among the continuous and the discrete (permutation) space. $|N|$-dimensional vectors in the continuous Cartesian space are used for positions and velocities. The discrete representation of the particles' positions is done in the permutation space. They present methods to transform the positions from one space to the other. They alternate between the two spaces until a stopping condition is reached. The particle's position and velocity are updated in the continuous space. Then, they move to the discrete space, where a local search procedure is applied to all particles' positions. Two local search procedures are tested in their algorithms: the 2-swap and the 2-opt (Flood, 1956). After that, they make the reverse transformation to the continuous space. In order to avoid premature convergence, Pang et al. (2004a) use a chaotic operator. This operator changes randomly the position and velocity in the continuous space, multiplying these vectors by a random number. Four versions of their algorithm are applied to four benchmark instances with 14 to 51 cities: burma14, eil51, eil76 and berlin52. The algorithm variations comprise the presence or not of chaotic variables and the two local search procedures. In the set of instances tested, the results showed that the version that includes chaotic variables and the 2-opt local search presented the best results.

Pang et al. (2004b) present a fuzzy-based PSO algorithm for the TSP. The position of each particle is a matrix $P = [p_{ij}]$, where $p_{ij} \in (0,1)$ represents the degree of membership of the i-th city to the j-th position of a given tour. The velocity is also defined as a matrix and the operations resulting from equations (2) and (3) are defined accordingly. A method to decode the matrix position to a tour solution is presented. The value associated with each particle is the length of the tour represented by the particle's position. They apply their algorithm to instances burma14 and berlin52. No average results or comparisons with other algorithms are reported.

A hybrid approach that joins PSO, Genetic Algorithms and Fast Local Search is presented by Machado & Lopes (2005) for the TSP. The positions of the particles represent TSP tours as permutations of $|N|$ cities. The value assigned to each particle (fitness) is the rate between a constant D_{min} and the cost of the tour represented in the particle's position. If the optimal solution is known, then D_{min} equals the optimal tour cost. If the optimum is not known, D_{min} is set to 1. Velocity is defined regarding only $pbest_p$ and $gbest_p$ and the equation of velocity is reduced to equation (7). The distance between two positions is calculated with a version of the Hamming distance for permutations. With the use of equation (7) for velocity, the particles tend to converge to $pbest_p$ and $gbest_p$. At each iteration step, the average distance between all particles and the best global solution is computed. If this distance is lower than $0.05|N|$, then random positions are generated for all particles. The same occurs when some subset of particles is close enough. If a subset of particles is close enough to the best local solution, then the positions of the particles of the considered subset are generated randomly. The solutions are recombined by means of the OX operator and then submitted to the fast local search procedure introduced by Voudouris & Tsang (1999). The hybrid PSO is applied to the following symmetric TSP benchmark instances: pr76, rat195, pr299, pr439, d657, pr1002, d1291, rl1304, d2103.

$$v_p(t) = c_1.rand_1.(pbest_p(t\text{-}1) - x_p(t\text{-}1)) + c_2.rand_2.(gbest_p(t\text{-}1) - x_p(t\text{-}1)) \quad (7)$$

Goldbarg et al. (2006a) present a PSO algorithm for the TSP where the idea of distinct velocity operators is introduced. The velocity operators are defined according to the possible movements a particle is allowed to do. In the previous section, three alternatives for movements are identified. The three alternatives can be divided into two categories: independent and dependent moves. The independent move concerns the first parcel of equations (1) and (3). The other two parcels of those equations depend on $pbest_p$ and $gbest_p$, thus referring to dependent moves. Based on those movement classes, Goldbarg et al. (2006a) use local search procedures as velocity operators for independent moves and path-relinking (Glover et al., 2000) for dependent moves. At each iteration step, one of the three alternative moves is assigned to a particle and the correspondent velocity operator is applied in order to modify the particles position. For each particle, only one type of movement is allowed per iteration. A probability is assigned to each movement alternative. Initially, independent moves are more likely to occur than dependent moves. During the algorithm execution, the probabilities are modified, such that the probabilities assigned to the dependent moves are increased and the probability assigned to independent moves is decreased. This algorithmic proposal obtained very promising results. It was applied to 35 benchmark TSP instances with 51 to 7397 cities. The results were comparable to the results of state-of-the-art algorithms for the TSP. A detailed discussion of this approach and the results it obtained is presented in section 3.

Yuan et al. (2007) and Shi et al. (2007) propose extensions for the approach presented by Wang et al. (2003). Both algorithms define subtraction in terms of sequences of 2-swap operations as defined in the path-relinking velocity operator presented by Goldbarg et al. (2006a), including some uncertainty for the exchange of two elements.

Yuan et al. (2007) propose new concepts for "chaos variables" and memory for particles. The memory of each particle is an $|N|$-dimensional vector of chaos variables. The chaos variables are numbers in the interval (0,1) and are generated with a method proposed by the authors. Based on the memory list of a particle p, they define the permutation that represents p's position. They sort the elements of the memory list. The resulting order leads to a permutation of the elements in the memory list. This permutation is the representation of p's position. They apply their algorithm to four benchmark instances with 14 to 51 cities: burma14, oliver30, att48, eil51. The results obtained for instances oliver30 and att48 are compared with the results obtained by algorithms based on: Simulated Annealing, Genetic Algorithm and Ant Colony Systems. Their algorithm outperforms the others regarding quality of solution of these two instances.

Shi et al. (2007) adds to their algorithm a procedure that aims at eliminating edge crossings in the TSP tours represented by the particles' positions. They apply their algorithm to five benchmark instances: eil51, berlin52, st70, eil76 and pr70.

Zhong et al. (2007) present a PSO approach where a mutation factor (c_3) is introduced in the formula that updates the particle's position (equation (2)). The new formula is presented in equation (8). The factor introduces some diversity in the algorithm. The position of a particle is represented as a set of edges instead of a permutation as in the previous approaches. The velocity is defined as a list of edges with a probability associated with each element of the list. During the iterations if $pbest_p$ is identical to $gbest_p$ then, $pbest_p$ is not replaced by the current position of p. The authors apply their algorithm to six benchmark TSP instances: burma14, eil51, eil76, berlin52, kroA100 and kroA200. The results are compared with the results of Pang et al. (2004a) and with an Ant Colony Optimization algorithm. They show that their algorithm outperforms the others regarding average solutions.

$$x_p(t) = c_3.rand.x_p(t\text{-}1) + v_p(t) \tag{8}$$

Fang et al. (2007) present a PSO algorithm for the TSP where an annealing scheme is used to accept the movement of a particle. They apply their algorithm to instances oliver30 and att48. The results are compared with the results of algorithms based on: Simulated Annealing, Genetic Algorithms and Ant Colony. In the two instances tested, their algorithm presents the best average results.

A comparison among some of the previous algorithms and the approach proposed in this chapter is presented in the next section.

3. New velocity operators for discrete PSO

In PSO algorithms the velocity is the basic mechanism for accomplishing the search in the space of solutions of optimization problems. In most applications, the particles' positions represent the solutions of the investigated problem. The positions are updated by means of velocity operators that direct the search to promising regions of the space of solutions. There are two classes of movement a particle is allowed to do: independent and dependent moves. Independent moves are those in which the particle moves without knowing any other positions besides its own on the current instant. This type of movement depends only on the current particle position and on a velocity operator. The other case arises when the particle needs to know the position of *pbest* or *gbest*. This distinction between the movements leads us to a unary and a binary concept for velocity operators. In the unary operations only one particle is accepted as input. The particle's position is transformed according to a unary velocity operator. The binary operations accept two particles and alter the position of one of them considering the position of the other. In this context, m-ary operations can be defined where m particles are accepted and the position of one of them is altered considering the positions of the remaining m-1 particles, in accordance with an m-ary velocity operator.

In order to modify the position of a given particle, the velocity operators are identified with heuristic methods. Basically, two approaches are utilized for designing the search strategies: the improvement methods and the metaheuristic techniques. As defined by Burkard (2002), the local search algorithms constitute the class of improvement methods. Given a neighborhood structure defined over a search space, a local search procedure begins with a solution and search the neighborhood of the current solution for an improvement. The metaheuristics are general frameworks for heuristics design. A review of the TSP and some well known methods utilized to solve it are presented by Gutin & Punnen (2002).

In this chapter, any search strategy where a given solution is transformed with no knowledge of other solutions is a unary velocity operator. Search strategies where a solution interacts with other m-1 solutions are classified as m-ary velocity operators. For example, local search and mutation are defined as unary velocity operators, recombination of two solutions, such as crossover in Genetic Algorithms, and path-relinking are defined as binary velocity operators and recombination operations among m solutions, such as in Scatter Search algorithms (Glover et al., 2000), are defined as m-ary velocity operators.

The proposed approach is illustrated with unary and binary velocity operators utilizing local search and path-relinking strategies, respectively.

Path-relinking is an intensification technique which ideas were originally proposed by Glover (1963) in the context of methods to obtain improved local decision rules for job shop scheduling problems (Glover et al., 2000). The strategy consists in generating a path between two solutions creating new intermediary solutions. This idea is very close to the movement of a particle from one position to another. Given an origin solution, x_1, and a target solution, x_2, a path from x_1 to x_2 leads to a sequence x_1, x_1 (1), x_1 (2), …, x_1 (r) = x_2, where $x_1(i+1)$ is obtained from $x_1(i)$ by a move that introduces in $x_1(i+1)$ an attribute that reduces the distance between attributes of the origin and target solutions.

The framework of PSO for discrete optimization problems proposed by Goldbarg et al. (2006a, 2006b) is shown in figure 2. In this proposal equation (3) is replaced by equation (9), where v_1 is a unary velocity operator, v_2 and v_3 are binary velocity operators. The coefficients c_0, c_1 and c_2 have the same meaning stated previously and the signal $\oplus$ represents a composition.

$$v_p(t) = c_0 v_1(x_p(t\text{-}1)) \oplus c_1 v_2(pbest_p(t\text{-}1), x_p(t\text{-}1)) \oplus c_2 v_3(gbest_p(t\text{-}1), x_p(t\text{-}1)) \quad (9)$$

In initial applications of the proposed approach, only one of the three primitive moves is associated to each particle of the swarm at each iteration step (Goldbarg et al., 2006a, 2006b). Thus, $c_0, c_1, c_2 \in \{0,1\}$ and $c_0 + c_1 + c_2 = 1$ in equation (9). The assignment is done randomly. Initial probabilities are associated with each possible move and, during the execution, these probabilities are updated. Initially, a high value is set to pr_1, the probability of particle p to follow its own way, a lower value is set to pr_2, the probability of particle p goes towards $pbest_p$ and the lowest value is associated with the third option, to go towards $gbest_p$. The algorithm utilizes the concept of social neighborhood and the $gbest_p$ of all particles is associated with the best current solution, $gbest$. The initial values set to pr_1, pr_2 and pr_3 are 0.9, 0.05 and 0.05, respectively. As the algorithm runs, pr_1 is decreased and the other probabilities are increased. At the final iterations, the highest value is associated with the option of going towards $gbest$ and the lowest probability is associated with the first move option.

```
procedure Discrete_PSO
   /* Define initial probabilities for particles' moves:*/
   pr1 ← a1 /*to follow its own way*/
   pr2 ← a2 /*to go towards pbest*/
   pr3 ← a3 /*to go towards gbest*/
   /* a1+ a2+ a3=1 */
   Initialize the population of particles
   do
     for each particle p
         value_p ← Evaluate(x_p)
         if (value(x_p) < value(pbest_p)) then
            pbest_p ← x_p
         if (value(x_p) < value(gbest) ) then
            gbest ← x_p
     end_for
     for each particle p
        velocity_p ← define_velocity(pr1, pr2, pr3)
        x_p ← update(x_p,velocity_p)
     end_for
     /* Update probabilities*/
     pr1 = pr1×0.95; pr2 = pr2×1.01; pr3 = 1-( pr1+ pr2)
   while (a stop criterion is not satisfied)
```

Fig. 2. Pseudo-code of PSO for discrete optimization problems

In the application to the TSP, Goldbarg et al. (2006a) implement two versions of the PSO algorithm defined by two local search procedures utilized to implement v_1. In the first version a local search procedure based on an inversion neighborhood is used. The Lin-Kernighan (Lin & Kernighan, 1973) neighborhood is used in the second version. In both versions v_2 and v_3 are implemented with the same path-relinking procedure. The particles' positions are represented as permutations of the $|N|$ cities.

In the inversion neighborhood, given a sequence $x_1 = (n_1, \ldots, n_i, n_{i+1}, \ldots, n_{j-1}, n_j, \ldots, n_{|N|})$ and two indices i and j, the sequence x_2 is x_1's neighbor if $x_2 = (n_1, \ldots, n_j, n_{j-1}, \ldots, n_{i+1}, n_i, \ldots, n_{|N|})$. The difference between indices i and j varies from 1 to $|N|$-1. When v_1 is applied to a particle p, the local search procedure starts inverting sequences of two elements in p's position, then sequences of three elements are inverted, and so on.

The Lin-Kernighan neighborhood is a recognized efficient improvement method for the TSP. The basic LK algorithm has a number of decisions to be made and depending on the strategies adopted by programmers distinct implementations of this algorithm may result on different performances. The literature contains reports of many LK implementations with widely varying behavior (Johnson & McGeoch, 2002). The work of Goldbarg et al. (2006a) uses the LK implementation of Applegate et al. (1999).

The path-relinking implemented for the binary velocity operators exchanges adjacent elements of the origin solution. The permutations are considered as circular lists. At first, the origin solution is rotated until its first element be equal the first element of the target solution. Then the second element of the target solution is considered. The correspondent element in the origin solution is shifted left until reaching the second position in the sequence that represents the solution. The process continues until the origin solution reaches the target solution. This procedure leads to time complexity $O(n^2)$. The path-relinking is applied simultaneously from the origin to the target solution and vice-versa (back and forward). Swap-left and swap-right operations are used. The permutation sequence representing the best solution found replaces the position of the considered particle. An example of the path-relinking procedure is shown in figure 3.

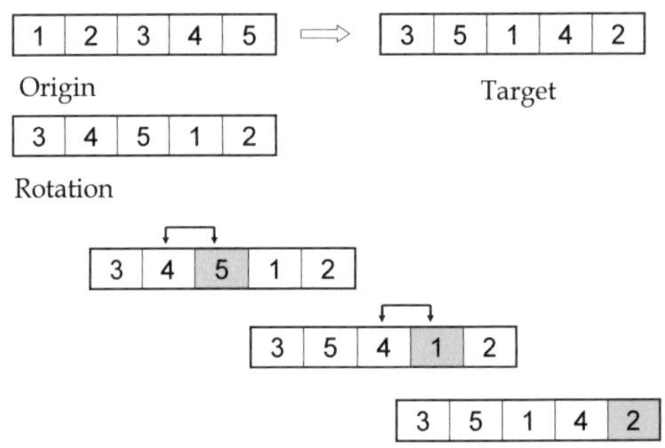

Fig. 3. Path-relinking

In the following, a discussion about the results obtained by PSO proposals for the TSP is presented. PSO-INV and PSO-LK denote the two algorithmic versions of the proposed approach with the inversion and the LK neighborhoods, respectively. These algorithms run on a Pentium IV with 3.0 GHz, 1 Gb using Linux. The maximum processing times are 60 seconds for instances with $|N| < 1000$ and 300 seconds for instances with $1000 \leq |N| < 5000$. Other three stop criteria are used: to find the optimal solution, to reach a maximum number of iterations (200) or to reach a maximum number of iterations with no improvement of the best current solution (20). The population has 20 particles. Once most papers report results for instance eil51, berlin52 and eil76, table 1 shows a comparison between the proposed approach and other PSO algorithms concerning these instances. The compared algorithms are listed in the first column of table 1. The traced lines represent results not reported in the correspondent work. Results in table 1 are given in terms of the percent difference from the optimal solution (*gap*), calculated with equation (10), where *av* and *optimal* denote, respectively, the average solution found by the investigated algorithm and the best solution known for the correspondent instance.

$$gap = \frac{av - optimal}{optimal} \times 100 \tag{10}$$

Only Pang et al. (2004) and Zhong et al. (2007) report average processing times. Pang et al. (2004) use a Pentium IV with 2 GHz, 256 Mb running Windows 2000. Zhong et al. (2007) use a Celeron with 2.26 GHz, 256 Mb, running Windows XP. Running time comparisons are, in general, difficult to make, even when the codes are developed in the same machines and the same compiler options are used. A re-implementation of those algorithms could introduce errors and the results obtained with the new implementations could produce results that differ largely from the published ones. The proposed algorithm was executed in a platform superior than the other algorithms of table 1. Nevertheless, even if the processing times of the other algorithms were divided by a factor of 3 (an estimate that favors those algorithms), table 1 shows that the two versions of the proposed algorithm exhibit processing times significantly lower than the others.

Instance	Algorithm	Min	Average	T(s)
eil51	Pang et al. (2004a)	---	3.498	30
	Shi et al. (2007)	0.235	2.575	---
	Zhang et al. (2007)	---	2.529	---
	Zhong et al. (2007)	0.235	1.793	4.06
	PSO-INV	0.704	2.582	0.16
	PSO-LK	0	0	< 0.01
berlin52	Pang et al. (2004a)	---	2.151	120
	Shi et al. (2007)	0	3.846	---
	Zhong et al. (2007)	0	0.753	4.12
	PSO-INV	0	2.592	0.17
	PSO-LK	0	0	< 0.01
eil76	Pang et al. (2004a)	---	4.222	60
	Shi et al. (2007)	1.487	4.167	---
	Zhong et al. (2007)	0.372	2.550	11.59
	PSO-INV	2.416	4.656	0.40
	PSO-LK	0	0	0.01

Table 1. Results of distinct PSO approaches

Although the inversion neighborhood is not specialized for the TSP, table 1 shows that PSO-INV exhibits better average results than the algorithms of Pang et al. (2004) and Shi et al. (2007) for instances eil51 and berlin52, respectively. Concerning the group of tested instances PSO-INV presents results that are comparable with the results presented by Pang et al. (2004a), Zhang et al. (2007) and Shi et al. (2007). Except for the PSO-LK, the algorithm presented by Zhong et al. (2007) outperforms the others regarding quality of solution. A comparison between the results obtained for instances with more than 50 cities by the PSO-LK and the algorithm presented by Zhong et al. (2007) is shown in table 2. The proposed algorithm outperforms the algorithm of Zhong et al. (2007) regarding quality of solution and processing times in the five tested instances.

Instance	Zhong et al. (2007)			PSO-LK		
	Min	Average	T(s)	Min	Average	T(s)
eil51	0.002	1.793	4.06	0	0	0
berlin52	0	0.753	4.12	0	0	0
eil76	0.004	2.550	11.59	0	0	0.01
kroA100	0.001	1.914	23.95	0	0	0.02
kroA200	0.007	3.427	198.55	0	0	0.08

Table 2. Comparison between PSO-LK and the algorithm of Zhong et al (2007)

PSO-INV performs poorly when compared with PSO-LK. Table 3 presents a comparison, in terms of percent deviation from the optimal solution, between the best and average results found by these two algorithms for 8 instances with 195 to 2103 cities. Table 3 shows that the PSO-LK outperforms PSO-INV with a significant difference among the results reported. This is not a surprise, since the local search procedure embedded in the former version is more powerful than the local search procedure of the latter.

Among the PSO approaches for the TSP, the hybrid algorithm presented by Machado & Lopes (2005) presents results for the largest instances. A comparison between the quality of solutions obtained by this algorithm (M&L) and the PSO-LK is shown in table 4, where is shown that the proposed approach outperforms the algorithm of Machado & Lopes (2005) in all tested instances. The average differences from the optimal solution obtained by Machado & Lopes (2005) and the PSO-LK regarding the tested instances are, respectively, 3.832 and 0.005.

Instances	PSO-INV		PSO-LK	
	Min	Av	Min	Av
rat195	5.8114	8.7581	0	0
pr299	5.8476	7.9952	0	0
pr439	4.4200	8.0111	0	0
d657	6.9656	9.6157	0	0
pr1002	9.8574	11.1900	0	0
d1291	13.2104	15.5505	0	0.0113
rl1304	10.4432	11.9942	0	0
d2103	16.7383	18.4180	0.0087	0.0267

Table 3. Quality of solutions obtained by the two versions of the proposed algorithm

Instance	M & L	PSO-LK
rat195	0.983	0
pr299	0.590	0
pr439	2.956	0
d657	3.849	0
pr1002	6.699	0
d1291	4.581	0.0113
rl1304	3.245	0
d2103	7.749	0.0267

Table 4. Quality of solutions obtained by Machado & Lopes (2005) and PSO-LK

Although the LK is a powerful neighborhood for the TSP, the good performance exhibited by the PSO-LK is not only due to the use of this neighborhood. The differences between the results obtained by the LK procedure and the PSO-LK algorithm are shown in table 4. This experiment aimed at finding out if the proposed PSO approach was able to improve the LK results. Table 5 shows the results for 30 symmetric instances. The cells with dark background show the results where an improvement with the PSO approach is obtained. Twenty independent runs of each algorithm were performed. Table 5 shows that all average solutions are improved. A statistical analysis shows that, in average, improvements of 88% and 89% were achieved on the best and average results, respectively. The Mann-Whitney U-test was applied to verify if the average solutions are statistically different. The Mann-Withney U-test, also called Mann-Whitney-Wilcoxon test or Wilcoxon rank-sum test, is a non-parametric test used to verify the null hypothesis that two samples come from the same population (Conover, 1971). The p-values obtained are shown in the last column of table 5.

Let av_{LK} and $av_{PSO\text{-}LK}$ denote the average solution obtained by the LK and the PSO-LK algorithms, respectively, then the p-values show that, with a level of significance of 0.05, the null hypothesis that verifies if $av_{LK} = av_{PSO\text{-}LK}$ is rejected for all instances.

Instance	LK		PSO-LK		p-value
	Min	Average	Min	Average	
pr439	0.0000	0.0463	0.0000	0.0000	0.004233
pcb442	0.0000	0.1119	0.0000	0.0000	0.018562
d493	0.0029	0.1216	0.0000	0.0000	0.000000
rat575	0.0295	0.1277	0.0000	0.0052	0.000000
p654	0.0000	0.0078	0.0000	0.0000	0.001932
d657	0.0020	0.1500	0.0000	0.0000	0.000000
rat783	0.0000	0.0704	0.0000	0.0000	0.000000
dsj1000	0.0731	0.2973	0.0027	0.0041	0.000000
pr1002	0.0000	0.1318	0.0000	0.0000	0.000000
u1060	0.0085	0.1786	0.0000	0.0049	0.000000
vm1084	0.0017	0.0669	0.0000	0.0052	0.000000
pcb1173	0.0000	0.1814	0.0000	0.0003	0.000000
d1291	0.0039	0.4333	0.0000	0.0113	0.000000
rl1304	0.0202	0.3984	0.0000	0.0000	0.000000
rl1323	0.0463	0.2300	0.0000	0.0079	0.000001
nrw1379	0.0547	0.1354	0.0018	0.0160	0.000000
fl1400	0.0000	0.1215	0.0000	0.0000	0.000021
fl1577	0.7371	2.2974	0.0000	0.0420	0.000000
vm1748	0.0903	0.1311	0.0000	0.0009	0.000000
u1817	0.1976	0.5938	0.0454	0.1408	0.000000
rl1889	0.1836	0.3844	0.0000	0.0165	0.000000
d2103	0.0597	0.3085	0.0087	0.0267	0.000000
u2152	0.2381	0.5548	0.0062	0.1135	0.000000
pr2392	0.0775	0.3904	0.0000	0.0112	0.000000
pcb3038	0.1598	0.2568	0.0123	0.0686	0.000000
fl3795	0.5665	1.0920	0.0000	0.0403	0.000000
fnl4461	0.0882	0.1717	0.0794	0.1155	0.000000
rl5915	0.3528	0.5343	0.0755	0.1554	0.000000
rl5934	0.2221	0.4761	0.0309	0.1545	0.000000
pla7397	0.1278	0.2912	0.0075	0.0253	0.000000

Table 5. Comparison between LK and PSO-LK

4. Composing velocity operators

The composition of velocities can be thought as an arrangement of velocity operators. This arrangement defines the sequence that determines the order of application of each velocity operator to a given particle. For example, let v_1, v_2, v_3 be the three velocity operators defined in the last section, A_1 and A_2 be two sequences of application of these velocity operators, $A_1=(v_1, v_2, v_3)$, $A_2=(v_3, v_1, v_2)$. Regardless the coefficients of equation (9), two examples of algorithms for the composition of the velocities are presented in figures 4(a) and 4(b). The meaning of those coefficients is explained further. In the algorithm shown in figure 4(a), the composition of velocities is implicit, once the results of the application of the velocity operators v_1 and v_2 are inputs for the next operation. A possible implementation for the composition of velocities with sequence A_2 is illustrated in figure 4(b), where a method to compose the results of each application of the velocity operators has to be defined.

(a)	(b)
procedure update_position(x_p, $pbest_p$, $gbest_p$)	procedure update_position(x_p, $pbest_p$, $gbest_p$)
$y_1 \leftarrow v_1(x_p)$	$y_1 \leftarrow v_3(x_p, gbest_p)$
$y_2 \leftarrow v_2(y_1, pbest_p)$	$y_2 \leftarrow v_1(x_p)$
$y_3 \leftarrow v_3(y_2, gbest_p)$	$y_3 \leftarrow v_2(x_p, pbest_p)$
return(y_3)	return($y_1 \oplus y_2 \oplus y_3$)

Fig. 4. Composition of velocities to update x_p with sequences (a) A_1 and (b) A_2

Besides the six ways to combine velocities v_1, v_2 and v_3, there is, still, the possibility of repeating velocity operators in the same sequence. For example, the sequence $A = (v_1,v_2,v_3,v_1)$ can be implemented with the algorithm of figure 4(a), replacing the statement *return*(y_3) by the statements $y_4 \leftarrow v_1(y_3)$ and *return*(y_4).

In order to accomplish the task of composing velocities, stopping conditions for the application of each velocity operator can also be defined. Let $A = (a_1, a_2, \ldots, a_m)$ be a sequence where each a_i, $1 \le i \le m$, is a pair (v_j, s_k), $v_j \in V$, the set of velocity operators, and s_k is v_j's stopping condition. Thus, given a sequence A with q elements, the first velocity operator is applied to particle p until reaching its corresponding stopping condition, then the process continues with the second velocity operator until the q-th element of sequence A.

In this work two velocity operators are considered: local search (v_1) and path-relinking (v_2=v_3). Some stopping conditions that can be adopted for v_1 are: to execute a maximum number of local search iterations, to find a solution that improves the input solution by a given amount, to find a local optimum (corresponds to a standard local search run). Some stopping conditions for v_2 are: to reach the target solution (corresponds to the standard path-relinking), to find a solution better than the origin and target solutions, to find a solution better than the worst among the two input solutions, to stop after a maximum number of iterations, or, given the distance d between the two input solutions, to stop after doing $\lfloor d/z \rfloor$ iterations, where z is an integer $z \le d$.

In this context, the coefficients of equation (9) can be thought as representing stopping conditions. For example, let c_0, c_1, c_2 be three numbers in the interval [0,1] and $itmax_1$, $itmax_2$, $itmax_3$ be the maximum number of iterations for the operations with velocities v_1, v_2 and v_3, respectively. Then $c_i \times v_{i+1}(\cdot)$, i = 0,1,2, represents the application of velocity operator v_{i+1} with a maximum of $c_i \times itmax_{i+1}$ iterations.

Consider the algorithm of figure 2, with the following modifications:

- pr_1, pr_2, pr_3 are the probabilities associated with compositions represented by sequences A_1, A_2 and A_3, respectively.
- The statements

  $velocity_p \leftarrow$ define_velocity(pr_1, pr_2, pr_3)

  $x_p \leftarrow$ update(x_p,$velocity_p$)

  are replaced by

  $comp_p \leftarrow$ define_composition(pr_1, pr_2, pr_3)

  $x_p \leftarrow$ update(x_p,$comp_p$)

In order to test the potential of composing velocities, two variants of the basic algorithm shown in figure 2 are investigated. The sequences A_1, A_2 and A_3 of the first algorithmic version are: $A_1 = ((v_1,s_1))$, $A_2 = ((v_2,s_2), (v_1,s_1))$, $A_3 = ((v_3,s_2), (v_1,s_1))$. The stopping conditions s_1

and s_2 are, respectively, to find a local optimum and to find a solution better than the worst among the two input solutions. Figure 5(a) shows an illustrative scheme of sequence A_2. Once the path-relinking is considered for v_2 and v_3, the scheme of figure 5(a) is also valid if v_2 is replaced by v_3. In the second variant of the basic algorithm the sequences are: $A_1 = ((v_1,s_1))$, $A_2 = ((v_2,s_2), (v_1,s_1), (v_2,s_3))$, $A_3 = ((v_3,s_2), (v_1,s_1),(v_3,s_3))$. The stopping condition s_3 is to reach the target solution. The illustrative scheme of the sequence A_3 (also valid for A_2) is shown in figure 5(b).

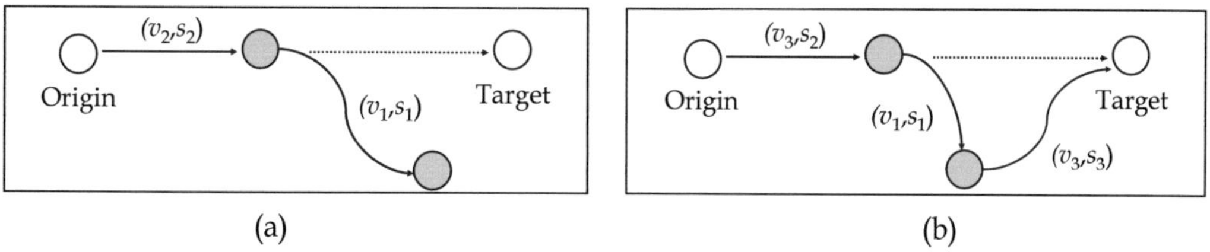

Fig. 5. Sequences (a) $A_2 = ((v_2,s_2), (v_1,s_1))$ and (b) $A_3 = ((v_3,s_2), (v_1,s_1),(v_3,s_3))$.

Tables 6 and 7 show a comparison between the results obtained by the basic PSO-LK and the first and second algorithmic versions, respectively. The elements of columns *Min* and *Av* are the percent deviation from the best known solution of the best and average solutions found by the correspondent algorithm in 20 independent runs. The average processing times in seconds are presented in column *T*(*s*). The cells with the best results have a dark background. The p-values shown in the last column of tables 6 and 7 are the result of the hypothesis test with the average values presented for each instance.

In preliminary experiments the values 10, 15, 20 and 25 were tested for the size of the swarm and the values 20, 50 and 100 were tested for the maximum number of iterations. The best trade-off between quality of solution and processing time was reached with 20 particles and maximum of 20 iterations. The tests were done in a Pentium IV, 3.0 GHz, 1 Gb of RAM.

Table 6 shows that both algorithmic versions find the best average solutions of 10 instances, the PSO-LK finds 1 best solution and the PSO-LK-C1 finds 6 best solutions. Observing the p-values of the 20 instances where different average solutions were found, the table shows that, with a level of significance 0.05, significant differences exist only for instances nrw1379 and pr2392. Thus, both versions present similar performance regarding quality of solution for the majority of the tested instances. Nevertheless, the processing times of the algorithmic version with the composition of velocities are significantly lower than those presented by the basic algorithmic version at 27 instances. The algorithm with the composition of velocities spends, in average, half the processing time spent by the basic algorithm. Thus with half of the processing effort, the algorithm is able to find solutions as good as the basic PSO-LK.

Similar results are observed in table 7. The PSO-LK and the PSO-LK-C2 find the best average solutions of 10 and 11 instances, respectively. Regarding the best solution found by each algorithm, table 7 shows that the PSO-LK-C2 finds 6 best results and the PSO-LK does not find any best result. The p-values of the 21 instances for which the algorithms found different average solutions show that a significant difference exists only for instance pr2392. In average, the processing times of PSO-LK-C2 are 1.27 times better than the ones presented by the PSO-LK.

Instances	PSO-LK			PSO-LK-C1			p-level
	Min	Av	T(s)	Min	Av	T(s)	
pr439	0	0	0.78	0	0	0.38	-----
pcb442	0	0	0.80	0	0	0.39	-----
d493	0	0	19.38	0	0	13.52	-----
rat575	0	0	6.47	0	0.0007	3.83	0.317318
p654	0	0	1.90	0	0	0.87	-----
d657	0	0	12.42	0	0	8.35	-----
rat783	0	0	5.25	0	0	1.92	-----
dsj1000	0.0027	0.0031	178.48	0.0027	0.0027	82.27	0.077143
pr1002	0	0	9.50	0	0	3.32	-----
u1060	0	0	38.18	0	0.0008	22.87	0.151953
vm1084	0	0.0010	34.74	0	0.0016	25.05	0.958539
pcb1173	0	0.0001	48.18	0	0.0003	32.65	0.156717
d1291	0	0	29.86	0	0	8.81	-----
rl1304	0	0	21.62	0	0	5.57	-----
rl1323	0	0.0092	225.32	0	0.0030	66.60	0.068481
nrw1379	0.0017	0.0085	417.80	0	0.0058	181.75	0.041205
fl1400	0	0	15.42	0	0	5.68	-----
fl1577	0	0.0135	461.99	0	0.0200	248.85	0.237805
vm1748	0	0.0018	854.17	0	0	382.28	0.317318
u1817	0	0.0863	789.18	0.0367	0.1068	410.16	0.297390
rl1889	0	0.0073	894.43	0	0.0037	348.68	0.229728
d2103	0	0.0043	1137.53	0	0.0123	417.53	0.751641
u2152	0	0.0717	1415.32	0	0.0711	512.12	0.989112
pr2392	0	0.0021	577.78	0	0	86.43	0.018578
pcb3038	0.0101	0.0396	323.94	0	0.0343	1772.8	0.336582
fl3795	0	0.0142	621.63	0	0.0214	131.10	0.636875
fnl4461	0.0296	0.0462	583.78	0.0104	0.0421	952.61	0.386402
rl5915	0.0122	0.0633	1359.25	0.0025	0.0435	1029.21	0.083396
rl5934	0.0012	0.0650	983.04	0	0.0797	1443.5	0.645471
pla7397	0.0075	0.0253	1563.22	0.0004	0.0348	826.38	0.158900

Table 6. Comparison between PSO-LK and PSO-LK-C1

Instances	PSO-LK			PSO-LK-C2			p-level
	Min	Av	T(s)	Min	Av	T(s)	
pr439	0	0	0.78	0	0	0.59	----
pcb442	0	0	0.80	0	0	0.6	----
d493	0	0	19.38	0	0	16.3	----
rat575	0	0	6.47	0	0.0007	4.17	0.317318
p654	0	0	1.90	0	0	1.46	----
d657	0	0	12.42	0	0	9.72	----
rat783	0	0	5.25	0	0	3.76	----
dsj1000	0.0027	0.0031	178.48	0.0027	0.0028	103.01	0.097603
pr1002	0	0	9.50	0	0	6.33	----
u1060	0	0	38.18	0	0.0013	26.88	0.075373
vm1084	0	0.0010	34.74	0	0.0016	29.57	0.958539
pcb1173	0	0.0001	48.18	0	0.0003	34.53	0.297961
d1291	0	0	29.86	0	0.0073	27.46	0.152088
rl1304	0	0	21.62	0	0	10.44	----
rl1323	0	0.0092	225.32	0	0.0055	127.55	0.618230
nrw1379	0.0017	0.0085	417.80	0	0.0080	259.99	0.587686
fl1400	0	0	15.42	0	0	11.2	----
fl1577	0	0.0135	461.99	0	0.1144	303.77	0.102963
vm1748	0	0.0018	854.17	0	0	485.22	0.317318
u1817	0	0.0863	789.18	0	0.0811	454.81	0.684114
rl1889	0	0.0073	894.43	0	0.0070	389.12	0.844488
d2103	0	0.0043	1137.53	0	0.0128	443.39	0.655928
u2152	0	0.0717	1415.32	0	0.0609	680.38	0.390349
pr2392	0	0.0021	577.78	0	0	145.84	0.018578
pcb3038	0.0101	0.0396	323.94	0.0036	0.0387	1930.7	0.849722
fl3795	0	0.0142	621.63	0	0.0285	408.86	0.381866
fnl4461	0.0296	0.0462	583.78	0.0148	0.0452	1148.8	0.108256
rl5915	0.0122	0.0633	1359.25	0.0109	0.0499	984.11	0.194137
rl5934	0.0012	0.0650	983.04	0	0.0659	1142.78	0.913724
pla7397	0.0075	0.0253	1563.22	0.0007	0.0298	763.47	0.684311

Table 7. Comparison between PSO-LK and PSO-LK-C2

A comparison between the performance, regarding quality of solution, of PSO-LK-C1 and four effective heuristics for the TSP is shown in tables 8 and 9, where 23 symmetric instances with $|N|$ ranging from 1000 to 7397 are considered. The heuristics are: the Nguyen, Yoshihara, Yamamori and Yasunada iterated Lin-Kernighan variant (reported at http://www.research.att.com/~dsj/chtsp/), ILK-NYYY, the iterated Lin-Kernighan variant presented by Johnson & McGeoch (1997), ILK-JM, the Tourmerge (Cook & Seymour, 2003) and the LK implementation presented by Helsgaun (2000), ILK-H. The results of the first three heuristics were obtained in the DIMACS Challenge page (at http://www.research.att.com/~dsj/chtsp/results.html).

The columns of table 8 corresponding to the ILK-NYYY and the ILK-JM show the best tours obtained in ten $|N|$ iterations runs. The table shows that the PSO-LK-C1 obtains better values than the ILK-NYYY and the ILK-JM at 13 and 16 instances, respectively. The ILK-NYYY presents the best minimal solution for instance dsj1000. The last line of table 8 shows the average results of the three algorithms. It is observed that, in average, the solutions obtained by the PSO-LK-C1 are, approximately, 8 and 24 times better than the solutions presented by the ILK-NYYY and the ILK-JM, respectively.

Instance	PSO-LK-C1	ILK-NYYY Nb10	ILK-JM Nb10
dsj1000	0.0027	0	0.0063
pr1002	0	0	0.1482
u1060	0	0.0085	0.0210
vm1084	0	0.0217	0.0217
pcb1173	0	0	0.0088
d1291	0	0	0
rl1304	0	0	0
rl1323	0	0.01	0
nrw1379	0	0.0247	0.0018
fl1400	0	0	0
fl1577	0	0	0
vm1748	0	0	0
u1817	0.0367	0.1643	0.2657
rl1889	0	0.0082	0.0041
d2103	0	0.0559	0
u2152	0	0	0.1743
pr2392	0	0.0050	0.1495
pcb3038	0	0.0247	0.1213
fl3795	0	0	0.0104
fnl4461	0.0104	0.0449	0.1358
rl5915	0.0025	0.0580	0.0168
rl5934	0	0.0115	0.1723
pla7397	0.0004	0.0209	0.0497
Mean	0.0023	0.0199	0.0569

Table 8. Best solutions of PSO-LK-C1 and two iterative LK

Table 9 shows a comparison between the best and average results found by the PSO-LK-C1, the Tourmerge and the ILK-H. Regarding the minimal values, the proposed algorithm presents better results than the Tourmerge at 6 of the 21 instances the latter algorithm reports results. The Tourmerge presents one minimal result better than the proposed algorithm. The ILK-H presents 4 minimal results that are better than the ones presented by the PSO-LK-C1. Compared with the former, the latter algorithm presents the best minimal results of 2 instances. Considering the average solutions, the PSO-LK-C1 presents better results than the Tourmerge and the ILK-H at 14 and 12 instances, respectively. The Tourmerge and the ILK-H present better average results than the PSO algorithm for 5 and 8 instances, respectively. The last line of table 9 summarizes the results of each column. The proposed algorithm presents the best statistics regarding the average solutions.

Instance	PSO-LK-C1		Tourmerge		ILK-H	
	Min	Average	Min	Average	Min	Average
dsj1000	0.0027	0.0027	0.0027	0.0478	0	0.035
pr1002	0	0	0	0.0197	0	0
u1060	0	0.0008	0	0.0049	0	0
vm1084	0	0.0016	0	0.0013	0	0.007
pcb1173	0	0.0003	0	0.0018	0	0.002
d1291	0	0	0	0.0492	0	0.033
rl1304	0	0	0	0.1150	0	0.019
rl1323	0	0.0030	0.01	0.0411	0	0.018
nrw1379	0	0.0058	0	0.0071	0	0.006
fl1400	0	0	0	0	0	0.162
fl1577	0	0.0200	0	0.0225	0	0.046
vm1748	0	0	0	0	0	0.023
u1817	0.0367	0.1068	0.0332	0.0804	0	0.078
rl1889	0	0.0037	0.0082	0.0682	0	0.002
d2103	0	0.0123	0.0199	0.3170	---	---
u2152	0	0.0711	0	0.0794	0	0.029
pr2392	0	0	0	0.0019	0	0
pcb3038	0	0.0343	0.0036	0.0327	0	0
fl3795	0	0.0214	0	0.0556	0	0.072
fnl4461	0.0104	0.0421	---	---	0	0.001
rl5915	0.0025	0.0435	0.0057	0.0237	0.009	0.028
rl5934	0	0.0797	0.0023	0.0104	0.005	0.089
pla7397	0.0104	0.0348	---	---	0	0.001
Mean	0.002291	0.019926	0.004076	0.046652	0.000636	0.029591

Table 9. Minimal and average results presented by PSO-LK-C1 and Tourmerge

5. Conclusion

This chapter summarized the research done to develop PSO algorithms for the TSP. Many of the PSO algorithms presented previously for the investigated problem do not tackle large instances and present results far from the best known heuristic solutions obtained by effective algorithms. The chapter presented an approach to design effective PSO algorithms for the TSP that can be extended to other discrete optimization problems. The new approach, first introduced by Goldbarg et al. (2006a), differentiates velocity operators according to the type of move the particle does. Additionally, methods to compose the velocity operators were proposed. Computational experiments with instances up to 7397 cities were presented. The results of those experiments show that the proposed method produces high quality solutions, when compared with four effective heuristics designed specifically for the investigated problem.

The composition of velocities allows building a number of possible implementations for the search strategies chosen to be used in the PSO algorithm. Therefore, rather than a metaheuristic, the Particle Swarm approach can be thought as a framework for heuristics hybridization in the context of discrete optimization problems.

6. Future works

In future works other methods to compose velocities and heuristics hybridization under the PSO framework will be investigated. Another idea to be explored in future researches is variable velocities. The proposed approach will be applied to the Generalized TSP and to the Bi-objective TSP.

7. References

Applegate, D.; Bixby, R.; Chvatal, V. & Cook, W. (1999). *Finding Tours in the TSP*, Technical Report TR99-05, Department of Computational and Applied Mathematics, Rice University

Burkard, R. E. (2002). The traveling salesman problem, In: *Handbook of Applied Optimization*, Pardalos, P.M. & Resende, M.G.C. (Ed.), pp. 616-624, Oxford University Press, ISBN: 0195125940, USA

Clerc, M. (1999). The swarm and the queen: Towards a deterministic and adaptive particle swarm optimization, *Proceedings of the 1999 Congress on Evolutionary Computation*, pp. 1951-1957, ISBN: 0780355369, Washington, DC, June 1999, IEEE

Clerc, M. (2004). Discrete particle swarm optimization, illustrated by the traveling salesman problem. In: *Studies in Fuzziness and Soft Computing New optimization techniques in engineering*, Babu, B.V. & Onwubolu, G.C. (Eds.), Vol. 141, , pp. 219–239, Springer ISBN: 978-3-5402-0167-0, Berlin

Coello, C.A.C.; Pulido, G.T. & Lechuga, M.S. (2004). Handling multiple objectives with particle swarm optimization, *IEEE Transactions on Evolutionary Computation*, Vol. 8, No. 3, pp. 256-279, ISSN: 1089-778X

Conover, W.J. (1971). *Practical Nonparametric Statistics*, Wiley, ISBN: 978-0-4711-6068-7, New York

Cook, W.J. & Seymour, P. (2003). Tour merging via branch-decomposition, *INFORMS Journal on Computing*, Vol. 15, pp. 233-248, ISSN: 1091-9856

Eberhart, R.C. & Shi, Y. (2000). Comparing inertia weights and constriction factors in particle swarm optimization. *Proceedings of the 2000 Congress on Evolutionary Computation*, Vol. 1, No. 2, pp. 84-88, ISBN: 0780363752, La Jolla, San Diego, CA , July 2000, IEEE, Piscataway, NJ

Eberhart, R. C. & Shi, Y. (2001) Particle swarm optimization: developments, applications and resources, *Proceedings of the 2001 Congress on Evolutionary Computation*, Vol. 1, pp. 81-86, ISBN: 0780366573, Seoul, South Korea, May 2001, IEEE, Piscataway, NJ

Fang, L.; Chen, P. & Liu, S. (2007). Particle swarm optimization with simulated annealing for TSP, *Proceedings of the 6th WSEAS International Conference on Artificial Intelligence, Knowledge Engineering and Data Bases*, Long, C. A.; Mladenov, V. M. & Bojkovic Z. (Eds.), pp. 206-210, ISBN: 978-9-6084-5759-1, Corfu Island, Greece, February 2007

Flood, M.M. (1956). The traveling-salesman problem, *Operations Research*, Vol. 4, pp. 61-75, ISSN: 0030-364X

Glover, F. (1963). Parametric *Combinations of Local Job Shop Rules*, Chapter IV, ONR Research Memorandum No. 117, Carnegie Mellon University, Pittsburgh

Glover, F.; Laguna, M. & Martí, R. (2000). Fundamentals of scatter search and path relinking. *Control and Cybernetics*, Vol. 29, No. 3, pp. 653-684, ISSN: 0324-8569.

Goldbarg, E.F.G; Souza, G.R. & Goldbarg, M.C. (2006a). Particle swarm for the traveling salesman problem, *Proceedings of the EvoCOP 2006*, Gottlieb, J. & Raidl, G.R. (Ed.), Lecture Notes in Computer Science, Vol. 3906, pp. 99-110, ISBN: 3540331786, Budapest, Hungary, April 2006, Springer, Berlin

Goldbarg, E.F.G; Souza, G.R. & Goldbarg, M.C. (2006b). Particle swarm optimization for the bi-objective degree-constrained minimum spanning tree, *Proceedings of the 2006 Congress on Evolutionary Computation*, Vol. 1, pp. 420-427, ISBN: 0780394879, Vancouver, BC, Canada, July 2006, IEEE

Gutin, G. & Punnen, A.P. (2002). *Traveling Salesman Problem and Its Variations*, Kluwer Academic Publishers, ISBN: 0387444599, Dordrecht.

Helsgaun, K. (2000). An effective implementation of the Lin-Kernighan traveling salesman heuristic, *European Journal of Operational Research*, Vol. 126, pp. 106-130, ISSN: 0377-2217

Hendtlass, T. (2003). Preserving diversity in particle swarm optimization, Developments in Applied Artificial Intelligence, *Proceedings of the 16th International Conference on Industrial and Engineering Applications of Artificial Intelligence and Expert Systems IEA/AIE 2003*, Laughborough, UK, June 2003, In: Lecture Notes in Computer Science, Vol. 2718, pp. 4104-4108, ISBN: 978-3-5404-0455-2, Springer, Berlin

Heppner, F. & Grenander, U. (1990). A stochastic nonlinear model for coordinated bird flocks, In: *The Ubiquity of Caos*, Krasner, S. (Ed.), pp.233-238, ISBN: 0871683504, AAAS Publications, Washington, DC

Hu, X.; Eberhart, R.C. & Shi, Y. (2003). Swarm intelligence for permutation optimization: A case study of n-queens problem, *Proceedings of the 2003 IEEE Swarm Intelligence Symposium*, pp. 243-246, ISBN: 0780379144, Indianapolis, USA, April 2003, IEEE

Johnson, D. S. & McGeoch, L.A. (1997). The traveling salesman problem: A case study in local optimization, In: *Local Search in Combinatorial Optimization*, Aarts, E.H.L. & Lenstra, J.K., pp. 215-310, ISBN: 978-0-6911-1522-1, John Wiley & Sons, New York

Johnson, D. S. & McGeoch, L.A. (2002). Experimental analysis of heuristics for the STSP, In: *Traveling Salesman Problem and Its Variations*, Guttin, G. & Punnen, A.P. (Eds.), pp. 369-443 , ISBN: 1402006640, Kluwer Academic, Dordrecht

Kennedy, J. & Eberhart, R.C. (1995). Particle swarm optimization, *Proceedings of the IEEE International Conference on Neural Networks*, Vol. 4, pp. 1942-1948, ISBN: 0780327683, Perth, Western Australia November 1995, IEEE

Kennedy, J. & Eberhart, R.C. (1997) A discrete binary version of the particle swarm algorithm, *Proceedings of the IEEE International Conference on Systems, Man, and Cybernetics*, Vol. 5, No. 2, pp. 4104 - 4109, ISBN: 0780340531, Orlando, Florida, October 1997, IEEE

Kennedy, J. & Eberhart, R.C. (2001) *Swarm Intelligence*, Morgan Kaufmann, ISBN: 1558605959, San Francisco, CA.

Lin, S. & Kernighan, B. (1973). An effective heuristic algorithm for the traveling-salesman problem, *Operations Research*, Vol. 21, pp. 498-516, ISSN: 0030-364X

Machado, T.R. & Lopes, H.S. (2005). A hybrid particle swarm optimization model for the traveling salesman problem, In: *Natural Computing Algorithms*, Ribeiro, H.; Albrecht, R.F. & Dobnikar, A. (Eds.), pp. 255-258, ISBN: 3211249346, Springer, Wien

Onwubolu, G.C. & Clerc, M. (2004). Optimal path for automated drilling operations by a new heuristic approach using particle swarm optimization, *International Journal of Production Research*, Vol. 42, No. 3, pp. 473–491, ISSN: 0020-7543

Pang, W.; Wang, K.; Zhou, C.; Dong, L.; Liu, M.; Zhang, H. & Wang, J. (2004a) Modified particle swarm optimization based on space transformation for solving traveling salesman problem, In: *Proceedings of the Third International Conference on Machine Learning and Cybernetics*, Shangai, China, August 2004, pp. 2342-2346, ISBN: 0780384032, IEEE

Pang, W.; Wang, K.; Zhou, C. & Dong, L. (2004b) Fuzzy discrete particle swarm optimization for solving traveling salesman problem, In: *Proceedings of the Fourth International Conference on Computer and Information Technology*, Wuhan, China, September 2004, pp. 796-800, ISBN: 0769522165, IEEE

Reeves, W.T. (1983). Particle systems technique for modeling a class of fuzzy objects. *ACM Transactions on Graphics*, Vol. 17, No. 3, pp. 359-376, ISSN: 0730-0301

Reynolds, C. W. (1987). Flocks, herds and schools: A distributed behavioural model. *Computer Graphics*, Vol. 21, No. 4, pp. 24-34, ISBN: 0897912276

Shi, Y. & Eberhart, R. C. (1998). Parameter selection in particle swarm optimization, In *Evolutionary Programming VII: Proceedings of Seventh International Conference on Evolutionary Programming - EP98*, San Diego, California, USA, March 1998, Lecture Notes in Computer Science, Vol. 1447, pp. 591-600, ISBN: 3540648917, Springer-Verlag, New York

Shi, X.H.; Liang, Y.C.; Lee, H.P.; Lu, C. & Wang, Q.X. (2007). Particle swarm optimization-based algorithms for TSP and generalized TSP, *Information Processing Letters*, Vol. 103, pp. 169-176, ISSN: 0020-0190

Voudouris, C. & Tsang, E. (1999). Guide local search and its application to the traveling salesman problem, *European Journal of Operational Research*, Vol. 113, pp. 469-499, ISSN: 0377-2217

Yuan, Z.; Yang, L.; Wu, Y.; Liao, L. & Li, G. (2007). Chaotic particle swarm optimization algorithm for Traveling Salesman Problem, In: *Proceedings of the IEEE International Conference on Automation and Logistics*, Jinan, China, August 2007, pp. 1121-1124., ISBN: 978-1-4244-1531-1, IEEE

Zhong, W.; Zhang, J. & Che, W. (2007). A novel discrete particle swarm optimization to solve traveling salesman problem, In: *Proceedings of the 2007 IEEE Congress on Evolutionary Computation*, Singapore, September 2007, pp. 3283-3287, ISBN: 978-1-4244-1340-9, IEEE

5

A Modified Discrete Particle Swarm Optimization Algorithm for the Generalized Traveling Salesman Problem

Mehmet Fatih Tasgetiren[1], Yun-Chia Liang[2], Quan-Ke Pan[3] and P. N. Suganthan[4]
[1]*Department of Operations Management and Business Statistics, Sultan Qaboos University Muscat,*
[2]*Department of Industrial Engineering and Management, Yuan Ze University,*
[3]*College of Computer Science, Liaocheng University, Liaocheng,*
[4]*School of Electrical and Electronic Engineering, Nanyang Technological University,*
[1]*Sultanate of Oman*
[2]*Taiwan, R.O.C*
[3]*P.R. China*
[4]*Singapore*

1. Introduction

A variant of the traveling salesman problem (**TSP**) is known as the generalized traveling salesman problem (**GTSP**), where a tour does not necessarily visit all the nodes since the set N of nodes is divided into m sets or clusters, $N_1,..,N_m$ with $N_1 \cup .. \cup N_m = N$ and $N_j \cap N_k = \phi$ if $j \neq k$. The objective is to find a minimum tour length containing at least a node from each cluster N_j. Several applications of the **GTSP** can be found in postal routing [1], computer file processing [2], order picking in warehouses [3], process planning for rotational parts [4], and the routing of clients through welfare agencies [5]. Furthermore, many other combinatorial optimization problems can be reduced to the **GTSP** problem [1]. **TSP** is *NP*-Hard and hence the **GTSP** is *NP*-hard because if the set N of nodes is partitioned into $|N|$ subsets with each containing one node, it results in a **TSP**.

Regarding the literature for the **GTSP**, it was first addressed in [2, 5, 6]. Exact algorithms can be found in Laporte *et al.* [7, 8], Laporte & Nobert [9], Fischetti *et al.* [10, 11], and others in [12, 13]. On the other hand, several worthy heuristic approaches are applied to the **GTSP**. Noon [3] presented several heuristics for the **GTSP** among which the most promising one is an adaptation of the well-known nearest-neighbor heuristic for the **TSP**. Similar adaptations of the farthest-insertion, nearest-insertion, and cheapest-insertion heuristics are proposed in Fischetti *et al.* [11]. **GI3** (Generalized Initilialization, Insertion, and Improvement) is one of the most sophisticated heuristics, which is developed by Renaud & Boctor [14]. **GI3** is a generalization of the **I3** heuristic presented in Renaud *et al.* [15]. The application of the metaheuristic algorithms specifically to the **GTSP** is very rare in the litearture. A random key genetic algorithm (**RKGA**) is proposed by Snyder & Daskin [16], which ignited the metaheuristic research on the **GTSP**. In the **RKGA**, random key representation is used and solutions generated by the **RKGA** are improved by using two local search heuristics namely, 2-opt and "swap" procedures. Note that their "swap" procedure provides a speed-up method in the search process. It is basically concerned with removing a node *j* from a tour, and inserting all possible nodes *k*'s from the corresponding cluster in an edge (u,v) in a tour (i.e., between the node u and the node v) with a modified nearest-neighbor criterion. They have been separately implemented by embedding them in the *level-I improvement* and *level-II improvement* procedures.

For each individual in the population, they store the original (pre-improvement) cost and the final cost after improvements have been made. When a new individual is created, they compare its pre-improvement cost to the pre-improvement cost of the individual at position $p \times N$ in the previous (sorted) population, where $p \in [0,1]$ is a parameter of the algorithm and $p = 0.05$ in Snyder & Daskin [16]. These two improvement procedures are implemented as follows:

1. If the new solution is worse than the pre-improvement cost of this individual, the *level-I improvement* is used by applying one 2-opt exchange and one "swap" procedure (assuming a profitable one can be found) and store the resulting individual.
2. On the other hand, if the new solution is better, the *level-II improvement* is used by applying *2-opt* until no profitable *2-opt* can be found, then applying "*swap*" procedures until no profitable swaps can be found, and repeat until no improvements have been made in a given pass.

The RKGA focuses on designing the local search to spend more time on improving solutions that seem promising in comparison to previous solutions and to spend less time on the others. In both *level-I* and *level-II* improvement, a "*first-improving*" strategy is employed where the first move of a given type improving the objective value is implemented, rather than searching for the best such move before choosing one. Thereafter, Tasgetiren *et al.* [17, 18, 19] presented a discrete particle swarm optimization algorithm a genetic algorithm (**GA**) and an iterated greedy algorithm, respectively whereas Silberholz & Golden proposed another genetic algorithm in [20] which is denoted as **mrOXGA**.

The **GSTP** may deal with either symmetric where the distance from node *j* to node *k* is the same as the distance from *k* to *j* or asymmetric distances where the distance from node *j* to node *k* is not the same as the distance from *k* to *j*. In this paper, meta-heuristics are presented to solve the **GTSP** on a standard set of benchmark instances with symmetric distances.

Particle swarm Optimization (**PSO**) is one of the most recent evolutionary meta-heuristic methods, which receives growing interest from the researchers. It is based on the metaphor of social interaction and communication such as bird flocking and fish schooling. **PSO** was first introduced to optimize various continuous nonlinear functions by Eberhart & Kennedy [21]. Distinctly different from other evolutionary-type methods such as **GA** and **ES**, **PSO** algorithms maintain the members of the entire population through the search procedure. In a PSO algorithm, each individual is called a *particle*, and each particle moves around in the multi-dimensional search space with a velocity constantly updated by the particle's own experience, the experience of the particle's neighbors, or the experience of the whole swarm. That is, the search information is socially shared among particles to direct the population towards the best position in the search space. The comprehensive surveys of the **PSO** algorithms and applications can be found in Kennedy *et al.* [22] and Clerc [23].

In this paper, a **DPSO** algorithm is presented to solve the **GTSP** on a standard set of benchmark instances with symmetric distances. Furthermore, the **DPSO** algorithm is hybridized with local search improvement heuristics to intensify the search process; hence to further improve the solution quality.

The remaining chapter is organized as follows. Section 2 introduces the **DPSO** algorithm and its basic components. Section 3 presents the computational results on benchmark problems. Finally, Section 4 summarizes the concluding remarks.

2. Discrete particle swarm optimization algorithm

In the standard **PSO** algorithm, all particles have their position, velocity, and fitness values. Particles fly through the *m*-dimensional space by learning from the historical information emerged from the swarm population. For this reason, particles are inclined to fly towards better search area over the course of evolution. Let *NP* denote the swarm size represented as $x^k = \left[x_1^k, x_2^k, \ldots, x_{NP}^k\right]$. Then each particle in the swarm population has the following attributes: A current position represented as $x_i^k = \left[x_{i1}^k, x_{i2}^k, \ldots, x_{im}^k\right]$; a current velocity represented as $v_i^k = \left[v_{i1}^k, v_{i2}^k, \ldots, v_{im}^k\right]$; a current personal best position represented as $p_i^k = \left[p_{i1}^k, p_{i2}^k, \ldots, p_{im}^k\right]$; and a current global best position represented as $g^k = \left[g_1^k, g_2^k, \ldots, g_m^k\right]$. Assuming that the function f is to be minimized, the current velocity of the *jth* dimension of the *ith* particle is updated as follows.

$$v_{ij}^k = w^{k-1} v_{ij}^{k-1} + c_1 r_1 \left(p_{ij}^{k-1} - x_{ij}^{k-1}\right) + c_2 r_2 \left(g_j^{k-1} - x_{ij}^{k-1}\right) \tag{1}$$

where w^k is the inertia weight which is a parameter to control the impact of the previous velocities on the current velocity; c_1 and c_2 are acceleration coefficients and r_1 and r_2 are uniform random numbers between [0,1]. The current position of the *jth* dimension of the *ith* particle at the generation k is updated using the previous position and current velocity of the particle as follows:

$$x_{ij}^k = x_{ij}^{k-1} + v_{ij}^k \tag{2}$$

The personal best position of each particle is updated using

$$p_i^k = \begin{cases} p_i^{k-1} & \text{if} \quad f\left(x_i^k\right) \geq f\left(p_i^{k-1}\right) \\ x_i^k & \text{if} \quad f\left(x_i^k\right) < f\left(p_i^{k-1}\right) \end{cases} \tag{3}$$

Finally, the global best position found so far in the swarm population is obtained for $1 \leq i \leq NP$ as

$$g^k = \begin{cases} \arg\min_{p_i^k} f\left(P_i^k\right) & \text{if} \quad \min f\left(p_i^k\right) < f\left(g^{k-1}\right) \\ g^{k-1} & \text{else} \end{cases} \tag{4}$$

Standard **PSO** equations cannot be used to generate binary/discrete values since positions are real-valued. Pan *et al.* [24, 25, 26] have presented a **DPSO** optimization algorithm to tackle the binary/discrete spaces, where particles are updated as follows:

$$x_i^k = c_2 \oplus CR\left(c_1 \oplus CR\left(w \oplus F_\rho\left(x_i^{k-1}\right), p_i^{k-1}\right), g^{k-1}\right) \tag{5}$$

The update equation (5) consists of three components: The first component is $a_i^k = w \oplus F_\rho\left(x_i^{k-1}\right)$, which represents the velocity of the particle. In the component $a_i^k = w \oplus F_\rho\left(x_i^{k-1}\right)$, F_ρ represents the mutation or perturbation operator with the mutation strength of ρ and the mutation probability of w. In other words, a uniform random number r is generated between 0 and 1. If r is less than w then the mutation operator is applied to generate a perturbed particle by $a_i^k = F_\rho\left(x_i^{k-1}\right)$, otherwise current particle is mutated as $a_i^k = insert\left(x_i^{k-1}\right)$. In addition, the mutation strength d is the degree of perturbation, i.e., single insert move or double insert move or some constructive heuristics generating distinct solutions and so on. In this paper, we employ the destruction and construction (**DC**) procedure of the IG algorithm in the mutation phase.

The second component is $b_i^k = c_1 \oplus CR\left(a_i^k, p_i^{k-1}\right)$, which is the "*cognition*" part of the particle representing the private thinking of the particle itself. In the component $b_i^k = c_1 \oplus CR\left(b_i^k, p_i^{k-1}\right)$, CR represents the crossover operator with the probability of c_1. Note that a_i^k and p_i^{k-1} will be the first and second parents for the crossover operator, respectively. It results either in $b_i^k = F_d\left(a_i^k, p_i^{k-1}\right)$ or in $b_i^k = a_i^k$ depending on the choice of a uniform random number.

The third component is $x_i^k = c_2 \oplus CR\left(b_i^k, g^k\right)$, which is the "*social*" part of the particle representing the collaboration among particles. In the component $x_i^k = c_2 \oplus CR\left(b_i^k, g^{k-1}\right)$, CR represents the crossover operator with the probability of c_2. Note that b_i^k and g^{k-1} will be the first and second parents for the crossover operator, respectively. It results either in $x_i^k = CR\left(b_i^k, g^{k-1}\right)$ or in $x_i^k = b_i^k$ depending on the choice of a uniform random number.

The basic idea behind the **DPSO** algorithm is to provide information exchange amongst the population members, personal best solutions and the global best solution.

However, combining the particle with both personal best and then global best solution through crossover operator may cause a particle losing some genetic information. Instead, we propose a modification to our **DPSO** algorithm in this paper utilizing either the "social" or "cognitive" genetic information during the particle update process. It is achieved as follows:

$$x_i^k = \begin{cases} CR(a_i^k, p_i^{k-1}) & if \quad r < c_1 \\ CR(a_i^k, g^{k-1}) & else \end{cases} \tag{6}$$

In other words, after mutation operator, the particle is updated by recombining the temporary mutated individual with either the personal best or global best solution depending on a search directing probability of c_1. For the **DPSO** algorithm, the *gbest* (global neighborhood) model of Kennedy *et al.* [22] was followed. The pseudo code of the **DPSO** algorithm with the local search is given in Fig. 1.

```
Procedure DPSO
Initialize parameters
Initialize particles of population
Evaluate particles of population
Apply local search to population individuals              %Optional
While (not termination) Do
    Find personal best
    Find global best
    Update particles of population
    Evaluate particles of population
    Apply local search to population individuals          %Optional
Endwhile
Return Global best
Endprocedure
```

Fig. 1. Generic Outline of DPSO Algorithm with Local Search.

2.1 Solution representation

We employ a path representation for the **GTSP** in this paper. In the path representation, each consecutive node is listed in order. An advantage of this representation is due to its simplicity in objective function evaluation since the total cost of a path can easily be calculated by summing the costs (distances) of each pair of adjacent nodes. However, a distadvantge of this representation is due to the fact that there is no quarantee that a randomly selected solution will be a valid **GTSP** tour because there is no quarantee that each cluster is represented exactly once in the path without some repair procedures. In order to handle the decision of which node should be chosen from a given cluster in the **GTSP** solution, we include both cluster and tour information in solutions. In other words, a **GTSP** solution consists of both an array of permutation of clusters (n_j) and an array of nodes (π_j) to be visited in m dimensions/clusters. In this way, each solution is guaranteed to be a GTSP solution. The solution representation together with the necessary distance information for calculating the objective function value $F(x)$ of the solution x is illustrated in Table 1 where $d_{\pi_j \pi_{j+1}}$ shows the distance from node π_j to node π_{j+1}. The initial solution is constructed in such a way that first a permutation of clusters is determined randomly, then since each cluster contains one or more nodes, a tour is established by randomly choosing a single node from each corresponding cluster. By including cluster information in solution representation, which node must be visited in a tour can be determined easily with either a random selection or a systematic way. For example, in the pair (n_j, π_j), n_j stands for the cluster in the jth dimension whereas π_j represents the node to be visited from cluster n_j.

	j	1	2	...	m-1	m	1
x	n_j	n_1	n_2	...	n_{m-1}	n_m	n_1
	π_j	π_1	π_2	...	π_{m-1}	π_m	π_1
	$d_{\pi_j \pi_{j+1}}$	$d_{\pi_1 \pi_2}$	$d_{\pi_2 \pi_3}$	...	$d_{\pi_{m-1} \pi_m}$	$d_{\pi_m \pi_1}$	
$F(x)=$	$\sum_{j=1}^{m} d_{\pi_j \pi_{j+1}} + d_{\pi_m \pi_1} =$	$d_{\pi_1 \pi_2}$ +	$d_{\pi_2 \pi_3}$ +	...	$d_{\pi_{m-1} \pi_m}$ +	$d_{\pi_m \pi_1}$	

Table 1. Solution Representation

As illustrated in Table 1, the objective function value of a solution x is the total tour length and given by

$$F(x) = \sum_{j=1}^{m-1} d_{\pi_j \pi_{j+1}} + d_{\pi_m \pi_1} \tag{1}$$

For example, consider a **GTSP** instance of **11EIL51** from **TSPLIB** library [27], which has fifty one nodes divided into eleven clusters. So the clusters are $N_1 = \{19,40,41\}$, $N_2 = \{3,20,35,36\}$, $N_3 = \{24,43\}$, $N_4 = \{33,39\}$, $N_5 = \{11,12,27,32,46,47,51\}$, $N_6 = \{2,16,21,29,34,50\}$, $N_7 = \{8,22,26,28,31\}$, $N_8 = \{13,14,18,25\}$, $N_9 = \{4,15,17,37,42,44,45\}$, $N_{10} = \{1,6,7,23,48\}$, and $N_{11} = \{5,9,10,30,38,49\}$. Table 2 illustrates a random **GTSP** solution with the distance information $d_{\pi_j \pi_{j+1}}$ and the objective function $F(x)$ for the instance **11EIL51**. In addition, the whole distance matrix and other detailed information about the instance **11EIL51** can be found in http://www.ntu.edu.sg/home/EPNSugan.

	j	1	2	3	4	5	6	7	8	9	10	11	1
x	n_j	10	5	7	2	6	11	4	9	1	8	3	10
	π_j	1	51	22	20	50	10	33	44	41	25	24	1
	$d_{\pi_j \pi_{j+1}}$	$d_{1,51}$	$d_{51,22}$	$d_{22,20}$	$d_{20,50}$	$d_{50,10}$	$d_{10,33}$	$d_{33,44}$	$d_{44,41}$	$d_{41,25}$	$d_{25,24}$	$d_{24,1}$	
$F(x)$	201	14	21	15	21	17	12	17	20	21	14	29	

Table 2. **GTSP** Solution for Instance **11EIL51**

As to the construction of the initial random solution as mentioned before, first a random permutation of clusters is established; then a corresponding node is randomly chosen from each cluster to establish the tour. To be more specific, for example, in Table 2, $n_2 = 5$ refers to the cluster N_5, and the corresponding node $\pi_2 = 51$ refers to the node 51 chosen randomly from the cluster N_5.

2.2 NEH heuristic

Due to the availability of the insertion methods that we have already proposed in [17, 18, 19], it is possible to apply the **NEH** heuristic of Nawaz *et al.* [28] to the **GTSP**. Without considering cluster information for simplicity, the **NEH** heuristic for the **GTSP** can be summarized as follows:

1. Determine an initial tour of nodes. Let this tour be x.
2. The first two nodes (that is, π_1 and π_2) are chosen and two possible partial tours of these two nodes are evaluated. Note that since a tour must be Hamiltanion cycle, partial tours will be evaluated with the first node being the last node, too. As an example, partial tours, (π_1, π_2, π_1) and (π_2, π_1, π_2) are evaluated.
3. Repeat the following steps until all nodes are inserted. In the *k*th step, node π_k at position k is taken and tentatively inserted into all the possible k positions of the partial tour that are already partially completed. Select these k tentative partial tours

that results in the minimum objective function value or a cost function suitably predefined.

To picture out how the **NEH** heuristic can be adopted for the **GTSP**, consider a solution with five nodes as $x = \{3,1,4,2,5\}$. The following example illustrates the implementation of the **NEH** heuristic for the **GTSP**:

1. Current solution is $x = \{3,1,4,2,5\}$.
2. Evaluate the first two nodes as follows: $\{3,1,3\}$ and $\{1,3,1\}$. Assume that the first partial tour has a better objective function value than the second one. So the current partial tour will be $\{3,1\}$.
3. Insertions:
   - Insert node 4 into three possible positions of the current partial tour as follows: $\{4,3,1,4\}$, $\{3,4,1,3\}$ and $\{3,1,4,3\}$. Assume that the best objective function value is with the partial tour $\{3,4,1,3\}$. So the current partial tour will be $\{3,4,1\}$.
   - Next, insert node 2 into four possible positions of the current partial tour as follows: $\{2,3,4,1,2\}$, $\{3,2,4,1,3\}$, $\{3,4,2,1,3\}$ and $\{3,4,1,2,3\}$. Assume that the best objective function value is with the partial tour $\{3,2,4,1,3\}$. So the current partial tour will be $\{3,2,4,1\}$.
   - Finally, insert node 5 into five possible positions of the current partial tour as follows: $\{5,3,2,4,1,5\}$, $\{3,5,2,4,1,3\}$, $\{3,2,5,4,1,3\}$, $\{3,2,4,5,1,3\}$ and $\{3,2,4,1,5,3\}$. Assume that the best objective function value is with the partial tour $\{3,2,4,5,1,3\}$. So the final complete tour will be $x = \{3,2,4,5,1\}$.

2.3 Destruction and construction procedure

We employ the destruction and construction (**DC**) procedure of the iterated greedy (**IG**) algorithm in [29] in the **DPSO** algorithm. In the destruction step, a given number d of nodes, randomly chosen and without repetition, are removed from the solution. This results in two partial solutions. The first one with the size d of nodes is called x^R and includes the removed nodes in the order where they are removed. The second one with the size $m-d$ of nodes is the original one without the removed nodes, which is called x^D. It should be pointed out that we consider each corresponding cluster when the destruction and construction procedures are carried out in order to keep the feasibility of the **GTSP** tour. Note that the perturbation scheme is embedded in the destruction phase where p nodes from x^R are randomly chosen without repetition and they are replaced by some other nodes from the corresponding clusters.

The construction phase requires a constructive heuristic procedure. We employ the **NEH** heuristic described in the previous section. In order to reinsert the set x^R into the destructed solution x^D in a greedy manner, the first node π_1^R in x^R is inserted into all possible $m-d+1$ positions in the destructed solution x^D generating $m-d+1$ partial solutions. Among these $m-d+1$ partial solutions including node π_1^R, the best partial solution with the minimum tour length is chosen and kept for the next iteration. Then the second node π_2^R in x^R is considered and so on until x^R is empty or a final solution is obtained. Hence x^D is again of size m.

To figure out how **DC** can be adopted for the **GTSP**, consider a solution with five nodes as $x = \{3,1,4,2,5\}$. Again, we do not consider cluster information for simplicity:

1. Current solution is $x = \{3,1,4,2,5\}$.
2. Remove nodes 1 and 5 randomly from the current solution to establish two partial solutions as $x^D = \{3,4,2\}$ and $x^R = \{1,5\}$.
3. Insert node 1 into **four** possible positions of the current partial tour $x^D = \{3,4,2\}$ as follows: $\{1,3,4,2,1\}$, $\{3,1,4,2,3\}$, $\{3,4,1,2,3\}$ and $\{3,4,2,1,3\}$. Assume that the best objective function value is with the partial tour $\{3,4,1,2,3\}$. So the current partial tour will be $x^D = \{3,4,1,2\}$.
4. Next, insert node 5 into **five** possible positions of the current partial tour $x^D = \{3,4,1,2\}$ as follows: $\{5,3,4,1,2,5\}$, $\{3,5,4,1,2,3\}$, $\{3,4,5,1,2,3\}$, $\{3,4,1,5,2,3\}$ and $\{3,4,1,2,5,3\}$. Assume that the best objective function value is with the final tour $\{5,3,4,1,2,5\}$. So the final complete tour will be $x = \{5,3,4,1,2\}$.

In order to highlight the difference between the **NEH** insertion and the one proposed in by Rosenkrantz *et al.* [30], we give the same example as follows:

1. Current solution is $x = \{3,1,4,2,5\}$
2. Revove nodes 1 and 5 randomly from the current solution to establish two partial solutions as $x^D = \{3,4,2\}$ and $x^R = \{1,5\}$.
3. Insert node 1 into **two** possible positions of the current partial tour $x^D = \{3,4,2\}$ as follows: $\{3,1,4,2,3\}$ and $\{3,4,1,2,3\}$ because there are only two edges in x^D. Assume that the best objective function value is with the partial tour $\{3,4,1,2,3\}$. So the current partial tour will be $x^D = \{3,4,1,2\}$.
4. Next, insert node 5 into **three** possible positions of the current partial tour $x^D = \{3,4,1,2\}$ as follows: $\{3,5,4,1,2\}$, $\{3,4,5,1,2,3\}$ and $\{3,4,1,5,2,3\}$ because there are only three edges in x^D. Assume that the best objective function value is with the final tour $\{3,5,4,1,2\}$. So the final complete tour will be $\{3,5,4,1,2,3\}$

As seen in the examples above, the **NEH** heuristic considers $(n+1)$ insertions at each step whereas the Rosenkrantz *et al.* [30] makes $(n-1)$ insertions in order to find a complete tour.

2.4 Insertion methods

The following insertion methods are proposed by the authors in [19]. These greedy speed-up methods are based on the insertion of the pair (n_k^R, π_k^R) into $m-d+1$ possible positions of a partial or destructed solution x^d. Note that as an example only a single pair is considered to be removed from the current solution, perturbed with another node from the same cluster and reinserted into the partial solution. For this reason, the destruction size and the perturbation strength are equal to one (i.e., $\rho = d = k = 1$). As a matter of fact, the insertion of node π_k^R into $m-d-1$ possible positions is actually proposed by Rosenkrantz *et al.* [30] for the **TSP**. Snyder & Daskin [16] have adopted it for the **GTSP**. It is based on the removal and the insertion of node π_k^R in an edge $\left(\pi_u^D, \pi_v^D\right)$ of a partial tour. However, it avoids the insertion of node π_k^R on the first and the last position of any given partial tour. We illustrate these possible three insertions using the partial solution x^D of the instance **11EIL51** having eleven clusters and nodes. Suppose that the pair $(5,51)$ is removed from the solution in Table 1; perturbed with node 27 from the same cluster N_5. So the current partial solution after removal and the pair to be reinserted are given in Tables 3A and 3B, respectively.

	j	1	2	3	4	5	6	7	8	9	10	1
x^D	n_j^D	10	7	2	6	11	4	9	1	8	3	10
	π_j^D	1	22	20	50	10	33	44	41	25	24	1
	$d_{\pi_j^D \pi_{j+1}^D}$	$d_{1,22}$	$d_{22,20}$	$d_{20,50}$	$d_{50,10}$	$d_{10,33}$	$d_{33,44}$	$d_{44,41}$	$d_{41,25}$	$d_{25,24}$	$d_{24,1}$	
$F\left(x^D\right)$	173	7	15	21	17	12	17	20	21	14	29	

Table 3A. Current Partial Solution

	k	1
x^R	n_k^R	5
	π_k^R	27

Table 3B. Partial Solution to Be Inserted

A. Insertion of pair $\left(n_k^R, \pi_k^R\right)$ *in the first position of the partial solution*

a. Remove $= d_{\pi_m^D \pi_1^D}$

b. Add $= d_{\pi_k^R \pi_1^D} + d_{\pi_m^D \pi_k^R}$

c. $F(x) = F\left(x^D\right) + \text{Add} - \text{Remove}$

Example A:

Remove $= d_{\pi_m^D \pi_1^D}$

Remove $= d_{\pi_{10}^D \pi_1^D}$

Remove $= d_{24,1}$

Add $= d_{\pi_k^R \pi_1^D} + d_{\pi_m^D \pi_k^R}$

Add $= d_{\pi_1^R \pi_1^D} + d_{\pi_{10}^D \pi_1^R}$

Add $= d_{27,1} + d_{24,27}$

$F(x) = F\left(x^D\right) + \text{Add} - \text{Remove}$

$$F(x)=d_{1,22}+d_{22,20}+d_{20,50}+d_{50,10}+d_{10,33}+d_{33,44}+d_{44,41}+d_{41,25}+d_{25,24}+d_{24,1}+d_{27,1}+d_{24,27}-d_{24,1}$$

$$F(x)=d_{1,22}+d_{22,20}+d_{20,50}+d_{50,10}+d_{10,33}+d_{33,44}+d_{44,41}+d_{41,25}+d_{25,24}+d_{27,1}+d_{24,27}$$

	j	1	2	3	4	5	6	7	8	9	10	11	1
x	n_j	**5**	10	7	2	6	11	4	9	1	8	3	5
	π_j	**27**	1	22	20	50	10	33	44	41	25	24	27
	$d_{\pi_j \pi_{j+1}}$	$d_{27,1}$	$d_{1,22}$	$d_{22,20}$	$d_{20,50}$	$d_{50,10}$	$d_{10,33}$	$d_{33,44}$	$d_{44,41}$	$d_{41,25}$	$d_{25,24}$	$d_{24,27}$	
$F(x)$	174	8	7	15	21	17	12	17	20	21	14	22	

Table 3C. Insertion of pair $(n_k^R, \pi_k^R)=(5,27)$ into the first position of partial solution

B. Insertion of pair (n_k^R, π_k^R) *in the last position of partial solution*

a. Remove $= d_{\pi_m^D \pi_1^D}$

b. Add $= d_{\pi_m^D \pi_k^R} + d_{\pi_k^R \pi_1^D}$

c. $F(x)=F(x^D)+\text{Add}-\text{Remove}$

Example B:

Remove $= d_{\pi_m^D \pi_1^D}$

Remove $= d_{\pi_{10}^D \pi_1^D}$

Remove $= d_{24,1}$

Add $= d_{\pi_m^D \pi_k^R} + d_{\pi_k^R \pi_1^D}$

Add $= d_{\pi_{10}^D \pi_1^R} + d_{\pi_1^R \pi_1^D}$

Add $= d_{24,27} + d_{27,1}$

$F(x)=F(x^D)+\text{Add}-\text{Remove}$

$$F(x)=d_{1,22}+d_{22,20}+d_{20,50}+d_{50,10}+d_{10,33}+d_{33,44}+d_{44,41}+d_{41,25}+d_{25,24}+d_{24,1}+d_{24,27}+d_{27,1}-d_{24,1}$$

$$F(x)=d_{1,22}+d_{22,20}+d_{20,50}+d_{50,10}+d_{10,33}+d_{33,44}+d_{44,41}+d_{41,25}+d_{25,24}+d_{24,27}+d_{27,1}$$

	j	1	2	3	4	5	6	7	8	9	10	11	1
x	n_j	10	7	2	6	11	4	9	1	8	3	**5**	10
	π_j	1	22	20	50	10	33	44	41	25	24	**27**	1
	$d_{\pi_j \pi_{j+1}}$	$d_{1,22}$	$d_{22,20}$	$d_{20,50}$	$d_{50,10}$	$d_{10,33}$	$d_{33,44}$	$d_{44,41}$	$d_{41,25}$	$d_{25,24}$	$d_{24,27}$	$d_{27,1}$	
$F(x)$	174	7	15	21	17	12	17	20	21	14	22	8	

Table 3D. Insertion of the pair $(n_k^R, \pi_k^R)=(5,27)$ into the last position of partial solution

Note that even though both tours generated in the examples ***A*** and ***B*** are different, the insertion of pair $(n_k^R, \pi_k^R) = (5,27)$ into the first and last positions of the partial solution x^D is equivalent to each other in terms of distance information that they have. In addition, note that both solutions are optimal.

C. Insertion of pair (n_k^R, π_k^R) *between the edge* (n_u^D, π_u^D) *and* (n_v^D, π_v^D)

a. Remove $= d_{\pi_u^D \pi_v^D}$

b. Add $= d_{\pi_u^D \pi_k^R} + d_{\pi_k^R \pi_v^D}$

c. $F(x) = F(x^D) + \text{Add} - \text{Remove}$

Example C:

$u = 6$

$v = 7$

$\text{Remove} = d_{\pi_u^D \pi_v^D}$

$\text{Remove} = d_{\pi_6^D \pi_7^D}$

$\text{Remove} = d_{33,44}$

$\text{Add} = d_{\pi_u^D \pi_k^R} + d_{\pi_k^R \pi_v^D}$

$\text{Add} = d_{\pi_6^D \pi_1^R} + d_{\pi_1^R \pi_7^D}$

$\text{Add} = d_{33,27} + d_{27,44}$

$F(x) = F(x^D) + \text{Add} - \text{Remove}$

$$F(x) = d_{1,22} + d_{22,20} + d_{20,50} + d_{50,10} + d_{10,33} + d_{33,44} + d_{44,41} + d_{41,25} + d_{25,24} + d_{24,1} + d_{33,27} + d_{27,44} - d_{33,44}$$

$$F(x) = d_{1,22} + d_{22,20} + d_{20,50} + d_{50,10} + d_{10,33} + d_{44,41} + d_{41,25} + d_{25,24} + d_{24,1} + d_{33,27} + d_{27,44}$$

	j	1	2	3	4	5	6	7	8	9	10	11	1
x	n_j	10	7	2	6	11	4	5	9	1	8	3	10
	π_j	1	22	20	50	10	33	27	44	41	25	24	1
	$d_{\pi_j \pi_{j+1}}$	$d_{1,22}$	$d_{22,20}$	$d_{20,50}$	$d_{50,10}$	$d_{10,33}$	$d_{33,27}$	$d_{27,44}$	$d_{44,41}$	$d_{41,25}$	$d_{25,24}$	$d_{24,1}$	
$F(x)$	223	7	15	21	17	12	41	33	20	21	14	22	

Table 3E. Insertion of the pair $(n_k^R, \pi_k^R) = (5,27)$ between pairs $(n_u^D, \pi_u^D) = (4,33)$ and $(n_v^D, \pi_v^D) = (9,44)$.

It is important to note that above insertion methods, especially insertion to the first and the last nodes, make the **NEH** heuristic applicable in the destruction and construction procedure to establish a final complete solution. For this reason, the insertion methods given above are neccessary for an **IG** algorithm to solve the **GTSP**.

2.5 Hybridization with local search

The hybridization of **DPSO** algorithm with local search heuristics is trivial. It can be achieved through the improvement of each solution generated in the construction phase by some local search methods. As improvement heuristics, a simple local search (**LS**) method and the 2-opt heuristic [31] were separately applied to the reconstructed solution. Note that the 2-opt heuristic is employed with the first improvement strategy in this study. Regarding the **LS** heuristic, we choose a simple one that is again based on the **DC** procedure. In other words, the destruction and construction procedures with the destruction size and the perturbation strength equal to one (i.e., $\rho = d = 1$) are used in the **LS** procedure whereas the **LS** size is fixed at $w = ncluster \times 5$ in order to intensify the search on the local minima. We will denote the hybrid **DPSO** algorithm with both local search improvement heuristics as **mDPSO** from now on. The pseudo code of the **LS** procedure is given in Fig. 2 whereas the proposed **mDPSO** algorithm is given in Fig. 3.

```
procedure  LS_GTSP(x)
        h := 1
        while  (h ≤ w)  do
                x* := DC(x)                         % d=1 and p=1
                if  (f(x*) ≤ f(x))  then
                        x := x*
                        h := 1
                else
                        h := h + 1
                endif
        endwhile
        return  x
endprocedure
```

Fig. 2. Local Search Employed

procedure DPSO_GTSP

Set c_1, w, NP, $t_{\max}$

$t_A := GetTickCount/1000$

$\Pi = \left(x_1^0, x_2^0, .., x_{NP}^0\right)$ %NEH_RANDOM population individuals and evaluate

$\underset{i:=1,2,..,NP}{f\left(x_i^0\right)}$ %Evaluate population

$p_i^0 = \underset{i:=1,2,..,NP}{x_i^0}$ %Initialize bestsofar population

$x_i^0 = \underset{i=1,2,..,NP}{two\_opt\left(x_i^0\right)}$ %Apply two-opt

$x_i^0 = \underset{i=1,2,..,NP}{LS\left(x_i^0\right)}$ %Apply LS local search

$g^0 = \underset{i=1,2,..,NP}{\arg\min}\left\{f\left(x_i^0\right)\right\}$ %Find gbest solution

$x_B := g^0$ %Set bestsofar

$k := 1$

$t_B := GetTickCount/1000$

while $((t_B - t_A) < t_{\max})$ *do*

$a_i^k = w \oplus DC_{d\rho}(x_i^{k-1})$, $i = 1,2,..,NP$ %Temporary population individual by destruction and construction

$x_B = \arg\min\{f(x_B), f(a_i^k)\}$, $i := 1,2,..,NP$ %Update bestsofar

$x_i^k = c_1 \oplus CR(a_i^k, p^{k-1}, g^{k-1})$, $i := 1,2,..,NP$ %Update population individual by Eq. [6]

$f(x_i^k)$, $i := 1,2,..,NP$ %Evaluate population

$p_i^k = \arg\min\{f(x_i^k), f(p_i^{k-1})\}$, $i := 1,2,..,NP$ %Update personal best

$x_i^k = two\_opt(x_i^k)$, $i = 1,2,..,NP$ %Apply two-opt

$x_i^k = LS(x_i^k)$, $i = 1,2,..,NP$ %Apply LS local search

$g_i^k = \arg\min\{f(p_i^k), f(g_i^{k-1})\}$, $i := 1,2,..,NP$ %Update global best solution

$x_B = \arg\min\{f(x_B), f(g^k)\}$ %Update bestsofar

$k := k + 1$

endwhile

return x_B

endprocedure

Fig. 3. **DPSO** Algorithm with Improvement Heuristics.

2.6 Crossover operator

In this paper, the traditional two-cut crossover operator is used in the **mDPSO** algorithm. The two-cut crossover operator is is illustrated in Table 4.

P_1	j	1	2	3	4	5	6	7	8	9	10	11	1
	n_j	10	5	7	2	**6**	**4**	**11**	9	8	1	3	10
	π_j	1	51	22	20	**50**	**33**	**10**	44	25	41	24	1
P_2	n_j	10	**6**	7	**11**	5	1	2	9	8	**4**	3	10
	π_j	1	**50**	22	**10**	27	41	20	44	25	**33**	24	1
O_1	j	1	2	3	4	5	6	7	8	9	10	11	1
	n_j	10	7	5	1	**6**	**4**	**11**	2	9	8	3	10
	π_j	1	22	27	41	**50**	**33**	**10**	20	44	25	24	1

Table 4. Two-Cut Crossover Operator.

2.7 Insert mutation operator

The insert mutation operator is basically related to first determining a cluster randomly, then removing the corresponding node from the tour of the individual, and replacing that particular node with another node from the same cluster randomly. As shown in Table 5, the cluster $n_2 = 5$ is randomly chosen and its corresponding node $\pi_2 = 51$ is replaced by the node $\pi_2 = 27$ from the same cluster $n_2 = 5$ using the GTSP instance of 11EIL51.

	j	1	**2**	3	4	5	6	7	8	9	10	11	1
	n_j	10	**5**	7	2	6	4	11	9	8	1	3	10
x	π_j	1	**51**	22	20	50	33	10	44	25	41	24	1
	j	1	**2**	3	4	5	6	7	8	9	10	11	1
x	n_j	10	**5**	7	2	6	4	11	9	8	1	3	10
	π_j	1	**27**	22	20	50	33	10	44	25	41	24	1

Table 5. Insert Mutation Operator

3. Computational results

We consider **RKGA** and **mrOXGA** for comparison in this paper since they produced some of the best heuristic results for the **GTSP**. The first benchmark set contains between 51 (11) and 442 (89) nodes (clusters) and the optimal objective function value for each of the problems is available. The second benchmark set contains between 493 (99) and 1084 (217) nodes. Since optimal solutions are not available for larger instances, we compare our results to Silberholz & Golden [20]. The **DPSO** algorithm was coded in Visual C++ and run on an Intel P IV 3.20GHz with 512MB memory. The population size was fixed at 30. The initial population is constructed randomly and then the **NEH** heuristic was applied to each random solution. Destruction size and perturbation strength were taken as 5 and 3, respectively. The traditional two-cut crossover is employed where the search direction and mutation probabilities are taken as $c_1 = 0.5$ and $w = 0.9$, respectively. The **DPSO** algorithm was terminated when the best so far solution was not improved after 50 consecutive generations. Five runs were carried out for each problem instance to report the statistics based on the relative percent deviations (Δ) from optimal solutions. For the computational effort consideration, t_{avg} denotes average **CPU** time in seconds to reach the best solution found so far during the run, i.e., the point of time that the best so far solution does not improve thereafter. n_{opt} stands for the number of optimal solutions found by each algorithm whereas f_{avg} represents the average objective function values out of five runs.

We compare the **mDPSO** algorithm to two genetic algorithms, namely, **RKGA** by Snyder & Daskin [16] and **mrOXGA** by Silberholz & Golden [20] where **RKGA** is re-implemented under the same machine environment. Table 6 summarizes the solution quality in terms of relative percent deviations from the optimal values and **CPU** time requirements for all three algorithms. Note that our machine has a similar speed as Silberholz & Golden [20]. A two-sided paired *t*-test which compares the results on Table 6 with a null hypothesis that the algorithms were identical generated *p*-values of 0.167 and 0.009 for **mDPSO** vs. **mrOXGA** and **mDPSO** vs. **RKGA**, suggesting near-identical results between **mDPSO** and **mrOXGA**. On the other hand, the paired *t*-test confirms that the differences between **mDPSO** and **RKGA** were significant on the behalf of **mDPSO** subject to the fact that **RKGA** was computationally less expensive than both **mDPSO** and **mrOXGA** when solely the optimal instances are considered.

	mDPSO			mrOXGA		RKGA	
Instance	n_{opt}	Δ_{avg}	t_{avg}	Δ_{avg}	t_{avg}	Δ_{avg}	t_{avg}
11EIL51	5	0.00	0.10	0.00	0.26	0.00	0.08
14ST70	5	0.00	0.12	0.00	0.35	0.00	0.07
16EIL76	5	0.00	0.13	0.00	0.37	0.00	0.11
16PR76	5	0.00	0.17	0.00	0.45	0.00	0.16
20KROA100	5	0.00	0.24	0.00	0.63	0.00	0.25
20KROB100	5	0.00	0.23	0.00	0.60	0.00	0.22
20KROC100	5	0.00	0.23	0.00	0.62	0.00	0.23
20KROD100	5	0.00	0.24	0.00	0.67	0.00	0.43
20KROE100	5	0.00	0.23	0.00	0.58	0.00	0.15
20RAT99	5	0.00	0.21	0.00	0.50	0.00	0.24
20RD100	5	0.00	0.23	0.00	0.51	0.00	0.29
21EIL101	5	0.00	0.19	0.00	0.48	0.00	0.18
21LIN105	5	0.00	0.25	0.00	0.60	0.00	0.33
22PR107	5	0.00	0.23	0.00	0.53	0.00	0.20
25PR124	5	0.00	0.41	0.00	0.68	0.00	0.26
26BIER127	5	0.00	0.44	0.00	0.78	0.00	0.28
28PR136	5	0.00	0.52	0.00	0.79	0.16	0.36
29PR144	5	0.00	0.46	0.00	1.00	0.00	0.44
30KROA150	5	0.00	0.47	0.00	0.98	0.00	0.32
30KROB150	5	0.00	0.60	0.00	0.98	0.00	0.71
31PR152	5	0.00	1.38	0.00	0.97	0.00	0.38
32U159	5	0.00	0.64	0.00	0.98	0.00	0.55
39RAT195	5	0.00	0.99	0.00	1.37	0.00	1.33
40D198	5	0.00	1.77	0.00	1.63	0.07	1.47
40KROA200	5	0.00	1.11	0.00	1.66	0.00	0.95
40KROB200	5	0.00	2.44	0.05	1.63	0.01	1.29
45TS225	2	0.05	1.75	0.14	1.71	0.28	1.09
46PR226	5	0.00	0.74	0.00	1.54	0.00	1.09
53GIL262	5	0.00	4.76	0.45	3.64	0.55	3.05
53PR264	5	0.00	1.11	0.00	2.36	0.09	2.72
60PR299	1	0.07	5.66	0.05	4.59	0.16	4.08
64LIN318	5	0.00	5.72	0.00	8.08	0.54	5.39
80RD400	4	0.02	13.66	0.58	14.58	0.72	10.27
84FL417	4	0.00	13.06	0.04	8.15	0.06	6.18
88PR439	3	0.00	16.15	0.00	19.06	0.83	15.09
89PCB442	3	0.15	28.59	0.01	23.43	1.23	11.74
Avg	4.64	0.01	2.92	0.04	2.99	0.13	2.00
Machine	P IV 3.20 GHz			P IV 3.00 GHz			

Table 6. Comparison for Optimal Instances

	mDPSO		mrOXGA		RKGA	
Instance	f_{avg}	t_{avg}	f_{avg}	t_{avg}	f_{avg}	t_{avg}
11EIL51	**174.0**	100.0	**174.0**	259.2	**174.0**	78.2
14ST70	**316.0**	120.0	**316.0**	353.0	**316.0**	65.6
16EIL76	**209.0**	130.0	**209.0**	369.0	**209.0**	106.4
16PR76	**64925.0**	170.0	**64925.0**	447.0	**64925.0**	156.2
20KROA100	**9711.0**	240.0	**9711.0**	628.2	**9711.0**	249.8
20KROB100	**10328.0**	230.0	**10328.0**	603.2	**10328.0**	215.6
20KROC100	**9554.0**	230.0	**9554.0**	621.8	**9554.0**	225.0
20KROD100	**9450.0**	240.0	**9450.0**	668.8	**9450.0**	434.4
20KROE100	**9523.0**	230.0	**9523.0**	575.0	**9523.0**	147.0
20RAT99	**497.0**	210.0	**497.0**	500.0	**497.0**	243.8
20RD100	**3650.0**	230.0	**3650.0**	506.2	**3650.0**	290.8
21EIL101	**249.0**	190.0	**249.0**	478.2	**249.0**	184.6
21LIN105	**8213.0**	250.0	**8213.0**	603.2	**8213.0**	334.4
22PR107	**27898.0**	230.0	27898.6	534.4	27898.6	197.0
25PR124	**36605.0**	410.0	**36605.0**	678.0	**36605.0**	259.0
26BIER127	**72418.0**	440.0	**72418.0**	784.4	**72418.0**	275.2
28PR136	**42570.0**	520.0	**42570.0**	793.8	42639.8	362.8
29PR144	**45886.0**	460.0	**45886.0**	1003.2	45887.4	437.6
30KROA150	**11018.0**	470.0	**11018.0**	981.2	**11018.0**	319.0
30KROB150	**12196.0**	600.0	**12196.0**	978.4	**12196.0**	712.4
31PR152	**51576.0**	1380.0	**51576.0**	965.4	**51576.0**	381.2
32U159	**22664.0**	640.0	**22664.0**	984.4	**22664.0**	553.2
39RAT195	**854.0**	990.0	**854.0**	1374.8	**854.0**	1325.0
40D198	**10557.0**	1770.0	**10557.0**	1628.2	10564.0	1468.6
40KROA200	**13406.0**	1110.0	**13406.0**	1659.4	**13406.0**	950.2
40KROB200	**13111.0**	2440.0	13117.6	1631.4	13112.2	1294.2
45TS225	**68376.0**	1750.0	68435.2	1706.2	68530.8	1087.4
46PR226	**64007.0**	740.0	**64007.0**	1540.6	**64007.0**	1094.0
53GIL262	**1013.0**	4760.0	1017.6	3637.4	1018.6	3046.8
53PR264	**29549.0**	1110.0	**29549.0**	2359.4	29574.8	2718.6
60PR299	22631.0	5660.0	**22627.0**	4593.8	22650.2	4084.4
64LIN318	**20765.0**	5720.0	**20765.0**	8084.4	20877.8	5387.6
80RD400	6362.4	13660.0	6397.8	14578.2	6407.0	10265.6
84FL417	**9651.2**	13060.0	9654.6	8152.8	9657.0	6175.2
88PR439	60099.4	16150.0	**60099.0**	19059.6	60595.4	15087.6
89PCB442	21690.0	28590.0	**21658.2**	23434.4	21923.0	11743.8
99D493	20118.6	23193.8	**20117.2**	35718.8	20260.4	14887.8
115RAT575	2419.8	33521.6	**2414.8**	48481.0	2442.4	46834.4
131P654	**27432.4**	39847.0	27508.2	32672.0	27448.4	46996.8
132D657	22714.6	64956.2	**22599.0**	132243.6	22857.6	58449.8
145U724	17422.8	141587.8	**17370.6**	161815.2	17806.2	59625.2
157RAT783	**3297.2**	114315.8	3300.2	152147.0	3341.0	89362.4
201PR1002	115759.4	231546.6	**114582.2**	464356.4	117421.2	332406.2
212U1060	**107316.4**	341759.6	108390.4	594637.4	110158.0	216999.8
217VM1084	**131716.8**	310097.4	131884.6	562040.6	133743.4	390115.6
Overal Avg	27553.3	31245.7	27554.3	50930.4	27741.3	30169.1

Table 7. Comparision to Silberholz & Golden [20]

Silberholz & Golden [20] provided larger problem instances ranging from 493 (99) to 1084 (217) nodes (clusters) where no optimal solutions are available. However, they provided the results of **mrOXGA** and **RKGA**. We compare the **mDPSO** results to those presented in Silberholz & Golden [20]. As seen in Table 7, **mDPSO** generated consistently better results than both **RKGA** and **mrOXGA** in terms of solution quality even if the larger instances are considered. In particular, 4 out 9 larger instances are further improved by **mDPSO**. The paired t-test on the objective function values on Table 7 confirms that the differences between **mDPSO** and **RKGA** were significant since p-value was 0.030 (null hypothesis is rejected) whereas **mDPSO** was equivalent to **mrOXGA** since p-value was 0.979. In terms of **CPU** times, the paired t-test on the **CPU** times confirms that the differences between **mDPSO** and **mrOXGA** were significant since the p-values was 0.040 whereas it was failed to reject the null hypothesis of being equal difference between **mDPSO** and **RKGA** since the p-value was 0.700. The paired t-test indicates that **mDPSO** was able to generate lower objective function values with less **CPU** times than **mrOXGA**. On the other hand, **mDPSO** yielded much better objective function values with identical **CPU** times than **RKGA**. Finally, the detailed statistics accumulated for the **mDPSO** algorithm during the runs are given in Table 8. Briefly, the statistics about the objective function values, **CPU** times, number of generations, average number of 2-opts, and average number of **DC**, respectively.

4. Conclusions

The **mDPSO** algorithm proposed employs the destruction and construction procedure of the iterated greedy algorithm (**IG**) in its mutation phase. Its performance is enhanced by employing a population initialization scheme based on an **NEH** constructive heuristic for which some speed-up methods previously developed by authors are used for greedy node insertions. Furthermore, the **mDPSO** algorithm is hybridized with local search heuristics to achieve further improvements in the solution quality. To evaluate its performance, the **mDPSO** algorithm is tested on a set of benchmark instances with symmetric Euclidean distances ranging from 51 (11) to 1084 (217) nodes (clusters) from the literature. Furthermore, the **mDPSO** algorithm was able to find optimal solutions for a large percentage of problem instances from a set of test problems in the literature. It was also able to further improve 4 out of 9 larger instances from the literature. Both solution quality and computation times are competitive to or even better than the best performing algorithms from the literature.

5. Acknowledgment

The first author dedicates this paper to Dr. Alice E. Smith from Industrial and Systems Engineering Department at Auburn University. He is grateful to Dr. Thomas Stützle from IRIDIA, University of Brussels, for his generosity in providing his IG code. We are also greatiful to Dr. Gregory Gutin and Daniel Karapetyan from University of London for preparing the larger GTSP instances. In addition, P. N. Suganthan acknowledges the financial support offered by the A*Star (Agency for Science, Technology and Research) under the grant # 052 101 0020.

Instance	f_{avg}	f_{min}	f_{max}	t_{avg}	t_{min}	t_{max}	g_{avg}	g_{min}	g_{max}	$2opt$	DC
11EIL51	174.0	174.0	174.0	0.1	0.1	0.2	1.0	1.0	1.0	2.0	7346.6
14ST70	316.0	316.0	316.0	0.1	0.1	0.1	1.0	1.0	1.0	2.0	10387.8
16EIL76	209.0	209.0	209.0	0.1	0.1	0.1	1.0	1.0	1.0	2.0	11026.4
16PR76	64925.0	64925.0	64925.0	0.2	0.2	0.2	1.0	1.0	1.0	2.0	14108.2
20KROA100	9711.0	9711.0	9711.0	0.2	0.2	0.3	1.0	1.0	1.0	2.0	19958.6
20KROB100	10328.0	10328.0	10328.0	0.2	0.2	0.3	1.0	1.0	1.0	2.0	18637.0
20KROC100	9554.0	9554.0	9554.0	0.2	0.2	0.3	1.0	1.0	1.0	2.0	18370.0
20KROD100	9450.0	9450.0	9450.0	0.2	0.2	0.3	1.0	1.0	1.0	2.0	19146.4
20KROE100	9523.0	9523.0	9523.0	0.2	0.2	0.3	1.0	1.0	1.0	2.0	19235.8
20RAT99	497.0	497.0	497.0	0.2	0.2	0.2	1.0	1.0	1.0	2.0	17025.2
20RD100	3650.0	3650.0	3650.0	0.2	0.2	0.2	1.0	1.0	1.0	2.0	18345.6
21EIL101	249.0	249.0	249.0	0.2	0.2	0.2	1.0	1.0	1.0	2.0	15256.0
21LIN105	8213.0	8213.0	8213.0	0.3	0.2	0.3	1.0	1.0	1.0	2.0	20275.6
22PR107	27898.0	27898.0	27898.0	0.2	0.2	0.2	1.0	1.0	1.0	2.0	17978.0
25PR124	36605.0	36605.0	36605.0	0.4	0.3	0.7	1.8	1.0	4.0	2.8	31702.0
26BIER127	72418.0	72418.0	72418.0	0.4	0.3	0.6	1.8	1.0	3.0	2.8	34417.4
28PR136	42570.0	42570.0	42570.0	0.5	0.4	0.8	2.0	1.0	4.0	3.0	39157.2
29PR144	45886.0	45886.0	45886.0	0.5	0.4	0.7	1.4	1.0	3.0	2.4	34640.6
30KROA150	11018.0	11018.0	11018.0	0.5	0.4	0.6	1.2	1.0	2.0	2.2	35139.2
30KROB150	12196.0	12196.0	12196.0	0.6	0.4	1.3	2.2	1.0	7.0	3.2	44800.0
31PR152	51576.0	51576.0	51576.0	1.4	0.5	2.3	6.6	1.0	13.0	7.6	102702.0
32U159	22664.0	22664.0	22664.0	0.6	0.5	1.0	2.2	1.0	5.0	3.2	47115.2
39RAT195	854.0	854.0	854.0	1.0	0.6	1.2	2.6	1.0	4.0	3.6	68885.4
40D198	10557.0	10557.0	10557.0	1.8	0.7	2.5	5.8	1.0	10.0	6.8	123194.6
40KROA200	13406.0	13406.0	13406.0	1.1	0.7	1.3	2.8	1.0	4.0	3.8	76493.0
40KROB200	13111.0	13111.0	13111.0	2.4	1.2	4.1	9.6	3.0	16.0	10.6	169724.4
45TS225	68376.0	68340.0	68400.0	1.7	0.7	3.3	6.2	1.0	16.0	37.2	418896.2
46PR226	64007.0	64007.0	64007.0	0.7	0.7	0.8	1.0	1.0	1.0	2.0	48324.4
53GIL262	1013.0	1013.0	1013.0	4.8	2.0	9.1	16.2	4.0	37.0	17.2	300605.2
53PR264	29549.0	29549.0	29549.0	1.1	1.0	1.4	1.2	1.0	2.0	2.2	68722.2
60PR299	22631.0	22615.0	22635.0	5.7	4.0	7.9	13.8	8.0	29.0	54.8	860095.2
64LIN318	20765.0	20765.0	20765.0	5.7	3.2	9.7	12.4	5.0	30.0	13.4	334602.4
80RD400	6362.4	6361.0	6368.0	13.7	6.7	17.3	18.6	8.0	30.0	29.6	911334.6
84FL417	9651.2	9651.0	9652.0	13.1	11.0	15.7	32.6	24.0	44.0	43.6	829024.2
88PR439	60099.4	60099.0	60100.0	16.2	8.2	24.8	28.4	9.0	48.0	49.4	1173370.8
89PCB442	21690.0	21657.0	21802.0	28.6	8.1	59.6	57.2	10.0	125.0	78.2	1813548.8
99D493	20118.6	20045.0	20271.0	23.2	9.7	39.6	30.4	7.0	67.0	81.4	2240001.4
115RAT575	2419.8	2388.0	2449.0	33.5	20.5	43.4	32.0	18.0	50.0	83.0	2681845.4
131P654	27432.4	27432.0	27433.0	39.8	11.8	54.7	58.0	12.0	83.0	109.0	2740248.6
132D657	22714.6	22543.0	22906.0	65.0	38.1	85.1	61.2	22.0	91.0	112.2	3891504.4
145U724	17422.8	17257.0	17569.0	141.6	64.8	209.1	100.2	38.0	171.0	151.2	6502515.2
157RAT783	3297.2	3283.0	3324.0	114.3	80.2	157.3	70.2	47.0	99.0	121.2	5182433.0
201PR1002	115759.4	114731.0	116644.0	231.5	131.5	325.1	70.2	40.0	125.0	121.2	7972666.2
212U1060	107316.4	106659.0	107937.0	341.8	169.7	514.4	125.4	65.0	208.0	176.4	10209723.6
217VM1084	131716.8	131165.0	132394.0	310.1	133.9	389.8	113.6	36.0	156.0	164.6	9468416.8
Avg	27553.3	27491.5	27617.2	31.2	15.9	44.2	20.1	8.5	33.4	34.0	1304065.5

Table 8. Experimental Data Collected for **mDPSO**

6. References

G. Laporte, A. Asef-Vaziri, C. Sriskandarajah, Some applications of the generalized travelling salesman problem, Journal of the Operational Research Society 47 (12) (1996) 461–1467.

A. Henry-Labordere, The record balancing problem—A dynamic programming solution of a generalized travelling salesman problem, Revue Francaise D Informatique DeRecherche Operationnelle 3 (NB2) (1969) 43–49.

C.E. Noon, The generalized traveling salesman problem, Ph.D. thesis, University of Michigan, 1988.

D. Ben-Arieh, G. Gutin, M. Penn, A. Yeo, A. Zverovitch, Process planning for rotational parts using the generalized traveling salesman problem, International Journal of Production Research 41 (11) (2003) 2581–2596.

J.P. Saskena, Mathematical model of scheduling clients through welfare agencies, Journal of the Canadian Operational Research Society 8 (1970) 185–200.

S.S. Srivastava, S. Kumar, R.C. Garg, P. Sen, Generalized traveling salesman problem through n sets of nodes, Journal of the Canadian Operational Research Society 7 (1970) 97–101.

G. Laporte, H. Mercure, Y. Nobert, Finding the shortest Hamiltonian circuit through n clusters: A Lagrangian approach, Congressus Numerantium 48 (1985) 277–290.

G. Laporte, H. Mercure, Y. Nobert, Generalized travelling salesman problem through n-sets of nodes—The asymmetrical case, Discrete Applied Mathematics 18 (2) (1987) 185–197.

G. Laporte, Y. Nobert, Generalized traveling salesman problem through n-sets of nodes—An integer programming approach, INFOR 21 (1) (1983) 61–75.

M. Fischetti, J.J. Salazar-Gonzalez, P. Toth, The symmetrical generalized traveling salesman polytope, Networks 26(2) (1995) 113–123.

M. Fischetti, J.J. Salazar-Gonza´lez, P. Toth, A branch-and-cut algorithm for the symmetric generalized travelling salesman problem, Operations Research 45 (3) (1997) 378–394.

A.G. Chentsov, L.N. Korotayeva, The dynamic programming method in the generalized traveling salesman problem, Mathematical and Computer Modelling 25 (1) (1997) 93–105.

C.E. Noon, J.C. Bean, A Lagrangian based approach for the asymmetric generalized traveling salesman problem, Operations Research 39 (4) (1991) 623–632.

J. Renaud, F.F. Boctor, An efficient composite heuristic for the symmetric generalized traveling salesman problem, European Journal of Operational Research 108 (3) (1998) 571–584.

J. Renaud, F.F. Boctor, G. Laporte, A fast composite heuristic for the symmetric traveling salesman problem, INFORMS Journal on Computing 4 (1996) 134–143.

L.V. Snyder and M.S. Daskin, A random-key genetic algorithm for the generalized traveling salesman problem, European Journal of Operational research 174 (2006) 38-53.

M.F. Tasgetiren, P.N. Suganthan, Q.-K. Pan, A discrete particle swarm optimization algorithm for the generalized traveling salesman problem, In the Proceedings of the 9th annual conference on genetic and evolutionary computation (GECCO2007), 2007, London, UK, pp.158-167.

M.F. Tasgetiren, P.N. Suganthan, Q.-K. Pan, Y.-C. Liang, A genetic algorithm for the generalized traveling salesman problem, In the Proceeding of the World Congress on Evolutionary Computation (CEC2007), 2007, Singapore, p:2382-2389.

M.F. Tasgetiren, P.N. Suganthan, Q.-K. Pan, Y.-C. Liang, A hybrid iterated greedy algorithm for the generalized traveling salesman problem, 2006, Under second revision by European Journal of Operational Research.

J. Silberholz, B. Golden, The generalized traveling salesman problem: A new genetic algorithm approach, In: Edward K. B. et al. (Eds.), Extending the horizons: Advances in Computing, Optimization and Decision Technologies. Vol. 37, Springer-Verlag, pp. 165-181.

R.C. Eberhart, J. Kennedy A new optimizer using particle swarm theory. Proceedings of the Sixth International Symposium on Micro Machine and Human Science, Nagoya, Japan, 1995. p. 39-43.

J. Kennedy, R. C. Eberhart, and Y. Shi, Swarm Intelligence. San Mateo, Morgan Kaufmann, CA, USA, 2001.

M. Clerc Particle Swarm Optimization, ISTE Ltd., France, 2006.

Q.-K. Pan, M.F. Tasgetiren, Y.-C. Liang, 2006a, Minimizing total earliness and tardiness penalties with a common due date on a single machine using a discrete particle swarm optimization algorithm. In: Proceedings of Ant Colony Optimization and Swarm Intelligence (ANTS2006), LNCS 4150, Springer-Verlag, pp. 460-467.

Q.-K. Pan, M.F. Tasgetiren, Y.-C. Liang, 2006b, A discrete particle swarm optimization algorithm for the permutation flowshop sequencing problem with makespan criterion. In: Proceedings of the 26th SGAI International Conference on Innovative Techniques and Applications of Artificial Intelligence (AI-2006), Cambridge, UK, pp. 19-31.

Q.-K. Pan, M.F. Tasgetiren, Y.-C. Liang, 2007a, A discrete particle swarm optimization algorithm for the no-wait flowshop scheduling problem with makespan and total flowtime criteria. Computers and Operations Research 35(9) (2008) 2807-2839.

G. Reinelt, TSPLIB—A traveling salesman problem library, ORSA Journal on Computing 4 (1996) 134–143.

M. Nawaz, E.E. Enscore Jr., I.A. Ham., Heuristic algorithm for the m-machine, n-job flow shop sequencing problem. OMEGA; 11(1) (1983) 91-95.

R. Ruiz and T. Stutzle, A simple and effective iterated greedy algorithm for the permutation flowshop scheduling problem, European Journal of Operational Research 174 (2006)38-53.

D. Rosenkrantz, R. Stearns, P. Lewis, Approximate algorithms for the traveling salesman problem. Proceedings of the 15th Annual Symposium of Switching and Automata Theory 1974 .33-42.

S. Lin, B.W. Kernighan, An effective heuristic algorithm for the traveling salesman problem Operations Research, 21 (1973) 498-516.

6

Solving TSP by Transiently Chaotic Neural Networks

Shyan-Shiou Chen[1] and Chih-Wen Shih[2]
[1]*Department of Mathematics, National Taiwan Normal University, Taipei,*
[2]*Department of Applied Mathematics, National Chiao Tung University, Hsinchu, Taiwan, R.O.C.*

1. Introduction

Inspired by the information processing of human neural systems, the artificial neural networks (ANNs) have been developed and applied to solve problems in various disciplines with varying degrees of success. For example, ANNs have been applied to memory storage, pattern recognition, categorization, error correction, decision making, and machine learning in object oriented machine. Various computational schemes and algorithms have been devised for solving the travelling salesman problem which is a difficult NP-hard combinatorial optimization problem. The use of ANN as a computational machine to solve combinatorial optimization problems, including TSP, dates back to 1985 by Hopfield and Tank (1985). Although the achievement of such an application broadens the capacity of ANNs, there remain several insufficiencies to be improved for such a computational task, cf. (Smith, 1999). They include that the computations can easily get trapped at local minimum of the objective function, feasibility of computational outputs, and suitable choice of parameters. Improvements of feasibility and solution quality for the scheme have been reported subsequently. Among them, there is a success in adding the chaotic ingredient into the network to enhance the global searching ability. Chaotic behavior is an inside essence of stochastic processes in nonlinear deterministic system. Recently, chaotic neural networks have been paid much attention to, and contribute toward solving TSP. Chaotic phenomena arise from nonlinear system, and the discrete-time analogue of Hopfield's model can admit such a dynamics. Notably, the discrete-time neural network models can also be implemented into analogue circuits, cf. (Hänggi et al., 1999 ; Harrer & Nossek, 1992).

The chapter aims at introducing recent progress in discrete-time neural network models, in particular, the transiently chaotic neural network (TCNN) and the advantage of adopting piecewise linear activation function. We shall demonstrate the use of TCNN in solving the TSP and compare the results with other neural networks. The chaotic ingredients improve the shortcoming of the previous ODE models in which the outputs strongly depend on the initial conditions and are easily trapped at the local minimum of objective function. There are transiently chaotic phase and convergent phase for the TCNN. The parameters for convergent phase are confirmed by the nonautonomous discrete-time LaSalle's invariant principle, whereas the ones for chaotic phase are derived by applying the Marotto's theorem. The Marotto's theorem which generalizes the Li-York's theorem on chaos from one-dimension to multi-dimension has found its best application in the discrete-time neural network model considered herein.

In Section 2, we will introduce the setting of solving the TSP by the neural networks, including the description of objective functions to be minimized at optimal routes, and the original work by Hopfield and Tank. In Section 3, we review the LaSalle's invariant principle, the Marotto's theorem, and introduce the discrete-time analogue of Hopfield's network. The recent progress in the transiently chaotic neural network is summarized in Section 4. We arrange some numerical simulations in applying the TCNN with piecewise linear activation function in Section 5. Finally, the chapter is concluded with some discussions.

2. Solving TSP via Hopfield neural network

Suppose there are N cities indexed by i= 1, 2,..., N and the distance between city i and city k is d_{ik}. The optimal solution to the TSP consists of an ordered list of the N cities. The list expresses the order of the cities visited and indicates the path with shortest total tour length. Let us describe how to map the TSP into the computational networks. For each city, its final location in the ordered list is to be specified by the asymptotic output states of a set of N neurons. For example, for a 10-city problem, if city i is the seventh city visited in an optimal solution, then it is represented by the corresponding outputs of 10 neurons:

$$0\,0\,0\,0\,0\,0\,1\,0\,0\,0.$$

Accordingly, N^2 neurons will be needed in the computational network for a N-city TSP. We thus arrange the outputs of these neurons into a $N\times N$ matrix. In such a representation, an ideal output matrix with only one entry equal to one in each row and in each column, and other entries all zero, will then correspond to a feasible solution of the TSP.
Thereafter, the TSP with N cities can be formulated as the following optimization problem:

$$\text{Minimize} \quad E(\mathbf{y}) = \frac{1}{2}\sum_{i=1}^{N}\sum_{j=1}^{N}\sum_{k=1}^{N} d_{ij} y_{ik}(y_{j(k-1)} + y_{j(k+1)}), \tag{1}$$

where matrix $\mathbf{y}=[y_{ij}]$ is constrained by

$$\sum_{i=1}^{N} y_{ij} = 1 \text{ and } \sum_{j=1}^{N} y_{ij} = 1, \tag{2}$$

for all i,j =1,...,N, and $y_{i0}=y_{iN}$ and $y_{i1}=y_{i(N+1)}$. The variables $y_{ij}\in[0,1]$, i,j =1,...,N, can also be regarded as the probability for the i th city to be visited the j th time. If every y_{ij} is either 0 or 1, then the constraint Eq. (2) means that every city must be visited only once. Under such a circumstances, the optimal solution of the objective function $E(\mathbf{y})$ equals the shortest distance of the traveling route. Notably, any shift of an optimal solution also yields an optimal solution (with the same shortest tour length). Thus, the optimal solution is not unique.
The main idea of using neural networks to solve TSP is to search the global minimum of the objective function which involves the data of TSP, through evolutions of the states of the network. Hopfield & Tank (1985) considered the following objective function

$$E(\mathbf{y})=\frac{\gamma_1}{2}\sum_{i=1}^{N}\sum_{j=1}^{N}\sum_{k\neq j}^{N}y_{ij}y_{ik}+\frac{\gamma_2}{2}\sum_{j=1}^{N}\sum_{i=1}^{N}\sum_{k\neq i}^{N}y_{ij}y_{kj}+\frac{\gamma_3}{2}(\sum_{i=1}^{N}\sum_{j=1}^{N}y_{ij}-N)^2 \tag{3}$$

$$+\frac{\gamma_4}{2}\sum_{i=1}^{N}\sum_{j=1}^{N}\sum_{k=1}^{N}d_{ij}y_{ik}(y_{j(k-1)}+y_{j(k+1)}). \tag{4}$$

Note that the minimum, i.e., zero, of (3) is attained at a feasible solution. They aimed at using the Hopfield network to locate the global minimum of this objective function. The Hopfield network is a continuous-time ODE system which consists of a fully interconnected system of computational elements or neurons arranged in, say, lattice L:

$$C_{\mathbf{i}}\frac{dx_{\mathbf{i}}}{dt}=-\frac{x_{\mathbf{i}}}{R_{\mathbf{i}}}+\sum_{\mathbf{j}\in L}w_{\mathbf{ij}}y_{\mathbf{j}}+I_{\mathbf{i}},\ \mathbf{i}\in L, \tag{5}$$

$$y_{\mathbf{i}}=g_{\mathbf{i}}(x_{\mathbf{i}}). \tag{6}$$

The synapse (or weight) between two neurons is defined by w_{ij}, which may be positive or negative depending on whether the action of neurons is in an excitatory or inhibitory manner; $x_{\mathbf{i}}$ is the internal state of neuron **i**, and $y_{\mathbf{i}}$ with $0\leq y_{\mathbf{i}}\leq 1$ is the external (output) state of neuron **i.** The parameter C_{i} (resp. R_{i}) is the input capacitance of the cell membrane (resp. the transmembrane resistance) of neuron **i**. The activation function g_{i} is a monotonically increasing function and thus has an inverse. Typical g_{i} is given by

$$g_{\mathbf{i}}(\xi)=\frac{1}{2}(1+\tanh(\xi/\varepsilon)),$$

where ε is a parameter controlling the slope of the activation function. The gradient descent dynamics of the neural network provides a decreasing property of the objective function for the TSP. For convenience of expression and derivation, we consider (5) on the one-dimensional array $\{1,2,\ldots,n\}$. There exists a Lyapunov function (energy function for the network)

$$V=-\frac{1}{2}\sum_{i=1}^{n}\sum_{j=1}^{n}w_{ij}y_iy_j-\sum_{i=1}^{n}I_iy_i+\sum_{i=1}^{n}\frac{1}{R_i}\int_0^{y_i}g_i^{-1}(\xi)d\xi. \tag{7}$$

The time derivative of V along a solution $\mathbf{x}(t)$ is computed as

$$\frac{dV}{dt}=-\sum_{i=1}^{n}\frac{dy_i}{dt}(\sum_{j=1}^{n}w_{ij}y_j-\frac{x_i}{R_i}+I_i)=-\sum_{i=1}^{n}\frac{dy_i}{dt}C_i\frac{dx_i}{dt}$$
$$=-C_i\sum_{i=1}^{n}[\frac{dg_i(x_i)}{dx_i}](\frac{dx_i}{dt})^2.$$

Due to the increasing property of the activation function g_i, we obtain

$$\frac{dV}{dt} \le 0, \text{and} \frac{dV}{dt} = 0 \text{ if } \frac{dx_i}{dt} = 0. \tag{8}$$

3. Discrete-time dynamical systems

Biological neurons are much more complicated than the simple threshold elements in ANNs. Chaotic behaviors have actually been observed experimentally in biological neurons, as pointed out in Aihara et al. (1990) and the references therein.

Discrete-time dynamical systems have attracted much attention in recent years, thanks to its capacity of applications and underlying sophisticated mathematical theory. Indeed, not only that discrete-time counterparts of classical theorems for continuous-time systems have been developed successfully, but also the chaotic behaviors for discrete-time systems can be characterized lucidly.

Due to the shortcomings that solutions get trapped at local minimum of objective function, and dependence of performance upon choosing initial conditions in continuous-time systems, researchers have attempted to introduce the chaotic ingredient into the networks. The stage was thus set for the development of discrete-time neural networks, cf. (Aihara et al., 1990; Chen & Aihara, 1995; Nozawa, 1992; Yamada & Aihara, 1997). In particular, Nozawa (1992) showed that the Euler approximation of the continuous-time Hopfield neural network with a negative self-feedback connection possesses chaotic dynamics, and has a much better searching ability in solving the TSP than the original continuous-time Hopfield neural network.

Notably, although it has been reported in (Bersini,1998; Bersini & Senser, 2002) that there exist chaotic behaviours in continuous-time Hopfield-type neural networks, it is still unknown whether the same concept or technique can be applied to the TSP problem.

We shall introduce the discrete-time Hopfield neural network in Subsection 3.1; then review the LaSalle's invariant principle for convergent dynamics and the Marotto's theorem for chaos, for discrete-time dynamical systems in Subsections 3.2, 3.3, respectively.

3.1 Discrete-time Hopfield neural networks

Discrete-time neural network model of Hopfield type can be described by the following equations: for $i = 1,\dots,n$,

$$x_i(t+1) = \mu x_i(t) + \sum_{j=1}^{n} w_{ij} y_j(t) + I_i. \tag{9}$$

Here, x_i is the internal state of neuron i; y_i is the output of neuron i; μ is the damping factor; w_{ii} is the self-feedback connection weight; w_{ij} is the connection weight from neuron j to neuron i; I_i is the input bias. The parameter μ (resp. ω_{ij}, I_i) in Eq. (9) can be compared to $1 - \frac{\Delta t}{C_i R_i}$ (resp. $\frac{\omega_{ij}\Delta t}{C_i}$, $\frac{I_i \Delta t}{C_i}$) in terms of the parameters in Eq. (5), where Δt is the discretization time step. System (9) is the Euler approximation of Eq. (5). There also exists a Lyapunov function for the discrete-time system (9):

$$V(\mathbf{y}) = -\frac{1}{2}\sum_{i=1}^{n}\sum_{j=1}^{n} w_{ij} y_i y_j - \sum_{i=1}^{n} I_i y_i - (\mu - 1)\sum_{i=1}^{n} \int_0^{y_i} g_i^{-1}(\xi) d\xi, \tag{10}$$

where again $y_i = g_i(x_i)$. It has been shown in (Chen & Aihara, 1997; Chen & Shih, 2002) that, under some conditions, the energy function (10) is decreasing along the solution of the system:

$$V(\mathbf{y}(t+1)) - V(\mathbf{y}(t)) \leq 0, \text{ for all } t \in \boldsymbol{N}.$$

Notably, the Lyapunov function (10) for the discrete-time network and the one (7) for the continuous-time network are quite similar. The existence of Lyapunov function basically guarantees the convergence of evolutions for the system to certain steady states, by the LaSalle's invariant principle. The transiently chaotic neural network is developed from this discrete-time network with transient chaos imbedded in. Before introducing the theory for the TCNN, let us review the LaSalle's invariant principle and the Marotto's theorem.

3.2 LaSalle's invariant principle

Long-time asymptotic behaviors of solutions for a dynamical system, such as neural network, are always important concerns. In 1960, LaSalle discovered the relation between Lyapunov function and Birkhoff limit set. Extended from the Lyapunov direct method, a uniform concept was developed to describe the asymptotic behaviors in terms of limit set. By the invariant property of limit set, a basic theory for the stability of motion of dynamical systems was derived. In this section, we review the invariant principle for both autonomous and non-autonomous discrete-time dynamical systems, cf. (LaSalle, 1976). First, we consider an autonomous difference equation

$$\mathbf{x}(t+1) = \mathbf{F}(\mathbf{x}(t)), \mathbf{x} \in R^n, t \in \boldsymbol{N}, \tag{11}$$

where $\mathbf{F}: R^n \to R^n$ is continuous. We assume that $\mathbf{x}^*$ is a fixed point (i.e. $\mathbf{F}(\mathbf{x}^*) = \mathbf{x}^*$). Suppose there exists a continuous, positive definite, and radially unbounded function $V: \bar{G} \to R, G \subset R^n$ with

$$\Delta V(\mathbf{x}) \leq 0, \forall \mathbf{x} \in G$$

where $\Delta V(\mathbf{x}) = V(\mathbf{F}(\mathbf{x})) - V(\mathbf{x})$, then every solution to Eq. (11) converges to the largest invariant set *M* contained in $\{\mathbf{x} \in G \mid \Delta V(\mathbf{x}) = 0\}$. If the set *M* only contains the equilibrium $\mathbf{x}^*$, then $\mathbf{x}^*$ is asymptotically stable. The function *V* satisfying $\Delta V(\mathbf{x}) \leq 0$ for all $\mathbf{x} \in G$ is said to be a *Lyapunov function* on set G.

Now we consider a discrete-time non-autonomous system. Let **N** be the set of positive integers. For a given continuous function $\mathbf{F}: \boldsymbol{N} \times R^n \longrightarrow R^n$, we consider the non-autonomous dynamical system

$$\mathbf{x}(t+1) = \mathbf{F}(t, \mathbf{x}(t)). \tag{12}$$

A sequence of points $\{\mathbf{x}(t) \mid t = 1, 2, \cdots\}$ in R^n is a solution of (12) if $\mathbf{x}(t+1) = \mathbf{F}(t, \mathbf{x}(t))$, for all $t \in \boldsymbol{N}$. Let $O_\mathbf{x} = \{\mathbf{x}(t) \mid t \in \boldsymbol{N}, \mathbf{x}(1) = \mathbf{x}\}$ be the orbit of **x**. We say that **p** is a ω-limit point of $O_\mathbf{x}$ if there exists a sequence of positive integers $\{t_k\}$ with $t_k \to \infty$ as $k \to \infty$, such that $\mathbf{p} = \lim_{k \to \infty} \mathbf{x}(t_k)$. Denote by $\omega(\mathbf{x})$ the set of all ω-limit points of $O_{\mathbf{x}}$. Let $\mathbf{N}_i$ represent the set of all positive integers larger than n_i, for some positive integer n_i. Let $\Omega \subseteq R^n$ and $\overline{\Omega}$ be its closure. For a function $V : N_0 \times \Omega \longrightarrow R$, we define $\dot{V}(t,\mathbf{x}) = V(t+1,\mathbf{F}(t,\mathbf{x})) - V(t,\mathbf{x})$ so that if $\{\mathbf{x}(t)\}$ is a solution of Eq. (12), then $\dot{V}(t,\mathbf{x}(t)) = V(t+1,\mathbf{x}(t+1)) - V(t,\mathbf{x}(t))$. V is said to be a *Lyapunov function* for (12) if

i. each $V(t,\cdot)$ is continuous, and

ii. for each $\mathbf{p} \in \overline{\Omega}$, there exists a neighborhood U of $\mathbf{p}$ such that $V(t,\mathbf{x})$ is bounded below for $\mathbf{x} \in U \cap \Omega$ and $t \in N_1$, $n_1 \geq n_0$, and

iii. there exists a non-degenerate continuous function $Q_0 : \overline{\Omega} \to R$ such that $\dot{V}(t,\mathbf{x}) \leq -Q_0(\mathbf{x}) \leq 0$ for all $\mathbf{x} \in \Omega$ and for all $t \in N_2$, $n_2 \geq n_1$,

or

iii.′ there exist a non-degenerate continuous function $Q_0 : \overline{\Omega} \to R$ and an equi-continuous family of functions $Q(t,\cdot) : \overline{\Omega} \to R$ such that $\lim_{t \to \infty} |Q(t,\mathbf{x}) - Q_0(\mathbf{x})| = 0$ for all $\mathbf{x} \in \Omega$ and $\dot{V}(t,\mathbf{x}) \leq -Q(t,\mathbf{x}) \leq 0$ for all $(t,\mathbf{x}) \in N_2 \times \Omega$, $n_2 \geq n_1$.

If there exists such a Lyapunov function V, then the LaSalle's invariant principle states that the ω-limit set of any point $\mathbf{x}$ lies in S_0, i.e. $\omega(\mathbf{x}) \subset S_0$, where

$$S_0 = \{\mathbf{x} \in \overline{\Omega} : Q_0(\mathbf{x}) = 0\}. \tag{13}$$

3.3 Marotto's theorem on chaos

Originally, a chaotic phenomenon was numerically found in the research of Lorenz on weather prediction in 1963. Later, the mathematical definition of chaos was initiated by Li & Yorke (1975) for one-dimensional continuous maps. A criterion of existence of chaos has been termed as "period three implies chaos" therein. More precisely, let $f : I \to I$ be a continuous map of the compact interval I of the real line R into itself; if f has a periodic point of period three, then f exhibits chaotic behavior. Three years later, the above result was generalized by Marotto (1978). He proposed the definition of "snapback repeller" and proved that "snapback repellers imply chaos" for multi-dimensional maps. The definition of snapback repeller was further clarified in (Marotto, 2005).

The theorem has provided the best analytic argument of chaos for multi-dimensional maps. The detailed description of chaos in the sense of Marotto is as follows. Let us define a system as $\mathbf{x}_{k+1} = F(\mathbf{x}_k)$ where $\mathbf{x}_k \in R^n$, and F is C^1 or piecewise C^1 with non-smooth points at suitable locations. A fixed point $\overline{\mathbf{x}}$ is said to be a *snapback repeller* (see Fig. 1) of F if all eigenvalues of $DF(\overline{\mathbf{x}})$ exceeding one in magnitude, and there exists a point $\mathbf{x}_0 \neq \overline{\mathbf{x}}$ in a repelling neighborhood of $\overline{\mathbf{x}}$, such that $F^m(\mathbf{x}_0) = \overline{\mathbf{x}}$ for some $m \in \mathbf{N}$, and

$\det(DF^j(\mathbf{x}_0)) \neq 0$, for all $1 \leq j \leq m$. If F has a snapback repeller, then the dynamical system defined by F is chaotic in the following sense: (i) There exists a positive integer m_0 such that for each integer $p \geq m_0$, F has p-periodic points. (ii) There exists a scrambled set, that is, an uncountable set L containing no periodic points such that the following pertains: (a) $F(L) \subset L$; (b) for every $\mathbf{y} \in L$ and any periodic point $\mathbf{x}$ of F,

$$\limsup_{k \to \infty} \| F^k(\mathbf{y}) - F^k(\mathbf{x}) \| > 0;$$

(c) for every $\mathbf{x}, \mathbf{y} \in L$ with $\mathbf{x} \neq \mathbf{y}$,

$$\limsup_{k \to \infty} \| F^k(\mathbf{y}) - F^k(\mathbf{x}) \| > 0;$$

(iii) There exists an uncountable subset L_0 of L such that for every $\mathbf{x}, \mathbf{y} \in L_0$,

$$\liminf_{k \to \infty} \| F^k(\mathbf{y}) - F^k(\mathbf{x}) \| = 0.$$

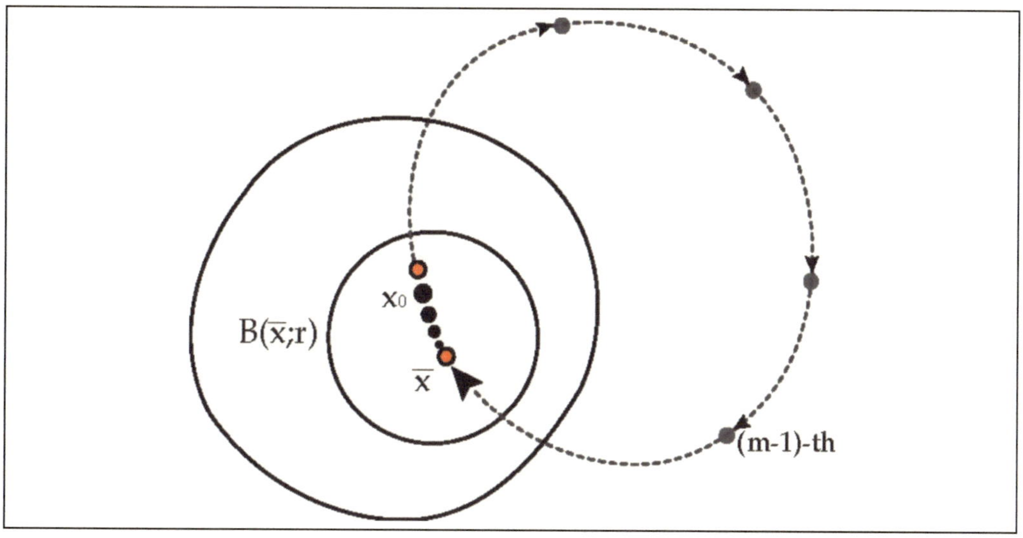

Fig. 1. Diagram of a snapback repeller. The point $\overline{X}$ is a snapback repeller. The point X_0 is a snapback point such that $F^m(X_0) = \overline{X}$ for some integer m. Note that the value of F at the (m-1)-th point is the snapback repeller $\overline{X}$.

Notably, (ii) (b) describes that any point in the scrambled set L does not converge to any periodic point of F under the iteration of F. It bears a sense that there only exist unstable periodic points in the system. (ii)(c) shows that there only exist unstable points in the scrambled set L. In other words, points in the scrambled set do not attract each other. (iii) describes that distances between the iterations of any pair of points in an uncountable subset of L approach zero. Although it seems that there exists no rule for the dynamical behavior, the behavior is controlled by the underlying deterministic system. It is not similar to the concept of randomness of a stochastic system. The chaotic behavior is very random but ordered.

Let us illustrate the existence of period-three points and a snap-back repeller in the sense of Li-Yorke and Marotto respectively, for the logistic map, $f_\mu(x) = \mu x(1-x), x \in [0,1]$, as an example. The period-three points and a snap-back repeller are presented in Fig. (2). There exists chaos in the sense of Li-Yorke (resp. Marotto) for the logistic map f_μ with $\mu = 4$.

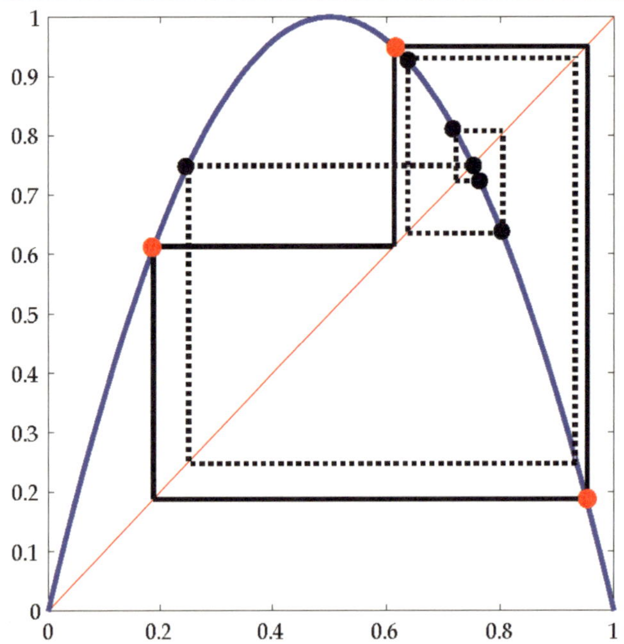

Fig. 2. The blue line is the graph of logistic map with $\mu = 4$. Black line illustrates the period 3 trajectory. The dotted line depicts a homoclinic orbit with snap-back points. This logistic map possesses Li-Yorke's and Marotto's chaos.

4. Transiently chaotic neural networks

The transiently chaotic neural network (TCNN) is equipped with a chaotic phase which prevails in the first stage of computation to enhance global searching and reduce the effect of variations from choosing initial values. This procedure can be realized by a suitable choice of parameters which typically starts from sufficiently large negative self-feedback connection weights. The process is then cooled down, as the self-feedback connection weights increases, while maintaining decreasing property of the energy (objective) function, and finally settles at a state with lower value of objective function. The characteristic of dynamical phenomena from chaotic phase to convergent phase is called "chaotic simulated annealing".

The TCNN, inherited from the Hopfield type network, was first proposed by Chen & Aihara (1995, 1997, 1999). Later, Chen & Shih (2002) performed a systematic analysis on the chaotic behaviors of the TCNN. The existence of chaos is proved by a geometrical formulation combined with the use of Marotto's theorem. The analysis has provided the ranges of parameters for the chaotic phase and convergent phase. Recently, Chen and Shih (2007) further extended the TCNN to the setting with piecewise linear activation function, which not only improves the performance of computation, but also admits more succinct and crystal mathematical description on the chaotic phase than the TCNN with the logistic activation function. Such a setting fits into the revised version of theorem in (Marotto, 2005) pertinently.

Let us describe the model equation for the TCNN.

$$x_i(t+1) = \mu x_i(t) - \omega_{ii}(t)[y_i(t) - a_{0i}] + \alpha[\sum_{j=1, j\neq i}^{n} \omega_{ij} y_j(t) + v_i], \tag{14}$$

$$|\omega_{ii}(t+1)| = |(1-\beta)\omega_{ii}(t)|, \tag{15}$$

for i=1,…,n, $t \in \mathbf{N}$, (positive integers), where x_i is the internal state of neuron i; y_i is the output of neuron i, which corresponds to x_i through an activation function; μ with $0 < \mu < 1$ is the damping factor of nerve membrane; ω_{ii} is the self-feedback connection weight; a_{0i} is the self-recurrent bias of neuron i; ω_{ij} is the connection weight from neuron j to neuron i; v_i is the input bias of neuron i; β with $0 < \beta < 1$, is the damping factor for ω_{ii}; α is a positive scaling parameter. Equation (15) represents an exponential cooling schedule in the annealing procedure. The activation function adopted in (Chen & Aihara, 1995; 1997; 1999) is the logistic function given by

$$y_i(t) = 1/[1 + \exp(-x_i(t)/\varepsilon)],$$

which is depicted in Fig. 3 (b).

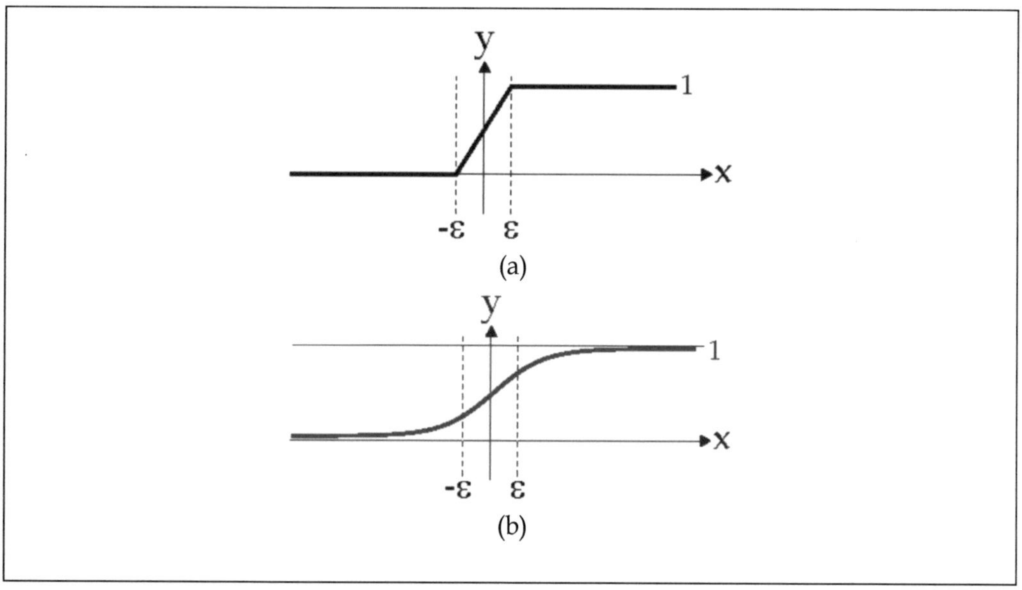

Fig. 3. The graphs of (a) the piecewise linear and (b) the logistic activation function.

One may also consider more general annealing process:

$$x_i(t+1) = \mu x_i(t) + (1-\beta)^{q(t)} \omega[y_i(t) - a_{0i}] + \alpha[\sum_{j=1, j\neq i}^{n} \omega_{ij} y_j(t) + v_i], \tag{16}$$

where i=1,...,n, $0 < \beta < 1$; $q(t)$ satisfies the condition that there exists an $n_1 \in \mathbf{N}$ such that $q(t) - t \geq 0$ for all $t > n_1$. The standard annealing process simply takes $q(t) = t$.

The disadvantage of using the logistic activation function is that the output values for some neurons may be neither close to one nor to zero, as demonstrated in Fig. (4). Although it is possible to avoid such a situation by choosing high gain of the logistic activation function, i.e., small ε, taking the piecewise linear output function (Fig. 3 (a)) leads to much better performance.

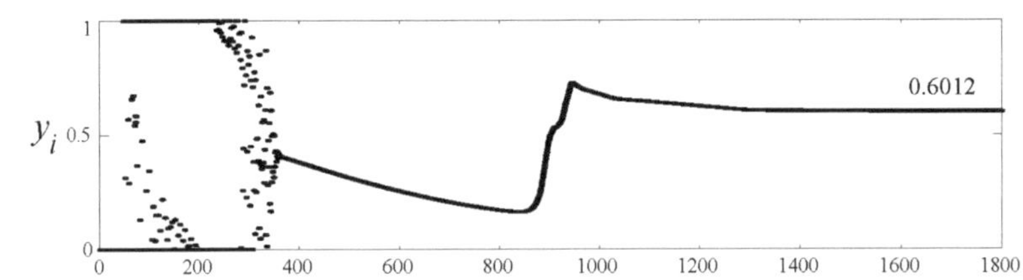

Fig. 4. An example that the TCNN with the logistic activation function has an infeasible solution, i.e., there exists an output entry y_i which approaches 0.6012, neither close to 1 nor to 0, after 1400 iterations.

4.1 Piecewise linear activation function

Chen & Shih (2007) proposed a transiently chaotic neural network (TCNN) with piecewise linear activation function, instead of the logistic one, as follows:

$$x_i(t+1) = \mu x_i(t) + (1-\beta)^{q(t)} \omega[y_i(t) - a_{0i}] + \sum_{j=1}^{n} w_{ij} y_j(t) + v_i, \tag{17}$$

where i=1,...,n, and x_i and y_i satisfy the following relation

$$y_i(t) = g_\varepsilon(x_i(t)) := [2 + |\frac{x_i(t)}{\varepsilon} + 1| - |\frac{x_i(t)}{\varepsilon} - 1|]/4, \varepsilon > 0, \tag{18}$$

That is, we consider the following time-dependent map on R^n:

$$F_i(t, \mathbf{x}) = \mu x_i + (1-\beta)^{q(t)} \omega[g_\varepsilon(x_i) - a_{0i}] + \sum_{j=1}^{n} \omega_{ij} g_\varepsilon(x_j) + v_i. \tag{19}$$

Corresponding to this piecewise linear activation function, for a fixed $\varepsilon > 0$, we partition the real line into the left (ℓ), middle (m), right (r) parts; namely,

$$\Omega_\ell := (-\infty, -\varepsilon), \Omega_{\mathrm{m}} := [-\varepsilon, \varepsilon], \Omega_{\mathrm{r}} := (\varepsilon, \infty). \tag{20}$$

Consequently, R^n can be partitioned into the following subsets:

$$\Omega_{q_1 \cdots q_n} = \{(x_1, \cdots, x_n) \in R^n \mid x_i \in \Omega_{q_i}; q_i = ``\mathrm{r}", ``\mathrm{m}", ``\ell"; i = 1, \cdots, n\}, \quad (21)$$

as illustrated in Fig. 5 for n=2. We may call $\Omega_{\mathrm{m}\cdots\mathrm{m}}$ the *interior region*, each $\Omega_{q_1 \cdots q_n}$, with $q_i = ``\ell", ``\mathrm{r}"$, for all i, an *saturated region*; each $\Omega_{q_1 \cdots q_n}$, with $q_i = ``\ell"$, or $``\mathrm{r}"$, for some i, and $q_j = ``\mathrm{m}"$ for some j, a *mixed region*.

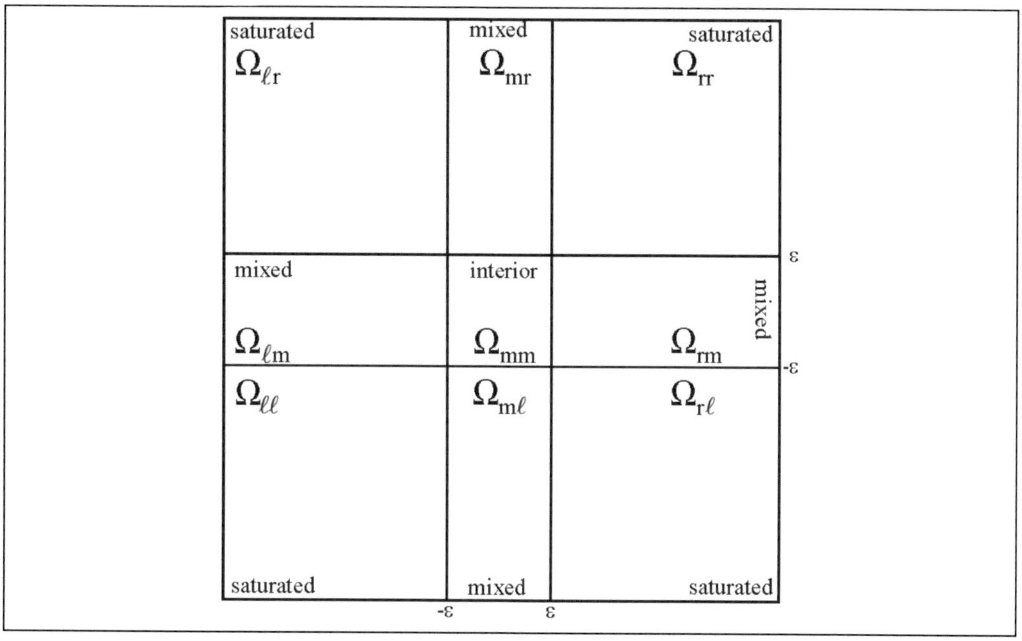

Fig. 5. Illustration of $\Omega_{q_1 q_2}$ in R^2, where q_1 and q_2 are $``\ell"$ or $``\mathrm{m}"$ or $``\mathrm{r}"$

Through introducing upper and lower bounds for the map (19), the existence of snap-back repellers in each of the 3^n regions, hence Marotto's chaos, for the system can be established. Let us quote the parameter conditions and the theorem. Consider

$$\text{(A)}\ \omega > 0,\ 0 < \tfrac{1-\mu}{\omega} < \tfrac{1}{2\varepsilon},\ -\tfrac{1-\mu}{\omega}\varepsilon - \tfrac{h}{\omega} + a_0 > 0,\ \tfrac{1-\mu}{\omega}\varepsilon + \tfrac{h}{\omega} + a_0 < 1,$$

$$\text{(B)}\ \mu\varepsilon + \omega(1 - a_0) - h > \tfrac{1}{\mu}[(\tfrac{1}{2}\omega - \omega a_0 + h)/(1 - \mu - \tfrac{\omega}{2\varepsilon}) - \omega + \omega a_0 - h].$$

Theorem 1 (Chen & Shih, 2007). If the parameters $(\mu, \omega, \varepsilon, a_{0i}, h_i)$, satisfy (A) and (B) with $a_0 = a_{0i}$, $h = h_i$, for every $i = 1, \ldots, n$, then there exist snap-back repellers for the TCNN with activation function (18).

On the other hand, system (17) admits a time-dependent Lyapunov function

$$V(t, \mathbf{x}) = -\frac{1}{2}\sum_{i=1}^{n}\sum_{j=1}^{n}\omega_{ij} y_i y_j - \sum_{i=1}^{n} v_i y_i - (\mu - 1)\varepsilon \sum_{i=1}^{n}(y_i^2 - y_i) + c^t, \quad (22)$$

where $y_i = g_\varepsilon(x_i)$, i=1,…,n, and 0< c <1. Note that V is globally Lipschitz, but not C^1. Let $W = [\omega_{ij}]_{n\times n}$. By applying the LaSalle's invariant principle, the following convergent theorem can be derived.

Theorem 2 (Chen & Shih, 2007). If $0 \le \mu \le 1$, $\varepsilon > 0$, $|\frac{1-\beta}{c}| < 1$ and the matrix $W + 2\varepsilon(1-\mu)I$ is positive-definite, then there exists $n_2 \in \mathbf{N}, n_2 > n_1$ so that $V(t+1, \mathbf{x}(t+1)) \le V(t, \mathbf{x}(t))$ for $t \ge n_2$ and V is a Lyapunov function for system (17) on $\mathbf{N}_2 \times R^n$.

The conditions for chaotic and convergent dynamical phases for the TCNN are all computable. The range of the parameters satisfying these conditions can also be depicted numerically. There are other advantages in adopting the piecewise linear activation function. Note that the feasible and optimal solutions lie in the saturated regions $\Omega_{q_1\cdots q_n}$, with $q_i =$ "ℓ", "r", for all i. One can further impose conditions so that the fixed points in the interior and mixed regions are unstable. Accordingly, iterations from almost any initial value converge to outputs with component equal to either 0 or 1. Details for these discussions can be found in (Chen & Shih, 2007).

On the other hand, the following objective function is considered in (Chen & Aihara, 1995)

$$E(\mathbf{y}) = \frac{\gamma_1}{2}[\sum_{i=1}^{N}(\sum_{k=1}^{N} y_{ik} - 1)^2 + \sum_{k=1}^{N}(\sum_{i=1}^{N} y_{ik} - 1)^2]$$

$$+\frac{\gamma_2}{2}\sum_{i=1}^{N}\sum_{j=1}^{N}\sum_{k=1}^{N} d_{ij} y_{ik}(y_{j(k-1)} + y_{j(k+1)}), \tag{23}$$

where γ_1 and γ_2 are parameters which are selected to reflect the relative importance of the constraints and the cost function of the tour length, respectively.

To apply the TCNN to the TSP, we reformulate the setting of TSP with two-dimensional indices into the one-dimensional form. Restated, by letting $s(i,j)=j+(i-1)N$, where N is the number of cities for the TSP, Eq. (23) becomes

$$E(\mathbf{y}) = -\frac{1}{2}\mathbf{y}\overline{W}\mathbf{y}^T - 2\gamma_1 I_{N^2\times N^2}\mathbf{y} + \gamma_1 N, \tag{24}$$

where, $I_{N^2\times N^2}$ is the identity matrix of size $N^2 \times N^2$, $\mathbf{y} = (y_1, \cdots, y_{s(i,j)}, \cdots, y_{N^2})$ and

$$\overline{W} = -\gamma_1[I_{N\times N} \otimes 1_{N\times N} + 1_{N\times N} \otimes I_{N\times N}] - \gamma_2 D \otimes B; \tag{25}$$

$1_{N\times N}$ is the matrix whose entries are all one, $D = [d_{ij}]^T$ and $B = [b_{ij}]$ with $b_{i,j} = 0$ except that $b_{i,i+1} = b_{i,i-1} = b_{1,N} = b_{N,1} = 1$; the $N^2 \times N^2$ block matrix $A \otimes B$ is defined by the formula $[A \otimes B]_{ij} = [a_{ij}B]$, where $A = [a_{ij}]$ and $B = [b_{ij}]$. The TCNN for the TSP is adjusted to

$$x_i(t+1) = \mu x_i(t) + (1-\beta)^{q(t)}\omega[y_i(t) - a_{0i}] + \sum_{j=1}^{N^2} W_{ij} y_j(t) + 2\gamma_1, \tag{26}$$

where $W = [W_{ij}] := \overline{W} - \text{diag}[\overline{W}]/2$, i=1,...,N^2. According to previous discussions, there is a Lyapunov function for Eq. (17):

$$V(t,\mathbf{y}) = -\frac{1}{2}\sum_{i=1}^{N^2}\sum_{j=1}^{N^2} W_{ij}y_iy_j - \sum_{i=1}^{N^2} 2\gamma_1 y_i - (\mu-1)\varepsilon\sum_{i=1}^{N^2}(y_i^2 - y_i) + c^t. \quad (27)$$

Notice that the Lyapunov function (27) can be compared to a constant shift of the objective function (24) when $|c|<1$, ε is sufficiently small and as t is large.

5. Numerical simulations

Let us describe the method to suitably choose the parameters in the numerical simulation. Due to the deterministic nature for the TCNN (17), parameters are selected such that its dynamical behaviors have some stable properties. Therefore, we take a parameter μ with $0< \mu < 1$ for boundedness of iterations for the TCNN. Set ω=0, and choose ε, a_{0i}, h, where $h = \max\{h_i : i = 1,\cdots,N^2\}$, $h_i = \sum_{k=1}^{N^2}\{|W_{ik}| + 2|\gamma_1|\}$, $i = 1,\cdots,N^2$, so that the TCNN with these parameters is in convergent phase. In convergent phase, any iteration is going to settle at a fixed point. Next, we let $|\omega|$ increase from 0 to see if parameters $(\mu,\varepsilon,\omega,a_{0i},h)$ enter the chaotic regime which has been justified in (Chen & Shih, 2002; 2007). These computations can be assisted by a computer programming. If the output matrix does not tend to a permutation matrix, one can enlarge slightly the parameter γ_1 in Eq. (25).

In this section, we quote the numerical simulations in (Chen & Shih, 2007) to demonstrate the computation performance of using the TCNN (17) to find the optimal route of the TSP. We consider the five cities $\{1,2,3,4,10\}$ with coordinates in Table 1. These are data from the ten-city TSP problem in (Hopfield & Tank, 1985). The positions of the ten cities and the optimal route are presented in Fig. 6.

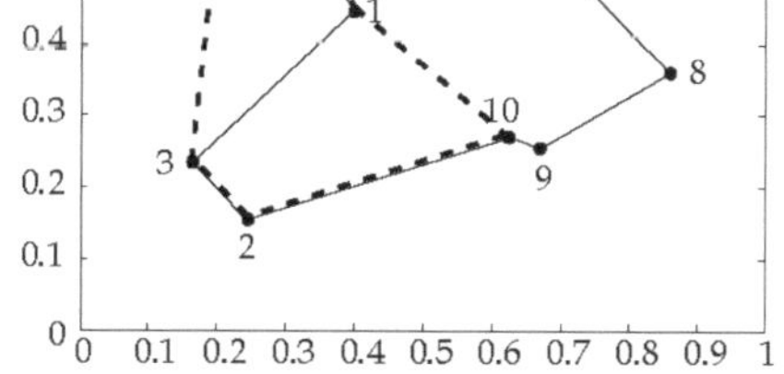

Fig. 6. Illustration of the locations of 10 cities for the Hopfield-Tank original data. The best way to travel for ten (resp. five) cities is in terms of the solid line (resp. dotted line) connection.

In our simulation, the parameters for the TCNN (17) are set as

$$\mu = 0.9;\ \beta = 0.005;\ \varepsilon = 0.01;\ a_{0i} = 0.65;$$

$$\omega = -0.08;\ \gamma_1 = 0.015,\ \gamma_2 = 0.015;\ q(t) = t.$$

Recall that coefficients γ_1 and γ_2 reflect the relative strength of the constraint and the tour length energy terms (23). An optimal route trajectory is demonstrated in Fig. 7. Our simulation indicates that the order of the best route for the TSP is $4 \mapsto 1 \mapsto 10 \mapsto 2 \mapsto 3$. The other best routes include $1 \mapsto 10 \mapsto 2 \mapsto 3 \mapsto 4$ and $4 \mapsto 3 \mapsto 2 \mapsto 10 \mapsto 1$. Actually, all of them represent the same loop. Three diagrams in Fig. 8 are plotted to show the evolutions of constraint part and tour length part in the objective function.

City No.	x-axis	y-axis
1	.4	.445
2	.245	.155
3	.165	.235
4	.225	.77
10	.625	.27

Table 1. Coordinates of positions for 5 cities.

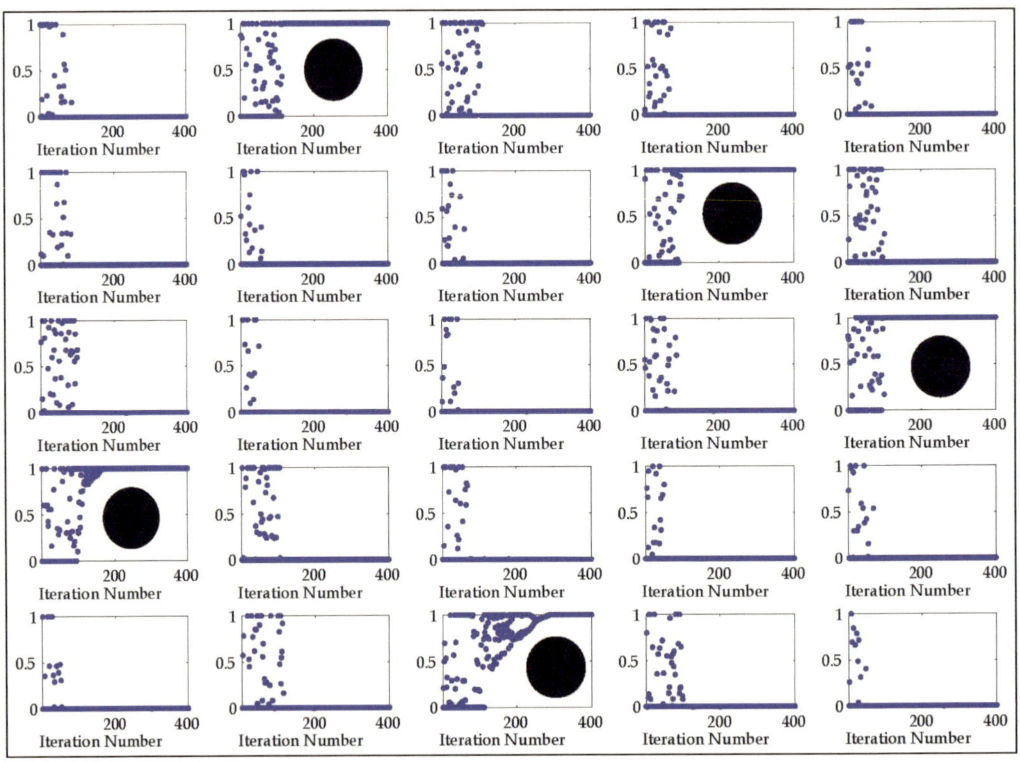

Fig. 7. Evolutions of outputs y_{ij} in Eq. (17). The trajectory approaches one, in the subfigures with a black point.

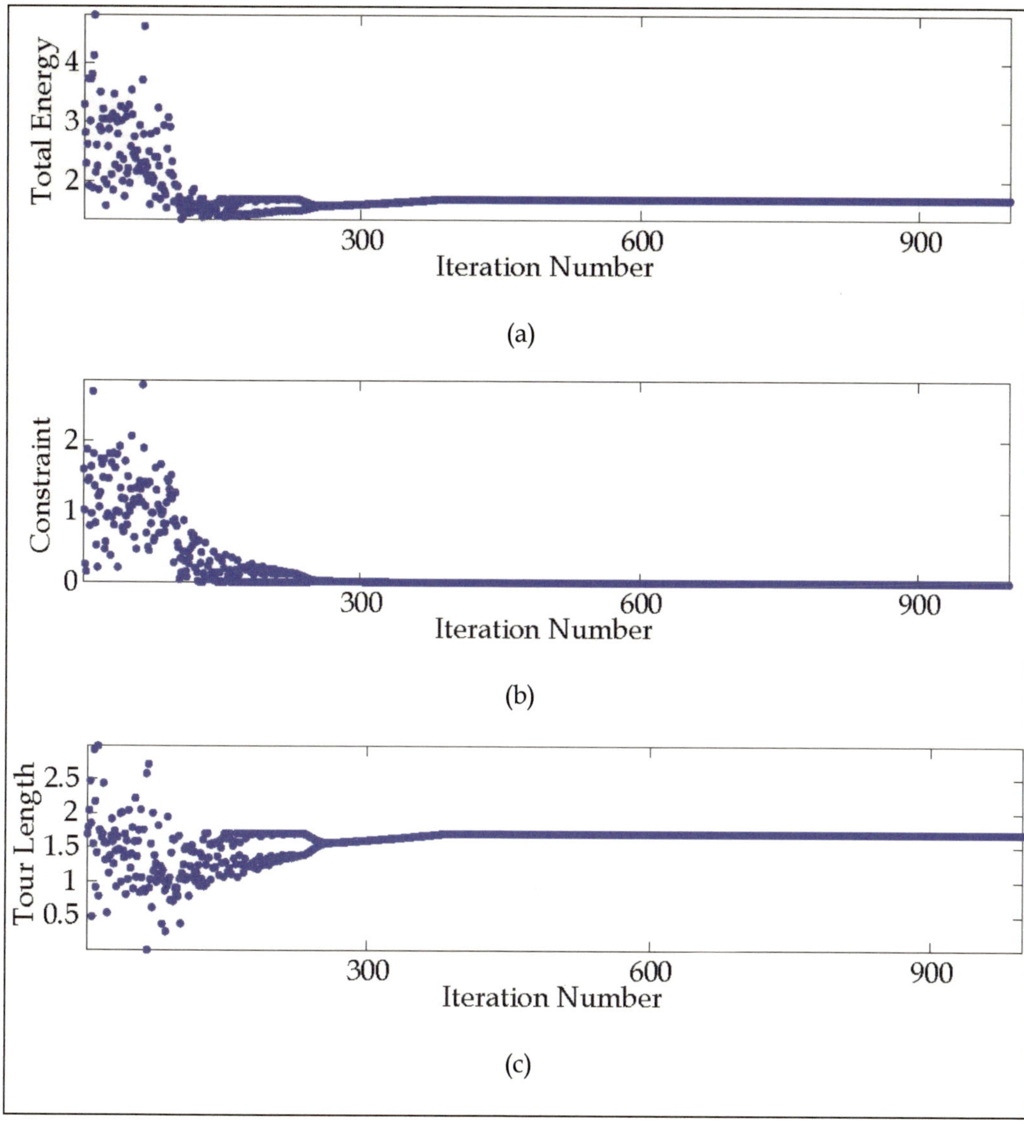

Fig. 8. Evolutions of (a) E, (b) the constraint term; (c) the tour-legnth term, in Eq. (23).

As another observation on the convergent and chaotic phases, we compute the Lyapunov exponents for the one-neuron equation:

$$x(t+1) = \mu x(t) + \omega[g_\varepsilon(x(t)) - a] + h, \omega = (1-\beta)^t \omega_0 \tag{28}$$

with parameters set as

$$\mu = 0.9; a = 0.65; \varepsilon = 0.01; h = 0.$$

Let us consider $\omega \in [\omega_0, 0]$ with $\omega_0 = -0.08$. If the system possesses a chaotic behavior, its maximal Lyapunov exponent is positive along the chaotic trajectory, and vice versa. The maximal Lyapunov exponent means the average of the maximal eigenvalue for linear part of the system along the chaotic trajectory in the ergodic sense. If the maximal Lyapunov exponent is negative, the system corresponds to stable phase. Notably, for a one-neuron map, there is only one Lyapunov exponent. The bifurcation diagram of Lyapunov exponent for the map (28) with parameters $\omega \in [\omega_0, 0]$ is shown in Fig. (9). It follows from Fig. (9) that there is a bifurcation point near $\omega_0 = -0.04$. In other words, the behavior changes near the point, and transforms from chaotic phase to stable phase. However, since our algorithm is based on $\omega = (1-\beta)^t \omega_0$, we also present the correspondence between iteration number t and parameter ω in Fig. (10). Similar computations can be applied to the multidimensional systems.

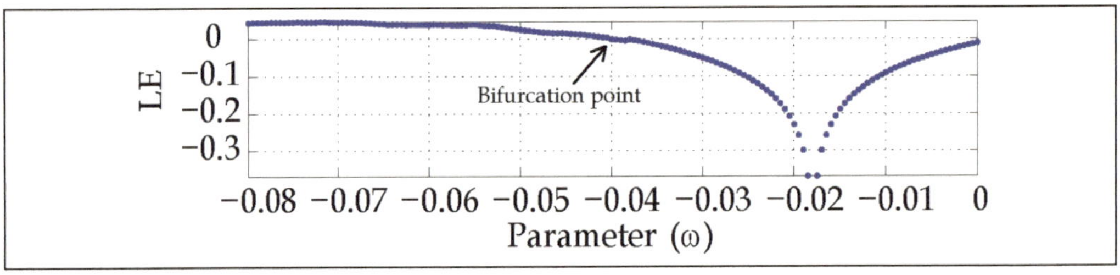

Fig. 9. Bifurcation diagram of Lyapunov exponent for one-dimensional map (28).

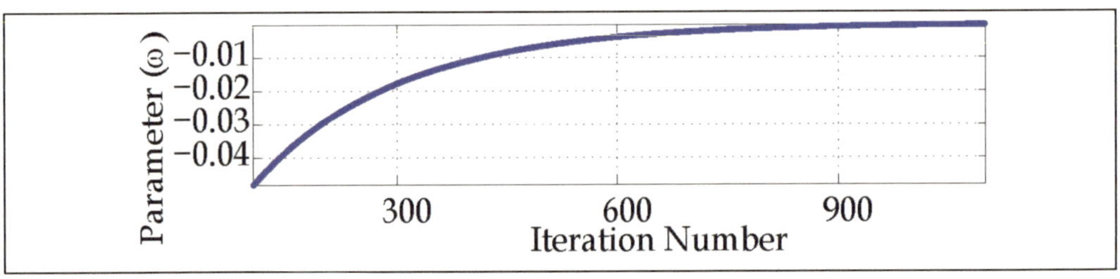

Fig. 10. Correspondence between iteration number t and parameter ω.

6. Conclusions

It has been more than two decades since artificial neural networks were employed to solve TSP. Among the efforts in improving the performance of this computational scheme, substantial achievements have been made in incorporating chaos into the system and developing mathematical analysis for finding the parameters in the chaotic regime and convergent regime. There are several advantages in employing the piecewise linear activation function. We have observed that the TCNN with piecewise linear activation function has better performance than with the logistic activation function in the

applications. In addition, the parameter conditions derived in this framework are much simpler than the ones for logistic activation functions.
There are certainly some further improvements to be developed; for example, in the decision of timing to cool down the process from the chaotic phase; observing and realization of the rotational symmetry and reversal symmetry in the solution structure, as well as conditions for stability of feasible solutions and instability of infeasible solutions.

7. Acknowledgements

This work is partially supported by The National Science Council, and the MOEATU program, of R.O.C. on Taiwan.

8. References

Aihara, K.; Takabe, T. & Toyoda, M. (1990). Chaotic neural network. *Phys. Lett. A*, 144, pp. 333-340.

Bersini, H. (1998). The frustrated and compositional nature of chaos in small Hopfield networks. *Neural Networks*, 11, pp. 1017-1025.

Bersini, H. & Senser, P. (2002). The connections between the grustrated chaos and the intermittency chaos in small Hopfield networks. *Neural Networks*, 15 , pp. 1197-1204.

Chen, L. & Aihara, K. (1995). Chaotic simulated annealing by neural network model with transient chaos. *Neural Networks*, 8, pp. 915-930.

Chen, L. & Aihara, K. (1997). Chaos and asymptotical stability in discrete-time neural networks. *Phys. D*, 104 , pp. 286-325.

Chen, L. & Aihara, K. (1999). Global searching ability of chaotic neural networks. *IEEE Trans. Circuits Systems I Fund. Theory Appl.*, 46 , pp. 974-993.

Chen, S. S. & Shih, C. W. (2002). Transversal homoclinic orbits in a transiently chaotic neural network. *Chaos*, 12, pp. 654-671.

Chen, S. S. & Shih, C. W. (2007). Transiently chaotic neural networks with piecewise linear output functions. *Chaos, Solitons & Fractals*, doi:10.1016/j.chaos.2007.01.103.

Hänggi, M.; Reddy, H. C. & Moschytz, G. S. (1999). Unifying results in CNN theory using delta operator. *IEEE International Symposium on Circuits and Systems*, 3, pp. 547-550.

Harrer, H. & Nossek, J. A. (1992). An analog implementation of discrete-time CNNs. *IEEE Transactions on Neural Networks*, 3, pp. 466-476.

Hopfield, J. J. & Tank, D. W. (1985). Neural computation of decisions in optimization problems. *Biol. Cybernet.*, 52, pp. 141-152.

LaSalle, J. P. (1976). The stability of dynamical systems. *Regional Conference Series in Applied Mathematics*. Philadelphia, PA:SIAM.

Li, T. & Yorke, J. (1975). Periodic three implies chaos. *Am Math Monthly*, 82, pp. 985-992.

Lorenz, E. (1963) Deterministic nonperiodic flow. *J. of Atmospheric Science*, 20, pp. 130-141.

Marotto, F. R. (1978). Snap-back repellers imply chaos in R^n . *J. Math. Anal. Appl.*, 63, pp. 199-223.

Marotto, F. R. (2005). On redefining a snap-back repeller. *Chaos Solitons & Fractals*, 25, pp. 25–28.

Nozawa, H. (1992). A neural network model as a globally coupled map and applications based on chaos. *Chaos*, 2, pp. 377–386.

Smith, K. (1999). Neural networks for combinatorial optimization: a review of more than a decade of research. *INFORMS J. on Computing*, 11(1), pp. 15–34.

Yamada, T. & Aihara, K. (1997) Nonlinear neurodynamics and combinatorial optimization in chaotic neural networks. *J. Intell. Fuzzy Syst.*, 5, pp. 53–68.

7

A Recurrent Neural Network to Traveling Salesman Problem

Paulo Henrique Siqueira, Sérgio Scheer, and Maria Teresinha Arns Steiner
Federal University of Paraná
Curitiba, Paraná,
Brazil

1. Introduction

One technique that uses Wang's Recurrent Neural Networks with the "Winner Takes All" principle is presented to solve two classical problems of combinatorial optimization: Assignment Problem (AP) and Traveling Salesman Problem (TSP).
With a set of appropriate choices for the parameters in Wang's Recurrent Neural Network, this technique appears to be efficient in solving the mentioned problems in real time. In cases of solutions that are very close to each other or multiple optimal solutions to Assignment Problem, the Wang's Neural Network does not converge. The proposed technique solves these types of problems by applying the "Winner Takes All" principle to Wang's Recurrent Neural Network, and could be applied to solve the Traveling Salesman Problem as well. This application to the Traveling Salesman Problem can easily be implemented, since the formulation of this problem is the same that of the Assignment Problem, with the additional constraint of Hamiltonian circuit.
Comparisons between some traditional ways to adjust parameters of Recurrent Neural Networks are made, and some proposals concerning to parameters with dispersion measures of the cost matrix coefficients to the Assignment Problem are shown. Wang's Neural Network with principle Winner Takes All performs only 1% of the average number of iterations of Wang's Neural Network without this principle. In this work 100 matrices with dimension varying of 3×3 to 20×20 are tested to choose the better combination of parameters to Wang's recurrent neural network.
When the Wang's Neural Network presents feasible solutions for the Assignment Problem, the "Winner Takes All" principle is applied to the values of the Neural Network's decision variables, with the additional constraint that the new solution must form a feasible route for the Traveling Salesman Problem.
The results from this new technique are compared to other heuristics, with data from the TSPLIB (Traveling Salesman Problem Library). The 2-opt local search technique is applied to the final solutions of the proposed technique and shows a considerable improvement of the results. The results of problem "dantzig42" of TSPLIB and an example with some iterations of technique proposed in this work are shown.
This work is divided in 11 sections, including this introduction. In section 2, the Assignment Problem is defined. In section 3, the Wang's recurrent neural network is presented and a

problem with multiple optimal solutions is shown. In section 4, the technique based on the "Winner takes all" principle is presented and an example of application to Assignment Problem is shown. In section 5, some alternatives for parameters of Wang's neural network to Assignment Problem are presented. In section 6 the results to 100 matrices are shown. In Section 7, it is presented the formulation of Traveling Salesman Problem. In section 8 the application of Wang's neural network with "Winner Takes all" is shown with five examples of TSPLIB. In Section 9, results to others problems of TSPLIB are compared to the ones obtained trhrough other techniques. Findings are presented in section 10, and section 11 contains the references.

2. The assignment problem

The objective of this problem is assigning a number of elements to the same number of positions, and minimizing the linear cost function. This problem is known in literature as Linear Assignment Problem or problem of Matching with Costs (Ajuha et al., 1993; Siqueira et al., 2004), and can be formulated as follows:

$$\text{Minimize } C = \sum_{i=1}^{n}\sum_{j=1}^{n} c_{ij}x_{ij} \tag{1}$$

$$\text{Subject to} \sum_{i=1}^{n} x_{ij} = 1 \text{ , } j = 1, 2, \ldots, n \tag{2}$$

$$\sum_{j=1}^{n} x_{ij} = 1 \text{ , } i = 1, 2, \ldots, n \tag{3}$$

$$x_{ij} \in \{0, 1\}, i, j = 1, 2, \ldots, n, \tag{4}$$

where c_{ij} and x_{ij} are, respectively, the cost and the decision variable associated to the assignment of element i to position j. The usual representation form of c in the Hungarian method is the matrix form. When $x_{ij} = 1$, element i is assigned to position j.
The objective function (1) represents the total cost to be minimized. The set of constraints (2) and (3) guarantees that each element i will be assigned for exactly one position j. The set (4) represents the zero-one integrality constraints of the decision variables x_{ij}. The set of constraints (4) can be replaced by:

$$x_{ij} \geq 0 \text{ , } i, j = 1, 2, \ldots, n. \tag{5}$$

Beyond traditional techniques, as the Hungarian method and the Simplex method, some ways of solving this problem has been presented in the last years. In problems of great scale, i.e., when the problem's cost matrix is very large, the traditional techniques do not reveal efficiency, because the number of restrictions and the computational time are increased.
Since the Hopfield and Tank's publication (Hopfield & Tank, 1985), lots of works about the use of Neural Networks to solving optimization problems had been developed (Matsuda, 1998; Wang, 1992 and 1997). The Hopfield's Neural Network, converges to the optimal solution of any Linear Programming problem, in particular for the AP.

Wang, 1992, considered a Recurrent Neural Network to solve the Assignment Problem, however, the necessary number of iterations to achieve an optimal solution is increased in problems of great scale. Moreover, in problems with solutions that are very close to each other or multiple optimal solutions, such network does not converge.
In this work, one technique based on the "Winner Takes All" principle is presented, revealing efficiency solving the problems found in the use of Wang's Recurrent Neural Network. Some criteria to adjust the parameters of the Wang's Neural Network are presented: some traditional ways and others that use dispersion measures between the cost matrix' coefficients.

3. The Wang's recurrent neural network to assignment problem

Consider the $n^2 \times 1$ vectors c^T, that contains all the rows of matrix c; x, that contains the decision elements x_{ij}, and b, that contains the number "1" in all positions. The matrix form of the problem described in (1)-(4) is due Hung & Wang, 2003:

$$\text{Minimize } C = c^T x \tag{6}$$

$$\text{Subject to } Ax = b \tag{7}$$

$$x_{ij} \geq 0,\ i, j = 1, 2, \ldots, n,$$

where matrix A has the following form:

$$A = \begin{bmatrix} I & I & \ldots & I \\ B_1 & B_2 & \ldots & B_n \end{bmatrix} \in \Re^{2n \times n^2}$$

where I is an $n \times n$ identity matrix, and each B_i matrix, for $i = 1, 2\ldots, n$, contains zeros, with exception of ith row, that contains the number "1" in all positions.
The Recurrent Neural Network proposed by Wang (published in Wang, 1992; Wang, 1997; and Hung & Wang, 2003) is characterized by the following differential equation:

$$\frac{du_{ij}(t)}{dt} = -\eta \sum_{k=1}^{n} x_{ik}(t) - \eta \sum_{l=1}^{n} x_{lj}(t) + \eta\theta_{ij} - \lambda c_{ij} e^{-\frac{t}{\tau}}, \tag{8}$$

where $x_{ij} = g(u_{ij}(t))$ and the equilibrium state of this Neural Network is a solution for the Assignment Problem, where g is the sigmoid function with a β parameter, i.e.,

$$g(u) = \frac{1}{1 + e^{-\beta u}}. \tag{9}$$

The threshold is defined as the $n^2 \times 1$ vector $\theta = A^T b = (2, 2, \ldots, 2)$. Parameters η, λ and τ are constants, and empirically chosen (Hung & Wang, 2003), affecting the convergence of the network. Parameter η serves to penalize violations in the problem's constraints' set, defined by (1)-(4). Parameters λ and τ control the objective function's minimization of the Assignment Problem (1). The Neural Network matrix form can be written as:

$$\frac{du(t)}{dt} = -\eta(Wx(t) - \theta) - \lambda c e^{-\frac{t}{\tau}}, \tag{10}$$

where $x = g(u(t))$ and $W = A^TA$. The convergence properties of Wang's Neural Network are demonstrated in Wang 1993, 1994 & 1995, and Hung & Wang, 2003.

3.1 Multiple optimal solutions and closer optimal solutions

In some cost matrices, the optimal solutions are very closer to each other, or in a different way, some optimal solutions are admissible. The cost matrix c given below:

$$c = \begin{pmatrix} 0.6 & 0.9 & 1 & 2.7 & 0 & 1 & 0.1 & 0 \\ 1 & 0 & 0.3 & 0.4 & 5.5 & 0.3 & 3.4 & 5.5 \\ 0 & 2.2 & 0.2 & 0.6 & 0.2 & 0.2 & 0 & 0.2 \\ 0.3 & 0.2 & 0 & 0.1 & 1.5 & 0 & 0.1 & 1.5 \\ 0.6 & 0.9 & 1 & 2.7 & 0 & 1 & 0.1 & 0 \\ 0 & 2.2 & 0.2 & 0.6 & 0.2 & 0.2 & 0 & 0.2 \\ 0.6 & 0.9 & 1 & 2.7 & 0 & 1 & 0.1 & 0 \\ 0 & 2.2 & 0.2 & 0.6 & 0.2 & 0.2 & 0 & 0.2 \end{pmatrix}, \qquad (11)$$

has the solutions x^* and $\hat{x}$ given below:

$$x^* = \begin{pmatrix} 0 & 0 & 0 & 0 & 0.33 & 0 & 0.33 & 0.33 \\ 0 & 1 & 0 & 0 & 0 & 0 & 0 & 0 \\ 0.5 & 0 & 0.25 & 0 & 0 & 0.25 & 0 & 0 \\ 0 & 0 & 0.5 & 0 & 0 & 0.5 & 0 & 0 \\ 0 & 0 & 0 & 0 & 0.33 & 0 & 0.33 & 0.33 \\ 0.5 & 0 & 0.25 & 0 & 0 & 0.25 & 0 & 0 \\ 0 & 0 & 0 & 0 & 0.33 & 0 & 0.33 & 0.33 \\ 0 & 0 & 0 & 0 & 0 & 0 & 0 & 0 \end{pmatrix} \text{ and } \hat{x} = \begin{pmatrix} 0 & 0 & 0 & 0 & 1 & 0 & 0 & 0 \\ 0 & 1 & 0 & 0 & 0 & 0 & 0 & 0 \\ 1 & 0 & 0 & 0 & 0 & 0 & 0 & 0 \\ 0 & 0 & 0 & 1 & 0 & 0 & 0 & 0 \\ 0 & 0 & 0 & 0 & 0 & 0 & 0 & 1 \\ 0 & 0 & 1 & 0 & 0 & 0 & 0 & 0 \\ 0 & 0 & 0 & 0 & 0 & 0 & 1 & 0 \\ 0 & 0 & 0 & 0 & 0 & 1 & 0 & 0 \end{pmatrix},$$

where x^* is found after 4,715 iterations using the Wang's neural network, and $\hat{x}$ is an optimal solution.

The solution x^* isn't feasible, therefore, some elements x_{ij}^* violate the set of restrictions (4), showing that the Wang's neural network needs adjustments for these cases. The simple decision to place unitary value for any one of the elements x_{ij}^* that possess value 0.5 in solution x^* can become unfeasible or determine a local optimal solution. Another adjustment that can be made is the modification of the costs' matrix' coefficients, eliminating ties in the corresponding costs of the variable x_{ij}^* that possess value different from "0" and "1". In this way, it can be found a local optimal solution when the modifications are not made in the adequate form. Hence, these decisions can cause unsatisfactory results.

4. Wang's neural network and "Winner Takes All" principle to assignment problem

The method considered in this work uses one technique based on the "Winner Takes All" principle, speeding up the convergence of the Wang's Neural Network, besides correcting eventual problems that can appear due the multiple optimal solutions or very closer optimal solutions (Siqueira et al., 2005).

The second term of equation (10), $Wx(t) - \theta$, measures the violation of the constraints to the Assignment Problem. After a certain number of iterations, this term does not suffer substantial changes in its value, evidencing the fact that problem's restrictions are almost satisfied. At this moment, the method considered in this section can be applied.

When all elements of x satisfy the condition $Wx(t) - \theta \leq \phi$, where $\phi \in [0, 2]$, the proposed technique can be used in all iterations of the Wang's Neural Network, until a good approach of the Assignment Problem be found. An algorithm of this technique is presented as follows:

Step 1: Find a solution x of the AP, using the Wang's recurrent neural network. If $Wx(t) - \theta \leq \phi$, then go to Step 2. Else, find another solution x.

Step 2: Given the matrix of decision x, after a certain number of iterations of the Wang's recurrent neural network. Let the matrix $\bar{x}$, where $\bar{x} = x$, $m = 1$, and go to step 3.

Step 3: Find the mth biggest array element of decision, $\bar{x}_{kl}$. The value of this element is replaced by the half of all elements sum of row k and column l of matrix x, or either,

$$\bar{x}_{kl} = \frac{1}{2}\left(\sum_{i=1}^{n} x_{il} + \sum_{j=1}^{n} x_{kj}\right). \tag{12}$$

The other elements of row k and column l become nulls. Go to step 4.

Step 4: If $m \leq n$, makes $m = m + 1$, and go to step 3. Else, go to step 5.

Step 5: If a good approach to an AP solution is found, stop. Else, make $x = \bar{x}$, execute the Wang's neural network again and go to Step 2.

4.1 Illustrative example

Consider the matrix below, which it is a partial solution of the Assignment Problem defined by matrix C, in (13), after 14 iterations of the Wang's recurrent neural network. The biggest array element of $\bar{x}$ is in row 1, column 7.

$$\bar{x} = \begin{pmatrix} 0.0808 & 0.0011 & 0.0168 & 0.1083 & 0.0514 & 0.0033 & {}^{*}0.422 & 0.3551 \\ 0.0056 & 0.2827 & 0.0168 & 0.1525 & 0.1484 & 0.1648 & 0.1866 & 0 \\ 0.1754 & 0.0709 & 0.0688 & 0.3449 & 0 & 0.3438 & 0.0425 & 0.0024 \\ 0.1456 & 0.2412 & 0.2184 & 0.0521 & 0.1131 & 0.0747 & 0.0598 & 0.1571 \\ 0.0711 & 0 & 0.2674 & 0.272 & 0.3931 & 0.0024 & 0.0306 & 0.0061 \\ 0.2037 & 0.2823 & 0.2956 & 0.0366 & 0 & 0.0025 & 0.0136 & 0.2186 \\ 0.1681 & 0.174 & 0.1562 & 0 & 0.3053 & 0.2016 & 0.0369 & 0.0144 \\ 0.1142 & 0.0031 & 0.0138 & 0.0829 & 0.0353 & 0.2592 & 0.251 & 0.2907 \end{pmatrix}$$

$$C = \begin{pmatrix} 1.4 & 6.1 & 3.1 & 0.4 & 2.2 & 4.4 & 0.1 & 0 \\ 1.3 & 0.2 & 3.3 & 0.2 & 1.2 & 0.4 & 1.5 & 8.2 \\ 1.7 & 2.9 & 2.8 & 0.1 & 9.8 & 0.4 & 4.2 & 6.8 \\ 0.5 & 0 & 0 & 1.0 & 1.1 & 0.9 & 2.4 & 0.9 \\ 2.8 & 7.7 & 1.2 & 0.5 & 0.9 & 6 & 4.6 & 5.9 \\ 0.5 & 0.2 & 0 & 1.8 & 8.5 & 4.9 & 4.4 & 0.9 \\ 0.6 & 0.7 & 0.7 & 6.9 & 0.1 & 0 & 3.2 & 3.8 \\ 1.4 & 5.4 & 3.7 & 1.1 & 3 & 0 & 1.3 & 0.7 \end{pmatrix} \tag{13}$$

After the update of this element through equation (12), the result given below is found. The second biggest element of $\overline{x}$ is in row 5, column 5.

$$\overline{x}=\begin{pmatrix} 0 & 0 & 0 & 0 & 0 & 0 & 1.0412 & 0 \\ 0.0056 & 0.2827 & 0.0168 & 0.1525 & 0.1484 & 0.1648 & 0 & 0 \\ 0.1754 & 0.0709 & 0.0688 & 0.3449 & 0 & 0.3438 & 0 & 0.0024 \\ 0.1456 & 0.2412 & 0.2184 & 0.0521 & 0.1131 & 0.0747 & 0 & 0.1571 \\ 0.0711 & 0 & 0.2674 & 0.272 & {}^{*}0.393 & 0.0024 & 0 & 0.0061 \\ 0.2037 & 0.2823 & 0.2956 & 0.0366 & 0 & 0.0025 & 0. & 0.2186 \\ 0.1681 & 0.174 & 0.1562 & 0 & 0.3053 & 0.2016 & 0 & 0.0144 \\ 0.1142 & 0.0031 & 0.0138 & 0.0829 & 0.0353 & 0.2592 & 0 & 0.2907 \end{pmatrix}$$

After the update of all elements of $\overline{x}$, get the following solution:

$$\overline{x}=\begin{pmatrix} 0 & 0 & 0 & 0 & 0 & 0 & 1.0412 & 0 \\ 0 & 1.0564 & 0 & 0 & 0 & 0 & 0 & 0 \\ 0 & 0 & 0 & 1.0491 & 0 & 0 & 0 & 0 \\ 1.0632 & 0 & 0 & 0 & 0 & 0 & 0 & 0 \\ 0 & 0 & 0 & 0 & 1.0446 & 0 & 0 & 0 \\ 0 & 0 & 1.0533 & 0 & 0 & 0 & 0. & 0 \\ 0 & 0 & 0 & 0 & 0 & 1.0544 & 0 & 0 \\ 0 & 0 & 0 & 0 & 0 & 0 & 0 & 1.0473 \end{pmatrix}.$$

This solution is presented to the Wang's neural network, and after finding another x solution, a new $\overline{x}$ solution is calculated through the "Winner Takes All" principle.
This procedure is made until a good approach to feasible solution is found. In this example, after more 5 iterations, the matrix $\overline{x}$ presents one approach of the optimal solutions:

$$\overline{x}=\begin{pmatrix} 0 & 0 & 0 & 0 & 0 & 0 & 0.9992 & 0 \\ 0 & 0.9996 & 0 & 0 & 0 & 0 & 0 & 0 \\ 0 & 0 & 0 & 0.9994 & 0 & 0 & 0 & 0 \\ 0.999 & 0 & 0 & 0 & 0 & 0 & 0 & 0 \\ 0 & 0 & 0 & 0 & 0.9985 & 0 & 0 & 0 \\ 0 & 0 & 1 & 0 & 0 & 0 & 0. & 0 \\ 0 & 0 & 0 & 0 & 0 & 1.0003 & 0 & 0 \\ 0 & 0 & 0 & 0 & 0 & 0 & 0 & 0.9991 \end{pmatrix}.$$

Two important aspects of this technique that must be taken in consideration are the following: the reduced number of iterations necessary to find a feasible solution, and the absence of problems related to the matrices with multiple optimal solutions. The adjustments of the Wang's neural network parameters are essential to guarantee the convergence of this technique, and some forms of adjusting are presented on the next section.

5. The parameters of Wang's recurrent neural network

In this work, the used parameters play basic roles for the convergence of the Wang's neural network. In all the tested matrices, $\eta = 1$ had been considered, and parameters τ and λ had been calculated in many ways, described as follows (Siqueira et al., 2005).
One of the most usual forms to calculate parameter λ for the AP can be found in Wang, 1992, where λ is given by:

$$\lambda = \eta / C_{\max}, \tag{14}$$

where $C_{\max} = \max\{c_{ij};\ i, j = 1, 2, \ldots, n\}$.
The use of dispersion measures between the c matrix coefficients had revealed to be efficient adjusting parameters τ and λ. Considering δ as the standard deviation between the c cost matrix' coefficients, the parameter λ can be given as:

$$\lambda = \eta / \delta. \tag{15}$$

Another way to adjust λ is to consider it a vector, defined by:

$$\bar{\lambda} = \eta\left(\frac{1}{\delta_1}, \frac{1}{\delta_2}, \ldots, \frac{1}{\delta_n}\right), \tag{16}$$

where δ_i, for $i = 1, 2\ldots, n$, represents the standard deviation of each row of the matrix c. Each element of the vector $\bar{\lambda}$ is used to update the corresponding row of the x decision matrix. This form to calculate λ revealed to be more efficient in cost matrices with great dispersion between its values, as shown by the results presented in the next section.
A variation of the expression (14), that uses the same principle of the expression (16), is to define λ by the vector:

$$\bar{\lambda} = \eta\left(\frac{1}{c_{1\max}}, \frac{1}{c_{2\max}}, \ldots, \frac{1}{c_{n\max}}\right), \tag{17}$$

where $c_{i\max} = \max\{c_{ij};\ j = 1, 2, \ldots, n\}$, for each $i = 1, 2, \ldots, n$. This definition to λ also produces good results in matrices with great dispersion between its coefficients.
The parameter τ depends on the necessary number of iterations for the convergence of the Wang's neural network. When the presented correction "Winner Takes All" technique isn't used, the necessary number of iterations for the convergence of the Wang's neural netowork varies between 1,000 and 15,000 iterations. In this case, τ is a constant, such that:

$$1{,}000 \le \tau \le 15{,}000. \tag{18}$$

When the "Winner Takes All" correction is used, the necessary number of iterations varies between 5 and 300. Hence, the value of τ is such that:

$$5 \le \tau \le 300. \tag{19}$$

In this work, two other forms of τ parameter adjustment had been used, besides considering it constant, in the intervals showed in expressions (18) and (19). In one of the techniques, τ is given by:

$$\bar{\tau} = \frac{1}{\mu}(\mu_1\delta_1, \mu_2\delta_2, ..., \mu_n\delta_n), \tag{20}$$

where μ_i are the coefficients average of ith row of matrix c, δ_i is the standard deviation of ith row of matrix c, and μ is the average between the values of all the coefficients of c.
The second proposal of adjustment for τ uses the third term of definition of neural network of Wang (8). When $c_{ij} = c_{\max}$, the term $-\lambda_i c_{ij} \exp(-t/\tau_i) = k_i$ must satisfied $g(k_i) \cong 0$, so x_{ij} has minor value, minimizing the final cost of the Assignment Problem. Isolating τ, and considering $c_{ij} = c_{\max}$ and $\lambda_i = 1/\delta_i$, where $i = 1, 2..., n$, τ is got, as follows:

$$\tau_i = \frac{-t}{\ln\left(\dfrac{-k_i}{\lambda_i\, c_{\max}}\right)}, \tag{21}$$

The parameters' application results given by (14)-(21) are presented on next section.

6. Results to assignment problem

In this work, 100 matrices (with dimensions varying of 3×3 until 20×20) had been used to test the techniques of adjustments to parameters presented in previous section, beyond the proposed "Winner Takes All" correction applied to the Wang's recurrent neural network. These matrices had been generated randomly, with some cases of multiple optimal solutions and very closer optimal solutions.
The results to 47 tested matrices with only one optimal global appear in Table 1, and results to 53 matrices with multiple optimal solutions and/or very closer optimal solutions appear in Table 2. Table 3 shown results to all matrices tested to Assignment Problem.
To adjust λ, the following expressions had been used on Tables 1, 2 and 3: (14) in the first and last column; (15) in the second column; (17) in the third column; and (16) in fourth and fifth columns. To calculate τ, the following expressions they had been used: (19) in the three firsts columns; (20) in the fourth column; (21) in the fifth column; and (18) in the last column. The results of the Wang's neural network application, without the use of the proposed correction in this work, are meet in the last column of Tables 1, 2 and 3. In the last row of the Tables 1, 2 and 3 the numbers of iterations of each technique is given by the average between the numbers of iterations found for all tested matrices.

parameter λ	$\lambda = \eta / c_{\max}$	$\lambda = \eta / \delta$	$\lambda_i = \eta / c_{i\max}$	$\lambda = \eta / \delta$	$\lambda_i = \eta / \delta_i$	$\lambda = \eta / c_{\max}$
parameter τ	$5 \le \tau \le 300$	$5 \le \tau \le 300$	$5 \le \tau \le 300$	$\tau_i = \dfrac{\mu_i \delta_i}{\mu}$	$\tau_i = \dfrac{-t}{\ln\left(\dfrac{-k_i}{\lambda_i c_{\max}}\right)}$	$1{,}000 \le \tau \le$ $\le 15{,}000$
global optimality	40	45	40	40	46	47
local optimality	7	2	7	7	1	0
infeasibility	0	0	0	0	0	0
global optim.(%)	85	96	85	85	98	100
average error (%)	2.35	0.98	0.74	5.10	0.02	0
iterations (average)	37	46	41	72	51	3,625

Table 1. Results for 47 matrices with only one optimal solution

parameter λ	$\lambda = \eta / C_{\max}$	$\lambda = \eta / \delta$	$\lambda_i = \eta / c_{i\max}$	$\lambda = \eta / \delta$	$\lambda_i = \eta / \delta_i$	$\lambda = \eta / C_{\max}$
parameter τ	$5 \le \tau \le 300$	$5 \le \tau \le 300$	$5 \le \tau \le 300$	$\tau_i = \frac{\mu_i \delta_i}{\mu}$	$\tau_i = \frac{-t}{\ln\left(\frac{-k_i}{\lambda_i c_{\max}}\right)}$	$1{,}000 \le \tau \le$ $\le 15{,}000$
global optimality	33	43	32	39	46	0
local optimality	20	10	21	14	7	0
infeasibility	0	0	0	0	0	53
global optim.(%)	62	81	60	74	87	0
average error (%)	4.87	1.63	6.37	4.79	2.14	-
iterations (average)	39	42	41	76	47	6,164

Table 2. Results for 53 matrices with multiple optimal solutions

The results had been considered satisfactory, and the adjustments of the parameters that result in better solutions for the "Winner Takes All" correction are those that use the standard deviation and the average between the elements of matrix of costs, and the use of parameters in vector form revealed to be more efficient for these matrices. The results shown in Tables 1, 2 and 3 reveal that the dispersion techniques between the coefficients of matrix c are more efficient for the use of the correction "Winner Takes All" in matrices with multiple optimal solutions.

parameter λ	$\lambda = \eta / C_{\max}$	$\lambda = \eta / \delta$	$\lambda_i = \eta / c_{i\max}$	$\lambda = \eta / \delta$	$\lambda_i = \eta / \delta_i$	$\lambda = \eta / C_{\max}$
parameter τ	$5 \le \tau \le 300$	$5 \le \tau \le 300$	$5 \le \tau \le 300$	$\tau_i = \frac{\mu_i \delta_i}{\mu}$	$\tau_i = \frac{-t}{\ln\left(\frac{-k_i}{\lambda_i c_{\max}}\right)}$	$1{,}000 \le \tau \le$ $\le 15{,}000$
global optim.(%)	73	88	72	79	92	47
local optimality	27	12	28	21	8	0
infeasibility	0	0	0	0	0	53
average error (%)	3.17	1.19	2.57	5.00	0.71	-
iterations (average)	38	44	41	74	49	4,970

Table 3. Results for all matrices

The pure Wang's neural network has slower convergence when the adjustments described by (15)-(17) and (19)-(21) are applied for the parameters λ and τ, respectively. Better results are found with combination of parameters (16) and (21), as shown in Tables 1, 2 and 3. This combination is used to solve the Traveling Salesman Problem.

These results shows that the "Winner Takes All" principle, applied to the Wang's neural network, produces good results to Assignment Problem, mainly in matrices with multiple optimal solutions. The parameters to Wang's neural network presented in section 5 show the efficiency of this technique for great scale problems, because the average number of iterations necessary to find feasible solutions for the Assignment Problem was considerably reduced, compared to the pure Wang's neural network.

The application of "Winner Take All" principle to Wang's recurrent neural network to solve the Traveling Salesman Problem is presented on next sections.

7. The traveling salesman problem

The formulation of Traveling Salesman Problem is the same of Assignment Problem, with the additional constraint of Hamiltonian circuit, i.e., the feasible route must form a cycle which visits each city exactly once, and returns to the starting city:

$$\text{Minimize } C = \sum_{i=1}^{n}\sum_{j=1}^{n} c_{ij}x_{ij} \quad (22)$$

$$\text{Subject to } \sum_{i=1}^{n} x_{ij} = 1, \quad j = 1, 2, \ldots, n \quad (23)$$

$$\sum_{j=1}^{n} x_{ij} = 1, \quad i = 1, 2, \ldots, n \quad (24)$$

$$x_{ij} \in \{0, 1\}, \quad i, j = 1, 2, \ldots, n \quad (25)$$

$$\tilde{x} \text{ forms a Hamiltonian cycle} \quad (26)$$

where the vector $\tilde{x}$ has the whole sequence of the route that was found, i.e., the solution for the Traveling Salesman Problem.

The Traveling Salesman Problem is a classical problem of combinatorial optimization in the Operations Research area. The purpose is to find a minimum total cost Hamiltonian cycle (Ahuja et al.,1993). There are several practical uses for this problem, such as Vehicle Routing (Laporte, 1992) and Drilling Problems (Onwubolu & Clerc, 2004).

This problem has been used during the last years as a basis for comparison in order to improve several optimization techniques, such as Genetic Algorithms (Affenzeller & Wanger, 2003), Simulated Annealing (Budinich, 1996), Tabu Search (Liu et al., 2003), Local Search (Bianchi et al., 2005), Ant Colony (Chu et al., 2004) and Neural Networks (Leung et al., 2004; Siqueira et al., 2007).

The main types of Neural Network used to solve the Traveling Salesman Problem are: Hopfield's Recurrent Networks (Wang et al., 2002) and Kohonen's Self-Organizing Maps (Leung et al., 2003). In a Hopfield's Network, the main idea is to automatically find a solution for the Traveling Salesman Problem by means of an equilibrium state of the equation system defined for the Traveling Salesman Problem. By using Kohonen's Maps for the Traveling Salesman Problem, the final route is determined through the cities corresponding to those neurons that have weights that are closest to the pair of coordinates ascribed to each city in the problem.

Wang's recurrent neural network with the "Winner Takes All" principle can be applied to solve the Traveling Salesman Problem on this way: solving this problem as if it were an Assignment Problem by means of the Wang's neural network, and, furthermore, using the "Winner Takes All" principle on the solutions found with the Wang's neural network, with the constraint that the solutions found must form a feasible route for the Traveling Salesman

Problem. The parameters used for the Wang's neural network are those that show the best solutions for the Assignment Problem, as shown on Tables 1, 2 and 3 of previous section.
The solutions found with the heuristic technique proposed in this work are compared with the solutions from the Self-Organizing Maps (SOM) and the Simulated Annealing (SA) for the symmetrical TSP, and with other heuristics for the asymmetrical TSP. The 2-opt Local Search technique (Bianchi et al., 2005) is used to improve the solutions found with the technique proposed in this work. The data used for the comparisons are from the TSPLIB database (Reinelt, 1991).

8. Wang's neural network and "Winner Takes All" principle to traveling salesman problem

The algorithm presented on section 4 to Assignment Problem can be easily modified to solve the Traveling Salesman Problem:

Step 1: Determine a maximum number of routes r_{max}. Find a solution x to Assignment Problem using the Wang's neural netowork. If $Wx(t) - \theta \leq \phi$, then go to Step 2. Otherwise, find another solution x.

Step 2: Given the decision matrix, consider matrix $\bar{x}$, where $\bar{x} = x$, $m = 1$ and go to Step 3.

Step 3: Choose a row k in decision matrix $\bar{x}$. Do $p = k$, $\tilde{x}$ (m) = k and go to Step 4.

Step 4: Find the biggest element of row k, $\bar{x}_{kl}$. This element's value is given by the half of the sum of all elements of row k and of column l of matrix x, i.e.,

$$\bar{x}_{kl} = \frac{1}{2}\left(\sum_{i=1}^{n} x_{il} + \sum_{j=1}^{n} x_{kj}\right). \tag{27}$$

The other elements of row k and column l become null. So that sub-routes are not formed, the other elements of column k must also be null. Do $\tilde{x}(m + 1) = l$; to continue the Traveling Salesman Problem route, make $k = l$ and go to Step 5.

Step 5: If $m < n$, then make $m = m + 1$ and go to Step 4. Otherwise, do

$$\bar{x}_{kp} = \frac{1}{2}\left(\sum_{i=1}^{n} x_{ip} + \sum_{j=1}^{n} x_{kj}\right), \tag{28}$$

$\tilde{x}(n + 1) = p$, determine the route's cost, C, and go to Step 6.

Step 6: If $C < C_{min}$, then do $C_{min} = C$ and $x = \bar{x}$. Make $r = r + 1$. If $r < r_{max}$, then run the Wang's neural network again and go to Step 2, otherwise Stop.

8.1 Illustrative examples applied to problems of TSPLIB

Consider the symmetrical Traveling Salesman Problem with 14-city instances burma14, due Zaw & Win (Reinelt, 1991), as shown in Fig. 1. After 17 iterations, the Wang's neural network presents the following solution for the Assignment Problem:

$$
\bar{x} = \begin{pmatrix}
0 & 0.17 & 0.04 & 0.02 & 0.02 & 0.02 & 0.03 & 0.16 & 0.15 & 0.16 & 0.14 & 0.02 & 0.06 & 0.04 \\
0.18 & 0 & 0.09 & 0.03 & 0.01 & 0.02 & 0.03 & 0.14 & 0.1 & 0.13 & 0.1 & 0.02 & 0.05 & 0.06 \\
0.04 & 0.09 & 0 & 0.24 & 0.06 & 0.07 & 0.05 & 0.04 & 0.02 & 0.02 & 0.02 & 0.09 & 0.04 & 0.19 \\
0.02 & 0.04 & 0.22 & 0 & 0.2 & 0.12 & 0.06 & 0.02 & 0.01 & 0.01 & 0.02 & 0.13 & 0.04 & 0.12 \\
0.02 & 0.03 & 0.08 & 0.17 & 0 & 0.18 & 0.1 & 0.03 & 0.02 & 0.02 & 0.02 & 0.13 & 0.07 & 0.07 \\
0.02 & 0.02 & 0.07 & 0.13 & 0.23 & 0 & 0.12 & 0.02 & 0.02 & 0.01 & 0.02 & 0.2 & 0.07 & 0.09 \\
0.03 & 0.03 & 0.04 & 0.05 & 0.09 & 0.15 & 0 & 0.05 & 0.03 & 0.02 & 0.04 & 0.14 & 0.23 & 0.09 \\
{*0.18} & 0.14 & 0.04 & 0.02 & 0.02 & 0.02 & 0.04 & 0 & 0.14 & 0.12 & 0.15 & 0.02 & 0.08 & 0.04 \\
0.14 & 0.1 & 0.03 & 0.01 & 0.02 & 0.02 & 0.04 & 0.12 & 0 & 0.23 & 0.22 & 0.02 & 0.06 & 0.03 \\
0.14 & 0.12 & 0.03 & 0.02 & 0.03 & 0.02 & 0.04 & 0.11 & 0.19 & 0 & 0.17 & 0.02 & 0.06 & 0.03 \\
0.14 & 0.09 & 0.03 & 0.01 & 0.02 & 0.02 & 0.04 & 0.13 & 0.22 & 0.21 & 0 & 0.02 & 0.06 & 0.03 \\
0.02 & 0.03 & 0.09 & 0.14 & 0.16 & 0.21 & 0.12 & 0.03 & 0.02 & 0.01 & 0.02 & 0 & 0.07 & 0.12 \\
0.06 & 0.05 & 0.03 & 0.03 & 0.04 & 0.08 & 0.24 & 0.1 & 0.07 & 0.03 & 0.08 & 0.08 & 0 & 0.08 \\
0.03 & 0.06 & 0.2 & 0.14 & 0.05 & 0.1 & 0.09 & 0.05 & 0.02 & 0.01 & 0.02 & 0.13 & 0.08 & 0
\end{pmatrix}
$$

In this decision matrix, a city is chosen to start the route, for instance, city 8, this is, $p = 8$. In row p of the decision matrix the biggest element is chosen, thus defining the Traveling Salesman's destiny when he leaves city p. The biggest element of row p is in column 1, therefore, $k = p = 8$ and $l = 1$. After the decision matrix $\bar{x}$ is updated by means of equation (27), the route goes on with $k = 1$:

$$
\bar{x} = \begin{pmatrix}
0 & {*0.17} & 0.04 & 0.02 & 0.02 & 0.02 & 0.03 & 0.16 & 0.15 & 0.16 & 0.14 & 0.02 & 0.06 & 0.04 \\
0 & 0 & 0.09 & 0.03 & 0.01 & 0.02 & 0.03 & 0.14 & 0.1 & 0.13 & 0.1 & 0.02 & 0.05 & 0.06 \\
0 & 0.09 & 0 & 0.24 & 0.06 & 0.07 & 0.05 & 0.04 & 0.02 & 0.02 & 0.02 & 0.09 & 0.04 & 0.19 \\
0 & 0.04 & 0.22 & 0 & 0.2 & 0.12 & 0.06 & 0.02 & 0.01 & 0.01 & 0.02 & 0.13 & 0.04 & 0.12 \\
0 & 0.03 & 0.08 & 0.17 & 0 & 0.18 & 0.1 & 0.03 & 0.02 & 0.02 & 0.02 & 0.13 & 0.07 & 0.07 \\
0 & 0.02 & 0.07 & 0.13 & 0.23 & 0 & 0.12 & 0.02 & 0.02 & 0.01 & 0.02 & 0.2 & 0.07 & 0.09 \\
0 & 0.03 & 0.04 & 0.05 & 0.09 & 0.15 & 0 & 0.05 & 0.03 & 0.02 & 0.04 & 0.14 & 0.23 & 0.09 \\
1.01 & 0 & 0 & 0 & 0 & 0 & 0 & 0 & 0 & 0 & 0 & 0 & 0 & 0 \\
0 & 0.1 & 0.03 & 0.01 & 0.02 & 0.02 & 0.04 & 0.12 & 0 & 0.23 & 0.22 & 0.02 & 0.06 & 0.03 \\
0 & 0.12 & 0.03 & 0.02 & 0.03 & 0.02 & 0.04 & 0.11 & 0.19 & 0 & 0.17 & 0.02 & 0.06 & 0.03 \\
0 & 0.09 & 0.03 & 0.01 & 0.02 & 0.02 & 0.04 & 0.13 & 0.22 & 0.21 & 0 & 0.02 & 0.06 & 0.03 \\
0 & 0.03 & 0.09 & 0.14 & 0.16 & 0.21 & 0.12 & 0.03 & 0.02 & 0.01 & 0.02 & 0 & 0.07 & 0.12 \\
0 & 0.05 & 0.03 & 0.03 & 0.04 & 0.08 & 0.24 & 0.1 & 0.07 & 0.03 & 0.08 & 0.08 & 0 & 0.08 \\
0 & 0.06 & 0.2 & 0.14 & 0.05 & 0.1 & 0.09 & 0.05 & 0.02 & 0.01 & 0.02 & 0.13 & 0.08 & 0
\end{pmatrix}
$$

The biggest element of row 1 in matrix $\bar{x}$ is in column 2, therefore, $l = 2$. This procedure is executed until all rows are updated, thus defining the route: $\tilde{x} = (8, 1, 2, 10, 9, 11, 13, 7, 6, 5, 4, 3, 14, 12, 8)$, as shown in Fig. 1a, with a cost of 34.03, which represents an average error of 10.19%.

$$\bar{x} = \begin{pmatrix}
0 & 0.99 & 0 & 0 & 0 & 0 & 0 & 0 & 0 & 0 & 0 & 0 & 0 & 0 \\
0 & 0 & 0 & 0 & 0 & 0 & 0 & 0 & 0 & 0.99 & 0 & 0 & 0 & 0 \\
0 & 0 & 0 & 0 & 0 & 0 & 0 & 0 & 0 & 0 & 0 & 0 & 0 & 0.99 \\
0 & 0 & 0.99 & 0 & 0 & 0 & 0 & 0 & 0 & 0 & 0 & 0 & 0 & 0 \\
0 & 0 & 0 & 0.99 & 0 & 0 & 0 & 0 & 0 & 0 & 0 & 0 & 0 & 0 \\
0 & 0 & 0 & 0 & 1.01 & 0 & 0 & 0 & 0 & 0 & 0 & 0 & 0 & 0 \\
0 & 0 & 0 & 0 & 0 & 1.00 & 0 & 0 & 0 & 0 & 0 & 0 & 0 & 0 \\
1.01 & 0 & 0 & 0 & 0 & 0 & 0 & 0 & 0 & 0 & 0 & 0 & 0 & 0 \\
0 & 0 & 0 & 0 & 0 & 0 & 0 & 0 & 0 & 0 & 1.01 & 0 & 0 & 0 \\
0 & 0 & 0 & 0 & 0 & 0 & 0 & 0 & 0.99 & 0 & 0 & 0 & 0 & 0 \\
0 & 0 & 0 & 0 & 0 & 0 & 0 & 0 & 0 & 0 & 0 & 0 & 0.99 & 0 \\
0 & 0 & 0 & 0 & 0 & 0 & 0 & 0.99 & 0 & 0 & 0 & 0 & 0 & 0 \\
0 & 0 & 0 & 0 & 0 & 0 & 1.00 & 0 & 0 & 0 & 0 & 0 & 0 & 0 \\
0 & 0 & 0 & 0 & 0 & 0 & 0 & 0 & 0 & 0 & 0 & 1.00 & 0 & 0
\end{pmatrix}$$

This solution is presented to the Wang's neural network, by making $x = \bar{x}$. After more 16 iterations the neural network the following decision matrix is presented:

$$\bar{x} = \begin{pmatrix}
0 & 0.18 & 0.05 & 0.02 & 0.02 & 0.02 & 0.03 & 0.19 & 0.16 & 0.18 & 0.15 & 0.02 & 0.07 & 0.04 \\
0.19 & 0 & 0.11 & 0.03 & 0.02 & 0.02 & 0.03 & 0.18 & 0.12 & 0.15 & 0.11 & 0.02 & 0.07 & 0.07 \\
0.03 & 0.09 & 0 & 0.23 & 0.06 & 0.07 & 0.04 & 0.04 & 0.02 & 0.02 & 0.02 & 0.07 & 0.05 & 0.17 \\
0.02 & 0.04 & 0.26 & 0 & 0.23 & 0.14 & 0.06 & 0.03 & 0.02 & 0.03 & 0.02 & 0.11 & 0.05 & 0.12 \\
0.02 & 0.03 & 0.09 & 0.18 & 0 & 0.2 & 0.1 & 0.03 & 0.02 & 0.03 & 0.02 & 0.12 & 0.09 & 0.07 \\
0.01 & 0.02 & 0.07 & 0.1 & 0.21 & 0 & 0.09 & 0.02 & 0.01 & 0.01 & 0.01 & 0.14 & 0.07 & 0.07 \\
0.03 & 0.03 & 0.05 & 0.05 & 0.11 & 0.18 & 0 & 0.06 & 0.04 & 0.02 & 0.04 & 0.13 & 0.28 & 0.1 \\
0.17 & 0.14 & 0.04 & 0.02 & 0.02 & 0.02 & 0.04 & 0 & 0.14 & 0.12 & 0.14 & 0.02 & 0.08 & 0.04 \\
0.13 & 0.1 & 0.03 & 0.01 & 0.02 & 0.02 & 0.03 & 0.13 & 0 & 0.25 & 0.21 & 0.01 & 0.07 & 0.03 \\
0.13 & 0.13 & 0.04 & 0.02 & 0.03 & 0.02 & 0.03 & 0.12 & 0.2 & 0 & 0.17 & 0.02 & 0.06 & 0.03 \\
0.12 & 0.09 & 0.03 & 0.01 & 0.02 & 0.02 & 0.03 & 0.13 & 0.21 & 0.21 & 0 & 0.01 & 0.07 & 0.02 \\
0.02 & 0.02 & 0.09 & 0.12 & 0.15 & 0.2 & 0.09 & 0.03 & 0.01 & 0.01 & 0.01 & 0 & 0.07 & 0.1 \\
0.07 & 0.06 & 0.04 & 0.03 & 0.05 & 0.09 & 0.25 & 0.13 & 0.08 & 0.04 & 0.08 & 0.07 & 0 & 0.09 \\
0.04 & 0.08 & 0.26 & 0.15 & 0.06 & 0.12 & 0.09 & 0.06 & 0.03 & 0.02 & 0.03 & 0.13 & 0.1 & 0
\end{pmatrix},$$

Through the "Winner Takes All" principle, an approximation for the optimal solution of this problem is found with the route: $\tilde{x} = (2, 1, 10, 9, 11, 8, 13, 7, 12, 6, 5, 4, 3, 14, 2)$, with a cost of 30.88 (Fig. 2b).

$$\overline{x} = \begin{pmatrix} 0 & 0 & 0 & 0 & 0 & 0 & 0 & 0 & 0 & 0.99 & 0 & 0 & 0 & 0 \\ 1.00 & 0 & 0 & 0 & 0 & 0 & 0 & 0 & 0 & 0 & 0 & 0 & 0 & 0 \\ 0 & 0 & 0 & 0 & 0 & 0 & 0 & 0 & 0 & 0 & 0 & 0 & 0 & 0.99 \\ 0 & 0 & 0.99 & 0 & 0 & 0 & 0 & 0 & 0 & 0 & 0 & 0 & 0 & 0 \\ 0 & 0 & 0 & 0.99 & 0 & 0 & 0 & 0 & 0 & 0 & 0 & 0 & 0 & 0 \\ 0 & 0 & 0 & 0 & 1.01 & 0 & 0 & 0 & 0 & 0 & 0 & 0 & 0 & 0 \\ 0 & 0 & 0 & 0 & 0 & 0 & 0 & 0 & 0 & 0 & 0 & 0.99 & 0 & 0 \\ 0 & 0 & 0 & 0 & 0 & 0 & 0 & 0 & 0 & 0 & 0 & 0 & 0.99 & 0 \\ 0 & 0 & 0 & 0 & 0 & 0 & 0 & 0 & 0 & 0 & 1.01 & 0 & 0 & 0 \\ 0 & 0 & 0 & 0 & 0 & 0 & 0 & 0 & 0.99 & 0 & 0 & 0 & 0 & 0 \\ 0 & 0 & 0 & 0 & 0 & 0 & 0 & 0.99 & 0 & 0 & 0 & 0 & 0 & 0 \\ 0 & 0 & 0 & 0 & 0 & 1.01 & 0 & 0 & 0 & 0 & 0 & 0 & 0 & 0 \\ 0 & 0 & 0 & 0 & 0 & 0 & 1.00 & 0 & 0 & 0 & 0 & 0 & 0 & 0 \\ 0 & 1.00 & 0 & 0 & 0 & 0 & 0 & 0 & 0 & 0 & 0 & 0 & 0 & 0 \end{pmatrix}$$

Consider the symmetrical Traveling Salesman Problem with 42-city instance by Dantzig (Reinelt, 1991), as shown in Fig. 3 and 4. This problem contains coordinates of cities in the United States, and after 25 epochs the condition $Wx(t) - \theta \leq \phi$ is satisfied with $\phi = 0.01$ and the Wang's neural network presents the first solution $\tilde{x}_1$ for the Traveling Salesman Problem, as shown in Fig. 3a.

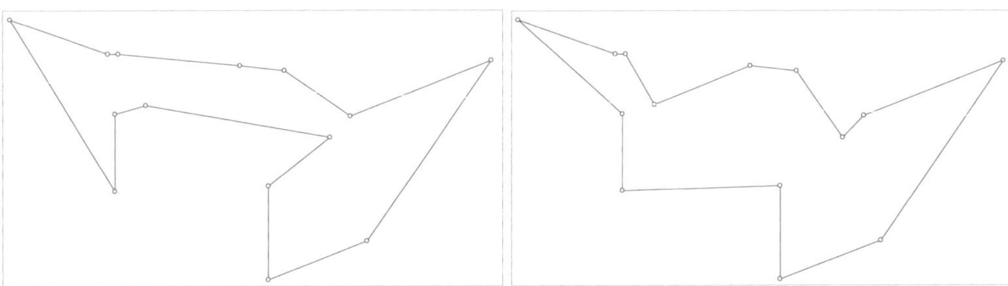

(a) (b)

Fig. 2. (a) Feasible solution found to burma14 through the proposed method, with an average error of 10.19%. (b) Optimal solution found through the proposed method

The solution $\tilde{x}_1$ is presented to Wang's neural network, and after 20 iterations an improved solution is reached, with the average error decreasing from 19.56% to 0.83% as shown in Fig. 3a and 3b.

An improvement to heuristic Wang's neural network is the application of local search 2-opt heuristic on Step 5 of the algorithm shown in this section. This application is made after the expression (27), to the Wang's neural network solution in the algorithm, just as an improvement. The results of Wang's neural network with 2-opt on problem dantzig42 is shown in Fig. 4, where after 72 epochs an optimal solution is found.

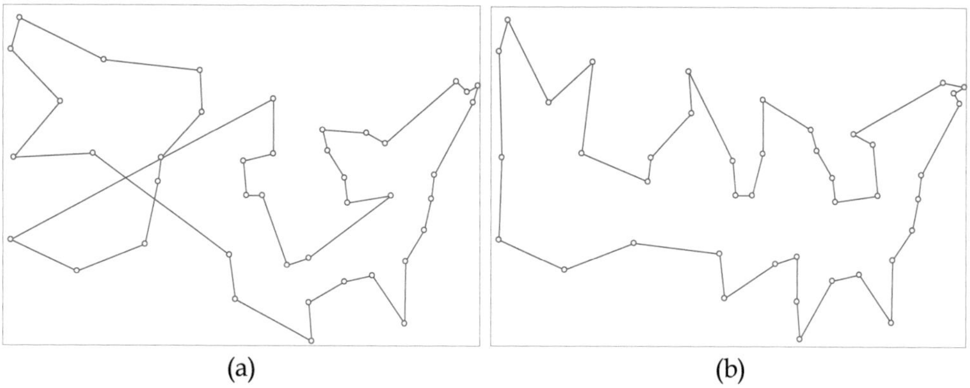

Fig. 3. Solutions found to dantzig42 data without 2-opt improvement. (a) First feasible tour found through the proposed heuristic, with an average error of 19.56%. (b) Tour with 0.83% of average error, after 29 iterations.

Others examples of results found to symmetrical Traveling Salesman problems are (Reinelt, 1991): the 58-city instance of Brazil, due Ferreira, shown in Fig. 5; the 532-city instances of United States due Padberg and Rinaldi, shown in Fig. 6; and the drilling problem u724 due Reinelt, shown in Fig. 7.

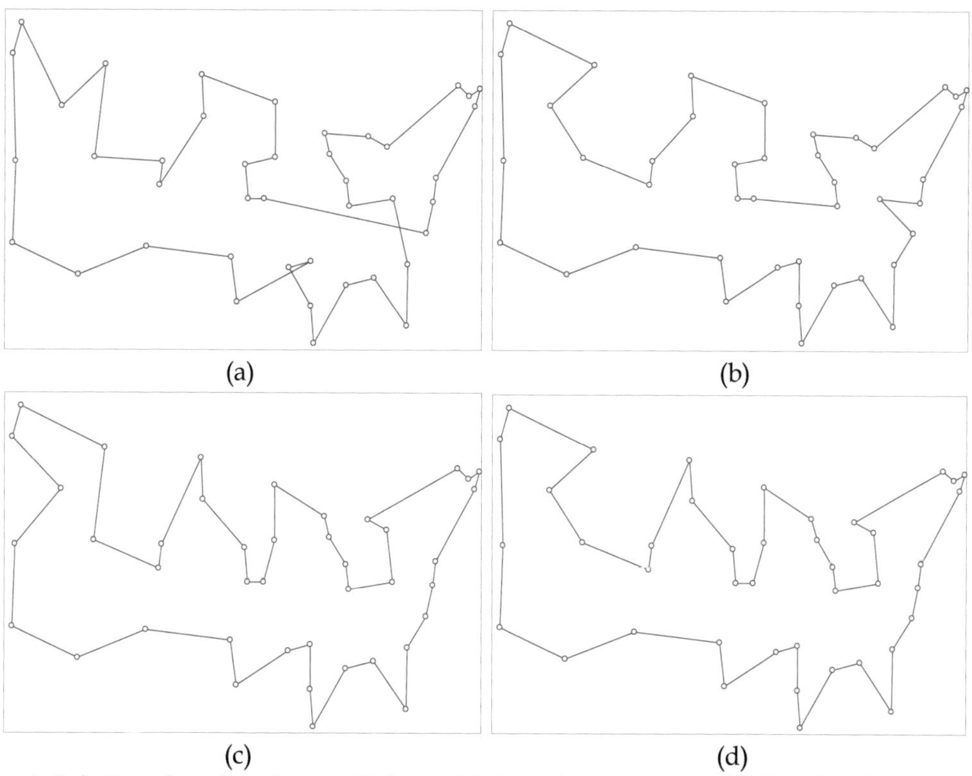

Fig. 4. Solutions found to dantzig42 data with 2-opt improvement. (a) First feasible solution found, in 26 epochs and average error of 8.77%. (b) 36 epochs and error 1.5%. (c) 45 epochs and error 0.57%. (d) 72 epochs and optimal solution found.

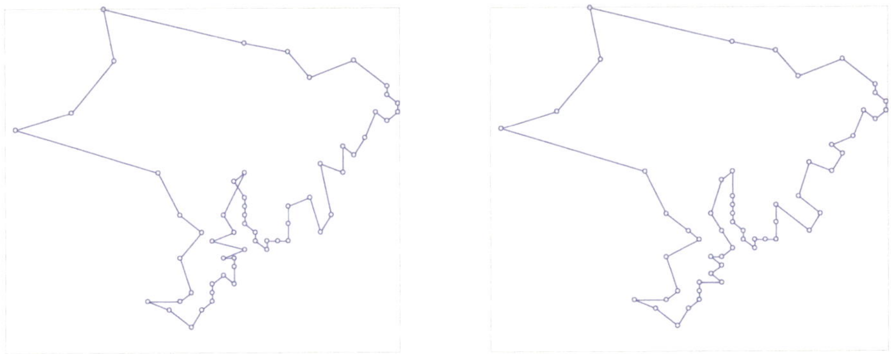

(a) (b)

Fig. 5. Solutions found to brazil58 data. (a) Feasible solution found without local search improvement with 81 epochs and average error of 2.9%. (b) Optimal solution found with 2-opt improvement with 88 epochs.

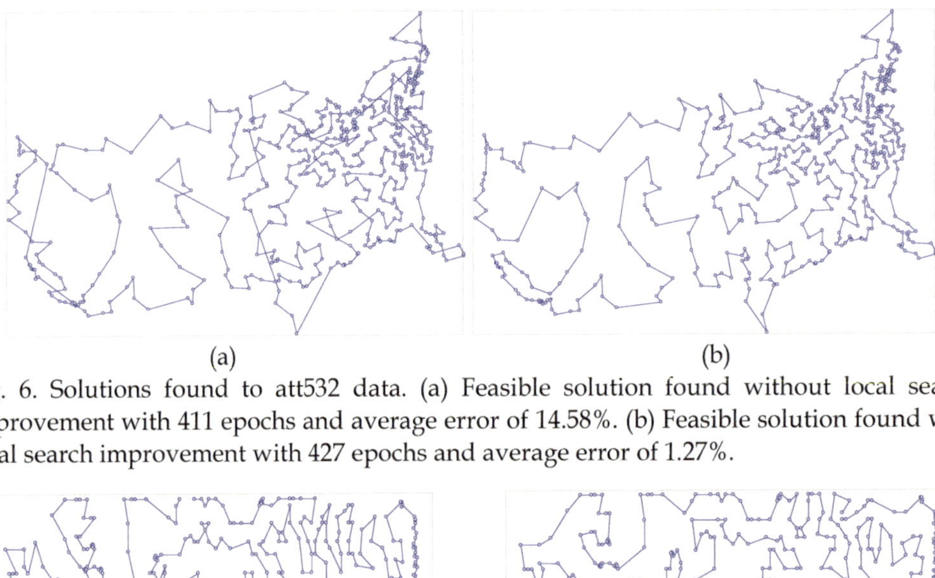

(a) (b)

Fig. 6. Solutions found to att532 data. (a) Feasible solution found without local search improvement with 411 epochs and average error of 14.58%. (b) Feasible solution found with local search improvement with 427 epochs and average error of 1.27%.

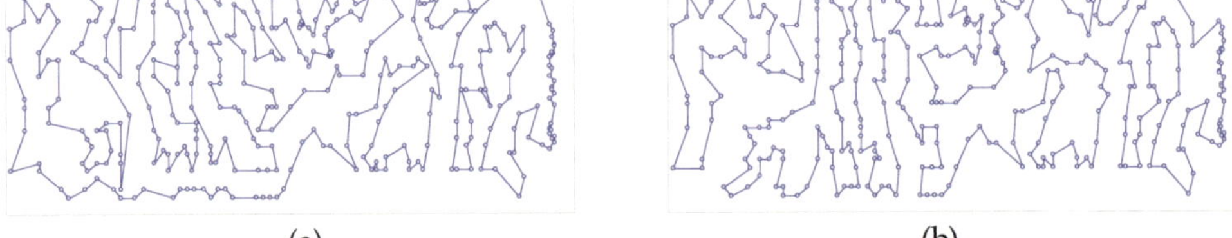

(a) (b)

Fig. 7. Solutions found to u724 data. (a) Feasible solution found without local search improvement with 469 epochs and average error of 16.85%. (b) Feasible solution found with local search improvement with 516 epochs and average error of 6.28%.

The next Section shows the results of applying this technique to some of the TSPLIB's problems for symmetrical and asymmetrical Traveling Salesman problems.

9. Comparisons of technique proposed with others heuristics to some TSPLIB's problems

The results found with the technique proposed to problems of TSPLIB with symmetrical cases are compared with Self Organizing Maps and Simulated Annealing results. In asymmetrical problems of TSPLIB, the technique proposed are compared with heurist of insertion of arcs. In both cases the local search technique was applied to results found with Wang's Recurrent Neural Network with "Winner Takes All".

For symmetrical problems, the following methods were used to compare with the technique presented in this work:

- the method that involves statistical methods between neurons' weights of Self Organizing Maps (Aras et al., 1999) and has a global version (KniesG: Kohonen Network Incorporating Explicit Statistics Global), where all cities are used in the neuron dispersion process, and a local version (KniesL), where only some represented cities are used in the neuron dispersion step;
- the Simulated Annealing technique (Budinich, 1996), using the 2-opt improvement technique;
- Budinich's Self Organizing Map, which consists of a traditional Self Organizing Map applied to the Traveling Salesman Problem, presented in Budinich, 1996;
- the expanded Self Organizing Map (ESOM), which, in each iteration, places the neurons close to their corresponding input data (cities) and, at the same time, places them at the convex contour determined by the cities (Leung et al., 2004);
- the efficient and integrated Self Organizing Map (eISOM), where the ESOM procedures are used and the winning neuron is placed at the mean point among its closest neighboring neurons(Jin et al., 2003);
- the efficient Self Organizing Map technique (SETSP), which defines the updating forms for parameters that use the number of cities of problem (Vieira et al., 2003);
- and Kohonen's cooperative adaptive network (CAN) uses the idea of cooperation between the neurons' close neighbors and uses a number of neurons that is larger than the number of cities in the problem (Cochrane & Beasley, 2003).

The computational complexity of the proposed heuristic is $O(n^2 + n)$ (Wang, 1997), considered competitive when compared to the complexity of mentioned Self Organizing Map, which have complexity $O(n^2)$ (Leung et al., 2004). The CAN technique has a computational complexity of $O(n^2\log(n))$ (Cochrane & Beasley, 2003), while the Simulated Annealing technique has a complexity of $O(n^4\log(n))$ (Liu et al., 2003).

The results for the proposed heuristic in this paper, together with the 2-opt improvement, presented an average error range from 0 to 3.31%, as shown in the 2-opt column of Table 4. The methods that use improvement techniques to their solutions are Simulated Annealing, CAN and Wang's neural network with "Winner Takes All".

The technique proposed in this paper, with 2-opt, present better results that Simulated Annealing and CAN methods in almost every problem, with the only exception in the *lin105* problem. Without the improvement 2-opt, the results of problems *eil76, eil51, eil101* and *rat195* are better than the results of the other neural networks that do not use improvement techniques in its solutions.

In Table 4 are shown the average errors of the techniques mentioned above. The "pure" technique proposed in this work to Traveling Salesman Problem, the proposed technique with the 2-opt improvement algorithm, as well as the best (max) and worst (min) results of each problem considered are also shown.

TSP's name	n	optimal solution	average error (%)										
			for 8 algorithms presented on TSPLIB								WRNN with WTA		
			KniesG	KniesL	SA	Budinich	ESom	EiSom	Setsp	CAN	Max	Min	2-opt
eil51	51	430	2.86	2.86	2.33	3.10	2.10	2.56	2.22	**0.94**	1.16	1.16	0
st70	70	678.6	2.33	1.51	2.14	1.70	2.09	NC	1.60	**1.33**	4.04	2.71	0
eil76	76	545.4	5.48	4.98	5.54	5.32	3.89	NC	4.23	2.04	2.49	**1.03**	0
gr96	96	514	NC	NC	4.12	2.09	**1.03**	NC	NC	NC	6.61	4.28	0
rd100	100	7,910	2.62	2.09	3.26	3.16	1.96	NC	2.60	**1.23**	7.17	6.83	0.08
eil101	101	629	5.63	4.66	5.74	5.24	3.43	3.59	NC	**1.11**	7.95	3.02	0.48
lin105	105	14,383	1.29	1.98	1.87	1.71	0.25	NC	1.30	**0**	5.94	4.33	0.20
pr107	107	44,303	0.42	0.73	1.54	1.32	1.48	NC	0.41	**0.17**	3.14	3.14	0
pr124	124	59,030	0.49	**0.08**	1.26	1.62	0.67	NC	NC	2.36	2.63	0.33	0
bier127	127	118,282	3.08	2.76	3.52	3.61	1.70	NC	1.85	**0.69**	5.08	4.22	0.37
pr136	136	96,772	5.15	4.53	4.90	5.20	4.31	NC	4.40	**3.94**	6.86	5.99	1.21
pr152	152	73,682	1.29	0.97	2.64	2.04	0.89	NC	1.17	**0.74**	3.27	3.23	0
rat195	195	2,323	11.92	12.24	13.29	11.48	7.13	NC	11.19	**5.27**	8.82	5.55	3.31
kroa200	200	29,368	6.57	5.72	5.61	6.13	2.91	1.64	3.12	**0.92**	12.25	8.95	0.62
lin318	318	42,029	NC	NC	7.56	8.19	4.11	**2.05**	NC	2.65	8.65	8.35	1.90
pcb442	442	50,784	10.45	11.07	9.15	8.43	7.43	6.11	10.16	**5.89**	13.18	9.16	2.87
att532	532	27,686	6.8	6.74	5.38	5.67	4.95	3.35	NC	**3.32**	15.43	14.58	1.28

Table 4. Results of the experiments for the symmetrical problems of TSP, with techniques presented on TSPLIB: KniesG, KniesL, SA, Budinich's SOM, ESOM, EISOM, SETSP, CAN and a technique presented on this paper: WRNN with WTA. The solutions presented in bold characters show the best results for each problem, disregarding the results with the 2-opt technique. (NC = not compared)

For the asymmetrical problems, the techniques used to compare with the technique proposed in this work were (Glover et al., 2001):

- the Karp-Steele path methods (KSP) and general Karp-Steele (GKS), which begin with one cycle and by removing arcs and placing new arcs, transform the initial cycle into a

Hamiltonian one. The difference between these two techniques is that the GKS uses all of the cycle's vertices for the changes in the cycle's arcs;

- the path recursive contraction (PRC) that consists in forming an initial cycle and transforming it into a Hamiltonian cycle by removing arcs from every sub-cycle;
- the contraction or path heuristic (COP), which is a combination of the GKS and RPC techniques;
- the "greedy" heuristic (GR) that chooses the smallest arc in the graph, contracts this arc creating a new graph, and keeps this procedure up to the last arc, thus creating a route;
- and the random insertion heuristic (RI) that initially chooses 2 vertices, inserts one vertex that had not been chosen, thus creating a cycle, and repeats this procedure until it creates a route including all vertices.

TSP's name	n	optimal solution	average error (%)								
			for 6 algorithms						WRNN with WTA		
			GR	RI	KSP	GKS	PRC	COP	max	Min	2-opt
br17	17	39	102.56	**0**	**0**	**0**	**0**	**0**	**0**	**0**	0
ftv33	33	1,286	31.34	11.82	13.14	8.09	21.62	9.49	7.00	**0**	0
ftv35	35	1,473	24.37	9.37	1.56	**1.09**	21.18	1.56	5.70	3.12	3.12
ftv38	38	1,530	14.84	10.20	1.50	**1.05**	25.69	3.59	3.79	3.73	3.01
pr43	43	5,620	3.59	0.30	**0.11**	0.32	0.66	0.68	0.46	0.29	0.05
ftv44	44	1,613	18.78	14.07	7.69	5.33	22.26	10.66	2.60	**2.60**	2.60
ftv47	47	1,776	11.88	12.16	3.04	**1.69**	28.72	8.73	8.05	3.83	3.83
ry48p	48	14,422	32.55	11.66	7.23	**4.52**	29.50	7.97	6.39	5.59	1.24
ft53	53	6,905	80.84	24.82	12.99	12.31	18.64	15.68	3.23	**2.65**	2.65
ftv55	55	1,608	25.93	15.30	**3.05**	**3.05**	33.27	4.79	12.19	11.19	6.03
ftv64	64	1,839	25.77	18.49	3.81	2.61	29.09	**1.96**	2.50	2.50	2.50
ft70	70	38,673	14.84	9.32	1.88	2.84	5.89	1.90	2.43	**1.74**	1.74
ftv70	70	1,950	31.85	16.15	3.33	2.87	22.77	**1.85**	8.87	8.77	8.56
kro124p	100	36,230	21.01	12.17	16.95	8.69	23.06	8.79	10.52	**7.66**	7.66
ftv170	170	2,755	32.05	28.97	2.40	**1.38**	25.66	3.59	14.66	12.16	12.16
rbg323	323	1,326	8.52	29.34	**0**	**0**	0.53	**0**	16.44	16.14	16.14
rbg358	358	1,163	7.74	42.48	**0**	**0**	2.32	0.26	22.01	12.73	8.17
rbg403	403	2,465	0.85	9.17	**0**	**0**	0.69	0.20	4.71	4.71	4.71
rbg443	443	2,720	0.92	10.48	**0**	**0**	**0**	**0**	8.05	8.05	2.17

Table 5. Results of the experiments for the asymmetrical problems of TSP with techniques presented on TSPLIB: GR, RI, KSP, GKS, RPC, COP and a technique presented on this paper: WRNN with WTA. The solutions presented in bold characters show the best results for each problem, disregarding the results with the 2-opt technique.

Table 5 shows the average errors of the techniques described, as well as those of the "pure" technique presented in this work and of the proposed technique with the 2-opt technique.

The results of the "pure" technique proposed in this work are better or equivalent to those of the other heuristics mentioned above, for problems br17, ftv33, ftv44, ft53, ft70 and kro124p, as shown in Table 5. By using the 2-opt technique on the proposed technique, the best results were found for problems br17, ftv33, pr43, ry48p, ftv44, ft53, ft70 and kro124p, with average errors ranging from 0 to 16.14%.

10. Conclusions

This work presented the Wang's recurrent neural network with the "Winner Takes All" principle to solve the Assignment Problem and Traveling Salesman Problem. The application of parameters with measures of matrices dispersion showed better results to both problems.

The results of matrices to Assignment Problem had shown that the principle "Winner Takes all" solves problems in matrices with multiple optimal solutions, besides speed the convergence of the Wang's neural network using only 1% of necessary iterations of neural network pure.

Using the best combination of parameters, the average errors are only 0.71% to 100 tested matrices to Assignment Problem. Using these parameters solutions of Traveling Salesman Problem can be found.

By means of the Wang's neural network, a solution for the Assignment Problem is found and the "Winner Takes All" principle is applied to this solution, transforming it into a feasible route for the Traveling Salesman Problem. These technique's solutions were considerably improved when the 2-opt technique was applied on the solutions presented by the proposed technique in this work.

The data used for testing were obtained at the TSPLIB and the comparisons that were made with other heuristics showed that the technique proposed in this work achieves better results in several of the problems tested, with average errors below 16.14% to these problems.

A great advantage of implementing the technique presented in this work is the possibility of using the same technique to solve both symmetrical and asymmetrical Traveling Salesman Problem as well.

11. References

Affenzeller, M. & Wanger, S. (2003). A Self-Adaptive Model for Selective Pressure Handling within the Theory of Genetic Algorithms, *Proceedings of Computer Aided Systems Theory - EUROCAST 2003*, pp. 384-393, ISBN 978-3-540-20221-9, Las Palmas de Gran Canaria, Spain, February, 2003, Springer, Berlin

Ahuja, R.K.; Mangnanti, T.L. & Orlin, J.B. (1993). *Network Flows theory, algorithms, and applications*, Prentice Hall, ISBN ISBN 0-13-617549-X, New Jersey.

Aras, N.; Oommen, B.J. & Altinel, I.K. (1999). The Kohonen network incorporating explicit statistics and its application to the traveling salesman problem. *Neural Networks*, Vol. 12, No. 9, November 1999, pp. 1273-1284, ISSN 0893-6080

Bianchi, L.; Knowles, J. & Bowler, J. (2005). Local search for the probabilistic traveling salesman problem: Correction to the 2-p-opt and 1-shift algorithms. *European Journal of Operational Research*, Vol. 162, No. 1, April 2005, pp. 206-219, ISSN 0377-2217

Budinich, M. (1996). A self-organizing neural network for the traveling salesman problem that is competitive with simulated annealing. *Neural Computation*, Vol. 8, No. 2, February 1996, pp. 416-424, ISSN 0899-7667

Chu, S.C.; Roddick, J.F. & Pan, J.S. (2004). Ant colony system with communication strategies. *Information Sciences*, Vol. 167, No. 1-4, December 2004, pp. 63-76, ISSN 0020-0255

Cochrane, E.M. & Beasley, J.E. (2001). The Co-Adaptive Neural Network Approach to the Euclidean Travelling Salesman Problem. *Neural Networks*, Vol. 16, No. 10, December 2003, pp. 1499-1525, ISSN 0893-6080

Glover, F.; Gutin, G.; Yeo, A. & Zverovich, A. (2001). Construction heuristics for the asymmetric TSP. *European Journal of Operational Research*, Vol. 129, No. 3, March 2001, pp. 555-568, ISSN 0377-2217

Hung, D.L. & Wang, J. (2003). Digital Hardware realization of a Recurrent Neural Network for solving the Assignment Problem. *Neurocomputing*, Vol. 51, April, 2003, pp. 447-461, ISSN 0925-2312

Jin, H.D.; Leung, K.S.; Wong, M.L. & Xu, Z.B. (2003). An Efficient Self-Organizing Map Designed by Genetic Algorithms for the Traveling Salesman Problem, *IEEE Transactions On Systems, Man, And Cybernetics - Part B: Cybernetics*, Vol. 33, No. 6, December 2003, pp. 877-887, ISSN 1083-4419

Laporte, G. (1992). The vehicle routing problem: An overview of exact and approximate algorithms, *European Journal of Operational Research*, Vol. 59, No. 2, June 1992, pp. 345-358, ISSN ISSN 0377-2217

Leung, K.S.; Jin, H.D. & Xu, Z.B. (2004). An expanding self-organizing neural network for the traveling salesman problem. *Neurocomputing*, Vol. 62, December 2004, pp. 267-292, ISSN 0925-2312

Liu, G.; He, Y.; Fang, Y.; & Oiu, Y. (2003). A novel adaptive search strategy of intensification and diversification in tabu search, *Proceedings of Neural Networks and Signal Processing*, pp 428- 431, ISBN 0-7803-7702-8, Nanjing, China, December 2003, IEEE, China

Onwubolu, G.C. & Clerc, M. (2004). Optimal path for automated drilling operations by a new heuristic approach using particle swarm optimization. *International Journal of Production Research*, Vol. 42, No. 3, February 2004, pp. 473-491, ISSN 0020-7543

Reinelt, G. (1991). TSPLIB – A traveling salesman problem library. *ORSA Journal on Computing*, Vol. 3, No. 4, 1991, pp. 376-384, ISSN 0899-1499

Siqueira, P.H.; Scheer, S. & Steiner, M.T.A. (2005). Application of the "Winner Takes All" Principle in Wang's Recurrent Neural Network for the Assignment Problem. *Proceedings of Second International Symposium on Neural Networks – ISNN 2005*, pp. 731-738, ISBN 3-540-25912-0, Chongqing, China, May 2005, Springer, Berlin.

Siqueira, P.H.; Steiner, M.T.A. & Scheer, S. (2007). A new approach to solve the traveling salesman problem. *Neurocomputing*, Vol. 70, No. 4-6, January 2007, pp. 1013-102, ISSN 0925-2312

Siqueira, P.H.; Carnieri, C.; Steiner, M.T.A. & Barboza, A.O. (2004). Uma proposta de solução para o problema da construção de escalas de motoristas e cobradores de ônibus por meio do algoritmo do matching de peso máximo. *Gestão & Produção*, Vol.11, No. 2, May 2004, pp. 187-196, ISSN 0104-530X

Vieira, F.C.; Doria Neto, A.D. & Costa, J.A. (2003). An Efficient Approach to the Travelling Salesman Problem Using Self-Organizing Maps, *International Journal Of Neural Systems*, Vol. 13, No. 2, April 2003, pp. 59-66, ISSN 0129-0657

Wang, J. (1992). Analog Neural Network for Solving the Assignment Problem. *Electronic Letters*, Vol. 28, No. 11, May 1992, pp. 1047-1050, ISSN 0013-5194

Wang, J. (1997). Primal and Dual Assignment Networks. *IEEE Transactions on Neural Networks*, Vol. 8, No. 3, May 1997, pp. 784-790, ISSN 1045-9227

Wang, R.L.; Tang, Z. & Cao, Q.P. (2002). A learning method in Hopfield neural network for combinatorial optimization problem. *Neurocomputing*, Vol. 48, No. 4, October 2002, pp. 1021-1024, ISSN 0925-2312

8

Solving the Probabilistic Travelling Salesman Problem Based on Genetic Algorithm with Queen Selection Scheme

Yu-Hsin Liu
Department of Civil Engineering, National Chi Nan University
Taiwan

1. Introduction

The probabilistic travelling salesman problem (PTSP) is an extension of the well-known travelling salesman problem (TSP), which has been extensively studied in the field of combinatorial optimization. The goal of the TSP is to find the minimum length of a tour to all customers, given the distances between all pairs of customers whereas the objective of the PTSP is to minimize the expected length of the *a priori* tour where each customer requires a visit only with a given probability (Bertsimas, 1988; Bertsimas et al., 1990; Jaillet, 1985). The main difference between the PTSP and the TSP is that in the PTSP the probability of each node being visited is between 0.0 and 1.0 while in TSP the probability of each node being visited is 1.0. Due to the fact that the element of uncertainty not only exists, but also significantly affects the system performance in many real-world transportation and logistics applications, the results from the PTSP can provide insights into research in other probabilistic combinatorial optimization problems. Moreover, the PTSP can also be used to model many real-world applications in logistical and transportation planning, such as daily pickup-delivery services with stochastic demand, job sequencing involving changeover cost, design of retrieval sequences in a warehouse or in a cargo terminal operations, meals on wheels in senior citizen services, trip-chaining activities, vehicle routing problem with stochastic demand, and home delivery service under e-commerce (Bartholdi et al., 1983; Bertsimas et al., 1995; Campbell, 2006; Jaillet, 1988; Tang & Miller-Hooks, 2004).

Early PTSP computational studies, dating from 1985, adopted heuristic approaches that were modified from the TSP (e.g., nearest neighbor, savings approach, spacefilling curve, radial sorting, 1-shift, and 2-opt exchanges) (Bartholdi & Platzman, 1988; Bertsimas, 1988; Bertsimas & Howell, 1993; Jaillet, 1985, 1987; Rossi & Gavioli, 1987). With its less than satisfactory performance in yielding solution quality, researchers in the recent years switch to metaheuristic methods, such as ant colony optimization (Bianchi, 2006; Branke & Guntsch, 2004), evolutionary algorithm (Liu et al., 2007), simulated annealing (Bowler et al., 2003), threshold accepting (Tang & Miller-Hooks, 2004) and scatter search (Liu, 2006, 2007, 2008). Because the genetic algorithm (GA), a conceptual framework of the population-based metaheuristic method, has been shown to yield promising outcomes for solving various complicated optimization problems in the past three decades (Bäck et al., 1997; Davis, 1991;

Goldberg, 1989; Holland, 1992; Liu & Mahmassani, 2000), this study will propose an optimization procedure based on GA framework for solving the PTSP.
Mainly, the author of this chapter proposes and tests a new search procedure for solving the PTSP by incorporating the nearest neighbor algorithm, 1-shift and/or 2-opt exchanges for local search, selection scheme, and edge recombination crossover (ERX) operator into genetic algorithm (GA) framework. Specifically, the queen GA, a selection approach which was proposed recently and yielded promising results (Balakrishnan et al., 2006; Stern et al., 2006), will be tested against the traditional selection mechanisms (i.e., fitness-proportional, tournament, rank-based and elitist selections) for its comparative effectiveness and efficiency in solving the PTSP. Unlike traditional selection mechanisms used in GA which selects both parents from the entire population based on their fitness values, the queen GA creates a subgroup of better solutions (the queen cohort), and uses at least one of its members in each performed crossover. To validate the effectiveness and efficiency of the proposed algorithmic procedure, a set of heterogeneous (90 instances) and homogeneous (270 instances) PTSP test instances as used in the previous studies (Liu, 2006, 2007, 2008; Tang & Miller-Hooks, 2004) will be used as the base for comparison purpose.
The remainder of this chapter is organized as follows. In the next section, expressions for exactly and approximately evaluating the *a priori* tour for the PTSP are introduced. The details of the proposed algorithmic procedure for the PTSP are then described. The results of the numerical experiments are presented and discussed in the next section, followed by concluding comments.

2. Definition and evaluation of the PTSP

The PTSP is defined on a directed graph $G := (V, E)$, where $V := \{0, v_1, v_2, ..., v_n\}$ is the set of nodes or vertices, $E \subseteq V \times V$ is the set of directed edges. Node 0 represents the depot with the presence probability of 1.0. Each non-depot node v_i is associated with a presence probability p_i that represents the possibility that node v_i will be present in a given realization. Given a directed graph G, the PTSP is to find an *a priori* Hamiltonian tour with minimal expected length in G.

2.1 Exact evaluation for the *a priori* tour

Solving the PTSP mainly relies on computing the expected length of an *a priori* tour. The computation of the expected length of a specific *a priori* PTSP tour τ, denoted as $E[\tau]$, depends on the relative location of nodes on that tour and the presence probability of each node in a given instance. By explicitly considering all realizations based on the presence of each individual node, the expected length of tour τ can be calculated. For an n-node PTSP instance, a tour τ has 2^n possible realizations. The probability of realization r_j, $p(r_j)$, can be calculated based on the presence probability of each individual node. Let $L[r_j(\tau)]$ describe the tour length of τ for realization r_j under the assumption that nodes not in r_j are simply skipped in the tour. The expected tour length can then be formally described as

$$E[\tau] = \sum_{j=1}^{2^n} p(r_j) L[r_j(\tau)] \tag{1}$$

The computation of expected length based on Equation (1) is inefficient, because the computational complexity increases exponentially with an increasing number of nodes.

Therefore, Jaillet & Odoni (1988) proposed an approach to exactly calculate $E[\tau]$ in the complexity of $O(n^3)$ for the PTSP.

$$E[\tau]=\sum_{i=0}^{n}\sum_{j=i+1}^{n+1}\{d_{\tau(i)\tau(j)}p_{\tau(i)}p_{\tau(j)}\prod_{k=i+1}^{j-1}(1-p_{\tau(k)})\} \tag{2}$$

d_{ij} represents the distance between nodes i and j; $\tau(i)$ denotes the node that has been assigned the ith stop in tour τ and $p_{\tau(i)}$ is the probability of node $\tau(i)$. $\tau(0)$ and $\tau(n+1)$ represent node 0, which is the depot.

2.2 Approximate evaluation for the *a priori* tour

Even though (2) yields a polynomial evaluation time for the PTSP, the resulting $O(n^3)$ time for calculating $E[\tau]$ is still very long, especially for metaheuristic methods which need to repeatedly evaluate the objective function value $E[\tau]$. In this study, the proposed GA needs to repeatedly compare two solutions (i.e., the new solution before and after local search procedure, which is described in the next section) based on their values of $E[\tau]$. Therefore, the depth approximation originally proposed by Branke & Guntsch (2004) was adopted. The depth approximate evaluation of $E[\tau]$ shown in (3) have been used to significantly increase the computation efficiency under the scatter search framework (Liu, 2006).

$$E_{\lambda}^{AP}[\tau]=\sum_{i=1}^{n}\sum_{j=i+1}^{\min\{n+1,i+\lambda\}}\{d_{\tau(i)\tau(j)}p_{\tau(i)}p_{\tau(j)}\prod_{k=i+1}^{j-1}(1-p_{\tau(k)})\} \tag{3}$$

The only difference between (2) and (3) is the choice of truncation position λ in (3). Equation (3) will have the computational complexity of $O(n\lambda^2)$, instead of $O(n^3)$ in (2). It is easy to see that (3) becomes more accurate when λ increases. A larger value of λ, however, requires more computation efforts for the computation of (3). Equation (3) can perform a very good approximation of $E[\tau]$ with a smaller value of λ when the value of $p_{\tau(k)}$ gets larger, because $\prod_{k=i+1}^{j-1}(1-p_{\tau(k)})$ will yield a very small value and can be omitted. Nevertheless, Equation (3) will need a larger value of λ to perform a good approximation when the value of $p_{\tau(k)}$ is small. The approximation usually yields some errors in comparison to the exact evaluation. To overcome that, the two-stage comparison proposed by Liu (2008) intends to exactly evaluate the $E[\tau]$ value by using the depth approximation evaluation (Equation 3) in the first stage and the exact evaluation (Equation 2) in the second stage. The detailed use of the depth approximation evaluation shown in Equation (3) to accelerate the proposed algorithm is referred to Liu (2008).

3. Solution algorithm

The proposed GA consists of four components as shown in Fig. 1. They are the initialization, local search, selection scheme, and crossover. When starting to solve the PTSP (Generation 0, g = 0), initial solutions are generated based on the nearest neighbor algorithm, which are then improved by the local search. Then, a specific selection mechanism is called into place to further select solutions to be mated based on their solution quality (objective function value). Pairs of solutions are used to generate the new solutions via edge recombination crossover (ERX). The newly generated solutions are then improved using the local search. The solutions are allowed to evolve through successive generations until a termination criterion is met. The detailed description of the embedded components is illustrated in the following sections.

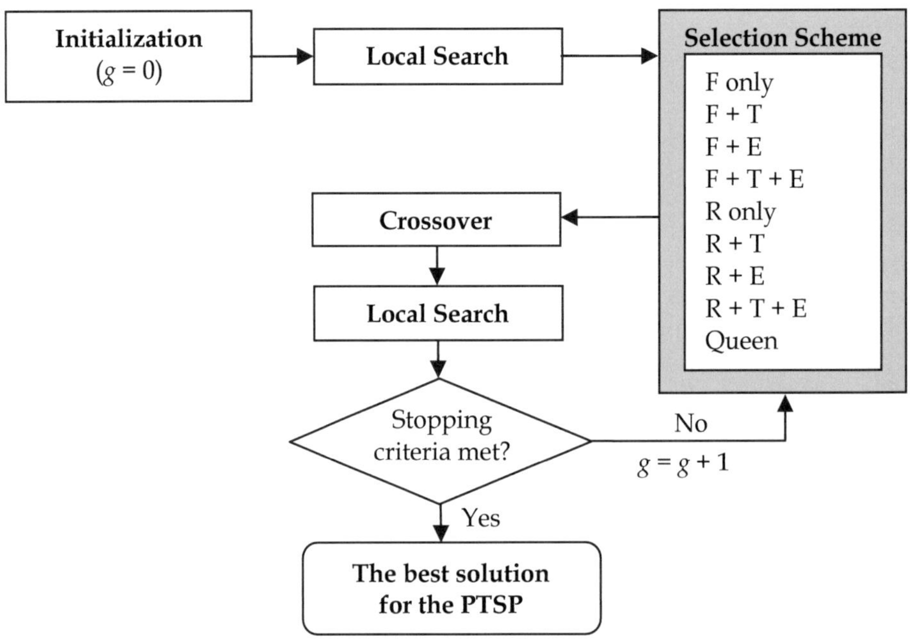

Fig. 1. The general procedure of the genetic algorithm for the PTSP.

3.1 Initialization

This procedure is designed to generate m initial solutions (m = 15 in this study). Considering a PTSP with n nodes (excluding the depot, node *0*), the farthest node, a_0, from node *0* is selected first and randomly inserted into a location between $(\lfloor (n+1)/2 \rfloor - 4)$ and $(\lfloor (n+1)/2 \rfloor + 4)$. The nearest neighbor algorithm is then used to build up the sequence of the tour. After selecting node a_0, the nearest node (a_1) from a_0 is selected and inserted in front of a_0. The second nearest node (a_2) from a_0 is selected and inserted behind a_0. Then, among the remaining nodes, the nearest node (a_3) from a_1 is selected and inserted in front of a_1, while the nearest node (a_4) from a_2 is selected and inserted behind a_2. The 1st initial solution (tour) is thus built by following the above rule and expressed as follows.

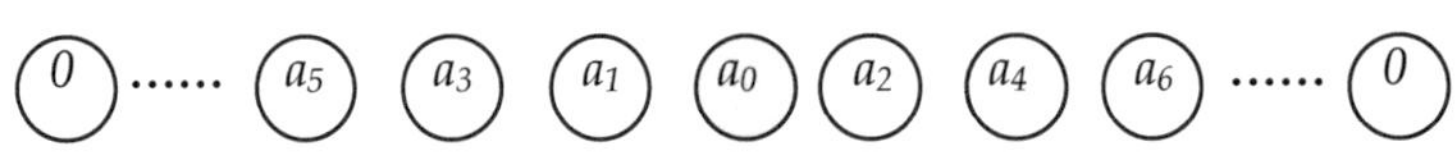

To create diverse solutions, the remaining initial solutions are generated using the above rule with slight modifications. The only difference lies in whenever l = 6, 12, 18, ..., instead of using the nearest node from a_{l-2}, a_l is randomly chosen from the first or second nearest node from a_{l-2}.

3.2 Local search

This component is used in an attempt to further enhance the solution generated via a local search procedure. As the previous study has investigated the performance of diversified local search strategy by stochastically selecting two different local search methods (i.e., 1-shift and 2-opt exchanges) and found that combining 1-shift and 2-opt (1-shift/2opt) is the most effective local search for the PTSP (Liu, 2008). Therefore, the 1-shift/2-opt is then adopted to improve the solution generated in the proposed GA algorithm.

The procedures of 1-shift and 2-opt exchanges are briefly summarized as follows. Given an *a priori* tour τ, its 1-shift neighborhood is the set of tours obtained by moving a node at position i to position j with the intervening nodes being accordingly shifted backwards one space. The 2-opt exchange is the set of tours obtained by reversing a section of τ.

The depth approximate evaluation of expected length of the *a priori* tour shown in (3) is then used to increase the computational efficiency. For a specific tour τ, $E_{\lambda}^{AP}[\tau]$ is always less than the value of $E[\tau]$ because of the truncation in calculating $E_{\lambda}^{AP}[\tau]$. Let τ_b and τ_a denote the *a priori* tour before and after a specific local search method, respectively. It means that no improvement has been found after the local search if $E_{\lambda}^{AP}[\tau_a] \geqq E[\tau_b]$. Equation (2) is used to exactly evaluate the solution after the local search if $E_{\lambda}^{AP}[\tau_a] < E[\tau_b]$. If the local search yields a better $E[\tau]$ value than the one from the original solution (i.e., $E[\tau_a] < E[\tau_b]$), the new solution (τ_a) will replace the original solution (τ_b). If no improvement has been found after the local search, no replacement will be made. The above procedure is repeated N_{LS} times for each solution (N_{LS} = 25 in this study).

3.3 Selection scheme

Selection scheme is the process of choosing the mating pairs from the current population and to create the new solutions based on crossover operator. To investigate the performance of the queen GA, four popularly used selection mechanisms are used as a benchmark in this study: fitness-proportional, rank-based, tournament, and elitism selections.

3.3.1 Fitness-proportional selection (F)

Under the fitness-proportional selection method, the probability of selecting a particular solution for reproduction is proportional to its own fitness (i.e., $E[\tau]$) relative to the average fitness of the entire current generation. With this selection method, the best solution tends to produce the largest amount of offspring and hence survive to future generations. This procedure can be regarded as a "biased" roulette wheel where each string in the current population occupies a roulette wheel slot sized in proportion to its fitness (Goldberg, 1989). Selection can be done by simply spinning the weighted roulette wheel, and fitter strings will have higher chances of being selected. This process can be simulated by the following expression:

$$q_k = \frac{1/f_k}{\sum_{t=1}^{m} 1/f_t} \tag{4}$$

where q_k is the probability of selecting solution k to produce offspring, and m is the population size. The f_k is the fitness value of the kth solution in the current generation.

Because the PTSP is a minimization problem, $1/f_k$ is used as the appropriate weight for the kth solution.

3.3.2 Rank-based selection (R)

Under the rank-based selection, the probability of selecting a particular solution for reproduction is determined by the rank of its fitness. This process can be simulated by the following expression:

$$q_k = \frac{1/r_k}{\sum_{t=1}^{m} 1/r_t} \tag{5}$$

where r_k is the rank of the fitness value for the kth solution.

3.3.3 Tournament selection (T)

Tournament selection, inspired by the competition in nature among individuals for the right to mate, picks two solutions using the proportional or rank-based selection from the population and the fittest one is selected for reproduction (Goldberg, 1989; Davis, 1991). Each solution can participate in an unlimited number of tournaments. The two winning solutions in the tournament are then subjected to the crossover operators.

3.3.4 Elitism (E)

Under the elitism selection strategy, the top N_e strings (N_e is determined by the analyst) of the current generation in terms of fitness value are kept and propagated to the next generation (Davis, 1991). The remaining solutions in the next generation are then generated based on the tournament selection method and the crossover operators. This procedure guarantees that the best solution in the next generation is not worse than the one in the current generation.

3.3.5 Queen GA

According to the concept of queen GA, the top N_{top} solutions in terms of its fitness value of the population are selected to be the members of queen. Then, one of the parents is chosen from the queen members and the other parent is randomly selected from the whole population excluding the already chosen member. These two selected parents are then mated based on the crossover operator. The queen members are dynamically updated based on the quality of the new solutions generated. A newly solution generated will become a queen member if the new solution has a better objective function value than the one with the worst objective value in the queen subset.

3.3.6 Experiment design of selection schemes

In addition to queen GA, eight schemes are designed by combining one or several selection methods from four popularly used selection mechanisms mentioned previously (i.e., fitness-proportional, rank-based, tournament, and elitism selection). Explicitly, since the tournament and elitism selections need to work with fitness-proportional (F) or rank-based (R) selection, eight selection schemes are designed and used in the numerical experiment in this study. They are fitness-proportional selection only (F), fitness-proportional and tournament selection (F+T), fitness-proportional and elitism selection (F+E), fitness-proportional, tournament and elitism selection (F+T+E), rank-based selection only (R), rank-based and tournament selection (R+T), rank-based and elitism selection (R+E), rank-based, tournament and elitism selection (R+T+E).

3.4 Edge recombination crossover (ERX)

The main purpose of this component is to create new solutions using a given pair of solutions generated by "selection". Based on the results from previous studies (Liu et al., 2007; Potvin, 1996), the edge recombination crossover (ERX) from genetic algorithms performed best when compared to other crossover strategies for both in TSP and PTSP. Therefore, ERX was adopted in this study.

ERX was proposed by Whitley et al. (1989) to solve the traditional TSP. A 5-node PTSP is used as an example to describe the procedure of ERX. Assuming that two solutions (tours) are chosen from the "selection"--(0, 4, 3, 1, 2, 0) and (0, 1, 2, 3, 4, 0), the edges connected to each node are as follows. For node 0, the first solution indicates that node 0 connects to nodes 2 and 4 and the second solution shows that node 0 connects to nodes 1 and 4. Therefore, node 0 connects to nodes 1, 2, and 4 by considering these two solutions. Similarly, node 1 connects to nodes 0, 2, 3; node 2 connects to nodes 0, 1, 3; node 3 connects to nodes 1, 2, 4; node 4 connects to nodes 0, 3. These are the initial edge lists for each node.

The operation of the ERX is described as follows. Assuming that node 0 is selected as the starting node for the new solution, all edges incident to node 0 must be deleted from the initial edge list. As described, from node 0 we can go to nodes 1, 2, or 4, while nodes 1 and 2 have two active edges and node 4 has only one active edge by deleting node 0 from the initial edge list. The node with the fewest active edge, node 4, is picked as the node next to node 0 in the new solution. Then, the edge list for the remaining nodes (nodes 1, 2, and 3) is further updated by deleting node 4. The updated edge list is node 1 (2, 3), node 2 (1, 3), and node 3 (1, 2). From node 4, we can only go to node 3 (as node 0 is already deleted from the list). Therefore, node 3 is chosen to be the node next to node 4 in the new solution. The new solution generated is further improved by the local search.

3.5 The procedure after the first generation

The newly generated solutions from the ERX and local search are used to update the population in terms of the objective function value. The above procedure is repeated until a termination criterion is met. However, if there are no solutions to be updated for the population in the current generation, the initialization is used to generate (m - m_1) new solutions in the next generation, but keeping m_1 high quality solutions ($m_1 = 2$, in this study). In addition, if the previous three generations converge to the same best solution, the local search is used to improve that "converged" solution by repeating N_{LS2} times to exhaustively search the neighborhood of that "converged" solution ($N_{LS2} = 300$, in this study).

4. Numerical experiments and results

There are two types of data sets, heterogeneous and homogeneous PTSP, used as numerical experiments in this study to examine the performance of different selection schemes under GA framework for the PTSP. First, 90 heterogeneous PTSP instances were generated by Tang & Miller-Hooks (2004) with size n = 50, 75, and 100. Three groups of problem sets categorized by different intervals of customer presence probabilities were created for each problem size (n = 50, 75, and 100). Presence probabilities of customer nodes were randomly generated from a uniform distribution on intervals (0.0, 0.2], (0.0, 0.5], (0.0, 1.0], one for each problem size. Second, there were 270 homogeneous PTSP instances generated by the author and used in the previous study of Liu (2008) with size n = 50, 75, and 100 associated with nine probability values (p = 0.1, 0.2, ..., 0.9). For both homogeneous and heterogeneous PTSP, the presence probability of the depot (node 0) was assigned as 1.0. Ten different problem instances were randomly generated for each presence probability of customer nodes. For each instance, the coordinates of one depot and n customer nodes (x_i, y_i) were generated based on a uniform distribution from $[0, 100]^2$. The Euclidean distance for each pair of nodes was calculated by using $d_{ij} = \sqrt{(x_i - x_j)^2 + (y_i - y_j)^2}$.

To compare the effectiveness among nine different selection schemes under GA framework, the preset maximum number of generations (G_{max}) was used as the termination criterion (G_{max} is set to be two times the number of nodes, i.e., $G_{max} = 2n$, in this study) for both heterogeneous and homogeneous PTSP. The average solution quality is examined and compared among nine different selection schemes. In this study, the proposed methods were used to solve each problem instance 30 times to enhance the robustness of the results. That is, the average statistics for the methods proposed in this study are based on a 300-run average. The numerical results of heterogeneous and homogeneous PTSP are discussed in Section 4.1 and 4.2, respectively.

4.1 Results of heterogeneous PTSP

4.1.1 Descriptive statistics of average $E[\tau]$ values obtained by the heterogeneous PTSP

Average $E[\tau]$ values found from nine different selection schemes for the heterogeneous PTSP are reported in Table 1. Definitions of terms used in the column headings are given as follows. n denotes problem size, which is the number of customer nodes. p represents the customer presence probability interval (0.0, p].

The best average value of $E[\tau]$ among the nine selection schemes (i.e., F, F+T, F+E, F+T+E, R, R+T, R+E, R+T+E, Queen) for each problem size with different presence probability interval is shown in shaded. As shown in Table 1, the average $E[\tau]$ values obtained by only using fitness-proportional (F) or rank-based (R) selection strategy are consistently worse than the ones obtained by the other seven selection strategies. The solution quality becomes much better when adding tournament (T) and/or elitism strategies to fitness-proportional (F) or rank-based (R) selection. It indicates that fitness-proportional (F) or rank-based (R) selection should combine tournament (T) and/or elitism strategies to obtain acceptable outcomes.

Moreover, except for p = 0.5 when n = 50, the average $E[\tau]$ values obtained by adding elitism to fitness-proportional (F) selection strategy (F+E) performs better than the ones obtained by adding tournament to fitness-proportional (F) selection strategy (F+T). Furthermore, except for p = 0.5, 1.0 when n = 50, the average $E[\tau]$ values obtained by adding elitism to rank-based (R) selection strategy (R+E) performs better than the ones obtained by adding tournament to rank-based (R) selection strategy (R+T). It reveals that the average $E[\tau]$ values obtained by keeping the best solution(s) to the successive generations can generally perform better than the ones obtained by only applying tournament selection to fitness-proportional (F) or rank-based (R) selection.

Finally, as shown in Table 1, the average $E[\tau]$ values obtained by adding elitism to fitness-proportional (F) or rank-based (R) selection strategy are similar to the ones obtained by combining both elitism and tournament to fitness-proportional (F) or rank-based (R) selection strategy. Overall, the queen, F+E, F+T+E, R+E, and R+T+E are better selection strategies and yielded similar average $E[\tau]$ value for the heterogeneous PTSP than the other four selection strategies.

n	p	F	F+T	F+E	F+T+E	R	R+T	R+E	R+T+E	Queen
50	0.2	225.110	224.854	224.839	224.832	224.868	224.838	224.835	224.834	224.831
	0.5	343.901	341.585	341.675	341.426	341.935	341.347	341.504	341.331	341.499
	1.0	459.504	450.583	450.235	450.964	452.853	449.539	450.916	451.383	451.272
75	0.2	267.731	266.071	265.943	265.958	266.239	265.970	265.929	265.959	265.958
	0.5	415.129	404.257	403.526	403.879	406.728	403.782	403.485	403.748	403.705
	1.0	555.256	534.013	527.832	527.421	540.306	529.276	527.300	527.295	526.765
100	0.2	304.779	301.318	300.859	300.873	301.791	301.084	300.830	300.825	300.837
	0.5	480.752	466.813	463.747	462.578	469.663	464.671	462.661	463.381	461.556
	1.0	684.758	649.544	626.749	625.105	660.210	641.668	625.056	624.490	624.144

Table 1. Computational Results for the Heterogeneous PTSP

4.1.2 Inferential statistics analysis of nine selection schemes for heterogeneous PTSP

Since the assumption of normal distribution is hardly met in minimization problems, the permutation test (Basso et al., 2007), instead of parametric tests, is adopted for statistical testing in the study. A Monte Carlo method with 10,000 permutations is used to obtain the approximate p-value of the permutation test. A set of two-sample permutation tests is conducted to investigate if any statistically significant differences exist between the best average $E[\tau]$ value obtained and the ones obtained by the other eight selection schemes. Table 2 shows the p-values of the permutation tests, where $\alpha = 0.05$ is considered statistically significant in this study.

Several important findings are obtained. First, according to the results of the permutation tests, the average $E[\tau]$ values obtained by fitness-proportional (F) or rank-based (R) selection strategy are significantly higher than the best ones obtained by the other seven selection schemes for all of the tested cases. Second, the average $E[\tau]$ values obtained by Queen GA performs best in four out of the nine tested cases, and where they are not the best performing scheme, the average $E[\tau]$ values are not statistically significant different to the best ones obtained by the other eight selection schemes, except for n = 50 and p = 1.0. Third, for most of the test cases (21 out of 27 cases), the average $E[\tau]$ values obtained by F+T+E, R+E and R+T+E are not statistically significant different to the best ones obtained by these nine selection schemes. Finally, generally speaking, the average $E[\tau]$ values obtained by F+T, F+E and R+T performs statistically worse than the best ones obtained by the nine selection schemes for most of the test cases (20 out of 27 cases), except for n = 50 and p = 1.0, where the average $E[\tau]$ value obtained by R+T performs statistically better than the other eight selection schemes.

n	p	F	F+T	F+E	F+T+E	R	R+T	R+E	R+T+E	Queen
50	0.2	0.0000	0.0000	0.0040	1.0000	0.0000	0.0000	0.1044	0.7157	–
	0.5	0.0000	0.0056	0.0016	0.2814	0.0000	0.8413	0.0742	–	0.0574
	1.0	0.0000	0.0001	0.0301	0.0003	0.0000	–	0.0037	0.0000	0.0009
75	0.2	0.0000	0.0000	0.2865	0.1025	0.0000	0.0000	–	0.1026	0.1526
	0.5	0.0000	0.0762	0.9371	0.4485	0.0000	0.4828	–	0.6295	0.6664
	1.0	0.0000	0.0000	0.2261	0.3782	0.0000	0.0003	0.4642	0.4745	–
100	0.2	0.0000	0.0000	0.0046	0.0896	0.0000	0.0000	0.6137	–	0.3041
	0.5	0.0000	0.0000	0.0000	0.0376	0.0000	0.0000	0.0259	0.0052	–
	1.0	0.0000	0.0000	0.0036	0.1991	0.0000	0.0000	0.2004	0.6788	–

Table 2. *p*-value of Permutation test for the Heterogeneous PTSP

4.1.3 Comparison among the best performing scheme obtained in the study, the Queen GA and previous studies

As indicated in the previous section, in eight out of the nine tested cases (except for n = 50 and p = 1.0), the Queen GA either performs best or its performance not statistically significant different from the best ones obtained by the other eight selection schemes. The Queen as well as the the best performing scheme obtained in the study are compared against the previous studies in this section. The heterogeneous PTSP data generated by Tang & Miller-Hooks (2004) has been investigated in several studies (Tang & Miller-Hooks, 2004; Liu, 2006, 2007, 2008). The best average $E[\tau]$ values as well as the corresponding average CPU time in these studies (Previous Best) are listed in Table 3. In Table 3, the definitions of n and p are the same as in Table 1. $E[\tau]$ denotes the average value of the expected length of the *a priori* PTSP tour. CPU is the average CPU running time in seconds. The "Previous Best" results for the heterogeneous PTSP data were obtained by Liu (2006, 2007, 2008), except for n = 50 and p = 0.5, which were obtained by Tang & Miller-Hooks (2004). In Liu's studies (as well as the results of this study), all implementations were performed on an Intel Pentium IV 2.8 GHz CPU personal computer with 512 MB memory (3479 MFlops), while TMH's study was based on a 10-run average and was conducted on a DEC AlphaServer 1200/533 computer with 1 GB memory (1277 MFlops). The best average value of $E[\tau]$ among the three compared sets for each problem size with different presence probability interval is shown in shaded.

n	p	Best in this study		Queen		Previous Best	
		E[τ]	CPU (s)	E[τ]	CPU (s)	E[τ]	CPU (s)
50	0.2	224.8313	28.7	224.8313	28.7	224.8314	45.4
	0.5	341.3313	16.8	341.4989	16.2	341.3000*	72.4*
	1.0	449.5391	6.5	451.2717	8.4	450.2215	12.4
75	0.2	265.9293	108.9	265.9581	118.5	265.9315	240.6
	0.5	403.4846	46.3	403.7050	50.1	403.2347	51.8
	1.0	526.7646	28.6	526.7646	28.6	527.1907	41.5
100	0.2	300.8245	288.1	300.8370	269.5	300.8495	689.9
	0.5	461.5559	115.6	461.5559	115.6	462.2678	121.2
	1.0	624.1439	68.8	624.1439	68.8	624.6369	96.7

*Running on DEC AlphaServer 1200/533 computer with 1 GB memory (1277 MFlops)

Table 3. Computational Results for the Heterogeneous PTSP

The results in Table 3 show that the best of the average $E[\tau]$ values obtained in this study are better than the ones obtained by the "Previous Best." The only exception is when p = 0.5 and n = 75. The best average $E[\tau]$ value yielded performs 0.06% worse than the one obtained by the previous study (Liu, 2008), when p = 0.5 and n = 75. Moreover, the computation efforts used to yield the best results in this study are all less than the one used in "Previous Best." It suggests that the GA solution framework proposed in this study is a promising method for solving the heterogeneous PTSP. As for the Queen GA, the results show that it performs better than the "Previous Best" in terms of average $E[\tau]$ value and computational effort when n = 100. It suggests that the Queen GA is capable of effectively and efficiently solving relatively large-sized heterogeneous PTSP.

4.2 Results of homogeneous PTSP

4.2.1 Descriptive statistics of average $E[\tau]$ values obtained by the homogeneous PTSP

Average $E[\tau]$ values found from nine different selection schemes for the homogeneous PTSP are reported in Table 4. In Table 4, the definitions of n and p are the same as in Table1. The best average value of $E[\tau]$ among the nine selection schemes (i.e., F, F+T, F+E, F+T+E, R, R+T, R+E, R+T+E, Queen) for each problem size with different presence probability is shown in shaded. As the similar results obtained in the heterogeneous PTSP, the average $E[\tau]$ values obtained by only using fitness-proportional (F) or rank-based (R) selection strategy are consistently worse than the ones obtained by the other seven selection strategies. The solution quality becomes much better when adding tournament (T) and/or elitism (E) strategies to fitness-proportional (F) or rank-based (R) selection. Moreover, except for p = 0.3 when n = 50, the average $E[\tau]$ values obtained by adding elitism to fitness-proportional (F) selection strategy (i.e., F+E) performs better than the ones obtained by adding tournament to fitness-proportional (F) selection strategy (i.e., F+T). Furthermore, except for p = 0.3, 0.4 when n = 50, the average $E[\tau]$ values obtained by adding elitism to rank-based (R) selection strategy (i.e., R+E) performs better than the ones obtained by adding tournament to rank-based (R) selection strategy (i.e., R+T). Finally, the average $E[\tau]$ values obtained by adding elitism to rank-based (R) selection strategy are similar to the ones obtained by combining both elitism and tournament to rank-based (R) selection strategy. Overall the queen, F+T+E, R+E, and R+T+E are better selection strategies and yielded similar average $E[\tau]$ value for the homogeneous PTSP than the other five selection strategies.

4.2.2 Inferential statistics analysis of nine selection schemes for homogeneous PTSP

A set of two-sample permutation tests is conducted to investigate if any statistically significant differences exist between the best average $E[\tau]$ value obtained and the ones obtained by the other eight selection schemes. Table 5 shows the p-values of the permutation tests, where $\alpha = 0.05$ is considered statistically significant in this study.

Several important findings are obtained. First, according to the results of the permutation tests, the average $E[\tau]$ values obtained by F only, R only and F+T are significantly higher than the best ones obtained by the other six selection schemes for all of the tested cases. Second, the average $E[\tau]$ values obtained by Queen GA performs best in 8 out of 27 tested cases, and where they are not the best performing scheme, the average $E[\tau]$ values are not statistically significant different to the best ones obtained by the other eight selection schemes, except for n = 75 and p = 0.6. Third, for most of the test cases (70 out of 81 cases), the average $E[\tau]$ values obtained by F+T+E, R+E and R+T+E are not statistically significant different to the best ones obtained by these nine selection schemes. Finally, the average $E[\tau]$ values obtained by F+E and R+T performs statistically worse than the best ones obtained by the nine selection schemes for most of the test cases (40 out of 54 cases).

n	p	F	F+T	F+E	F+T+E	R	R+T	R+E	R+T+E	Queen
50	0.1	233.907	233.550	233.497	233.493	233.584	233.513	233.492	233.492	233.492
	0.2	312.887	311.251	311.079	311.033	311.488	311.034	310.998	311.006	310.995
	0.3	371.020	366.525	366.788	366.170	367.575	366.097	366.424	366.632	366.492
	0.4	413.906	406.654	405.985	405.792	408.614	405.010	405.656	405.699	405.466
	0.5	467.415	456.167	453.551	453.791	459.147	454.205	453.581	453.486	453.204
	0.6	515.228	498.553	494.441	493.196	503.028	496.461	492.888	492.565	492.738
	0.7	537.288	519.762	510.409	509.883	525.096	516.295	509.516	509.762	509.492
	0.8	580.616	562.011	551.838	552.437	568.825	557.246	550.880	551.649	551.506
	0.9	586.400	565.562	562.089	561.712	572.469	561.706	560.520	561.090	561.496
75	0.1	277.591	276.112	275.827	275.822	276.302	275.976	275.824	275.819	275.820
	0.2	369.227	363.290	362.206	361.628	364.299	362.419	361.878	361.895	361.623
	0.3	460.647	448.300	444.228	444.268	451.166	446.191	444.101	444.083	444.365
	0.4	514.566	500.111	493.371	493.100	503.418	497.185	493.801	493.083	492.856
	0.5	563.640	537.817	526.367	525.293	546.373	532.653	525.790	525.704	525.308
	0.6	623.310	597.093	578.021	577.570	602.857	589.736	577.194	574.769	576.791
	0.7	666.105	638.798	621.849	620.450	648.911	632.238	619.659	618.957	619.248
	0.8	712.283	688.327	659.604	658.339	693.720	677.008	658.942	656.115	656.658
	0.9	757.030	722.544	690.629	690.952	733.558	711.425	690.537	690.196	690.150
100	0.1	310.330	306.549	305.727	305.682	307.103	306.172	305.685	305.676	305.682
	0.2	435.561	422.562	418.959	418.552	424.865	420.063	418.046	418.428	418.515
	0.3	526.932	507.731	497.024	496.876	512.953	502.780	496.402	497.076	497.298
	0.4	619.191	593.193	575.482	574.381	600.909	586.779	574.386	574.636	574.569
	0.5	679.219	648.563	618.385	616.023	657.506	637.732	617.572	616.625	616.519
	0.6	733.975	703.389	662.915	660.517	711.493	689.266	660.917	659.644	659.688
	0.7	809.507	775.264	730.042	726.416	786.035	761.061	726.758	727.200	726.707
	0.8	857.957	811.857	751.417	749.322	827.972	795.440	750.532	748.208	749.040
	0.9	880.283	844.058	791.853	790.753	856.049	830.113	791.278	789.900	788.850

Table 4. Computational Results for the Homogeneous PTSP

n	p	F	F+T	F+E	F+T+E	R	R+T	R+E	R+T+E	Queen
50	0.1	0.0000	0.0000	0.0075	0.7634	0.0000	0.0000	1.0000	1.0000	–
	0.2	0.0000	0.0000	0.0021	0.2200	0.0000	0.0945	0.9051	0.7110	–
	0.3	0.0000	0.0099	0.0048	0.6845	0.0000	–	0.1424	0.0095	0.0581
	0.4	0.0000	0.0000	0.0070	0.0409	0.0000	–	0.0904	0.0404	0.1295
	0.5	0.0000	0.0000	0.4667	0.1794	0.0000	0.0211	0.3636	0.5619	–
	0.6	0.0000	0.0000	0.0108	0.4328	0.0000	0.0000	0.6682	–	0.7860
	0.7	0.0000	0.0000	0.2819	0.5964	0.0000	0.0000	0.9782	0.7682	–
	0.8	0.0000	0.0000	0.1894	0.0571	0.0000	0.0000	–	0.3047	0.4021
	0.9	0.0000	0.0000	0.1670	0.1866	0.0000	0.2785	–	0.4873	0.1266
75	0.1	0.0000	0.0000	0.0000	0.0045	0.0000	0.0000	0.0027	–	0.3458
	0.2	0.0000	0.0000	0.0030	0.9778	0.0000	0.0000	0.2195	0.1902	–
	0.3	0.0000	0.0000	0.7352	0.6279	0.0000	0.0000	0.9672	–	0.5809
	0.4	0.0000	0.0000	0.4570	0.7199	0.0000	0.0000	0.1626	0.7544	–
	0.5	0.0000	0.0000	0.1553	–	0.0000	0.0000	0.5710	0.5843	0.9881
	0.6	0.0000	0.0000	0.0000	0.0020	0.0000	0.0000	0.0009	–	0.0112
	0.7	0.0000	0.0000	0.0068	0.1305	0.0000	0.0000	0.4880	–	0.7738
	0.8	0.0000	0.0000	0.0037	0.0406	0.0000	0.0000	0.0171	–	0.5933
	0.9	0.0000	0.0000	0.6335	0.4054	0.0000	0.0000	0.7243	0.9652	–
100	0.1	0.0000	0.0000	0.0000	0.3462	0.0000	0.0000	0.1212	–	0.2154
	0.2	0.0000	0.0000	0.0194	0.1442	0.0000	0.0000	–	0.2872	0.2267
	0.3	0.0000	0.0000	0.3428	0.4848	0.0000	0.0000	–	0.2666	0.2004
	0.4	0.0000	0.0000	0.1009	–	0.0000	0.0000	0.9924	0.7035	0.7599
	0.5	0.0000	0.0000	0.0045	–	0.0000	0.0000	0.0663	0.4873	0.4821
	0.6	0.0000	0.0000	0.0100	0.4620	0.0000	0.0000	0.2514	–	0.9728
	0.7	0.0000	0.0000	0.0012	–	0.0000	0.0000	0.7460	0.4101	0.7955
	0.8	0.0000	0.0000	0.0038	0.3420	0.0000	0.0000	0.0453	–	0.4636
	0.9	0.0000	0.0000	0.0149	0.1190	0.0000	0.0000	0.0362	0.3671	–

Table 5. *p*-value of Permutation test for the Homogeneous PTSP

5. Concluding comments

In this chapter, a genetic algorithm is developed to solve the PTSP. The effectiveness and efficiency of nine different selection schemes were investigated for both the heterogeneous and homogeneous PTSP. Extensive computational tests were performed and the permutation test was adopted to test the statistical significance of the nine selection schemes. Several important findings are obtained. First, fitness-proportional (F) or rank-based (R) selection should combine tournament (T) and/or elitism strategies to obtain acceptable outcomes for both the heterogeneous and homogeneous PTSP. Second, the average $E[\tau]$ values obtained by keeping the best solution(s) to the successive generations can generally perform better than the ones obtained by only applying tournament selection to fitness-proportional (F) or rank-based (R) selection for both the heterogeneous and homogeneous PTSP. Third, the queen, F+T+E, R+E, and R+T+E are better selection strategies and yielded similar average $E[\tau]$ value for the heterogeneous and homogeneous PTSP than the other five selection strategies. Finally, the numerical results showed that the proposed solution procedure can further enhance the performance of the method proposed by previous studies in most of the tested cases for the heterogeneous PTSP in terms of objective function value and computation time. These findings showed the potential of the proposed GA in effectively and efficiently solving the large-scale PTSP.

6. Acknowledgement

This work was supported primarily by the National Science Council of Taiwan under Grant NSC 96-2416-H-260-008. The author is indebted to Dr. Elise Miller-Hooks for providing me with the test instances to be used in this paper.

7. References

Bäck , T.; Fogel, D. B. & Michalewicz, Z. (1997). *Handbook of Evolutionary Computation*, Oxford University Press, 0-75030392-1, Bristol, UK.

Balakrishnan, P. V.; Gupta, R. & Jacob, V. S. (2006). An investigation of mating and population maintenance strategies in hybrid genetic heuristics for product line designs. *Computers & Operations Research,* Vol. 33, No. 3, 639-659, ISSN: 0305-0548.

Bartholdi, J. J. & Platzman, L. K. (1988). Heuristics based on spacefilling curves for combinatorial problems in Euclidean space. *Management Science,* Vol. 34, No. 3, 291-305, ISSN: 0025-1909.

Bartholdi, J. J.; Platzman, L. K.; Collins, R. L. & Warden, W. H. (1983). A minimal technology routing system for meals on wheels. *Interfaces,* Vol. 13, No. 3, 1-8, ISSN: 0092-2102.

Basso, D.; Chiarandini, M. & Salmaso L. (2007). Synchronized permutation tests in replicated I × J designs. *Journal of Statistical Planning and Inference,* Vol. 137, No. 8, 2564-2578, ISSN: 0378-3758.

Bertsimas, D. (1988). *Probabilistic combinatorial optimization problems,* Ph.D. dissertation, Massachusetts Institute of Technology, MA, USA.

Bertsimas, D.; Chervi, P. & Peterson, M. (1995). Computational approaches to stochastic vehicle routing problems. *Transportation Science,* Vol. 29, No. 4, 342-352, ISSN: 0041-1655.

Bertsimas, D. & Howell, L. (1993). Further results on the probabilistic traveling salesman problem. *European Journal of Operational Research,* Vol. 65, No. 1, 68-95, ISSN: 0377-2217.

Bertsimas, D.; Jaillet, P. & Odoni, A. R. (1990). A priori optimization. *Operations Research,* Vol. 38, No. 6, 1019-1033, ISSN: 0030-364X.

Bianchi, L. (2006). *Ant colony optimization and local search for the probabilistic traveling salesman problem: a case study in stochastic combinatorial optimization.* Ph.D. dissertation, Université Libre de Bruxelles, Brussles, Belgium.

Bowler, N. E.; Fink, T. M. A. & Ball, R. C. (2003). Characterization of the probabilistic traveling salesman problem. *Physical Review E*, Vol. 68, 036703, ISSN: 1539-3755.

Branke, J. & Guntsch, M. (2004). Solving the probabilistic TSP with ant colony optimization. *Journal of Mathematical Modelling and Algorithms*, Vol. 3, No. 4, 403-425, ISSN: 1570-1166.

Campbell, A. M. (2006). Aggregation for the probabilistic traveling salesman problem. *Computers & Operations Research*, Vol. 33, No. 9, 2703-2724, ISSN: 0305-0548.

Davis, L. (1991). *Handbook of Genetic Algorithms*. Van Nostrand Reinhold, ISBN: 0442001738, New York.

Goldberg, D. E. (1989). *Genetic Algorithms in Search, Optimization, and Machine Learning*, Addison-Wesley, ISBN: 0201157675, Reading, PA.

Holland, J. H. (1992). *Adaptation in Natural and Artificial Systems: An Introductory Analysis with Applications to Biology, Control, and Artificial Intelligence*, MIT Press, ISBN: 0262581116, Boston, MA.

Jaillet, P. (1985). *Probabilistic traveling salesman problems*, Ph.D. dissertation, Massachusetts Institute of Technology, MA, USA.

Jaillet, P. (1987). Stochastic routing problems, In: *Advanced school on stochastics in combinatorial optimization*, Andreatta, G., Mason, F. & Serafini, P. (Ed.), 192-213, World Scientific Publisher, ISBN: 9971504561, Singapore.

Jaillet, P. (1988). A priori solution of a traveling salesman problem in which a random subset of the customers are visited. *Operations Research*, Vol. 36, No. 6, 929-936, ISSN: 0030-364X.

Jaillet, P. & Odoni, A. R. (1988). The probabilistic vehicle routing problem, In: *Vehicle routing: methods and studies*, Golden, B. L. & Assad, A. A. (Ed.), 293-318, North-Holland, ISBN: 0444704078, Amsterdam.

Liu, Y-H. (2006). A scatter search based approach with approximation evaluation for the heterogeneous probabilistic traveling salesman problem, *Proceedings of 2006 IEEE Congress on Evolutionary Computation (CEC 2006)*, pp. 1603-1609, Vancouver, Canada.

Liu, Y.-H. (2007). A hybrid scatter search for the probabilistic traveling salesman problem. *Computers & Operations Research*, Vol. 34, No. 10, 2949-2963, ISSN: 0305-0548.

Liu, Y.-H. (2008). Diversified local search strategy under scatter search framework for the probabilistic traveling salesman problem. *European Journal of Operational Research*, Vol. 191, No. 2, 332-346, ISSN: 0377-2217.

Liu, Y.-H.; Jou, R.-C., Wang, C.-C. & Chiu, C.-S. (2007). An evolutionary algorithm with diversified crossover operator for the heterogeneous probabilistic TSP. *Lecture Notes in Artificial Intelligence*, 4617, 351-360, Springer, ISBN: 3540737286, Berlin.

Liu, Y.-H. & Mahmassani, H. S. (2000). Global maximum likelihood estimation procedure for multinomial probit model parameters. *Transportation Research, Part B*, Vol. 34B, No. 5, 419-449, ISSN: 0191-2615.

Potvin, J. Y. (1996). Genetic algorithms for the traveling salesman problem. *Annals of Operations Research*, Vol. 63, 339-370, ISSN: 0254-5330.

Rossi, F. & Gavioli, I. (1987). Aspects of heuristic method in the probabilistic traveling salesman problem, In: *Advanced school on stochastics in combinatorial optimization*, Andreatta, G., Mason, F. & Serafini, P. (Ed.), 214-227, World Scientific Publisher, ISBN: 9971504561, Singapore.

Stern, H.; Chassidim, Y. & Zofi, M. (2006). Multiagent visual area coverage using a new genetic algorithm selection scheme. *European Journal of Operational Research,* Vol. 175, No. 3, 1890-1907, ISSN: 0377-2217.

Tang, H. & Miller-Hooks, E. (2004). Approximate procedures for the probabilistic traveling salesperson problem. *Transportation Resesearch Record,* Vol. 1882, 27-36, ISSN: 0361-1981.

Whitley, D.; Starkweather, T. & Fuquay, D. (1989). Scheduling problems and traveling salesmen: the genetic edge recombination operator. *Proceedings of the Third International Conference on Genetic Algorithms (ICGA '89),* pp. 133-140, ISBN: 1558600663, Fairfax, Virginia, June, 1989, Morgan Kaufmann, Palo Alto, CA.

9

Niche Pseudo-Parallel Genetic Algorithms for Path Optimization of Autonomous Mobile Robot - A Specific Application of TSP

Zhihua Shen and Yingkai Zhao
Faculty of Engineering, The University of Melbourne
Faculty of Automation, The Nanjing University of Technology

1. Introduction

Path planning of autonomous mobile robot is pivotal technique for machine intelligence, which aims to find a non-collision path from initial position to objective position according to evaluation functions in an obstacle space[1]. It can be described as traveler salesman problem (TSP), a typical combination optimization problem, which belongs to the well-known NP-hard optimization[2]. The mathematical definition can be regarded as a map G = (V, E), where each line $e \in E$ has a nonnegative power $\omega(e)$. The aim is to find out a Hamilton circle noted with C of map G in order to obtain a minimum power $W(C)=\sum_{e \in E(C)} \omega(e)$.
Some traditional methods such as greed arithmetic, vicinage arithmetic and dynamic programming algorithm[3] do not behave a good performance on combination explosion aroused by rapid increment in exponent within a solution set of mathematic model, also known as the very quick accretion in both aspects of space and time complication along with the increase of degrees. A very promising direction is the genetic algorithm (GA) except for the traditional methods. Genetic algorithm is numerical optimization method[4] based on the theory of genetics and natural selection. It is a generally probabilistic and adaptable concept for problem solving, especially suitable for solving difficulty optimization and evolution problems, where traditional methods are less efficient.
An advanced genetic algorithm, niche pseudo-parallel genetic algorithm (NPPGA) is presented based on simple genetic algorithm (SGA), niche genetic algorithm (NGA) and parallel genetic algorithm (PGA) to further improve the GA for robot path optimization. Research on NPPGA is available for lots of practical problems such as path routing optimization, nets organization, job distribution, scheduling optimization etc.

2. Mechanism of niche pseudo-parallel genetic algorithms

The foundation of NPPGA is genetic algorithm, which is a class of global, adaptable, and probabilistic search optimization and revolution algorithm gleaned from the model of organic evolution and also simulates the genetics and evolution of biologic population in nature. GA adopts naturally evolutionary model such as selection, crossover, mutation, deletion and transference. Mathematically, this evolutionary process is a typical algorithm to find out the optimal solution via iteration search among multi-element in a NP set. As an optimal method applied with biologic genetics and evolutionary mechanism [5], GA totally embodies a classical biologically evolutionary theory depicted as natural selection. Simple genetic algorithm can be defined as $SGA= (M, C, F, M_o, P_s, P_c, P_m, T)$ [3], where C is a fixed bit-string code, F is a fitness evaluation function, M_o is an initial population of biologic colony and P_s, P_c, P_m are probabilities of selection, crossover and mutation respectively.

2.1 Proposal of NPPGA

Theoretically, genetic algorithm is able to trace on the optimal solution by a stochastic method on the sense of probability. On the contrary, GA has some prominent problems in practical application such as premature convergence, feebleness in local search, low rate of convergence etc. A simplex renewal from one population to another is hard to keep population diverse and avoid premature convergence.

Simple genetic algorithm is totally a stochastic method, which aims to settle with the problem where several different individuals are required to optimize in a cryptic and parallel process [6]. However, the rate of evolutionary process is still lower because of its essentially serial mechanism. In addition, before tracing on the globally optimal solution, the SGA may converge to a local one, which causes population trend to un-animousness and results in premature. To further improve the GA and avoid these disadvantages, we firstly divided original population into several groups known as pseudo- parallel operation to accelerate the rate of genetic algorithm computation and maintain the population diversity in order to reduce the rate of premature simultaneously. Based on the former step, niche genetic mechanism is introduced into pseudo-parallel genetic algorithm to further restrain the premature phenomenon. A method based on sharing functions is proposed to transfer genetic information to keep population diversity and avert from rapid increment of some special individuals, in other words, we created several niches among the population by pseudo-parallel technique to complete the process both of local and global solution optimization.

2.2 Pseudo code and layered flow chart of NPPGA

The Pseudo code of NPPGA is showed as following.

Begin s:=0;

initialize $P(0) := \{x_1(0),\ldots,x_m(0)\} \in \Re^m$ *where* $\Re = \{0,1\}^l$;

evaluate $P(0) := \{\Phi(x_1(0)),\ldots,\Phi(x_m(0))\}$ *where* $\Phi(x_k(0)) = \delta(f(\gamma(x_k(0))), P(0))$;

while $(\Im P(t) \neq true)$ *do* t:=0; $P(t) := \{P_1(t), P_2(t),\ldots,P_i(t),\ldots,P_n(t)\}$;

while $(\Im P(i) \neq true)$ do

recombine: $x_k^{'}(t) := r_{\{p_c,z\}}^{'}(P_i(t))\ \forall k \in \{1,\ldots,m/n\}$;

mutate: $x_k^{''}(t) := m_{\{p_m\}}^{'}(x_k^{'})\ \forall k \in \{1,\ldots,m/n\}$

niche operator: $x_k^{'''}(t) := \wp_{\{\gamma\}}^{'}(x_k^{''}) \forall k \in \{1,\ldots,m/n\}$ *with formula(1) and (2);*

delete: $x_k^{''''}(t) := d_{\{\alpha\}}^{'}(x_k^{'''}) \forall k \in \{1,\ldots,m/n\}$;

evaluate: $P_i^{'''}(t) := \{x_i^{''''}(t),\ldots,x_{m/n}^{''''}(t)\} \in \Re^{m/n}; \{\Phi_i(x_1^{''''}(t)),\ldots,\Phi_i(x_{m/n}^{''''}(t))\}$

where $\Phi_i(x_k^{''''}(t)) = \delta(f(\gamma(x_k^{''''}(t))), P_i(t-\varpi))$;

select: $P_i(t+1) := s(P_i^{''''}(t))$

where $P_s(x_k^{''}(t)) = \Phi_i(x_k^{''''}(t)) / \sum_{j=1}^{m/n} \Phi_i(x_k^{''''}(t))$;

t:=t+1; end

information exchange: $P(s+1) = c\{P(s),\ P_i^{''''}(t)\}$; s=s+1; *end*

Fig. 1 describes the layered structure of NPPGA by a flow chart.

Fig. 1 Pseudo code of NPPGA

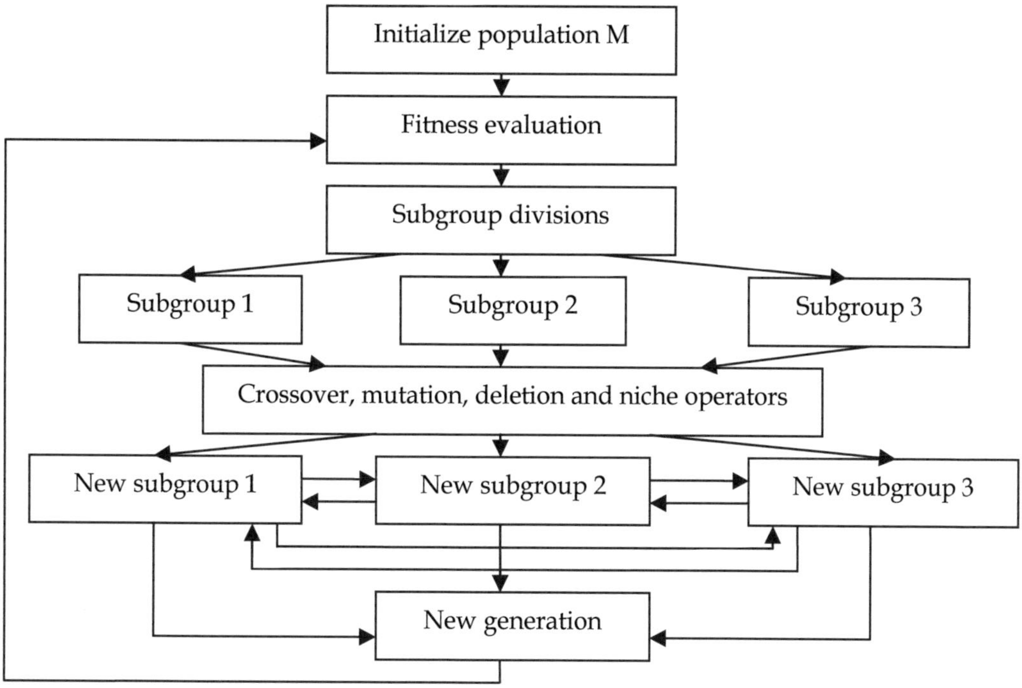

Fig. 1. Flow chart of NPPGA

2.3 Arithmetic description of NPPGA

Each step in niche pseudo-parallel genetic algorithms is demonstrated as following based on niche genetic algorithm and parallel genetic algorithm [3] [6]:

1. Initialize the genetic counter $t \leftarrow 0$;
2. Generate original population $P(t)$ made up of initial individuals which are divided into several subgroups in the form of $P(t)=\{P_1(t), P_2(t),\ldots,P_i(t),\ldots, P_n(t)\}$, where n is a integral number of subgroup.
3. Calculate each individual fitness function $F_j(j=1,2,\ldots,m/n)$ in every subgroup $P_i(t)(i=1,2,\ldots,n)$ of the population;
4. Execute independent evolution among each group $P(t)=\{P_1(t), P_2(t),\ldots,P_i(t),\ldots, P_n(t)\}$;
   i. Independently initialize evolutionary counter $s \leftarrow 1$ and select a subgroup fitness function to give an evaluation of each individual;
   ii. Make a lower taxis upon the individual fitness and storage q individuals in the former sequence where $q<m/n$;
   iii. Reproduce among $P_i(t)$ by the operator P_s in form of $P_i'(t) \leftarrow selection[P_i(t)]$;
   iv. Crossover among $P_i'(t)$ by the operator P_c in form of $P_i''(t) \leftarrow crossover[P_i'(t)]$;
   v. Mutate among $P_i''(t)$ by the operator P_m in form of $P_i'''(t) \leftarrow mutation\ [P_i''(t)]$;
   vi. Delete among $P_i'''(t)$ by the operator γ in form of $P_i''''(t) \leftarrow deletion[P_i'''(t)]$;

vii. Use a niche operator, which needs to combine $(m/n)-\gamma F[P_i'''(t)]$ individuals in the subgroup $P_i''''(t)$ with the former q excellent individuals that are saved early into a new population M_i including $(m/n)+q-\gamma F[P_i'''(t)]$ individuals, to wash out some inferior ones. When $\| X_i - X_j \| < L$, a Hamming distance is computed by

$$\| X_i - X_j \| = \sqrt{\sum_{k=1}^{m/n} (x_{ik} - x_{jk})^2}, \quad i = 1,2,...m/n+q-1,\ j = i+1,...m/n+q \tag{1}$$

L is the distance between contiguous generations. A penalty function $F_{\min(x_i,x_j)} = Penalty$ is used after comparing fitness between X_i and X_j. The penalty criterion is

$$F_i'(X) = \begin{cases} F_i(X) & (if(F_i(X) \geq F_j(X)) \& \| (X_i - X_j \| < L)) \\ F_i(X) - P(X) & (if(F_i(X) < F_j(X)) \& \| (X_i - X_j \| < L)) \end{cases} \tag{2}$$

viii. Realign in a lower sequence according to each fitness of (m/n)+q individuals and store former q individuals again;

ix. End niche heredity if evolutionary results fit with ending conditions, or renew independently evolutionary counter s←s+1 and turn to step iii while generating m/n individuals into next generation in step vii;

5. Transfer information usually with stepping-stone model, island model and neighborhood model among $P_i(t)(i=1,2,\ldots,n)$ to obtain the next generation $P(i+1) \leftarrow exchange\ [P(t), P_i'''(t)]$;
6. End parallel heredity when evolutionary results fit with ending conditions, otherwise, renew independently evolutionary counter $t \leftarrow t+1$ and turn to step (4).

3. Robot path optimization by NPPGA

It is well known that the problem of "Robot touring around Pekin" is typically practical application of TSP. Based on discussion in section 2, mechanism of niche pseudo-parallel genetic algorithm is investigated. In this section, NPPGA is used to solve the traveling salesman problem especially in the model of path optimization of robots. Each individual code is described in bit-strings of fixed length 18, which stands for paths between each two cities. Then an entire serial named chromosome $\vec{X}_i = (X_{i,1}, X_{i,2}, ..., X_{i,m})$ can be obtained in each individual space $S = \{X_{i,1}, X_{i,2}, ..., X_{i,m}\}^m$ that belongs to subgroup space $S^{m/n}$. The selection operator that is known as survival probabilities in solving path optimization is in the canonical form [6]

$$p_s = P\{T_s^\alpha(\vec{X}) = X_i\} = \frac{f^\alpha(X_i)}{\sum_{k=1}^{m/n} f^\alpha(X_k)} \tag{3}$$

To optimize the robotic paths, crossover operator, emphasized as the most important search operator of genetic algorithm, is introduce by[3]

$$P\{T_c(Y_{i,1}^k, Y_{i,2}^k) = X_k^{'}(n+1)\} = \begin{cases} {}^{kp_c}\!/_{m}, X_k^{'}(n+1) \neq Y_{i,1}^k and X_k^{'}(n+1) = AY_{i,1}^k + (I-A)Y_{i,2}^k \\ (1-p_c) + {}^{kp_c}\!/_{m}, X_k^{'}(n+1) = Y_{i,1}^k \\ 0, other \end{cases} \quad (4)$$

Small mutation and deletion rates are also used in solving this problem to guarantee that each individual do not differ genetically very much from its ancestor. In other words, it keeps the diversity of path space even though local convergence exists. Niche operator is demonstrated in Eqs. (1) and (2). Furthermore, we exchange different information of excellent path serials among subgroups based on islands model. All these parameters used in NPPGA are showed in table 1.

Parameters	Used in NPPGA
Selection rate	$\alpha=1$
Mutation operator	$P_m=0.0015$
Recombination operator	$P_r=\{0.72,4\}$
Deletion operator	$\gamma=0.0027$
Niche operator	Hamming Distance
Length per object variable	L=18
Population size	50

Table 1. Parameters of NPPGA

In the experiment, a single step NPPGA is used to solving the problem of path optimization and evolution of "Robot Tour". 8 optimal solutions can be obtained shown in table 2. The length of optimal path has been changed into standard units where (Remnant of optimal paths)= (length of paths)-(shortest distance) and (Ratio of relative paths) =(remnant)/(shortest distance).

Path	Path 1	Path 2	Path 3	Path 4	Path 5	Path 6	Path 7	Path 8
Length of optimal paths	96.17 (NPPGA)	96.79	97.20	97.59	98.48	98.75	102.17	102.77
Remnant of optimal paths	0 (NPPGA)	0.62	1.03	1.42	2.31	2.58	6.00	6.60
Ratio of relative path	0.26% (SGA)	0.86%	1.54%	2.2%	2.58%	3.73%	5.80%	6.92%
	0.18% (DPGA)	0.70%	1.32%	1.80%	1.93%	3.12%	5.95%	6.90%
	0% (NPPGA)	0.640%	1.071%	1.477%	2.042%	2.683%	6.239%	6.863%
Computation complexity	SGA	346 generations and 20760 count steps						
	DPGA	294 generations and 19500 count steps						
	NPPGA	276 generations and 16560 count steps						

Table 2. Experimental results in path optimization by single step NPPGA

According to experimental data, we illustrated an evolutionary process by niche pseudo-parallel genetic algorithm in figure 2. Compared with SGA and DPGA, the performance conducted by NPPGA is better. The computation complexity of NPPGA is 16560 count steps within 276 generations while SGA and DPGA are 20760 and 19500 respectively. Global optimization path other than local solution can be achieved by NPPGA when generations approach less than 300. Simultaneously, a remnant comparison is shown in Fig. 3. Although NPPGA has the peak error for some individual evolutionary processes caused by stochastic researching, it perform a lowest remnant error to the optimal path while the remnant of DPGA is a little bit large than NPPGA. The shortest route can be described in the following serial.

"start→dong_wu_yuan→zhong_guan_cun→yuan_ming_yuan→yi_he_yuan→xiang_shan→shi_san_ling→ba_da_ling→yong_he_gong→bei_hai_gong_yuan→gu_gong→tian_an_men→wang_fu_jing→beijing_zhan→tian_tan→shi_jie_gong_yuan→xi_dan→shi_ji_dan"

The total distance is 96.17 in standard units and actually shorter in practical robot tour.

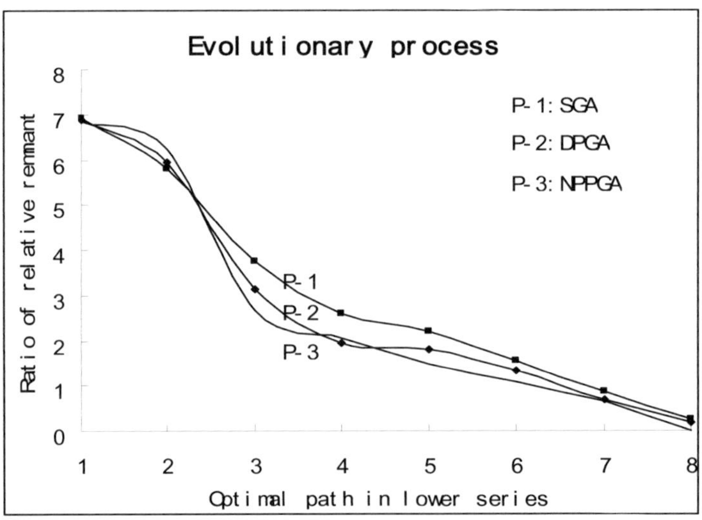

Fig. 2. Evolutionary process of NPPGA

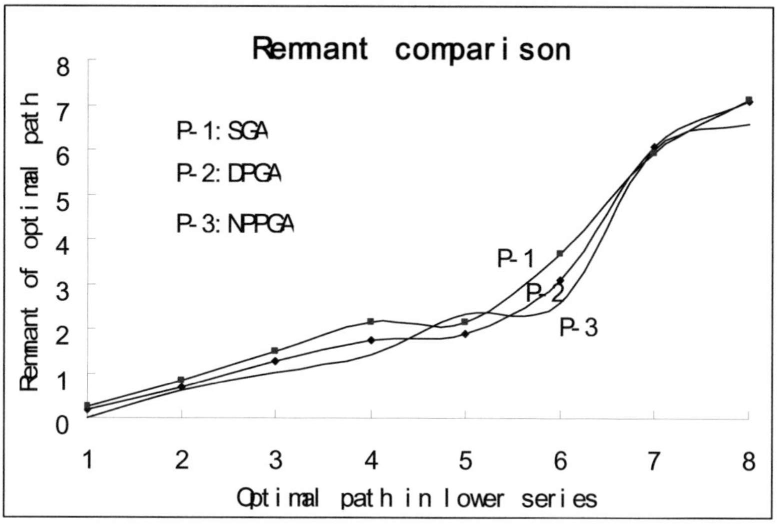

Fig. 3. Remnant comparison of NPPGA

4. Conclusion

The research, based on combination of niche genetic algorithm and pseudo parallel genetic algorithm, comes into being NPPGA technique which both considers the rate of genetic evolution and diversity of population. The strategy seems to be able to restrain the premature among population and closely cooperate with each other to improve the overall search performance. We presented NPPGA and used a single step NPPGA to figure out the optimal paths in "Robot tour around Pekin", which is a practical application of traveling salesman problem. Experiments show that the optimal route can be obtained. We believe that NPPGA and other advanced GAs will become a robust tool for path optimization and other potential applications.

5. References

Hu Y R, Yang S X. *Knowledge based genetic algorithm for path planning of a mobile robot* [A]. Proc. Of 2004 Robotics and Automation, IEEE international conference ICRA '04 [C]. New Orleans, USA, 2004, V(5):4350-4355.

Daoxiong Gong, Xiaogang Ruan. *A hybrid approach of GA and ACO for TSP [A]*. Intelligent Control and Automation, WCICA 2004. Fifth World Congress [C]. Hangzhou, China, 2004 V(3):2068- 2072.

Zhe Lei-lei, Chen Huan-yang. Mathematical Foundation of Computer Intelligence [M]. Science Publishing Company, Beijing, 2002, P:112-142.

Pullan, W. *Adapting the genetic algorithms to the traveling salesman problem [A]*. Evolutionary Computation CEC '03 Congress [C]. Canberra, Australia, 2003, 2(8):1029 - 1035.

Huai-Kuang Tsai, Jinn-Moon Yang, Yuan-Fang Tsai *et. al. An evolutionary algorithm for large traveling salesman problems [J]*. Systems, Man and Cybernetics, IEEE Transactions, 2004, 34(4):1718 - 1729.

Xiong Shengwu, Li Chengjun. *A distributed genetic algorithm to TSP [A]*. Intelligent Control and Automation Proceedings of the 4th World Congress [C]. Shanghai, China, 2002, 3(10): 1827-1830, 2002

10

The Symmetric Circulant Traveling Salesman Problem

Federico Greco and Ivan Gerace
Dipartimento di Matematica e Informatica, Università di Perugia, Italy

1. Introduction

An $n \times n$ matrix $D = d[i, j]$ is said to be circulant, if the entries $d[i, j]$ verifying $(j - i) = k \bmod n$, for some k, have the same value (for a survey on circulant matrix properties, see Davis (1979)). A directed (respectively, undirected) graph is circulant, if its adjacency matrix is circulant (respectively, symmetric, and circulant). Similarly, a weighted graph is circulant, if its weighted adjacency matrix is circulant.

In the last years, it had been often investigated if a graph problem becomes easier when it is restricted to the circulant graphs. For example, the Maximum Clique problem, and the Minimum Graph Coloring problem remain NP-hard, and not approximable within a constant factor, when the general instance is forced to be a circulant undirected graphs, as shown by Codenotti, et al. (1998). On the other hand, Muzychuk (2004) has proved that the Graph Isomorphism problem restricted to circulant undirected graphs is in P, while the general case is, probably, harder.

It is still an open question whether the Directed Hamiltonian Circuit problem, restricted to circulant (directed) graphs, remains NP-hard, or not. A solution in some special cases has been found by Garfinkel (1977), Fan Yang, et al. (1997), and Bogdanowicz (2005). The Hamiltonian Circuit problem admits, instead, a polynomial time algorithm on the circulant undirected graphs, as shown by Burkard, and Sandholzer (1991). It leads to a polynomial time algorithm for the Bottleneck Traveling Salesman Problem on the symmetric circulant matrices.

Finally, in Gilmore, et al. (1985) it is shown that the Shortest Hamiltonian Path problem is polynomial time solvable on the circulant matrices, while the general case is NP-hard. The positive results contained in Burkard, and Sandholzer (1991), and in Gilmore, et al. (1985) have encouraged the research on the Symmetric Circulant Traveling Salesman problem, that is, the Sum Traveling Salesman Problem restricted to the symmetric, and circulant matrices.

In this chapter we deal with such problem, called for short SCTSP. In §1–§3 the problem is introduced, and the notation is fixed. In §4–§6 an overview is given on the last 16 year results. Firstly, an upper bound (§4.1), a lower bound (§4.2), and a polynomial time 2-approximation algorithm for the general case of SCTSP (§4.3) are discussed. No better result concerning the computational complexity of SCTSP is known. Secondly, some sufficient theorems solving particular cases of SCTSP are presented (§5). Finally, §6 is devoted to a recently introduced subcase of SCTSP. §7 completes the chapter by presenting open problems, remarks, and future developments.

We list here some abbreviations used throughout the chapter:

- n denotes a positive integer greater than 1;
- $[m]$ denotes the set $\{1, 2, \ldots, m\}$, for any positive integer m;
- $a \equiv_m b$ denotes the relation $a \equiv b$ mod m, and $\langle a \rangle_m$ denotes the integer (a mod m), for any positive integer m, and for any two integers a, b;
- $(x_t)_{t=s'}^{s}$ denotes the tuple $(x_{s'}, x_{s'+1}, \ldots, x_s)$, for any two integers s, s' such that $s \geq s'$, and for any $(s - s' + 1)$ integers $x_{s'}, x_{s'+1}, \ldots, x_s$.

2. The symmetric circulant traveling salesman problem

Let $D = (d[i, j])$ be an $n \times n$ matrix. Assume that $d[i, j] = 0$, if $i = j$, and that $d[i, j]$ is a positive integer, if $i \neq j$. Let $\mathbb{Z}_n$ denote both its row index set, and its column index set. A **Hamiltonian tour** T for D is a cyclic permutation $T : \mathbb{Z}_n \rightarrow \mathbb{Z}_n$. The **(sum) cost** of T is the integer

$$sum_D(T) = \sum_{i=0}^{n-1} d[i, T(i)]. \tag{1}$$

The optimal sum cost of D is the integer

$$\text{opt}(D) = \min\{sum_D(T) : T \text{ is a Hamiltonian tour for } D\}. \tag{2}$$

The Sum Traveling Salesman Problem asks for finding opt(D). It is a well known NP-hard problem. Moreover, no performance guarantee polynomial time approximation algorithm for it is known.

An $n \times n$ matrix $D = (d[i, j])$ with entries in $\mathbb{N} \cup \{\infty\}$ is said to be **circulant**, if $d[i, j] = d[0, \langle j - i \rangle_n]$, for any $i, j \in \mathbb{Z}_n$. A **symmetric circulant matrix** is a circulant matrix which is also symmetric. As *Example 1* below suggests, a symmetric circulant matrix has a strong algebraic structure: It is fully determined by the entries in the first half of its first row.

Example 1 *The following two matrices are symmetric circulant.*

$$D_0 = \begin{pmatrix} 0 & 4 & 1 & 6 & 1 & 4 \\ 4 & 0 & 4 & 1 & 6 & 1 \\ 1 & 4 & 0 & 4 & 1 & 6 \\ 6 & 1 & 4 & 0 & 4 & 1 \\ 1 & 6 & 1 & 4 & 0 & 4 \\ 4 & 1 & 6 & 1 & 4 & 0 \end{pmatrix}, \quad D_1 = \begin{pmatrix} 0 & \infty & 2 & 6 & 2 & \infty \\ \infty & 0 & \infty & 2 & 6 & 2 \\ 2 & \infty & 0 & \infty & 2 & 6 \\ 6 & 2 & \infty & 0 & \infty & 2 \\ 2 & 6 & 2 & \infty & 0 & \infty \\ \infty & 2 & 6 & 2 & \infty & 0 \end{pmatrix}$$

Let $SC(\mathbb{N}^{n \times n})$ denote the set of all $n \times n$ symmetric circulant matrices with null principal diagonal entries, and positive integer entries otherwise. Note that $D_0 \in SC(\mathbb{N}^{6 \times 6})$, while $D_1 \notin SC(\mathbb{N}^{6 \times 6})$.

The Symmetric Circulant Traveling Salesman problem (for short, SCTSP) asks for finding opt(D), when D is a matrix in $SC(\mathbb{N}^{n\times n})$.

3. Definitions, and preliminaries

Let $D = (d[i, j])$ be a matrix in $SC(\mathbb{N}^{n\times n})$. For any $a \in [\lfloor n/2 \rfloor]$, the a-**stripe** of D is the set

$$D(a) = \{\{i, j\} \subset \mathbb{Z}_n : \langle j - i \rangle_n = a, \text{ or } \langle i - j \rangle_n = a\}. \quad (3)$$

The integer $d[0, a]$ is denoted by $d(a)$. It is called the a-**stripe cost** of D. Note that two different stripes have empty intersection.

If $T : \mathbb{Z}_n \rightarrow \mathbb{Z}_n$ is a Hamiltonian tour for D, then $sum_D(T)$ depends just on the stripe costs of D: For any $i \in \mathbb{Z}_n$, $\{i, T(i)\}$ belongs to $D(a_i)$, and costs $d(a_i)$, where $a_i = \min\{\langle i - T(i) \rangle_n, \langle T(i) - i \rangle_n\}$. Indeed, $a_i \leq \lfloor n/2 \rfloor$ holds by definition, and $a_i > 0$ holds, as T is a cyclic permutation. Thus, $T(i) \neq i$. Finally, the following statement holds:

$$\{i, j\} \in D(a) \Rightarrow d[i, j] = d(a), \qquad \forall\, i, j \in \mathbb{Z}_n,\ \forall\, a \in [\lfloor n/2 \rfloor]. \quad (4)$$

Indeed, if $\{i, j\} \in D(a)$, then either $\langle j - i \rangle_n = a$, or $\langle i - j \rangle_n = a$. In the first case, (4) holds, as D is circulant, and, thus, $d[i, j] = d[0, \langle j - i \rangle_n] = d[0, a]$. In the second case, (4) holds, as D is symmetric, and circulant, and, thus, $d[i, j] = d[j, i] = d[0, \langle i - j \rangle_n] = d[0, a]$.

Definition 2 *Let $D = (d[i, j])$ be a matrix in $SC(\mathbb{N}^{n\times n})$. The $\lfloor n/2 \rfloor$-tuple $\alpha_D = (a_t)_{t=1}^{\lfloor n/2 \rfloor}$ is a* **presentation** *for D, if $d(a_t) \leq d(a_{t+1})$, for any integer $1 \leq t < \lfloor n/2 \rfloor$, and $\{a_1, \ldots, a_{\lfloor n/2 \rfloor}\} = [\lfloor n/2 \rfloor]$.*

A presentation sorts the stripes of a matrix $D \in SC(\mathbb{N}^{n\times n})$ in non decreasing order with respect to their cost. Clearly, there exists just a presentation for D if and only if any two stripes have different stripe cost, and, thus, also the converse of (4) holds. In this case, we say that D has **distinct stripe costs**.

Example 3 *Let $\alpha_D = (a_t)_{t=1}^{\lfloor n/2 \rfloor}$ be a presentation for $D \in SC(\mathbb{N}^{n\times n})$. As observed by Garfinkel in (1977), the permutation $T_1 : \mathbb{Z}_n \rightarrow \mathbb{Z}_n$, defined as $T_1(i) = \langle i + a_1 \rangle_n$, for any $i \in \mathbb{Z}_n$, is a Hamiltonian tour for D if and only if $\gcd(n, a_1) = 1$. In this case T_1 is, clearly, optimal.*

Example 4 *Let $\alpha_D = (a_t)_{t=1}^{\lfloor n/2 \rfloor}$ be a presentation for $D \in SC(\mathbb{N}^{n\times n})$ such that $\gcd(n, a_1, a_2) > 1$. A Hamiltonian tour $T : \mathbb{Z}_n \rightarrow \mathbb{Z}_n$ for D such that $\{i, T(i)\} \in D(a_1) \cup D(a_2)$, for any $i \in \mathbb{Z}_n$, cannot exist since the set $\{a_1, a_2\}$ does not generate $\mathbb{Z}_n$.*

The previous examples suggest the following definition, that will play a crucial role in the next sections.

Definition 5 *Let $\alpha_D = (a_t)_{t=1}^{\lfloor n/2 \rfloor}$ be a presentation for $D \in SC(\mathbb{N}^{n\times n})$. The* **g -sequence** *of α_D is the tuple $g(\alpha_D) = (g_t(\alpha_D))_{t=0}^{\lfloor n/2 \rfloor}$ defined as follows:*

$$\begin{cases} g_0(\alpha_D) = n \\ g_t(\alpha_D) = \gcd(g_{t-1}(\alpha_D), a_t) = \gcd(n, a_1, \ldots, a_t), & \text{if } t \in [\lfloor n/2 \rfloor]. \end{cases} \quad (5)$$

Note that the g -sequence verifies the following properties:

$$g_t(\alpha_D) \text{ divides } g_{t'}(\alpha_D), \qquad \forall\, 0 \le t' \le t \le \lfloor n/2 \rfloor \quad (6)$$

$$g_t(\alpha_D) \le g_{t-1}(\alpha_D), \qquad \forall\, 1 \le t \le \lfloor n/2 \rfloor \quad (7)$$

$$g_{\lfloor n/2 \rfloor}(\alpha_D) = 1 \quad (8)$$

In particular (8) holds as $a_{\bar{t}} = 1$, for some $\bar{t} \in \lfloor n/2 \rfloor$. In the following, we write g_t instead of $g_t(\alpha_D)$ if the context is clear.

4. The circulant weighted undirected graph $G_\tau(\alpha_D)$

An usual way of representing a weighted undirected graph G with node set $\{0, 1, \ldots, m-1\}$ is its weighted adjacency matrix: An $m \times m$ symmetric matrix D_G whose general entry $d_G[i, j]$ corresponds either to 0, if $i = j$, or to the cost of $\{i, j\}$, if $\{i, j\}$ is an edge in G, or to ∞, in the other cases. If D_G is symmetric circulant, then G is said to be **circulant**.

On the converse, a matrix $D = (d[i, j])$ in $SC(\mathbb{N}^{n\times n})$ can be thought as the weighted adjacency matrix of a complete circulant weighted undirected graph. More precisely, any $A \subset [\lfloor n/2 \rfloor]$ determines a unique circulant weighted undirected graph having the following weighted adjacency matrix $D_A = (d_A[i, j])$:

$$d_A[i,j] = \begin{cases} 0, & \text{if } i = j; \\ d[i,j], & \text{if } \{i,j\} \in D(a), \text{ for some } a \in A; \\ \infty, & \text{otherwise.} \end{cases}$$

D_A is symmetric circulant, since $D \in SC(\mathbb{N}^{n\times n})$. Suppose, now, that a presentation $\alpha_D = (a_t)_{t=1}^{\lfloor n/2 \rfloor}$ for D is known. Since we are interested on a Hamiltonian tour for D with least possible cost, and α_D sorts the stripes in non decreasing order with respect to their cost, it is advisable to study the weighted undirected graph associated to the set $\{a_1, a_2, \ldots, a_\tau\}$, for any $\tau \in [\lfloor n/2 \rfloor]$.

Definition 6 Let D be a matrix in $SC(\mathbb{N}^{n\times n})$, and let $\alpha_D = (a_t)_{t=1}^{\lfloor n/2 \rfloor}$ be a presentation for it. Let us fix $\tau \in [\lfloor n/2 \rfloor]$. $G_\tau(\alpha_D)$ is the weighted undirected graph having $\mathbb{Z}_n$ as node set, $D(a_1) \cup \ldots \cup D(a_\tau)$ as edge set, and, finally, $d(a_t)$ as edge $\{i, j\}$ cost, if $\{i, j\} \in D(a_t)$, for some $t \in [\tau]$.

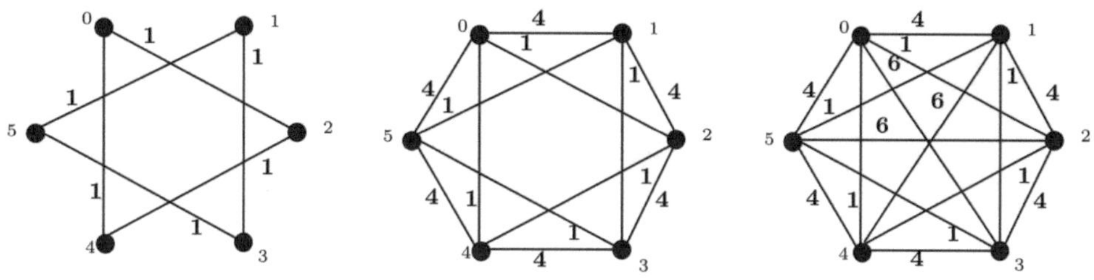

$G_1(\alpha_{D_0})$ $G_2(\alpha_{D_0})$ $G_3(\alpha_{D_0})$

Fig. 1. The circulant weighted undirected graphs $G_1(\alpha_{D_0})$, $G_2(\alpha_{D_0})$, $G_3(\alpha_{D_0})$

Example 7 *Let us consider the matrix $D_0 \in SC(\mathbb{N}^{6\times 6})$ defined in Example 1. The stripes of D_0 have the following costs: $d_0(1) = 4$, $d_0(2) = 1$, $d_0(3) = 6$. Hence, there exists a unique presentation $\alpha_{D_0} = (2, 1, 3)$. In Figure 1 the circulant weighted undirected graphs $G_1(\alpha_{D_0})$, $G_2(\alpha_{D_0})$, $G_3(\alpha_{D_0})$ are depicted.*

The path in $G_\tau(\alpha_D)$ of length l passing through the nodes $v_0, v_1, \ldots, v_l$ is denoted by $[v_0, v_1, \ldots, v_l]$. Say P such a path. v_0, and v_l are called, respectively, the starting point, and the ending point of P. The (sum) cost of P is

$$c_D(P) = \sum_{\lambda=1}^{l} d[v_{\lambda-1}, v_\lambda]. \tag{9}$$

The path $[u, u']$ is an **arc of** P if $u = v_{\lambda-1}$, and $u' = v_\lambda$, for some $\lambda \in [l]$. Let P^- denote the path $[v_l, v_{l-1}, \ldots, v_0]$, and, for any $v \in \mathbb{Z}_n$, let $(P + v)$ denote the path $[v_0 + v, v_1 + v, \ldots, v_l + v]$, where each sum is performed modulo n. Note that both P^-, and $(P + v)$ are well defined. Moreover, for any $\lambda \in [l]$, $d[v_{\lambda-1}, v_\lambda] = d[v_\lambda, v_{\lambda-1}]$ holds as $G_\tau(\alpha_D)$ is undirected, and $d[v_{\lambda-1}, v\_] = d[v_{\lambda-1} + v, v_\lambda + v]$ holds as $G_\tau(\alpha_D)$ is circulant. Hence, both $c_D(P) = c_D(P^-)$, and $c_D(P) = c_D(P + v)$ hold.

Finally, the path $[v_0, v_1]$ is an **arc in** $D(a_t)$, if $\{v_0, v_1\} \in D(a_t)$, for some $t \in [\tau]$.

A well known theorem due to Boesch, and Tindell (1984), and concerning the connectivity of a circulant weighted undirected graph can be restated for $G_\tau(\alpha_D)$ as follows.

Theorem 8 *Let $\alpha_D = (a_t)_{t=1}^{\lfloor n/2 \rfloor}$ be a presentation for $D \in SC(\mathbb{N}^{n\times n})$. Let us fix $\tau \in [\lfloor n/2 \rfloor]$. $G_\tau(\alpha_D)$ has g_τ pairwise isomorphic connected components. In particular, the set $\{v \in \mathbb{Z}^n : v \equiv_{g_\tau} i\}$ induces a different connected component, for any $i = 0, 1, \ldots, g_\tau - 1$. Finally, any connected component forms itself a circulant weighted undirected graph.*

PROOF. *(Sketch)* Let us fix a node $v_0 \in \mathbb{Z}_n$. A node $v \in \mathbb{Z}_n$ belongs to the same connected component of v_0 if and only if there exists a path in $G_\tau(\alpha_D)$ starting at v_0, and ending at v. Let P be a path starting at v_0. As the edge set of $G_\tau(\alpha_D)$ is $D(a_1/g_\tau) \cup \ldots \cup D(a_\tau/g_\tau)$, any arc $[u, u']$ of P is an arc in $D(a_t)$, and, thus, verifies $u \equiv_n u' \pm a_t$, for some $t \in [\tau]$ (see (3)). It follows that v is the ending point of a path starting at v_0 if and only if there exists integers $y_1, \ldots, y_\tau$ such that

$$v - v_0 \equiv_n \sum_{t=1}^{\tau} y_t \cdot a_t \equiv_n g_\tau \left(\sum_{t=1}^{\tau} y_t \cdot a_t / g_\tau \right). \tag{*}$$

As g_τ divides n by *Definition 5*, (*) implies that $v \equiv_{g_\tau} v_0$ holds.

On the other hand, if $v \equiv_{g_\tau} v_0$, then $(v - v_0) \equiv_n g_\tau b$, for some $b \in \mathbb{Z}$. It follows by definition of g_τ that $\gcd(n/g_\tau, a_1/g_\tau, \ldots, a_\tau/g_\tau) = 1$. Thus, by Euclid's lemma, there exists integers $y_1, \ldots, y_\tau$ such that $b \equiv_{n/g_\tau} \sum_{t=1}^{\tau} y_t \cdot a_t / g_\tau$. By substituting it in $(v - v_0) \equiv_n g_\tau \cdot b$, (*) follows. Hence, two nodes are in the same connected component if and only if they are equivalent modulo g_τ. Finally, any connected component is isomorphic to the circulant weighted undirected graph having $\mathbb{Z}_{n/g_\tau}$ as node set, $D(a_1/g_\tau) \cup \ldots \cup D(a_\tau/g_\tau)$ as edge set, and $d[g_\tau \cdot i, g_\tau \cdot j]$ as edge $\{i, j\}$ cost. □

A Hamiltonian path for a graph is a path passing exactly once through an node in the graph. A shortest Hamiltonian path starting at a node v is a least possible cost one among those having v as starting point. The next theorem is a direct consequence of a result of Bach, et al. (see *Chapter* 4 in Gilmore, et al. (1985)).

Theorem 9 *Let* $\alpha_D = (a_t)_{t=1}^{\lfloor n/2 \rfloor}$ *be a presentation for* $D \in SC(\mathbb{N}^{n \times n})$. *An algorithm setting* $v_0 = 0$, *and*

$$v_\lambda \in \arg \min_{u \notin \{v_0, \ldots, v_{\lambda-1}\}} \{t : \{v_{\lambda-1}, u\} \in D(a_t),\ t \in [\lfloor n/2 \rfloor]\}, \quad \forall 1 \le \lambda < n,$$

finds a shortest Hamiltonian path for $G_{\lfloor n/2 \rfloor}(\alpha_D)$ *starting at the node* 0. *Such path costs* $SHP(\alpha_D) = \sum_{t=1}^{\lfloor n/2 \rfloor} (g_{t-1} - g_t) \cdot d(a_t)$.

The algorithm described in *Theorem 9* is a non deterministic one. For example, both choices $v_1 = a_1$, and $v_1 = n - a_1$ are possible, as both arcs $\{0, a_1\}$, and $\{0, n-a_1\}$ are in $D(a_1)$. Moreover, it is a nearest neighbor ruled one: For any $1 \le \lambda < n$, and for any $u \notin \{v_0, \ldots, v_{\lambda-1}\}$, $d[v_{\lambda-1}, v_\lambda] \le d[v_{\lambda-1}, u]$ holds, as α_D is a presentation. *Example 10* below shows that the contribution given by α_D is fundamental, as it forces to insert in the solution arcs belonging to the same stripe as far as possible.

Example 10 *Let* $D = (d[i, j])$ *be a matrix in* $SC(\mathbb{N}^{6\times6})$ *having as strip costs* $d(1) = d(2) = 1$, *and* $d(3) = 2$. *Clearly,* [0, 1, 2, 3, 4, 5] *is a shortest Hamiltonian path of cost 5. An algorithm setting* $v_0 = 0$, *and following the nearest neighbor rule*

$$v_\lambda \in \arg \min_{u \notin \{v_0, \ldots, v_{\lambda-1}\}} \{d[v_{\lambda-1}, u]\}, \qquad \forall 1 \le \lambda < n,$$

may return the Hamiltonian path [0, 2, 3, 5, 4, 1] *of cost 6, since it indifferently inserts in the solution arcs in* $D(1)$ (i.e., [0, 2], *and* [3, 5]), *and arcs in* $D(2)$ (*i.e.,* [2, 3], *and* [4, 5]), *since* $d(1) = d(2) = 1$ *holds.*

Let us compute $SHP(\alpha_D)$ by the formula given in *Theorem 9*. It follows from *Definition 5* that $g_0 = n$, and that $g_1 = \gcd(n, a_1) < n$, as a_1 is a stripe, and, then, $a_1 \le \lfloor n/2 \rfloor$. Hence, the first summand is always greater than 0. And what about the other summands? As (6) holds, there exist at most r indexes t, for some $r \le \log_2 n$, such that $g_t < g_{t-1}$ holds. Hence, at most r summands in $SHP(\alpha_D)$ are greater than 0. Finally, as (7), and (8) hold, there exists an index $\overline{t}$ such that $g_t = 1$ holds if and only if $t \ge \overline{t}$. Therefore, the t-th summand for any $t > \overline{t}$ is equal to 0. Hence, just a few number of stripes could be involved in the construction of a shortest Hamiltonian path for $G_{\lfloor n/2 \rfloor}(\alpha_D)$ starting at 0. It suggests the following definition.

Definition 11 *Let* $\alpha_D = (a_t)_{t=1}^{\lfloor n/2 \rfloor}$ *be a presentation for* $D \in SC(\mathbb{N}^{n\times n})$.

The r -tuple $(a_{\zeta_j})_{j=1}^{r}$ *is the* **stripe sequence** *(for short,* **s.s.***)* of α_D, *if* $\zeta_{j+1} < \zeta_j$, *for any* $1 \le j < r$, *and* $\{\zeta_1, \ldots, \zeta_r\} = \{t \in [\lfloor n/2 \rfloor] : g_t(\alpha_D) < g_{t-1}(\alpha_D)\}$. ζ_j *is called the j* **-th s.s. index** *of* α_D, *for any* $j \in [r]$.

Note that the higher is j, the lower is ζ_j, and the higher is $g_{\zeta_j}(\alpha_D)$. In particular,

$$\begin{cases} \zeta_1 = \min\{t \in [\lfloor n/2 \rfloor] : g_t(\alpha_D) = g_{\lfloor n/2 \rfloor}(\alpha_D) = 1\} \\ \zeta_r = 1 \end{cases} \tag{10}$$

For any $1 \le j < r$, the integer $g_{\zeta_{j+1}}(\alpha_D)/g_{\zeta_j}(\alpha_D)$ is denoted by $h_j(\alpha_D)$. In the following, we write h_j instead of $h_j(\alpha_D)$ if the context is clear.

5. Bounds for the general case of SCTSP

In this section the most remarkable results regarding the general case of SCTSP are reported. Unfortunately, such results do not allow to prove neither that SCTSP is in P, nor that it is an NP-hard problem.

5.1 An upper bound for SCTSP

The first author explicitly dealing with SCTSP is Van der Veen (1992). Its heuristic **HT1** is a polynomial time algorithm for SCTSP in the case in which the matrix in input has distinct stripe costs. Van der Veen computes the cost of the Hamiltonian tour returned by **HT1** just in some cases. Gerace, and Greco (2008b) propose the procedure **H**, a restyling of Van der Veen's procedure. The main difference is the input instance: While **HT1** accepts just matrices in $SC(\mathbb{N}^{n\times n})$ with distinct stripe costs, **H** works on any matrix in $SC(\mathbb{N}^{n\times n})$, once a presentation for it is given. In the following, we explain how **H** works.

Let D be a matrix in $SC(\mathbb{N}^{n\times n})$, and let $\alpha_D = (a_t)_{t=1}^{\lfloor n/2 \rfloor}$ be a presentation for it. For any $\tau \in [\lfloor n/2 \rfloor]$, let $\Delta_\tau(\alpha_D)$ be the connected component of $G_\tau(\alpha_D)$ containing the node 0. It follows by *Theorem 8* that its node set, say it $V_\tau(\alpha_D)$, is $\{v \in \mathbb{Z}_n : v \equiv_{g_\tau} 0\}$

First of all, we describe a procedure **HP** returning on input (α_D, τ) a Hamiltonian path for $\Delta_\tau(\alpha_D)$ starting at the node 0. **HP** corresponds to *Steps 2–3* of **HT1**.

Suppose that $\tau = 1$. For any $0 \le \lambda < n/g_1$, let $v_\lambda = \langle \lambda \cdot a_1 \rangle_n$. Note that $v_\lambda \equiv_{g_1} 0$. Let **HP**$(\alpha_D, 1)$ = $[v_0, v_1, \ldots, v_{n/g_1 - 1}]$. Since $g_1 = \gcd(n, a_1)$ by *Definition 5*, it follows that **HP**$(\alpha_D, 1)$ passes through any node in $V_1(\alpha_D)$. Thus, it is a Hamiltonian path for $\Delta_1(\alpha_D)$.

Suppose, now, that $\tau > 1$. Let $P_0 = \mathbf{HP}(\alpha_D, \tau - 1)$. We distinguish two cases. If $g_{\tau-1} = g_\tau$, then P_0 is a Hamiltonian path also for $\Delta_\tau(\alpha_D)$ by *Theorem 8*. In this case $\mathbf{HP}(\alpha_D, \tau)$ returns P_0. Otherwise, $g_{\tau-1} > g_\tau$ holds. As $g_\tau = \gcd(g_{\tau-1}, a_\tau)$, and $v \in V_{\tau-1}(\alpha_D)$ if and only if $v \equiv_{g_{\tau-1}} 0$, it follows that

$$V_\tau(\alpha_D) = \{\langle v + \mu a_\tau \rangle_n : v \in V_{\tau-1}(\alpha_D), \mu = 0, 1, \ldots, g_{\tau-1}/g_\tau - 1\}. \quad (**)$$

Let z denote the ending point of P_0, and h the integer $g_{\tau-1} / g_\tau$. For any $\mu \in [h-1]$, let u_μ denote the integer $\langle \mu(z+a_\tau) \rangle_n$, and P_μ the path (P_0+u_μ). Finally, let P be the path obtained by linking $P_0, P_1, \ldots, P_{h-1}$ by the arcs $[\langle u_\mu - a_\tau \rangle_n, u_\mu]$, for any $\mu \in [h-1]$. $\mathbf{HP}(\alpha_D, \tau)$ returns P. Note that P passes through any node in $V_\tau(\alpha_D)$, as P_0 passes through any node in $V_{\tau-1}(\alpha_D)$, and (**) holds. Hence, it is a Hamiltonian path for $\Delta_\tau(\alpha_D)$.

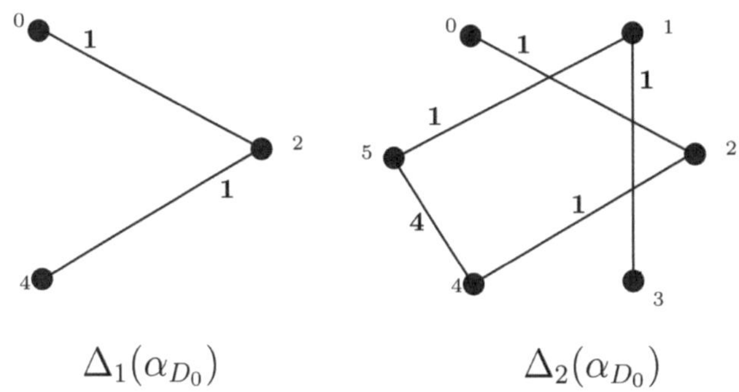

Fig. 2. *Shortest Hamiltonian paths for* $\Delta_1(\alpha_{D_0})$, *and for* $\Delta_2(\alpha_{D_0})$ *starting at* 0

Example 12 *Let us consider the matrix* $D_0 \in SC(\mathbb{N}^{6\times 6})$ *defined in Example 1. Its unique presentation is* $\alpha_{D_0} = (2, 1, 3)$, *and* $G_1(\alpha_{D_0})$, *and* $G_2(\alpha_{D_0})$ *are depicted in Figure 1. The path shown in Figure 2 are returned, respectively, by executing* $\mathbf{HP}(\alpha_{D_0}, 1)$, *and* $\mathbf{HP}(\alpha_{D_0}, 2)$.

Remark. *Let* $\tau \in [\lfloor n/2 \rfloor]$. *The path* $HP(\alpha_{D_0}, \tau) = [v_0, v_1, \ldots v_{n_{g_{\tau-1}}}]$ *verifies* $v_0 = 0$, *and* $v_\lambda \in \arg \min_{u \notin \{v_0, \ldots, v_{\lambda-1}\}} \{t : \{v_{\lambda-1}, u\} \in D(a_t), t \in [\tau]\}$, *for any* $1 \le \lambda < n/g_\tau$. *Thus,* **HP** *is a deterministic nearest neighbor ruled algorithm. By applying Kruskal's algorithm to* $\Delta_\tau(\alpha_D)$, *a minimum spanning tree* T, *whose weight is equal to the cost of* $\mathbf{HP}(\alpha_D, \tau)$, *is obtained. Thus,* **HP** (α_D, τ) *is a shortest Hamiltonian path for* $\Delta_\tau(\alpha_D)$ *starting at the node* 0 *(see also* Corollary *6 in Gilmore, et al. (1985)).*

Let us define, now, the procedure **H**.

Procedure H.

Instance. A matrix $D \in SC(\mathbb{N}^{n\times n})$, and a presentation α_D for D.

Step a. Execute $\mathbf{Pr}(\alpha_D, 1)$.
Step b. Let $H = [v_0, v_1, \ldots, v_{n-1}, v_0]$ be the Hamiltonian cycle obtained in *Step a*. Return the Hamiltonian tour $T_H: \mathbb{Z}_n \rightarrow \mathbb{Z}_n$ for D, defined as follows: $T_H(v_\lambda) = v_{\langle \lambda+1 \rangle_n}$, for any $\lambda \in \mathbb{Z}_n$.

Procedure Pr.

Instance. A presentation $\alpha_D = (a_t)_{t=1}^{\lfloor n/2 \rfloor}$, and an integer $j \geq 1$.

Step 1. Let $\zeta_1, \ldots, \zeta_r$ denote the s.s. indexes of α_D. If $j = 1$, compute ζ_1.

Step 2. If $\zeta_j = 1$, compute $h_j = g_0 / g_1$. Set $v_0 = 0$, and $v_\lambda = \langle v_{\lambda-1} + a_{\zeta_j} \rangle_n$, for any $1 \leq \lambda < h_j$. Return the cycle $[v_0, v_1, \ldots, v_{h_j-1}, v_0]$.

Step 3. Compute ζ_{j+1}, and $h_j = g_{\zeta_{j+1}} / g_{\zeta_j}$. Execute **HP**($\alpha_D$, ζ_{j+1}). Let P_0 be the obtained path. Find an arc $[u, u']$ of P_0 verifying $(u' - u) \equiv_n a_{\zeta_{j+1}}$. By deleting it, the paths Q_0, and R_0 are obtained. Let $u_\lambda = \langle \lambda \cdot a_{\zeta_j} \rangle_n$, for any $\lambda = 1, \ldots, h_j - 1$. Set $Q_\lambda = (Q_0 + u_\lambda)$, $R_\lambda = (R_0 + u_\lambda)$, for any $\lambda = 1, \ldots, h_j - 2$, and, finally, $P_{h_j-1} = (P_0 + u_{h_j-1})$.

Step 4. If h_j is even, link up $P_0, Q_1, R_1, Q_2, R_2, \ldots, Q_{h_j-2}, R_{h_j-2}, P_{h_j-1}$ by $2(h_j - 1)$ arcs in $D(a_{\zeta_j})$, as shown in Figure 3. Return the obtained cycle.

Step 5. Execute **Pr**(α_D, j+1). Let C_{j+1} be the obtained cycle. Find in C_{j+1} an arc $[v, v']$ such that $(v' - v) \equiv_n a_{\zeta_{j+1}}$. By deleting it a path K_0^* is obtained. Set $K_0 = (K_0^* + w)$, where $w = \langle u' - v' \rangle_n$.

Step 6. Link up $K_0, Q_1, R_1, Q_2, R_2, \ldots, Q_{h_j-2}, R_{h_j-2}, P_{h_j-1}$ by $2(h_j - 1)$ arcs in $D(a_{\zeta_j})$, as shown in *Figure* 3. Return the obtained cycle. ■

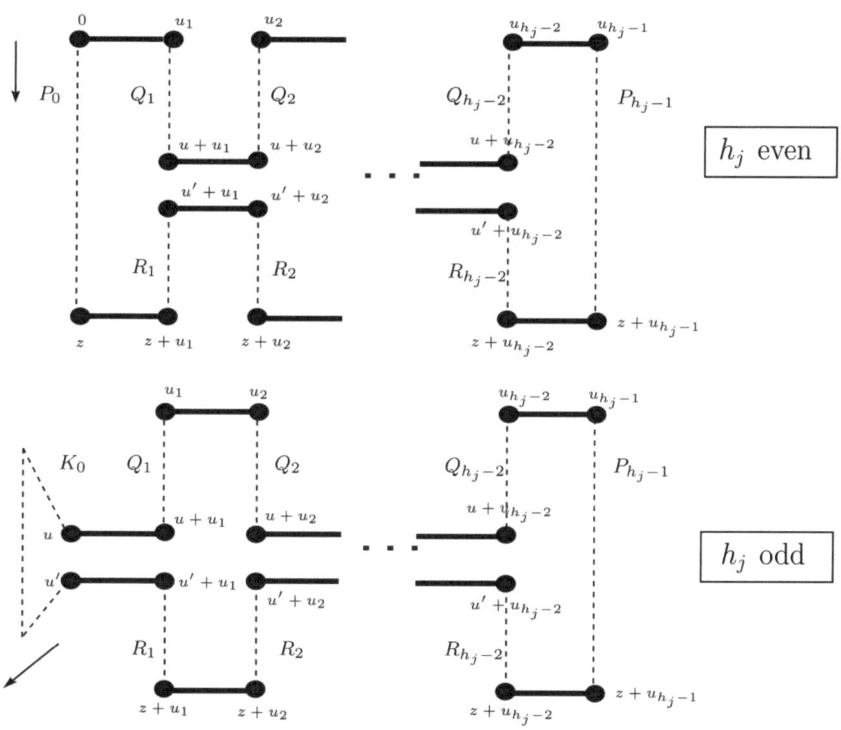

Fig. 3. **Pr**(α_D, j) in the case h_j even (above), and h_j odd (below). Note that h_j is the number of connected components of $G_{\zeta_{j+1}}(\alpha_D)$ contained in $\Delta_{\zeta_j}(\alpha_D)$.

HP(α_D, τ) contains an arc $[u, u']$ such that $(u' - u) \equiv_n a_\tau$ if and only if $g_{\tau-1} > g_\tau$ holds, that is, if and only if τ is a s.s. index of α_D. Hence, *Step 3* of **Pr** is well defined. Gerace, and Greco (2008b) prove that **H** is a correct polynomial time procedure, and that the cost of **H**(D, α_D) is time $O(n)$ computable (without running **H**) by the next theorem.

Theorem 13 *Let* α_D *be a presentation for a matrix* $D \in SC(\mathbb{N}^{n\times n})$, *let* $(a_{\zeta_j})_{j=1}^{r}$ *be its s.s., and let* $\rho = \max\{j \in [r] : g_{\zeta_j}$ is odd$\}$. *If* $\hat{\rho}$ *denotes the integer* $\min\{r - 1, \rho\}$, *then the Hamiltonian tour* **H**(D, α_D) *costs*

$$SHP(\alpha_D) + d(a_{\zeta_1}) + \sum_{j=1}^{\hat{\rho}}(h_j - 2)\cdot(d(a_{\zeta_j}) - d(a_{\zeta_{j+1}})).$$

As a consequence of *Theorem 13*, the integer

$$UB(D) = \min\{sum_D(\mathbf{H}(D, \alpha_D)) \ : \ \alpha_D \text{ is a presentation for } D\}. \tag{11}$$

is an upper bound for opt(D). If there exists just a presentation α_D for D, and **Pr**(α_D, 1) ends immediately with no more recursive calling, $UB(D)$ is equal to the upper bound given in Van der Veen (1992), *Theorem* 7.2.5.

In the general case D admits more than a presentation. As *Example 14*, and *Example 15* below show, the cost of the Hamiltonian tour returned by **H** depends on the presentation. Since the number of the presentations for D could be exponential in n, $UB(D)$ is not efficiently computable by determining sum_D(**H**(D, α_D)), for any presentation α_D.

Example 14 *Let* $n = 108$, *and let D be the matrix in* $SC(\mathbb{N}^{n\times n})$ *having as stripe costs* $d(36) = 1$, $d(8) = d(16) = d(27) = 2$, *and* $d(k) = 3 + k$, *for any other* $k \in [54]$. *We consider just two of the six possible presentations for D: the one verifying* $a_1 = 36$, $a_2 = 27$, $a_3 = 16$, $a_4 = 8$ *is denoted by* $\alpha_D = (a_t)_{t=1}^{54}$ *; the one verifying* $b_1 = 36$, $b_2 = 8$, $b_3 = 16$, $b_4 = 27$ *is denoted by* $\beta_D = (b_t)_{t=1}^{54}$ *. Let us denote by* $(a_{\zeta_j})_{j=1}^{r}$, *(respectively, by* $(b_{\xi_k})_{k=1}^{s}$ *the s.s. of* α_D *(respectively, of* β_D*). Let us compute* sum_D(**H**(D, α_D)), and sum_D(**H**(D, β_D)) *by following the arrows in the two schemes reported in* Figure 4 *(the differences between them are pointed out in bold). Such schemes are obtained by making use of (5), of (10), of* Theorem 9, *and of* Theorem 13. *Note that* sum_D(**H**(D, α_D)) > sum_D(**H**(D, β_D)).

Example 15 *Let* $n = 135$, *and let D be the matrix in* $SC(\mathbb{N}^{n\times n})$ *verifying* $d(45) = 1$, $d(5) = d(9) = 2$, *and* $d(k) = 3 + k$, *for any other* $k \in [52]$. *There exist exactly two presentations for D. Let* $\alpha_D = (a_t)_{t=1}^{67}$ *be the one verifying* $a_1 = 45$, $a_2 = 5$, $a_3 = 9$, *and let* $\beta_D = (b_t)_{t=1}^{67}$ *be the one verifying* $b_1 = 45$, $b_2 = 9$, $b_3 = 5$. *As above, let* $(a_{\zeta_j})_{j=1}^{r}$, *(respectively,* $(b_{\xi_k})_{k=1}^{s}$ *denotes the s.s. of* α_D *(respectively, of* β_D*), and let us compute* sum_D(**H**(D, α_D)), *and* sum_D(**H**(D, β_D)) *by following the arrows in the two schemes reported in* Figure 5 *(the differences are pointed out in bold). Note that* sum_D(**H**(D, α_D)) > sum_D(**H**(D, β_D)) *also in this case.*

In both examples **H**(D, β_D) costs less than **H**(D, α_D)). In the former, the presentation β_D sorts the stripes having the same cost in a way that $g_t(\beta_D)$ remains even as long as possible. In fact, $g_2(\alpha_D)$ is odd, while $g_2(\beta_D)$ is even. In the latter, n is an odd number. Thus, $g_t(\beta_D)$, and $g_t(\alpha_D)$

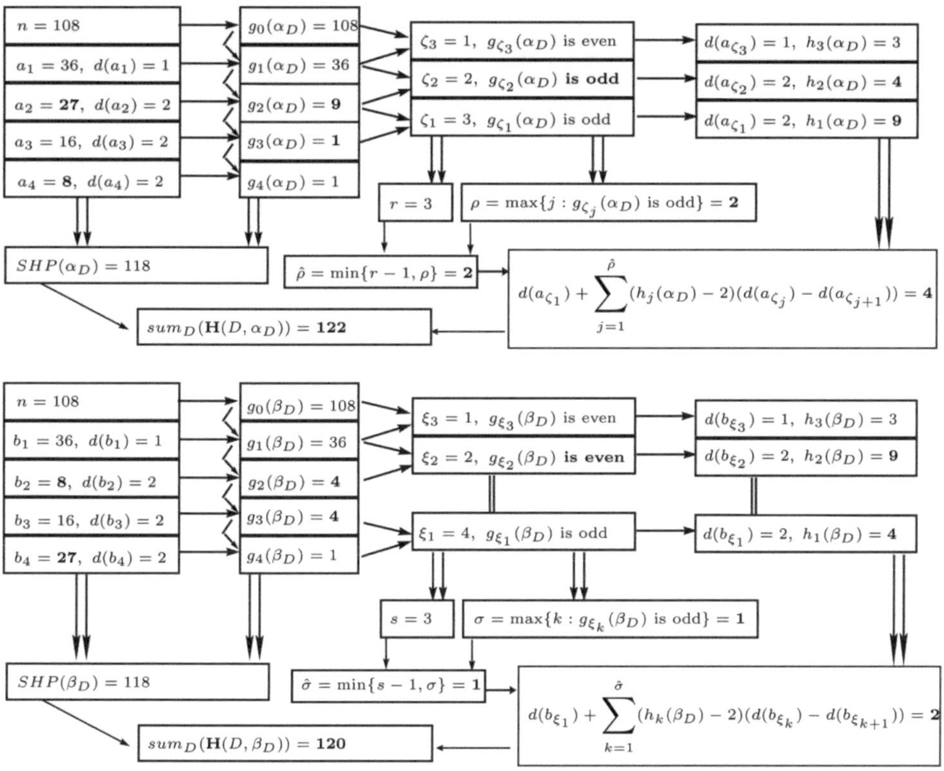

Fig. 4. How to compute $sum_D(\mathbf{H}(D, \alpha_D))$, and $sum_D(\mathbf{H}(D, \beta_D))$ in Example 14.

are necessarily odd, for any $t \in [\lfloor n/2 \rfloor]$. Anyway, β_D sorts the stripes having the same cost in a way that $g_2(\beta_D)$ is as great as possible.
Such considerations suggest the following definition.

Definition 16 *Let* **D** *be a matrix in* **SC**$(\mathbb{N}^{n\times n})$, *and let* $\beta_D = (\mathbf{b}_t)_{t=1}^{\lfloor n/2 \rfloor}$ *be a presentation for D.* β_D *is* **sharp** *if* $g_t(\beta_D)$ *odd implies that* $g_t(\alpha_D)$ *is an odd integer less than, or equal to* $g_t(\beta_D)$, *for any* $t \in [\lfloor n/2 \rfloor]$, *and for any other presentation* α_D *for D.*

A sharp presentation for a matrix in $SC(\mathbb{N}^{n\times n})$ is time $O(n \log n)$ computable by the procedure **SP** reported below.

Procedure SP.

Instance. A matrix D in $SC(\mathbb{N}^{n\times n})$.

Step 1. Set $S = [\lfloor n/2 \rfloor]$, $g = n$, and $t = 1$. Sort in non decreasing order the stripe costs of D. Let $(d_t)_{t=1}^{\lfloor n/2 \rfloor}$ the tuple so obtained.

Step 2. While there exists $a \in S$ such that $d(a) = d_t$, and $\gcd(g, a)$ is even set $b_t = a$, $S = S \setminus a$, $g = \gcd(g, a)$, and $t = t + 1$.

Step 3. While $S \neq 0$, extract from $S \cap \{a' : d(a') = d_t\}$ the element a maximizing $\gcd(g, a')$. Set $b_t = a$, $S = S \setminus a$, $g = \gcd(g, a)$, and $t = t + 1$.

Step 4. Return the presentation $(b_t)_{t=1}^{\lfloor n/2 \rfloor}$. ■

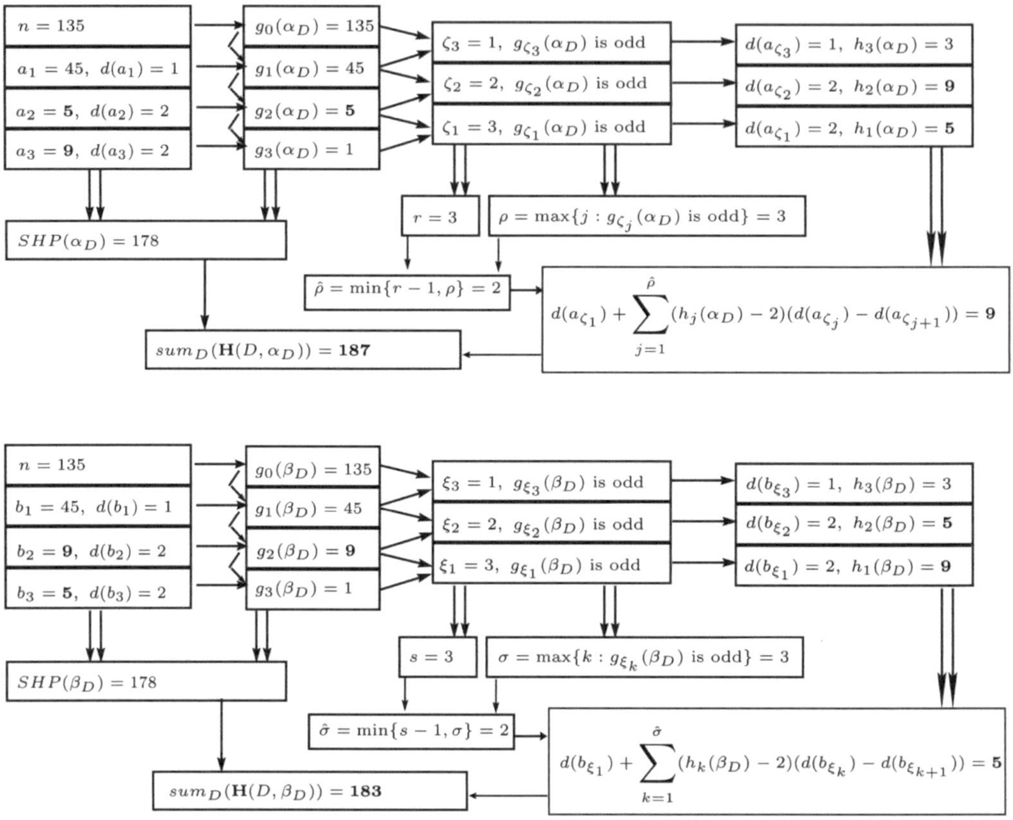

Fig. 5. *How to compute* $sum_D(\mathbf{H}(D, \alpha_D))$, *and* $sum_D(\mathbf{H}(D, \beta_D))$ *in* Example 15.

Let $\beta_D = \mathbf{SP}(D)$. Gerace, and Greco (2008b) prove that $UB(D) = sum_D(\mathbf{H}(D, \beta_D))$ holds, as β_D is sharp. Since $sum_D(\mathbf{H}(D, \beta_D))$ is time $O(n)$ computable (see *Theorem 13*), it follows that $UB(D)$ is a time $O(n \log n)$ computable upper bound for opt(D).

5.2 A lower bound for SCTSP

Let D be a matrix in $SC(\mathbb{N}^{n \times n})$. If D has distinct stripe costs, *Theorem* 7.4.2 in Van der Veen (1992) gives a lower bound for opt(D). By the same argument, *Theorem 17* below shows that any presentation for D leads to a lower bound.

Theorem 17 Let α_D be a presentation for a matrix $D \in SC(\mathbb{N}^{n \times n})$, and let $(a_{\zeta_j})_{j=1}^{r}$ be its s.s.. Then, $SHP(\alpha_D) + d(a_{\zeta_1}) \le \text{opt}(D)$ holds.

PROOF. Let us fix an optimal Hamiltonian tour $T : \mathbb{Z}_n \to \mathbb{Z}_n$ for D. Setting $v_0 = T(0)$, and $v_\lambda = T(v_{\lambda-1})$, for any integer $1 \le \lambda < n$, naturally induces a Hamiltonian cycle $H_T = [v_0, v_1, \ldots, v_{n-1}, v_0]$ for $G_{\lfloor n/2 \rfloor}(\alpha_D)$. It follows from (1), and from (9) that $c_D(H_T) = sum_D(T)$. If no arc $[u, v]$ of H_T would verify $\{u, v\} \in \bigcup_{t=\zeta_1}^{\lfloor n/2 \rfloor} D(a_t)$, then H_T would be a Hamiltonian cycle also for $G_{\zeta_1 - 1}(\alpha_D)$, a weighted undirected graph having $g_{\zeta_1 -1} > 1$ connected components, as a consequence of *Theorem 8*, and of *Definition 11*. Hence, there exists an arc $[u, v]$ in H_T such that $c_D([u, v]) = d[u, v] \geq d(a_{\zeta_1})$. By deleting $[u, v]$ from H_T a Hamiltonian path P for $G_{\lfloor n/2 \rfloor}(\alpha_D)$ is obtained. Clearly, $c_D(P) \geq SHP(\alpha_D)$ holds. Thus,

$$sum_D(T) = c_D(H_T) = c_D(P) + c_D([u, v]) \geq SHP(\alpha_D) + d(a_{\zeta_1}).$$

As $sum_D(T) = \text{opt}(D)$, the claim follows. □

Let $\beta_D = (b_t)_{t=1}^{\lfloor n/2 \rfloor}$ be a presentations for D, possibly different from α_D. Since $\{a_1, \ldots, a_{\lfloor n/2 \rfloor}\} = [\lfloor n/2 \rfloor] = \{b_1, \ldots, b_{\lfloor n/2 \rfloor}\}$, the weighted undirected graphs $G_{\lfloor n/2 \rfloor}(\alpha_D)$, and $G_{\lfloor n/2 \rfloor}(\beta_D)$ coincide by *Definition 6*. It follows from *Theorem 9* that $SHP(\alpha_D) = SHP(\beta_D)$ holds. As shown by Gerace, and Greco (2008b), $d(a_{\zeta_1}) = d(b_{\xi_1})$ also holds, where b_{ξ_1} denote the 1-st s.s. index of β_D.
It follows from *Theorem 17* that the integer

$$LB(D) = SHP(\alpha_D) + d(a_{\zeta_1}) \tag{12}$$

is a well defined lower bound for opt(D) holds not depending on the chosen presentation

5.3 A 2-approximation algorithm for SCTSP

A first 2-approximation algorithm for the general case of SCTSP is reported Gerace, and Irwing (1998). For any matrix $D \in SC(\mathbb{N}^{n \times n})$, such algorithm makes use of the construction proposed by Burkard, and Sandholzer (1991) for solving the Hamiltonian circuit problem in a circulant undirected graph. The returned Hamiltonian tour has a costs greater than, or equal to $UB(D)$.
By the procedure **SP**, a sharp presentation β_D for D can be found in polynomial time. If we apply **H** on input (D, β_D), a Hamiltonian tour for D of cost $UB(D)$ is obtained in polynomial time. Let **H*** denote the algorithm that, given D, returns $\mathbf{H}(D, \beta_D)$. Clearly, **H*** is a 2-approximation algorithm for SCTSP. Gerace, and Greco (2008b) proves that the analysis of **H*** is tight.

6. When the optimal cost is equal to the lower bound

Let D be a matrix in $SC(\mathbb{N}^{n \times n})$. Let α_D be a presentation for it, and let $(a_{\zeta_j})_{j=1}^{r}$ be its s.s.. *Theorem 18* below extends some results appearing in Van der Veen (1992), and in Gerace, and Irwing (1998). It is inspired by the following remark: According to (12), there exists a Hamiltonian tour for D of cost $LB(D)$ if and only if there exists a shortest Hamiltonian path for $G_{\lfloor n/2 \rfloor}(\alpha_D)$ starting at the node 0, and ending at a node v such that the arc $[v, 0]$ costs $d(a_{\zeta_1})$. Note that $[v, 0]$ is not necessary an arc in $D(a_{\zeta_1})$, if more than a stripe costs $d(a_{\zeta_1})$.

Theorem 18 *Let* $D = (d[i, j])$ *be a matrix in* $SC(\mathbb{N}^{n \times n})$. *Suppose that there exists a presentation* α_D *for* D *having* $(a_{\zeta_j})_{j=1}^{r}$ *as s.s., and that there exists* $v \in \mathbb{Z}_n$ *verifying* $d[v, 0] = d(a_{\zeta_1})$, *and*

$$v \equiv_n \sum_{j=r}^{1} (g_{\zeta_j - 1}/g_{\zeta_j} - 1)(2\gamma_j - g_{\zeta_j}) \cdot a_{\zeta_j},$$

for some integers $\gamma_r, \ldots, \gamma_2, \gamma_1$ *such that* $0 \le j \le g_{\zeta_1}$ *holds, for any* $j \in [r]$. *Then,* opt(D) = $LB(D)$ *holds.*

If D has distinct stripe costs, then the converse also holds.

PROOF. *(Sketch)* Let α_D be a presentation satisfying the hypotheses for some suitable integers v, $\gamma_r, \ldots, \gamma_2, \gamma_1$. Since α_D is fixed, Theorem 7.3.1 in Van der Veen (1992) implies that there exists a shortest Hamiltonian path P for $G_{\lfloor n/2 \rfloor}(\alpha_D)$ starting at 0, and ending at v. Let H be the Hamiltonian cycle for $G_{\lfloor n/2 \rfloor}(\alpha_D)$ obtained by composing P with the arc $[v, 0]$. Since $d[v, 0] = d(a_{\zeta_1})$, and *Theorem 9* holds, H costs $SHP(\alpha_D) + d(a_{\zeta_1}) = LB(D)$. H naturally induces a Hamiltonian tour T_H verifying $c_D(H) = sum_D(T_H)$. It follows from *Theorem 17* that opt(D) = $LB(D)$.

Suppose that D has distinct stripe costs, and that opt(D) = $LB(D)$. Let α_D be the unique presentation for D, and let $(a_{\zeta_j})_{j=1}^{r}$ be its s.s.. Let $T : \mathbb{Z}_n \rightarrow \mathbb{Z}_n$ be a Hamiltonian tour for D of cost $LB(D)$, and let $i \in \mathbb{Z}_n$ be an integer maximizing $d[i, T(i)]$. Clearly, $d[i, T(i)] \ge d(a_{\zeta_1})$ holds (see also the proof of *Theorem 17*). Let P be the Hamiltonian path obtained by deleting the arc $[i, T(i)]$ from the Hamiltonian cycle for $G_{\lfloor n/2 \rfloor}(\alpha_D)$ induced by T. Since P starts at the node $T(i)$, and ends at the node i, $(P - T(i))$ is a Hamiltonian path starting at 0, and ending at $v = \langle i - T(i) \rangle_n$. It follows from *Theorem 9* that $(P - T(i))$ is a shortest one, since $c_D(P) = c_D(P - T(i))$, and

$$c_D(P) = LB(D) - d[i, T(i)] = SHP(\alpha_D) + d(a_{\zeta_1}) - d[i, T(i)] \le SHP(\alpha_D).$$

Moreover, $d[i, T(i)] = LB(D) - SHP(\alpha_D) = d(a_{\zeta_1})$ is verified. As D is circulant, $d[v, 0] = d[i, T(i)] = d(a_{\zeta_1})$ also holds. As D has distinct stripe costs, *Theorem* 7.3.1 in Van der Veen (1992) implies that $v \equiv_n \sum_{j=r}^{1} (g_{\zeta_j - 1}/g_{\zeta_j} - 1)(2\gamma_j - g_{\zeta_j}) \cdot a_{\zeta_j}$, for some integers $\gamma_r, \ldots, \gamma_2, \gamma_1$ such that $0 \le \gamma_j \le g_j$ holds, for any $j \in [r]$. The second claim of the theorem is thus proved. □

As already observed, the number of presentation for a matrix $D \in SC(\mathbb{N}^{n \times n})$ could be exponential in n. Hence, an algorithm based on the sufficient condition given in *Theorem 18* cannot efficiently determine if opt(D) = $LB(D)$ holds. *Proposition 19* below gives some conditions implying opt(D) = $LB(D)$, once a presentation for D is fixed. In Garfinkel (1977) (respectively, in Van der Veen (1992)) appears a condition similar to condition (b) (respectively, to condition (c)). Finally, condition (d) is a consequence of *Theorem 18*.

Proposition 19 Let $D = (d[i, j])$ be a matrix in $SC(\mathbb{N}^{n \times n})$. Let $\_D$ be a presentation for it, and let $(a_{\zeta_j})_{j=1}^{r}$ be its s.s.. If one of the following condition occurs, then opt(D) = $LB(D)$ holds:

a) $d(a_{\zeta_r}) = d(a_{\zeta_1})$;

b) $r = 1$;

c) $r \geq 2$, and $g_{\zeta_2} = 2$;

d) $r \geq 2$, and there exist $r-1$ integers $y_r, \ldots, y_2$ verifying $0 \leq y_j \leq g_{\zeta_j}$, for any $2 \leq j \leq r$, and

$$\sum_{j=r}^{2}(g_{\zeta_j-1}/g_{\zeta_j} - 1)(g_{\zeta_j} - 2y_j) \cdot a_{\zeta_j} + g_{\zeta_1-1}a_{\zeta_1} \equiv_n 0.$$

PROOF. (a) If $d(a_{\zeta_r}) = d(a_{\zeta_1})$, then $d(a_t) = d(a_{\zeta_r})$, for any $\zeta_r \leq t \leq 1$. In particular, $d(a_{\zeta_j}) = d(a_{\zeta_{j+1}})$ holds, for any $j \in [r-1]$. It follows from *Theorem 13* that $sum_D(\mathbf{H}(D, \alpha_D)) = SHP(\alpha_D) + d(a_{\zeta_1})$. The claim thus follows by making use of (12), and of *Theorem 17.*

(b) It is a subcase of condition (a): If $r = 1$, then $d(a_{\zeta_r}) = d(a_{\zeta_1})$.

(c) It follows from *Theorem 13* that, if $r \geq 2$, and $g_{\zeta_2} = 2$, then $\rho = 1$, and $\hat{\rho} = 1$. Since $g_{\zeta_1} = 1$ holds by (10), we have that $h_1 = g_{\zeta_2}/g_{\zeta_1} = 2$. Hence, $sum_D(\mathbf{H}(D, \alpha_D)) = SHP(\alpha_D) + d(a_{\zeta_1})$ is verified. The claim thus follows by making use of (12), and of *Theorem 17.*

(d) Let us set $\gamma_1 = 1$, and $\gamma_j = g_{\zeta_j} - y_j$, for any $2 \leq j \leq r$. Trivially, $g_{\zeta_j} - 2y_j = 2_j - g_{\zeta_j}$ holds, for any $2 \leq j \leq r$. Since $g_{\zeta_1} = 1$, also $g_{\zeta_1} = 2\gamma_1 - g_{\zeta_1} = 1$ is verified. It follows from the hypothesis that

$$\sum_{j=r}^{2}(g_{\zeta_j-1}/g_{\zeta_j} - 1)(2\gamma_j - g_{\zeta_j}) \cdot a_{\zeta_j} + g_{\zeta_1-1}(2\gamma_1 - g_{\zeta_1}) \cdot a_{\zeta_1} \equiv_n 0.$$

$g_{\zeta_1-1} a_{\zeta_1}$ can be written as $(g_{\zeta_1-1}/g_{\zeta_1} - 1)a_{\zeta_1} + a_{\zeta_1}$. Hence,

$$\sum_{j=r}^{1}(g_{\zeta_j-1}/g_{\zeta_j} - 1)(2\gamma_j - g_{\zeta_j}) \cdot a_{\zeta_j} \equiv_n -a_{\zeta_1} \equiv_n n - a_{\zeta_1}.$$

Let $v = n - a_{\zeta_1}$. As $d[v, 0] = d(a_{\zeta_1})$ holds, α_D, and v verifies the hypotheses of *Theorem 18*. The claim thus follows. □

7. 2-striped symmetric circulant matrices

Let D be a matrix in $SC(\mathbb{N}^{n\times n})$, let $\alpha_D = (a_t)_{t=1}^{\lfloor n/2 \rfloor}$ be a presentation for it, and let τ be a fixed integer in $[\lfloor n/2 \rfloor]$. Any Hamiltonian tour $T: \mathbb{Z}_n \rightarrow \mathbb{Z}_n$ such that $\{i, T(i)\} \in D(a_t)$, for some $i \in \mathbb{Z}_n$, and some $t \geq \tau$, verifies $sum_D(T) \geq SHP(\alpha_D) + d(a_\tau)$. Indeed, if P denotes the Hamiltonian path obtained by deleting the arc $[i, T(i)]$ from the Hamiltonian cycle for $G_{\lfloor n/2 \rfloor}(\alpha_D)$ induced by T, then $c_D(P) \geq SHP(\alpha_D)$, and $sum_D(T) \geq c_D(P) + d(a_\tau)$. Any such tour is not optimal if $SHP(\alpha_D) + d(a_\tau) > UB(D)$ holds, since a Hamiltonian tour for D of cost $UB(D)$ always exists (see §4). Thus, we may ignore the a_t-stripe, for any $t \geq \tau$, if $d(a_\tau) > UB(D) - SHP(\alpha_D)$ holds.

Note that any other a-stripe cannot be a priori ignored, even if no presentation for D contains a in its s.s.. Thus, a first step for solving SCTSP is analyzing the case in which each presentation for D has the same s.s., and any stripe not belonging to the s.s. can be ignored.

Definition 20 A matrix $D \in SC(\mathbb{N}^{n\times n})$ is an s-**striped** matrix, for some $s \geq 1$, if a presentation $\alpha_D = (a_t)_{t=1}^{\lfloor n/2 \rfloor}$ for it verifies the following properties:

(i) $(a_s, a_{s-1}, \ldots, a_1)$ is the s.s. of α_D, and $d(a_t) < d(a_{t+1})$, for any $t \in [s]$;

(ii) $d(a_{s+1}) > UB(D) - SHP(\alpha_D)$.

Definition 20 does not depend on the presentation. Indeed, let $\beta_D = (b_t)_{t=1}^{\lfloor n/2 \rfloor}$ be a presentation for D, possibly different from α_D. As both α_D, and β_D sort in non decreasing order the multi-set containing the stripe costs of D, then $d(a_t) = d(b_t)$ holds, for any $t \in [\lfloor n/2 \rfloor]$. In particular, $d(b_{s+1}) = d(a_{s+1})$, and, thus, $d(b_{s+1})$ verifies property (*ii*). As a consequence of property (*i*), no other stripe different from a_t costs $d(a_t)$, for any $t \in [s]$. Hence, $a_t = b_t$, and $g_t(\alpha_D) = g_t(\beta_D)$ hold, for any $t \in [s]$, and, thus, $(a_s, a_{s-1}, \ldots, a_1)$ is also the s.s. of β_D.
The case $s = 1$ is trivial: condition (b) in *Proposition 19* holds, and thus opt(D) = $LB(D)$. In this section we deal with the case $s = 2$.

By $D(n; d_1, d_2; a_1, a_2)$ we denote the 2-striped matrix in $SC(\mathbb{N}^{n\times n})$ verifying $d(a_1) = d_1$, and $d(a_2) = d_2$, for some presentation $\alpha_D = (a_t)_{t=1}^{\lfloor n/2 \rfloor}$. As any two presentations have (a_2, a_1) as s.s., we denote by g_1 the integer $g_1(\alpha_D) = \gcd(n, a_1)$, and by G_1, and G_2 the weighted undirected graphs $G_1(\alpha_D)$, and $G_2(\alpha_D)$. Note that $g_1 > 1$, and that $\gcd(g_1, a_2) = 1$, as a consequence of *Definition 20*, applied for $s = 2$.
The weighted adjacency matrix of G_2 is a symmetric circulant matrix with two stripes, according to the definition given in Gerace, and Greco (2008a). Aim of this section is restating for the 2-striped matrices in $SC(\mathbb{N}^{n\times n})$ the results obtained in Gerace, and Greco (2008a). Let D be the matrix $D(n; d_1, d_2; a_1, a_2)$. As a consequence of *Theorem 9*, of *Theorem 17*, and of (11) (respectively, of *Theorem 9*, and of (12)), the integer $UB(D)$ (respectively, $LB(D)$) verifies:

$$\begin{aligned} UB(D) &= (n - 2(g_1 - 1)) \cdot d_1 + 2(g_1 - 1) \cdot d_2; \\ LB(D) &= (n - g_1) \cdot d_1 + g_1 \cdot d_2. \end{aligned} \tag{13}$$

If $g_1 = 2$, condition (c) of *Proposition 19* implies that opt(D) = $LB(D)$.

Definition 21 *Let D be the matrix $D(n; d_1, d_2; a_1, a_2)$, and let $T : \mathbb{Z}_n \rightarrow \mathbb{Z}_n$ be an Hamiltonian tour for D. T is* **feasible** if $\{i, T(i)\} \in D(a_1) \cup D(a_2)$, *for any* $i \in \mathbb{Z}_n$.

Any stripe of D different from a_1, and a_2 can be ignored. Thus, an optimal Hamiltonian tour for D is also a feasible one. As a consequence of *Definition 6*, Hamiltonian cycles for G_2, and feasible Hamiltonian tours for D are in correspondence.
Let $T : \mathbb{Z}_n \rightarrow \mathbb{Z}_n$ be a feasible Hamiltonian tour for D, and let $H_T = [v_0, v_1, \ldots, v_{n-1}, v_0]$ be the Hamiltonian cycle for G_2 associated to T. $[v_\lambda, v_{\langle \lambda+1 \rangle_n}]$ is a $(+a_1)$-**arc**, for some $\lambda \in \mathbb{Z}_n$, if

$(v_{\langle\lambda+1\rangle_n} - v_\lambda) \equiv_n +a_1$ holds. In a similar way, $(-a_1)$-**arcs**, $(+a_2)$-**arcs**, and $(-a_2)$-**arcs** are defined. $\pi^+_{2,T}$ (respectively, $\pi^-_{2,T}$) denotes the number of $(+a_2)$-arcs (respectively, of $(-a_2)$-arcs). If $g_1 \geq 3$, $(\pi^+_{2,T} + \pi^-_{2,T})$ corresponds the number of arcs of H_T belonging to $D(a_2)$, as the next remark shows.

Remark. *An arc is at the same time a $(+a_2)$-arc, and a $(-a_2)$-arc if and only if $a_2 \equiv_n -a_2$, that is, if and only if n is even, and $a_2 = n/2$. As already observed, $g_1 = \gcd(n, a_1) > 1$, and $1 = \gcd(n, a_1, a_2) = \gcd(g_1, n/2)$ hold. Thus, $g_1 = 2$ holds if n is even, and $a_2 = n/2$.*

Theorem 22 Let D be the matrix $D(n; d_1, d_2; a_1, a_2)$. If $g_1 \geq 3$, there exists an optimal Hamiltonian tour T for D such that $(\pi^+_{2,T} - \pi^-_{2,T}) \in \{0, g_1\}$. In particular, if $(\pi^+_{2,T} - \pi^-_{2,T}) = 0$, then, $\text{opt}(D) = UB(D)$ holds.

PROOF. *(Sketch)* Let $S : \mathbb{Z}_n \to \mathbb{Z}_n$ be an optimal Hamiltonian tour for D. As $g_1 \geq 3$ holds, the number of arcs in $D(a_2)$ is $(\pi^+_{2,S} + \pi^-_{2,S})$. Since either $\{i, S(i)\} \in D(a_1)$, or $\{i, S(i)\} \in D(a_2)$ holds, for any $i \in \mathbb{Z}_n$, then

$$\text{opt}(D) = sum_D(S) = (n - (\pi^+_{2,S} + \pi^-_{2,S})) \cdot d_1 + (\pi^+_{2,S} + \pi^-_{2,S}) \cdot d_2.$$

Clearly, $LB(D) \leq sum_D(S) \leq UB(D)$ holds. Hence, it follows from (13), and from $d_1 < d_2$ that $g_1 \leq (\pi^+_{2,S} + \pi^-_{2,S}) \leq 2(g_1 - 1)$. On the other hand, $(\pi^+_{2,S} - \pi^-_{2,S}) \equiv_{g_1} 0$, since any arc in $D(a_2)$ links two different connected components of G_1, and the starting one coincides with the ending one. Hence, $(\pi^+_{2,S} - \pi^-_{2,S}) \in \{-g_1, 0, g_1\}$. If $(\pi^+_{2,S} - \pi^-_{2,S}) \in \{0, g_1\}$, it suffices to take $T = S$. If $(\pi^+_{2,S} - \pi^-_{2,S}) = -g_1$, it suffices to take $T = S^-$.

Suppose that $(\pi^+_{2,T} - \pi^-_{2,T}) = 0$. Since $(\pi^+_{2,T} + \pi^-_{2,T}) \leq 2(g_1 - 1)$ also holds, it follows that $0 \leq \pi^+_{2,T} = \pi^-_{2,T} \leq (g_1 - 1)$.

For any $i \in \mathbb{Z}_n$, the nodes i, and $T(i)$ belong to different connected components of G_1 if and only if $\{i, T(i)\} \in D(a_2)$. G_1 has g_1 connected components, and the Hamiltonian cycle H_T induced by T starts, and ends at the same connected components, after having passed through each other connected component. It follows that $\pi^+_{2,T} = \pi^-_{2,T} \geq (g_1 - 1)$ also holds. The claim, thus, follows. □

Theorem 23 *Let D be the matrix $D(n; d_1, d_2; a_1, a_2)$. Assume that $g_1 \geq 3$ holds.* Let $A_D = \{y \in \mathbb{Z} : 0 \leq y < n/g_1, (n/g_1 - 1)(g_1 - 2y)a_1 + g_1 a_2 \equiv_n 0\}$. *If A_D is not empty, let y_1, and y_2 be, respectively, the minimum, and the maximum of A_D, and let* $m = \min\{y_1 - g_1, n/g_1 - y_2\}$.

The following statements hold.

(i) *If A_D is empty, then* $\text{opt(D)} = \text{UB(D)}$.

(ii) *A_D is not empty, and $m \leq 0$ if and only if* $\text{opt(D)} = \text{LB(D)}$.

(iii) *If A_D is not empty, and $m > 0$, there exists a Hamiltonian tour for D of cost* $\text{LB(D)} + 2m \cdot (d_2 - d_1)$.

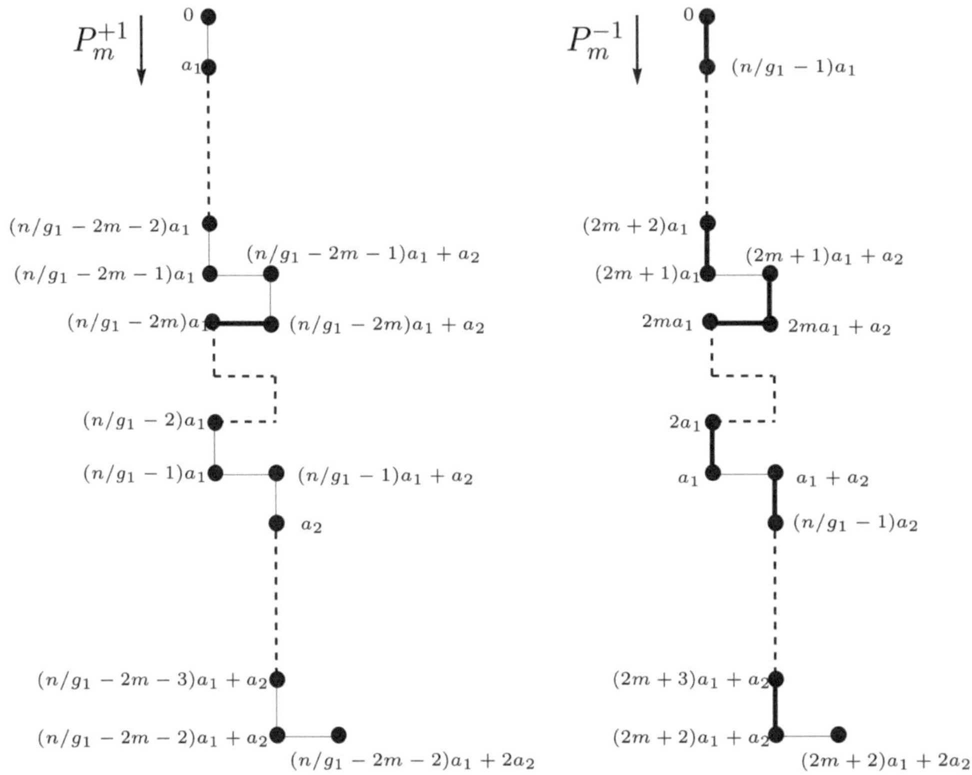

Fig. 6. P_m^{+1}, and P_m^{-1}, for a fixed $m > 0$

PROOF. *(Sketch)* If A_D is empty, it can be shown that no Hamiltonian tour T for D verifies $(\pi^{+}_{2,T} - \pi^{-}_{2,T}) = g_1$. Claim (*i*), thus, follows by Theorem 22.

Suppose that A_D is not empty, and that $m \le 0$ holds. As $(n/g_1 - y) > 0$ holds, for any $y \in A_D$, we have that $m = (y_1 - g_1)$. It follows from $m \le 0$ that y_1 verifies $0 \le y_1 \le g_1$, and from $y_1 \in A_D$ that $(n/g_1-1)(g_1-2y_1)a_1 + g_1 a_2 \equiv_n 0$. As (a_2, a_1) is the s.s. of any presentation for D, condition (d) of *Proposition 19* is verified. Thus, opt(D) = $LB(D)$ follows.
By arguing as in the proof of the second claim of *Theorem 18*, it can be shown that opt(D) = $LB(D)$ implies that there exists $y \in A_D$ such that $0 \le y \le g_1$. Clearly, $m \le 0$, in this case. Claim (*ii*) is thus proved.

Suppose that A_D is not empty, and that $m > 0$ holds. Then m is a positive integer less than $n/2g_1$. Let us denote by Δ_λ, for any $\lambda \in \mathbb{Z}_{g_1}$, the connected component of G_1 having as node set $\{v \in \mathbb{Z}_n : v \equiv_{g_1} \lambda a_2\}$.Let P_m^{+1}, and P_m^{-1} be the path in G_2 described in *Figure* 6[1]. They pass through any node in Δ_0, and in Δ_1, and cost $(2n/g_1 - 2m) \cdot d_1 + (2+2m) \cdot d_2$. For any $\lambda \in \mathbb{Z}_{g_1}$, let

[1] In the figures of this section, thin vertical lines represent $(+a_1)$-arcs, bold vertical lines represent $(-a_1)$-arcs, any other thin line represents a $(+a_2)$-arc, and, finally, any other bold line represents a $(-a_2)$-arcs.

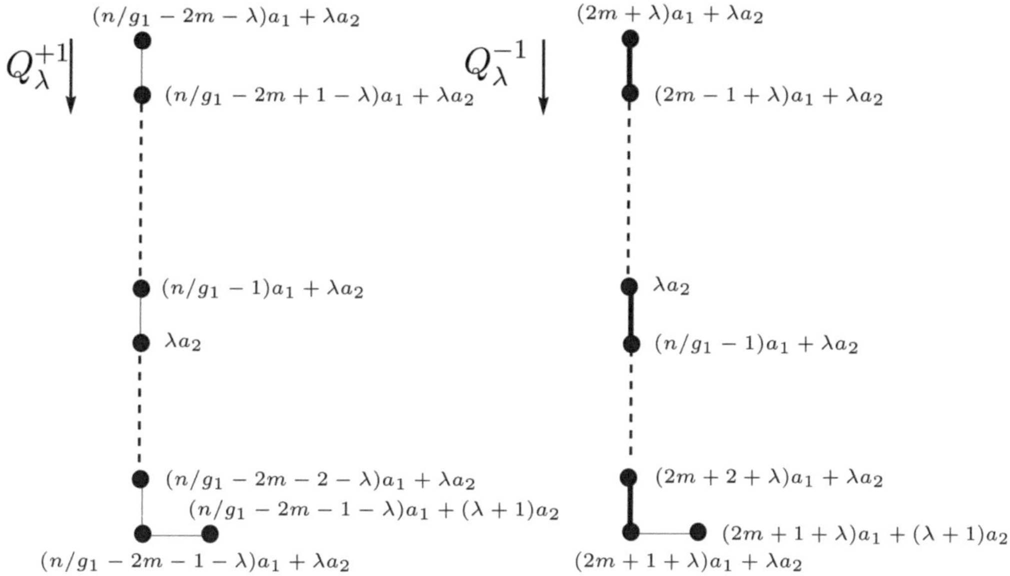

Fig. 7. Q_λ^{+1} , and Q_λ^{-1}, for a fixed $\lambda \in \mathbb{Z}_{g_1}$

Q_λ^{+1}, and Q_λ^{-1} be the path in G_2 described in *Figure* 7. They pass through any node in Δ_λ, and cost $c_D(Q_\lambda^\varepsilon) = (n/g_1 - 1) \cdot d_1 + d_2$. For $\varepsilon = +1,-1$, let H_m^ε be the path obtained by composing P_m^ε, Q_2^ε, . . . $Q_{g_1-1}^\varepsilon$. H_m^ε starts at the node 0, and passes through any node in G_2. Its cost verifies

$$c_D(H_m^\varepsilon) = c_D(P_m^\varepsilon) + (g_1 - 2)c_D(Q_m^\varepsilon) =$$
$$= (n - g_1 - 2m) \cdot d_1 + (g_1 + 2m) \cdot d_2 = LB(D) + 2m \cdot (d_2 - d_1).$$

If $m = y_1 - g_1$, H_m^{+1} is a Hamiltonian cycle for G_2, as its ending point is

$$v \equiv_n (2m + g_1)a_1 + g_1 a_2 \equiv_n (2y_1 - g_1)a_1 + g_1 a_2 \equiv_n 0.$$

If $m = n/g_1 - y_2$, II_m^{-1} is a Hamiltonian cycle for G_2 as its ending point is

$$v \equiv_n (2m + g_1)a_1 - g_1 a_2 \equiv_n (2y_2 - g_1)a_1 + g_1 a_2 \equiv_n 0.$$

The second part of claim (*ii*) thus follows, since either H_m^{+1}, or H_m^{-1} induced a Hamiltonian tour for D of the required cost. □

Example 24 *Let D_1 be the matrix $D(32; 1, 2; 8, 1)$. It is easy to verify that $g_1 = \gcd(32, 8) = 8$, and that $n/g_1 = 4$. The equation $3(8 - 2y)8 + 8 \equiv_{32} 0$ has no integer solutions. Thus, A_{D1} is empty. It follows from Theorem 23, and from (13) that* $\mathrm{opt}(D_1) = UB(D_1) = 46$.

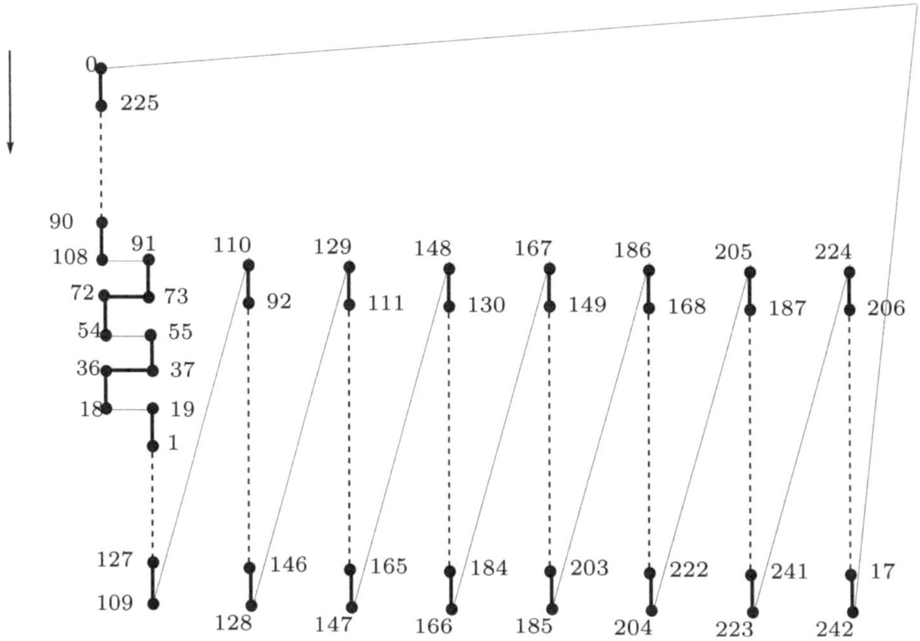

Fig. 8. The Hamiltonian cycle H_2^{-1} for $D(243; 18, 1; 1, 2)$

Let D_2 be the matrix $D(28; 1, 2; 7, 3)$. Note that $g_1 = \gcd(28, 7) = 7$, and that $n/g_1 = 4$. The equation $3(7-2y)7 + 21 \equiv_{28} 0$ is solved by any even integer. Thus, $A_{D_2} = \{0, 2\}$, and $m = \min\{0-4, 4-2\} = -4 \le 0$. It follows from Theorem 23, and from (13) that $\text{opt}(D_2) = LB(D_2) = 32$.
Let D_3 be the matrix $D(243; 18, 1; 1, 2)$. Note that $g_1 = \gcd(243, 18) = 9$, and that $n/g_1 = 27$. 25 is the unique integer solutions in $[0, 26]$ of the equation $(2y-9)18+9 \equiv_{243} 0$. Thus, $A_{D_3} = \{25\}$, and $m = \min\{25-9, 27-25\} = 2$. It follows from Theorem 23, and from (13) that H_2^{-1} induces a Hamiltonian tour for D_3 of cost 256, while $LB(D_3) = 252$, and $UB(D_3) = 259$. The Hamiltonian cycle H_2^{-1} is depicted in Figure 8.

Example 25 Let D_4 the matrix $D(45; 1, 2; 20, 9)$. It is easy to verify that $g_1 = 5$, $A_{D_4} = \{7\}$, and, thus, $m = 2$. Theorem 23 assures that a Hamiltonian tour for D_4 of cost 54 exists, while $UB(D_4) = 53$, as a consequence of (13).

Let us give an overview on the results presented in this section.
Let D be the matrix $D(n; d_1, d_2; a_1, a_2)$. If $g_1 = 2$, then $\text{opt}(D) = LB(D)$. If $g_1 \ge 3$, let A_D, and m be as in the hypothesis of *Theorem* 23. If A_D is empty, *Theorem* 23 assures that $\text{opt}(D) = UB(D)$. If A_D is not empty, and $m \le 0$ holds, then *Theorem* 23 assures that $\text{opt}(D) = LB(D)$. The converse also holds. Finally, if A_D is not empty, and $m > 0$ holds, then there exists a Hamiltonian tour of cost $LB(D) + 2m \cdot (d_2 - d_1)$. *Example 25* shows that such Hamiltonian tour is not necessarily an optimal one. Anyway, Gerace, and Greco Greco (2008a) conjecture that

$$\text{opt}(D) = \min\{UB(D), LB(D) + 2m \cdot (d_2 - d_1)\}.$$

8. Conclusions

In this chapter the attention has been focused on the Symmetric Circulant Traveling Salesman Problem (SCTSP), a subcase of the Traveling Salesman Problem explicitly introduced for the first time in 1992. The most remarkable results obtained in the last 16 years are reported: In the general case, there are given an upper bound, a lower bound, and a polynomial time 2-approximation algorithm; In the so-called 2-striped case, there are given an algebraic characterization for those matrices having the optimal cost equal either to the upper bound, or to the lower bound, and a new Hamiltonian tour construction for the remaining matrices.

At the moment the main research direction is that of generalizing to the s-striped case the results obtained in the 2-striped case. It seems the first necessary step in the direction of solving SCTSP.

To sum up, the problem of finding a polynomial time solution for SCTSP seems harder, and more interesting than it was expected. In general, it is less easy than it was expected dealing with circulant graphs, and with their algebraic structure. As a matter of fact, also showing that *Graph Isomorphism* is polynomial time solvable in the circulant graph case has required a forty year research.

9. References

F. Boesch and R. Tindell (1984). Circulant and their connectivities. *J. Graph Theory*, 8:487–499, 1984.

Z. Bogdanowicz (2005). Hamiltonian circuits in sparse circulant digraphs. *Ars Combinatoria*, 76:213–223, 2005.

R.E. Burkard and W. Sandholzer (1991). Efficiently solvable special cases of bottelneck traveling salesman problem. *Discrete Applied Mathematics*, 32:61–76, 1991.

B. Codenotti, I. Gerace, and S. Vigna (1998). Hardness results and spectral techniques for combinatorial problems on circulant graphs. *Linear Algebra and its Application*, 285:123–142, 1998.

P.J. Davis (1979), editor. *Circulant Matrices*. John Wiley & Sons, 1979.

R.S. Garfinkel (1977). Minimizing wallpaper waste, part 1: a class of traveling salesman problems. *Oper. Res.*, 25:741–751, 1977.

I. Gerace and F. Greco (2008a). The travelling salesman problem in symmetric circulant matrices with two stripes. *Math. Structures in Comp. Science*, 18:1–11, 2008.

I. Gerace and F. Greco (2008b). Bounds for the symmetric circulant traveling salesman problem. 2008. submitted for publication.

I. Gerace and R.W. Irving (1998). The traveling salesman problem in circulant graphs. Technical Report TR-1998-15, University of Glasgow, Department of Computing Science, June 1998.

R.C. Gilmore, E.L. Lawler, and D.B. Shmoys (1985). *Well-solvable solvable special cases (of the TSP), in: E.L. Lawler and J.K. Lenstra and A.H.G. Rinooy Ka D.B. Shmoys, eds, The traveling salesman problem*, chapter 4, pages 87–143. Wiley, Chichester, 1985.

M. Muzychuk (2004). A solution of the isomorphism problem for circulant graphs. *Proc. of the London Math. Society*, 88(3):1–41, 2004.

J.A.A. Van der Veen (1992). *Solvable Cases of the Traveling Salesman Problem with Various Objective Function*. PhD thesis, University of Groningen, Groningen, 1992.

Qi Fan Yang, R.E. Burkard, E. Çela, and G.J. Wöginger (1997). Hamiltonian cycles in circulant digraphs with two stripes. *Discrete Mathematics*, 176:233–254, 1997.